Devils and Realist vol.15

story by Madoka Takadono
art by Utako Yukihiro

Cast of characters

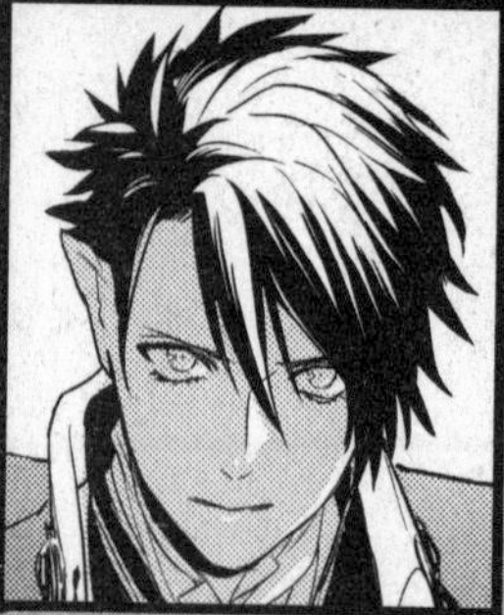

Dantalion
71st pillar and commander of thirty-six armies of Hell, he is Grand Duke of the Under-world. One of the candidates for representative king, he has joined up with Camio in an effort to crush Lucifer's plans.

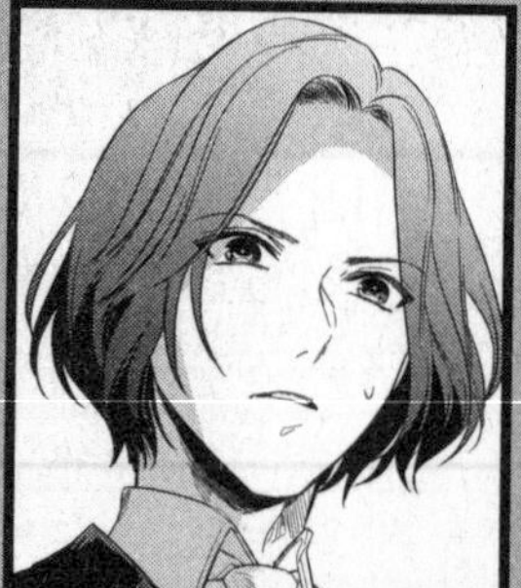

Kevin
William's capable yet gambling-addicted butler who is also a pastor at the academy. In truth, he is the angel Uriel who has been dispatched from Heaven.

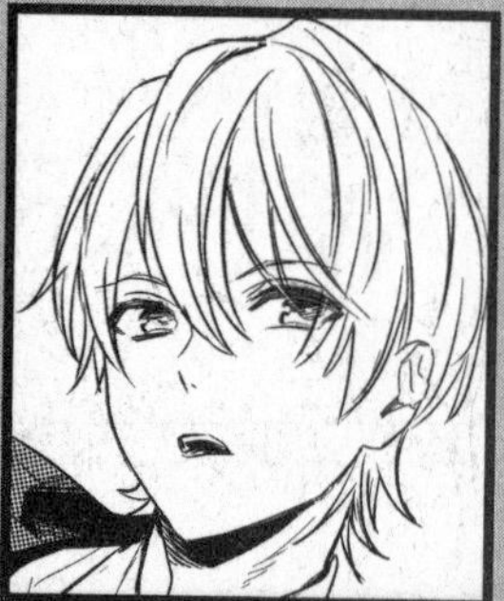

William
A brilliant realist from a famous noble family whose wealth was recently restored. As the descendant of King Solomon, he is the Elector with the authority to choose the representative of the King of Hell. Although he initially rejected this role, he has finally come to terms with it.

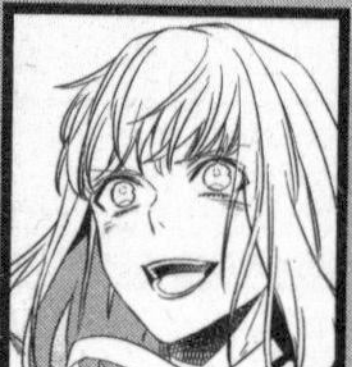

Michael
A vicious seraph who wanted to bring William to Heaven by administering the ecstasy. Betrayed by Metatron, he has lost both power and influence.

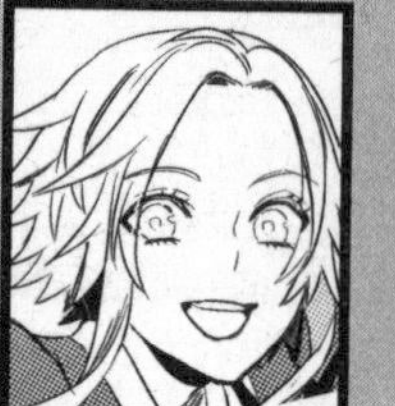

Sytry
Though Sytry was originally a candidate for representative King of Hell, Metatron has positioned him to be the successor to Gabriel.

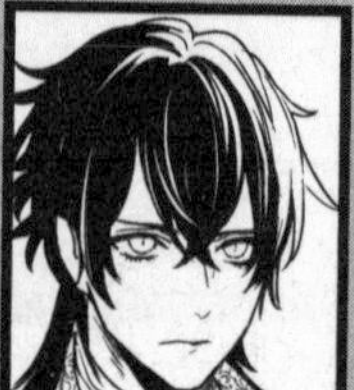

Camio
A candidate for representative king and a Great President of Hell. Camio hates Lucifer and detests the fact that he has inherited Lucifer's blood.

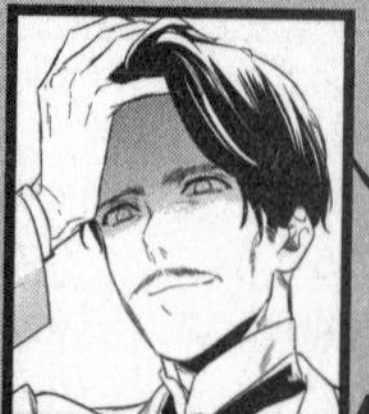

Barton
William's uncle. He murdered William's parents in his desire to inherit the soul of Solomon. One of the Four Horsemen of the Apocalypse.

The Story So Far

The demons Dantalion and Sytry appear suddenly before impoverished noble William to tell him that he is the Elector who will choose the representative king of Hell. After the demons join him at school as students, William's life becomes more and more entangled with the doings of Hell. But together with an announcement of an imminent three-way war involving Heaven, Hell, and Earth, Dantalion and the others vanish from school. Meanwhile, the Earth faces a crisis with the appearance of the Four Horsemen of the Apocalypse. As he works behind the scenes to prevent war on earth, William risks his life on a dive into Solomon's memories to save Sytry in Heaven and Dantalion in Hell...

Pillar 88

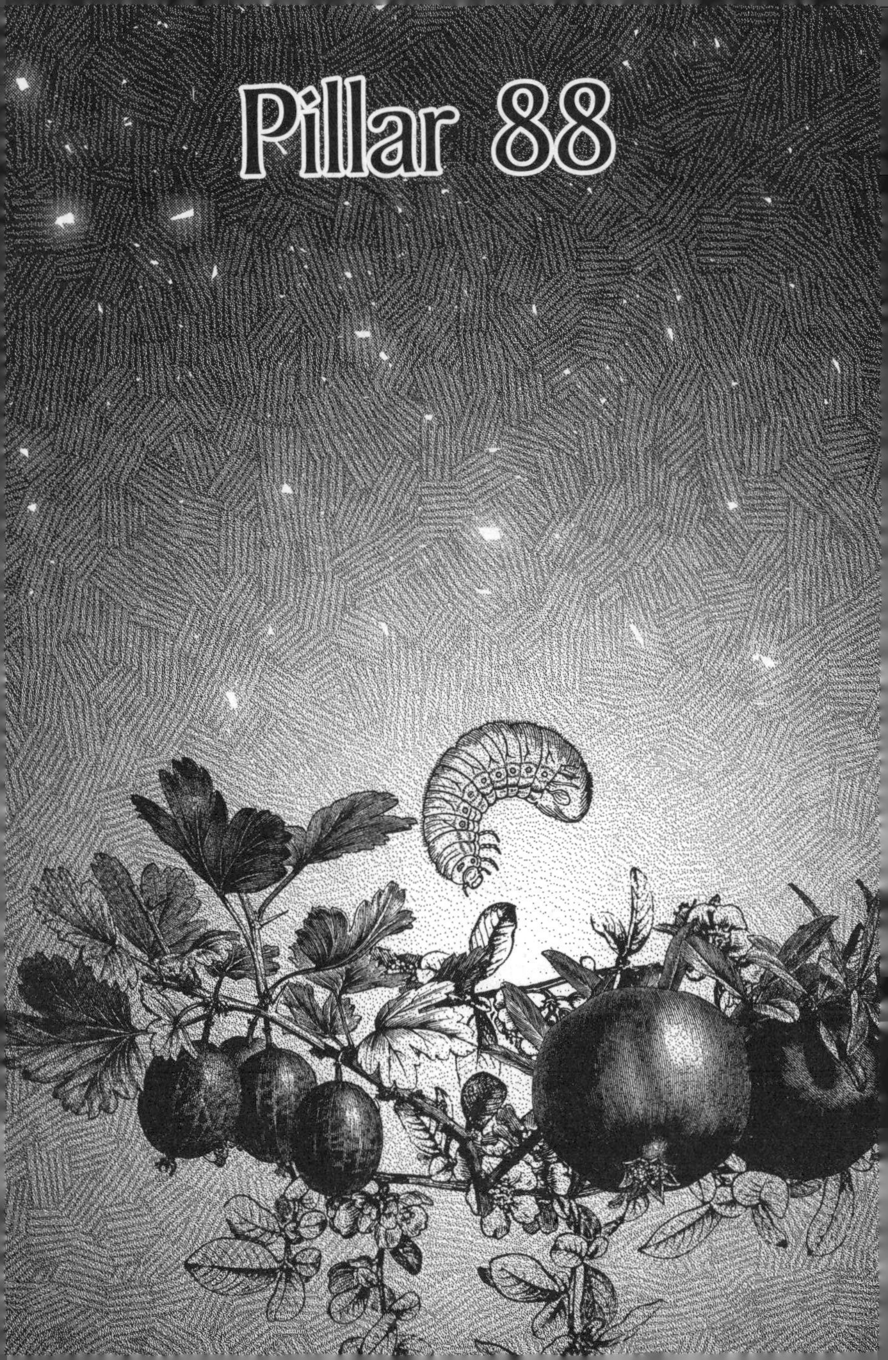

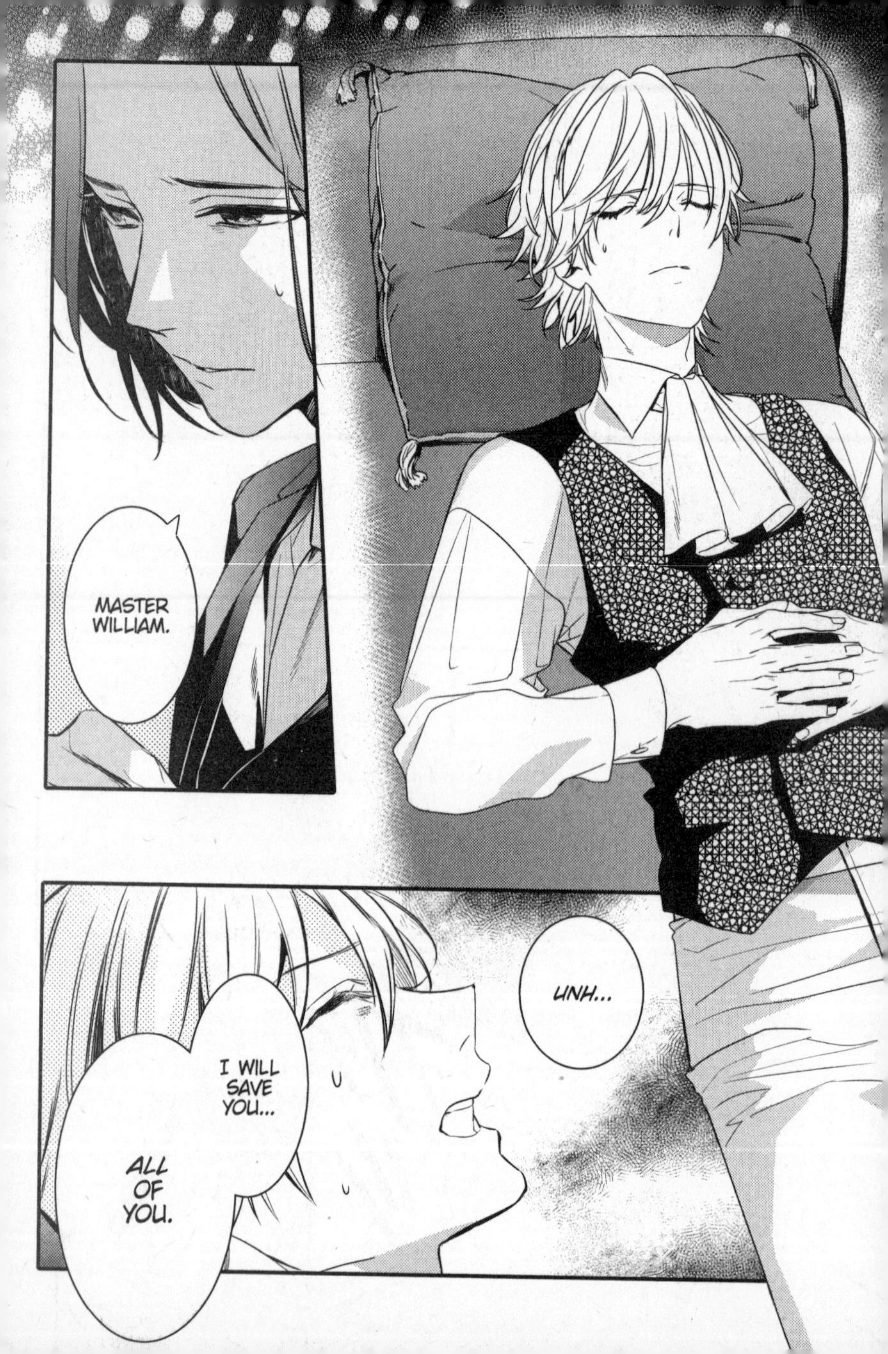
MASTER WILLIAM.
UNH...
I WILL SAVE YOU...
ALL OF YOU.

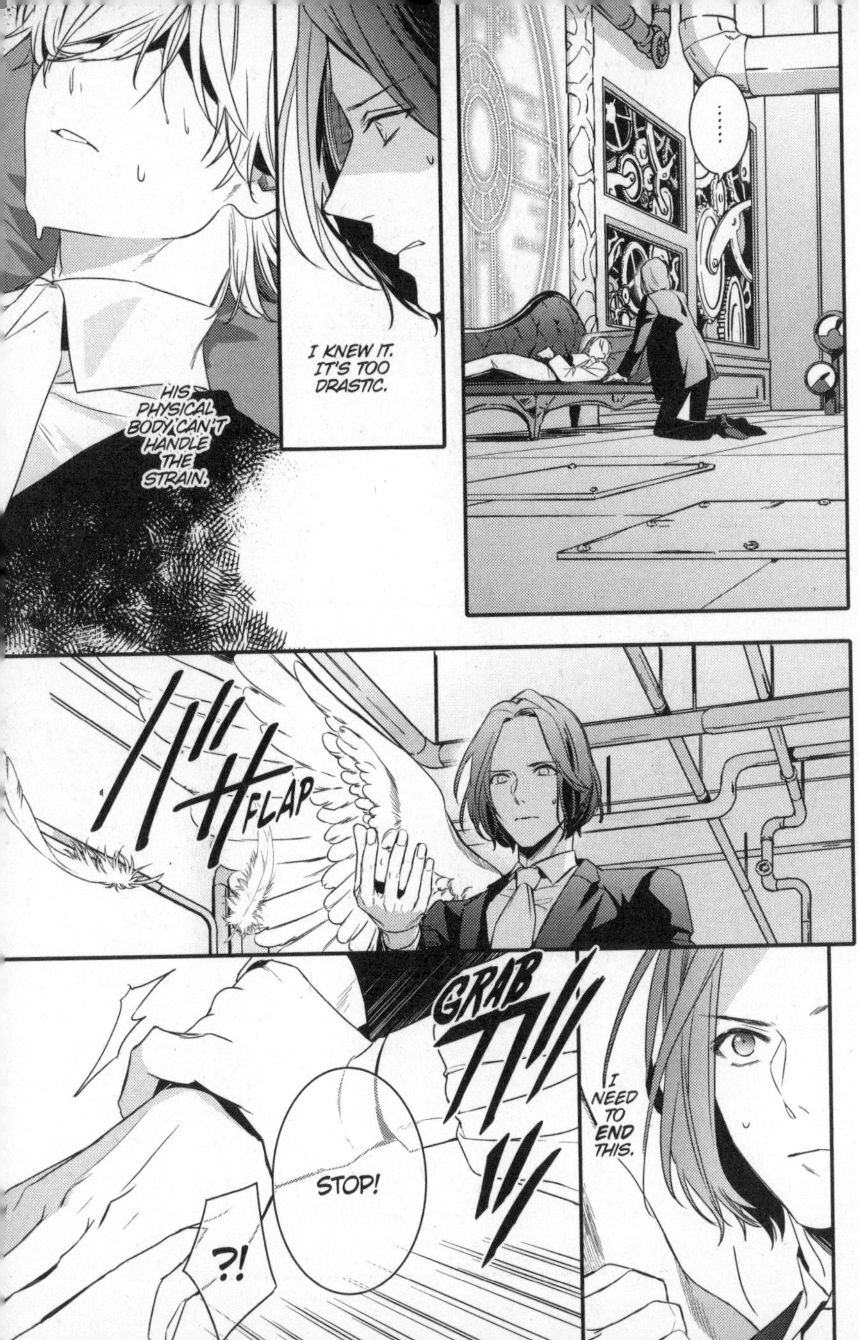
......
I KNEW IT. IT'S TOO DRASTIC.
HIS PHYSICAL BODY CAN'T HANDLE THE STRAIN.
FLAP
I NEED TO END THIS.
GRAB
STOP!
?!

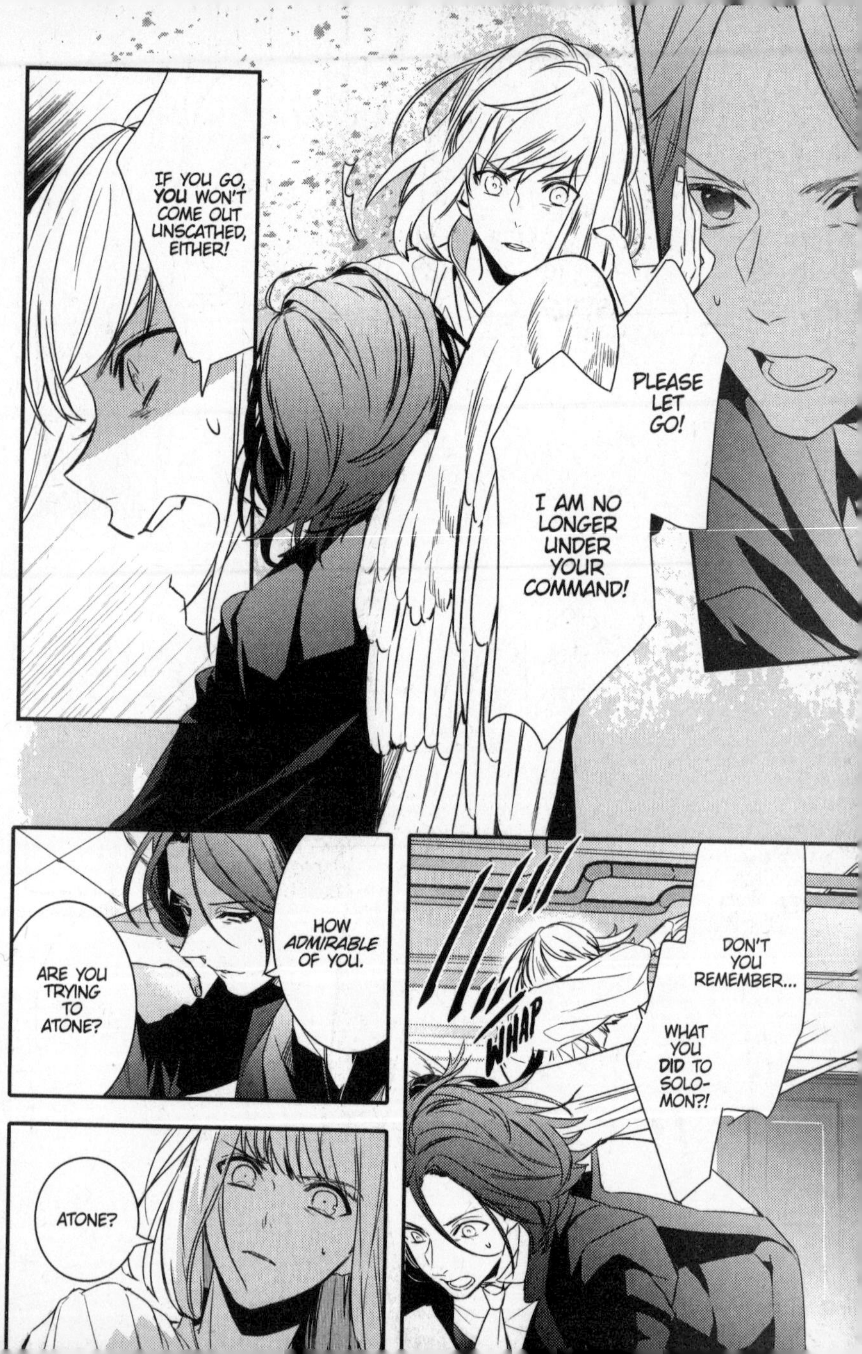
PLEASE LET GO!
I AM NO LONGER UNDER YOUR COMMAND!
IF YOU GO, YOU WON'T COME OUT UNSCATHED, EITHER!
WHAP
DON'T YOU REMEMBER...
WHAT YOU DID TO SOLO-MON?!
HOW ADMIRABLE OF YOU.
ARE YOU TRYING TO ATONE?
ATONE?

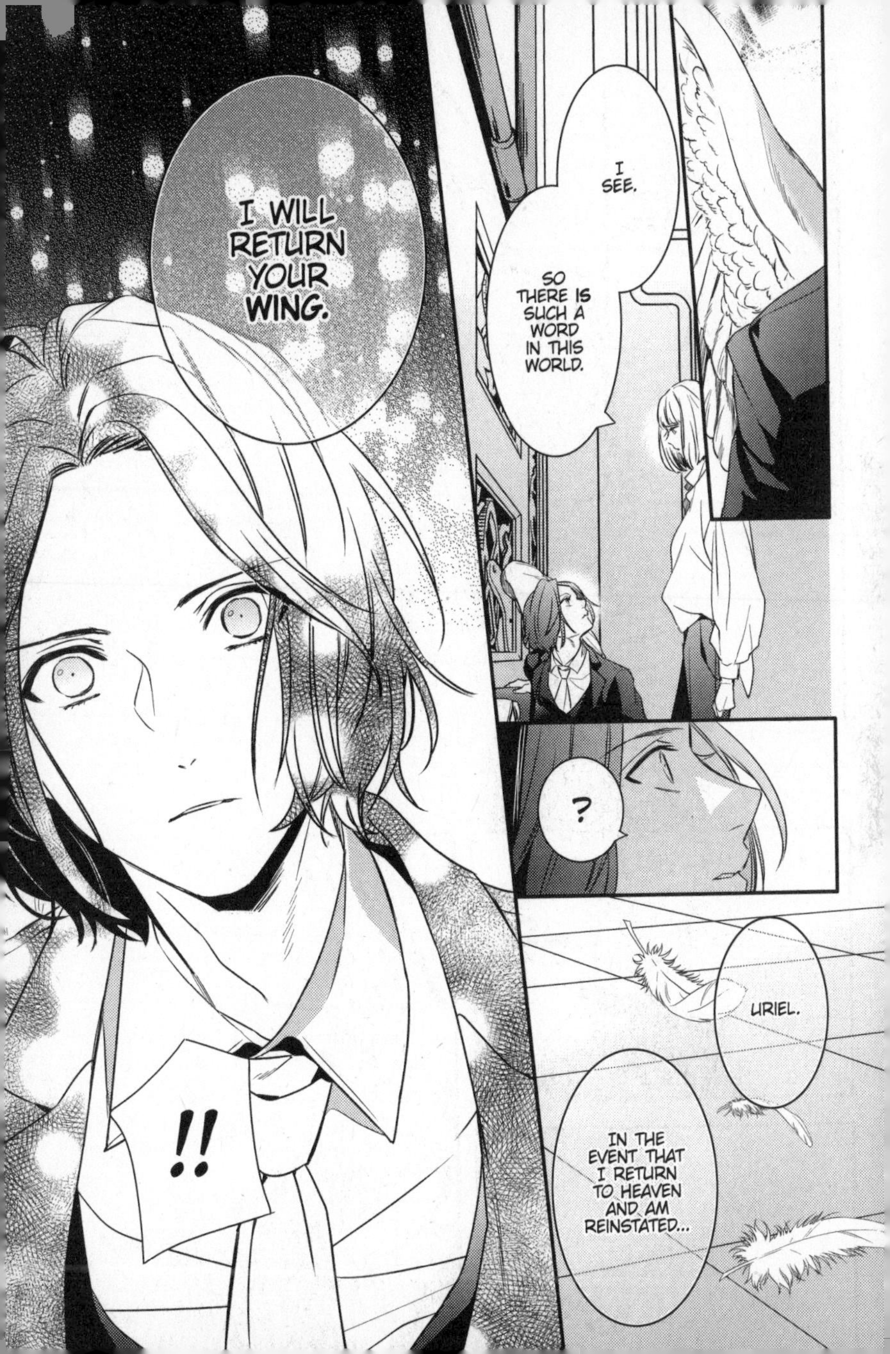
I SEE.
SO THERE IS SUCH A WORD IN THIS WORLD.
?
URIEL.
IN THE EVENT THAT I RETURN TO HEAVEN AND AM REINSTATED...
I WILL RETURN YOUR WING.
!!

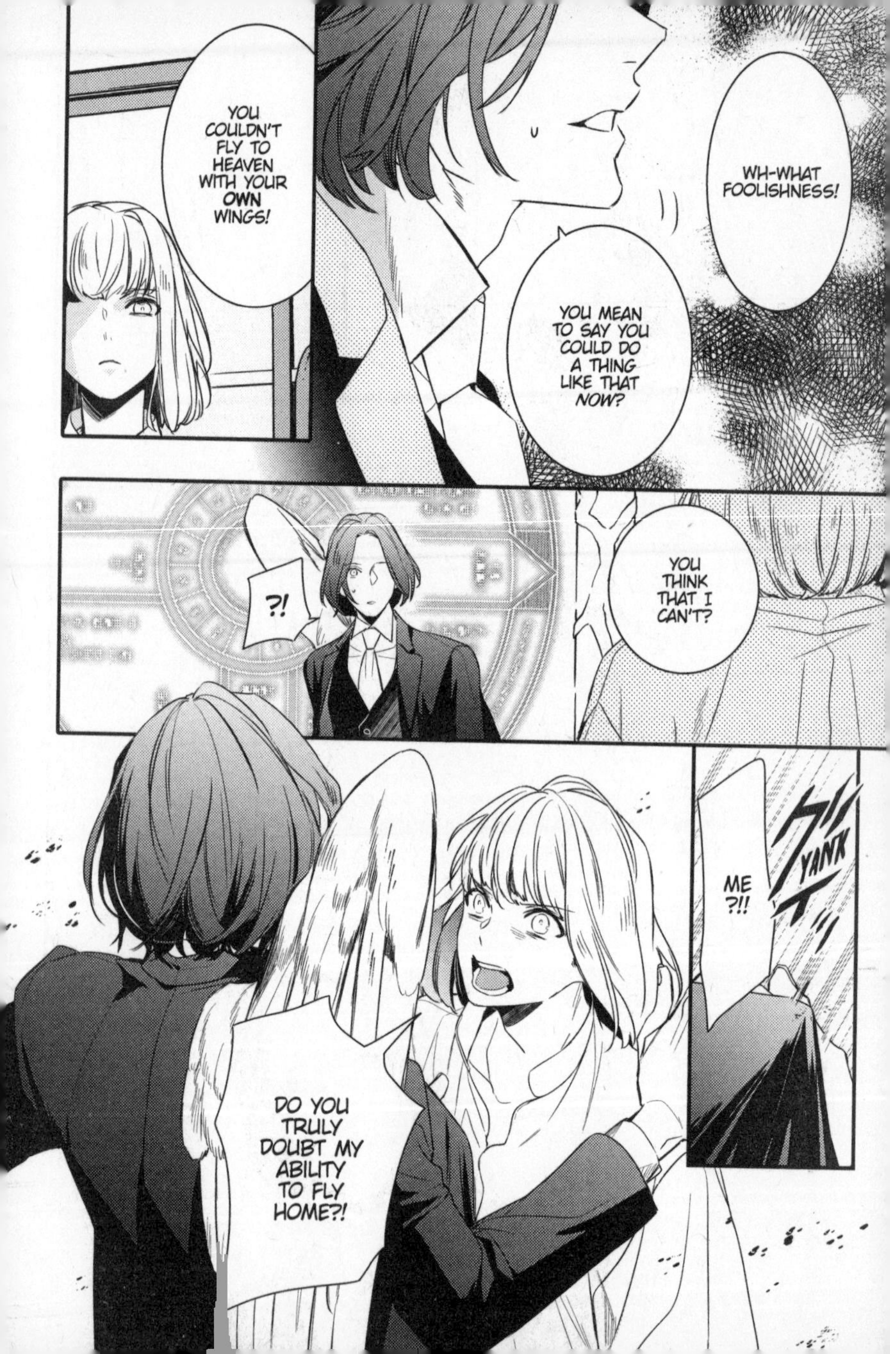
WH-WHAT FOOLISHNESS!
YOU MEAN TO SAY YOU COULD DO A THING LIKE THAT NOW?
YOU COULDN'T FLY TO HEAVEN WITH YOUR OWN WINGS!
YOU THINK THAT I CAN'T?
?!
ME ?!!
YANK
DO YOU TRULY DOUBT MY ABILITY TO FLY HOME?!

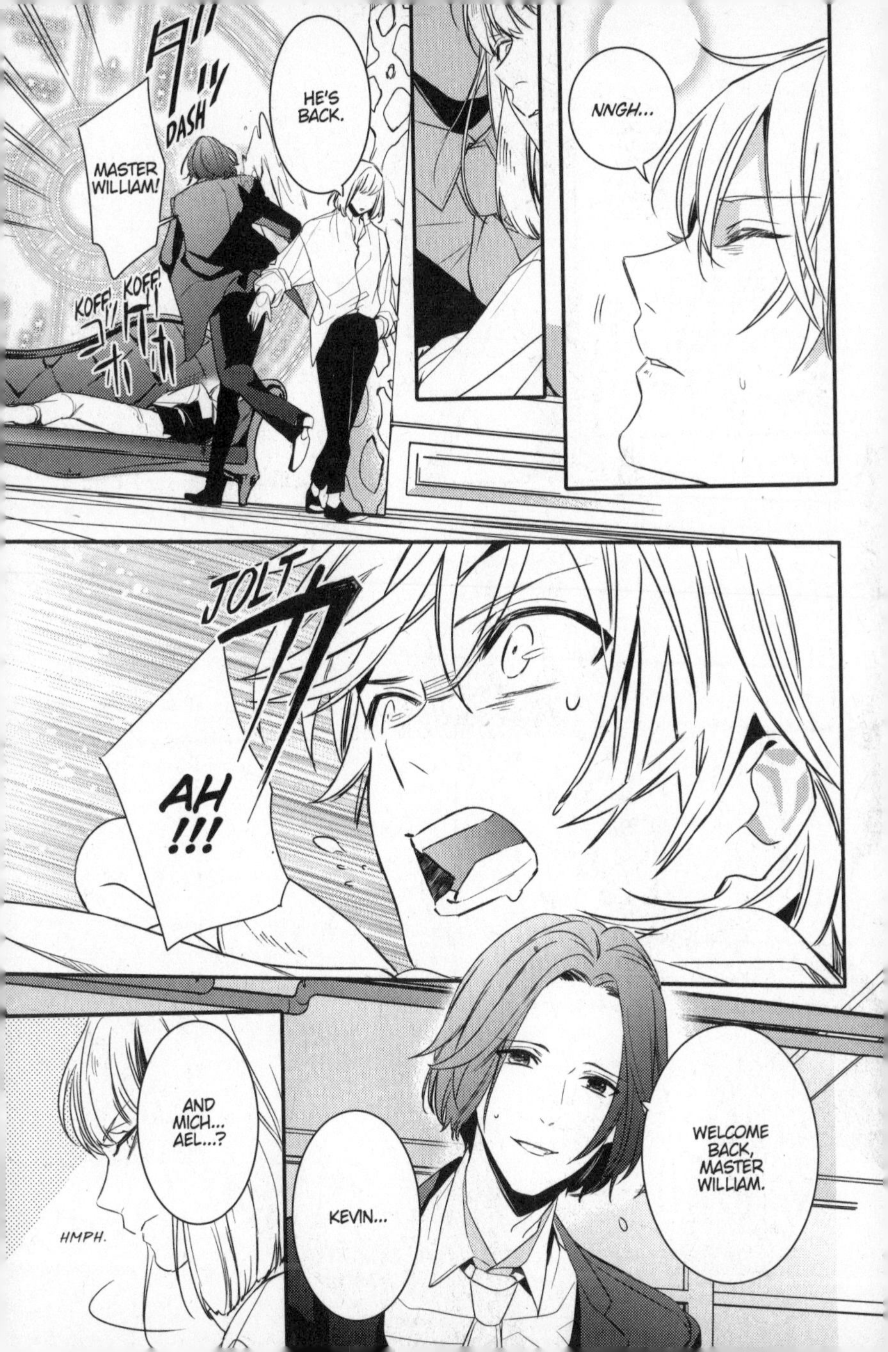
NNGH...
HE'S BACK.
DASH
MASTER WILLIAM!
KOFF! KOFF!
JOLT
AH !!!
WELCOME BACK, MASTER WILLIAM.
KEVIN...
AND MICH... AEL...?
HMPH.

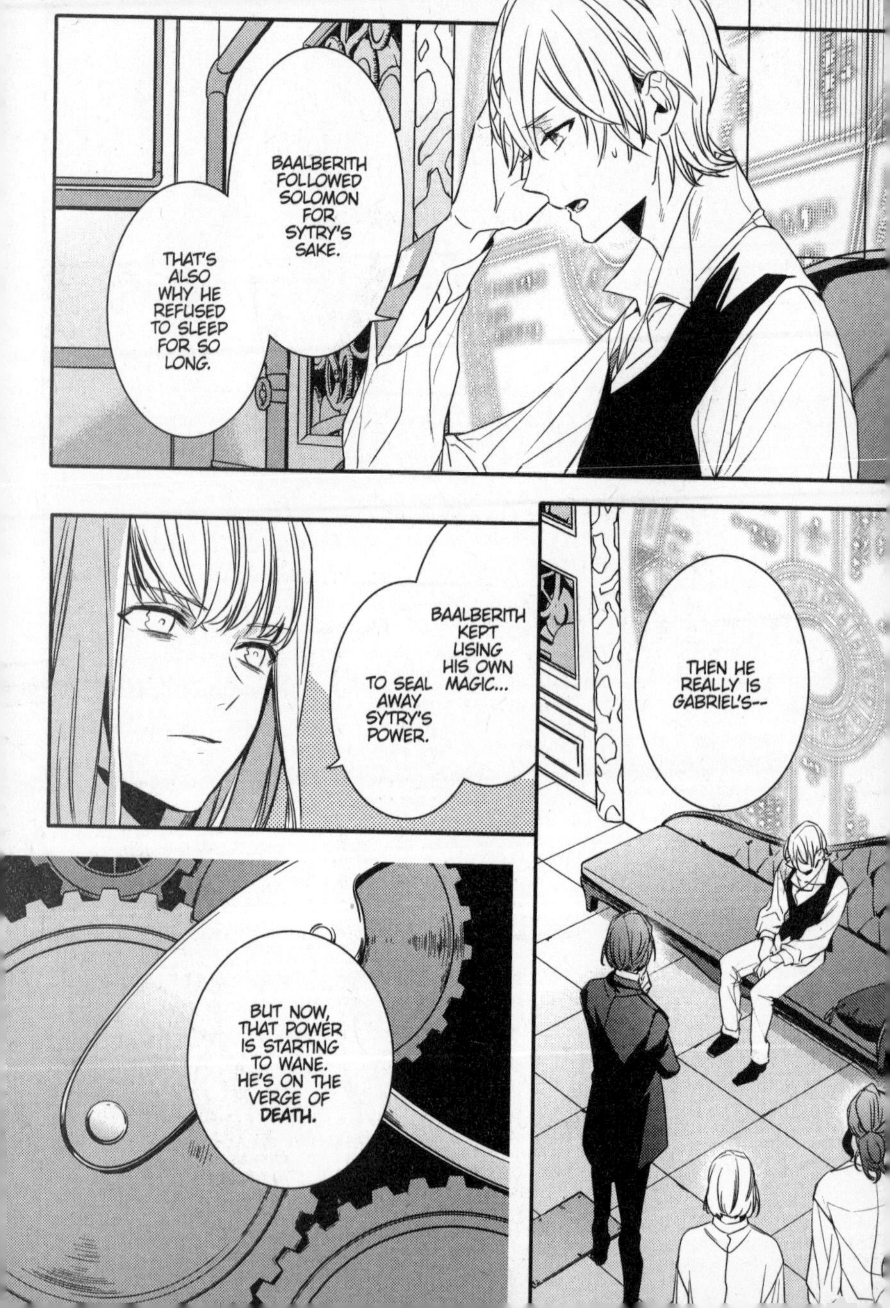
BAALBERITH FOLLOWED SOLOMON FOR SYTRY'S SAKE.
THAT'S ALSO WHY HE REFUSED TO SLEEP FOR SO LONG.
THEN HE REALLY IS GABRIEL'S--
BAALBERITH KEPT USING HIS OWN MAGIC...
TO SEAL AWAY SYTRY'S POWER.
BUT NOW, THAT POWER IS STARTING TO WANE. HE'S ON THE VERGE OF DEATH.

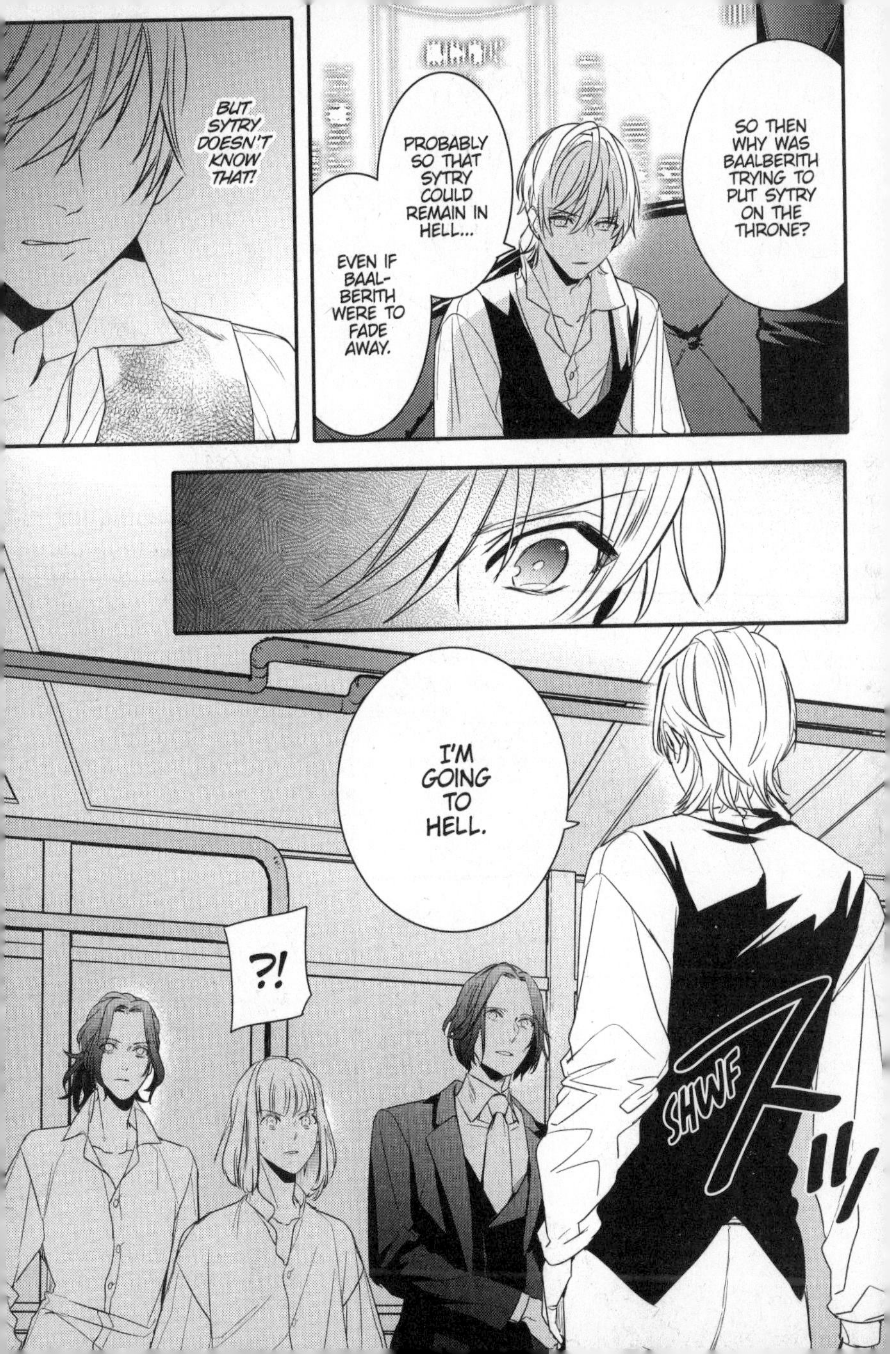
SO THEN WHY WAS BAALBERITH TRYING TO PUT SYTRY ON THE THRONE?
PROBABLY SO THAT SYTRY COULD REMAIN IN HELL...
EVEN IF BAAL-BERITH WERE TO FADE AWAY.
BUT SYTRY DOESN'T KNOW THAT!
I'M GOING TO HELL.
SHWF
?!

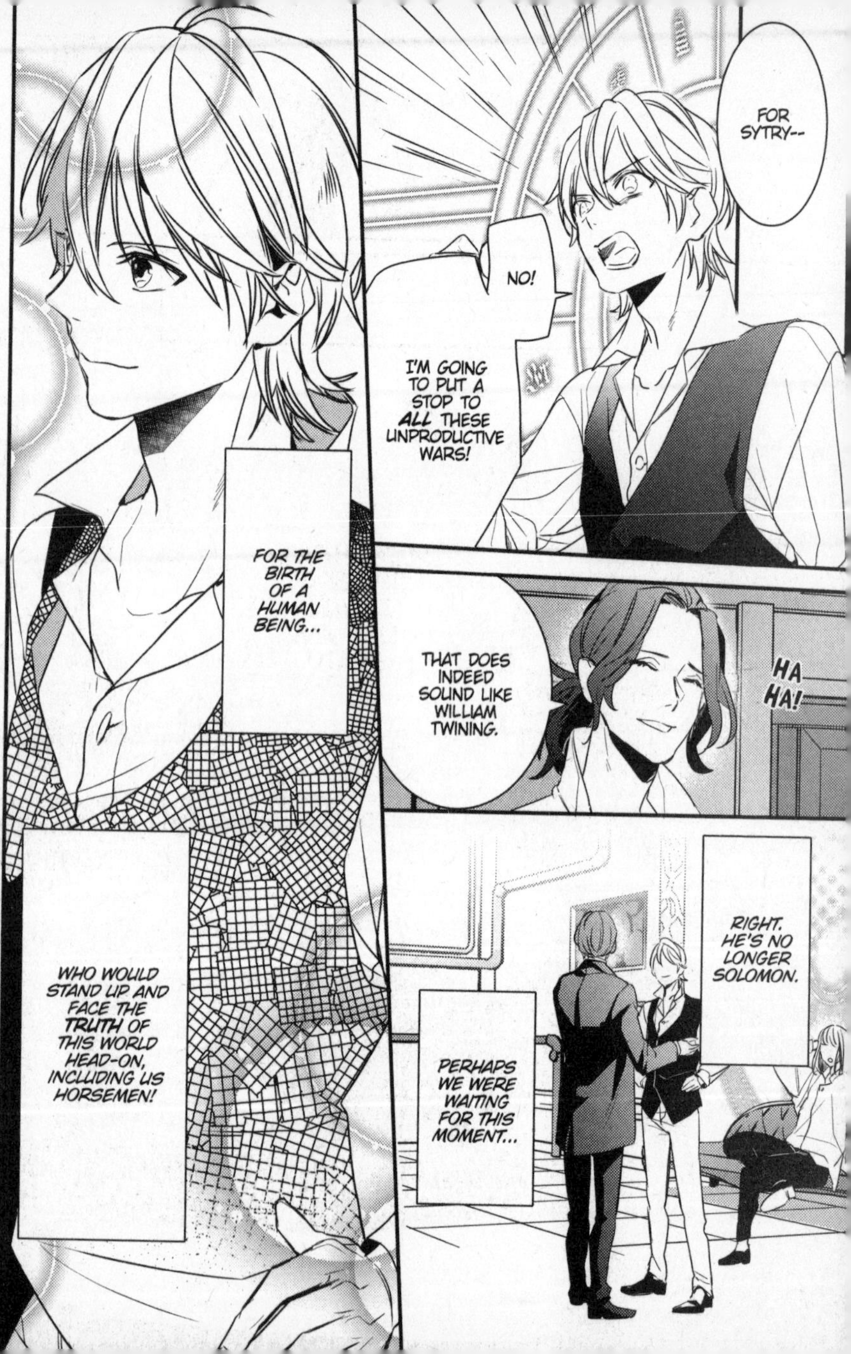
FOR SYTRY--
NO!
I'M GOING TO PUT A STOP TO **ALL** THESE UNPRODUCTIVE WARS!
HA HA!
THAT DOES INDEED SOUND LIKE WILLIAM TWINING.
RIGHT. HE'S NO LONGER SOLOMON.
PERHAPS WE WERE WAITING FOR THIS MOMENT...
FOR THE BIRTH OF A HUMAN BEING...
WHO WOULD STAND UP AND FACE THE **TRUTH** OF THIS WORLD HEAD-ON, INCLUDING US HORSEMEN!

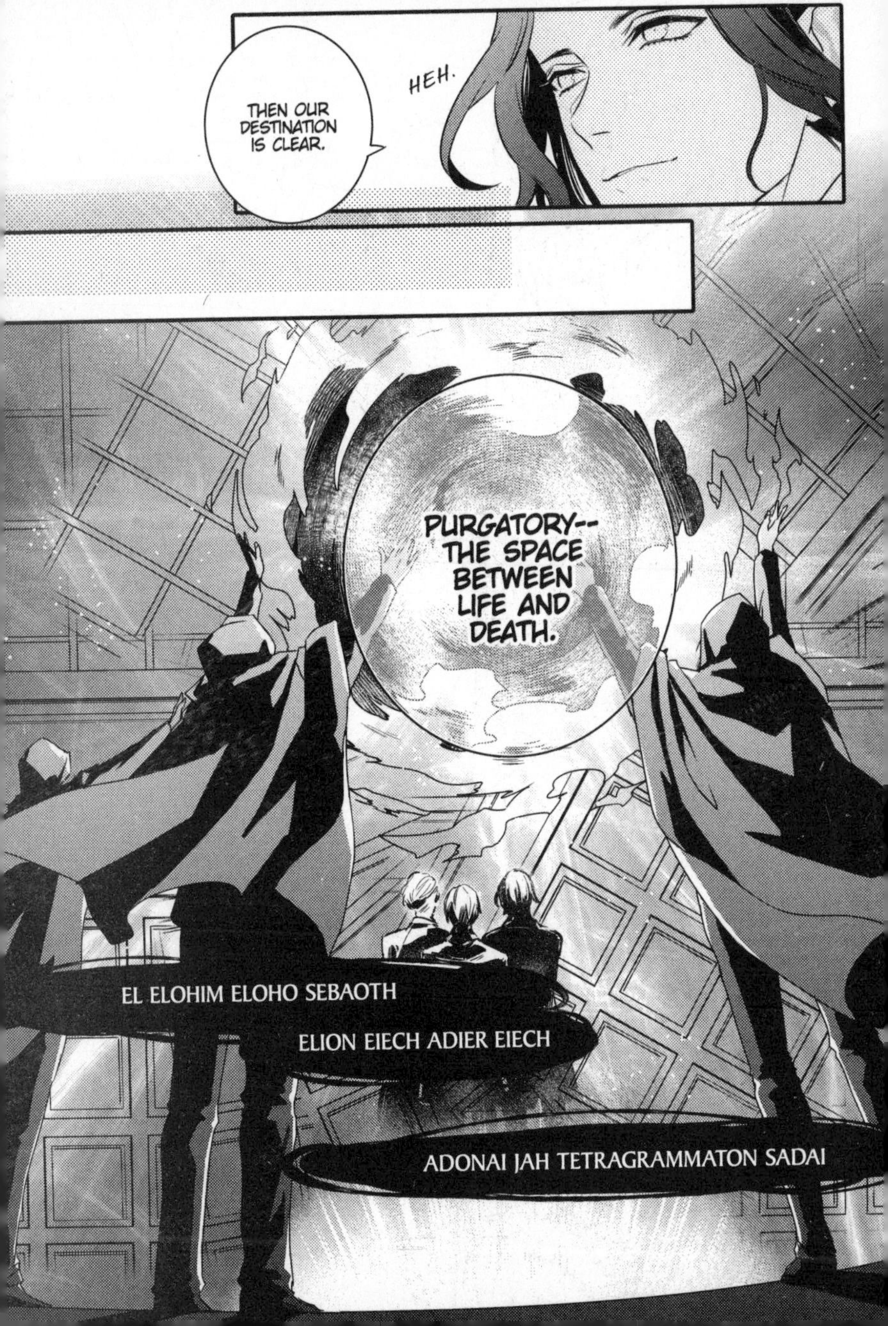
HEH.
THEN OUR DESTINATION IS CLEAR.
PURGATORY-- THE SPACE BETWEEN LIFE AND DEATH.
EL ELOHIM ELOHO SEBAOTH
ELION EIECH ADIER EIECH
ADONAI JAH TETRAGRAMMATON SADAI

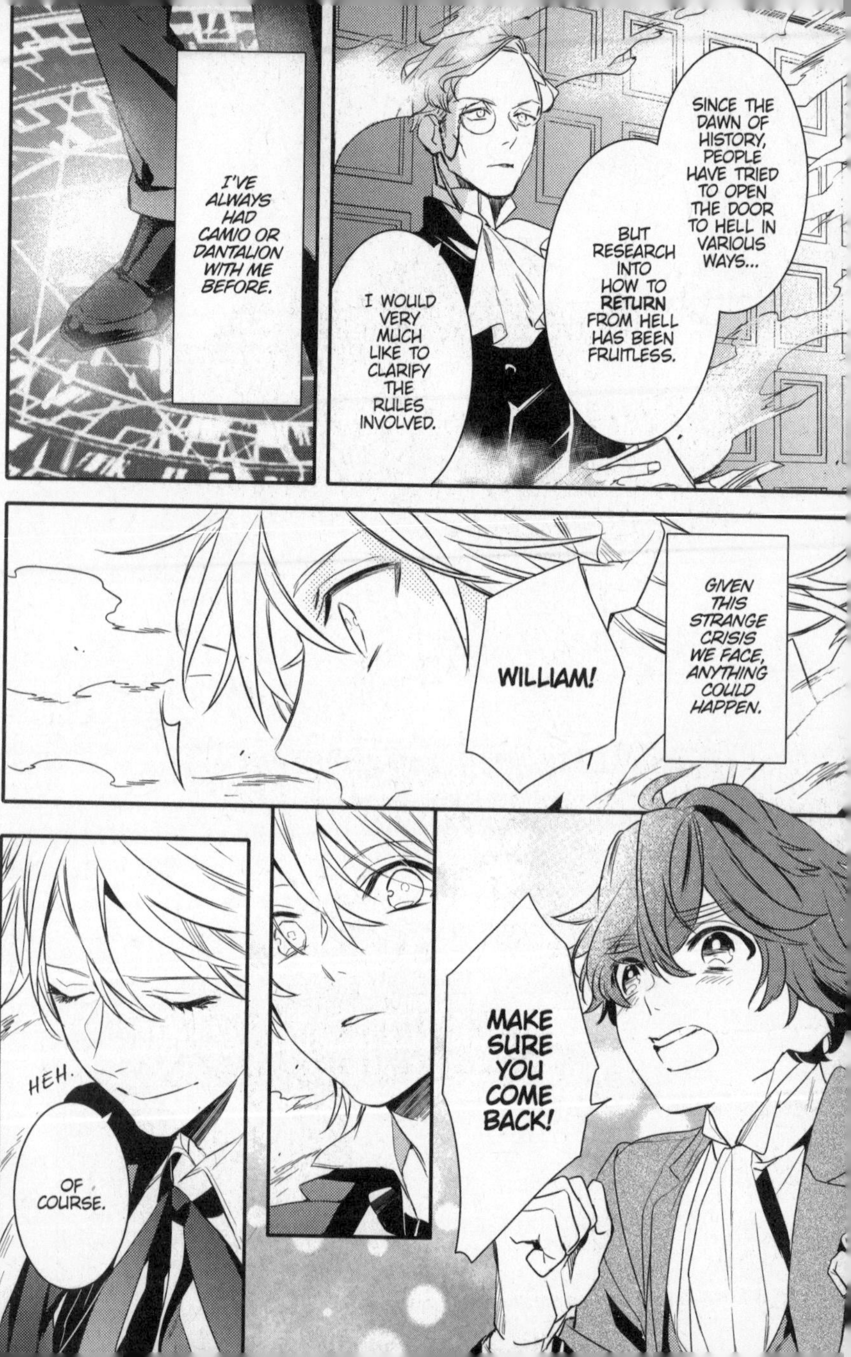
SINCE THE DAWN OF HISTORY, PEOPLE HAVE TRIED TO OPEN THE DOOR TO HELL IN VARIOUS WAYS...
BUT RESEARCH INTO HOW TO RETURN FROM HELL HAS BEEN FRUITLESS.
I WOULD VERY MUCH LIKE TO CLARIFY THE RULES INVOLVED.
I'VE ALWAYS HAD CAMIO OR DANTALION WITH ME BEFORE.
GIVEN THIS STRANGE CRISIS WE FACE, ANYTHING COULD HAPPEN.
WILLIAM!
MAKE SURE YOU COME BACK!
HEH.
OF COURSE.

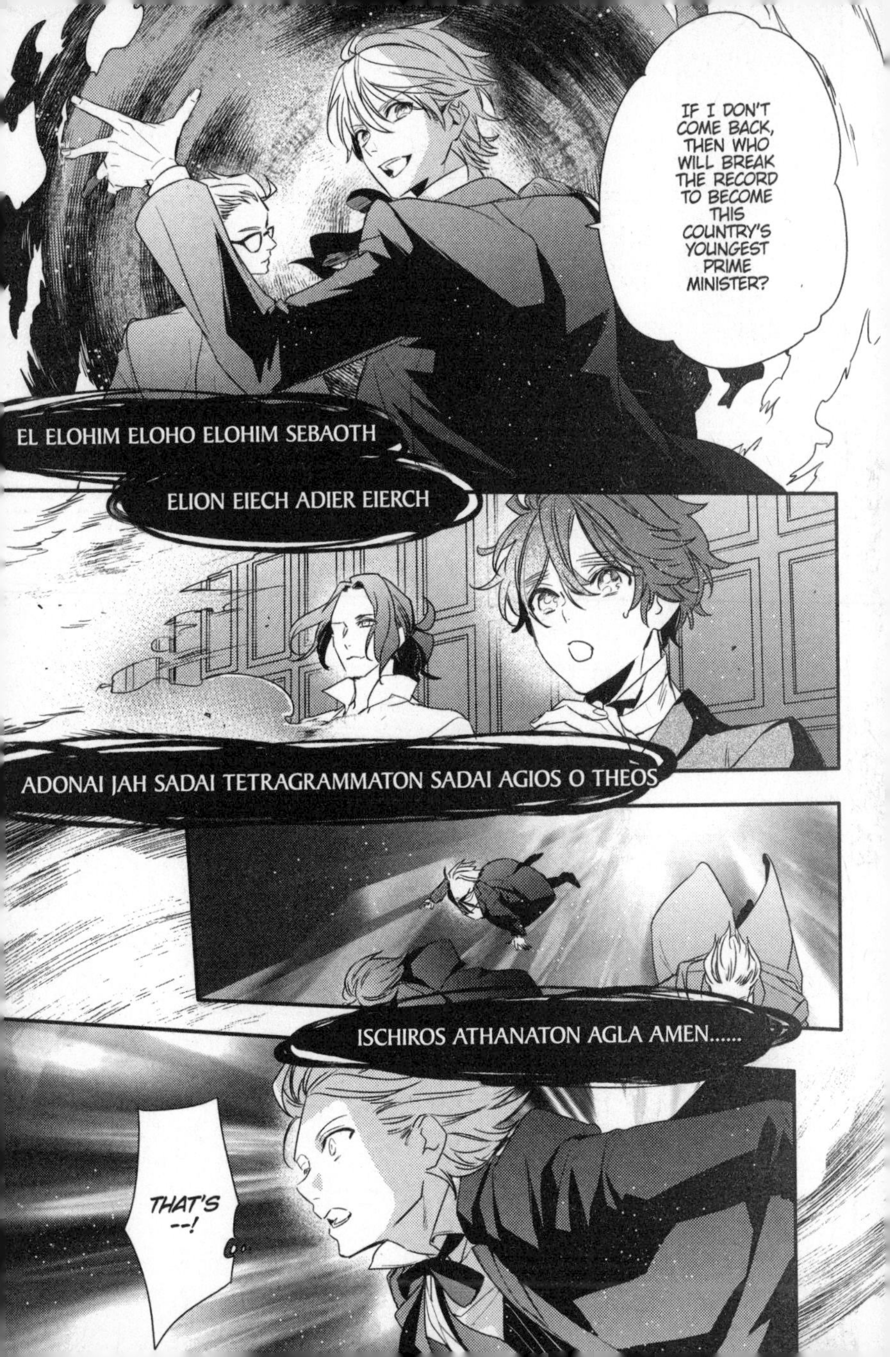
IF I DON'T COME BACK, THEN WHO WILL BREAK THE RECORD TO BECOME THIS COUNTRY'S YOUNGEST PRIME MINISTER?
EL ELOHIM ELOHO ELOHIM SEBAOTH
ELION EIECH ADIER EIERCH
ADONAI JAH SADAI TETRAGRAMMATON SADAI AGIOS O THEOS
ISCHIROS ATHANATON AGLA AMEN......
THAT'S --!

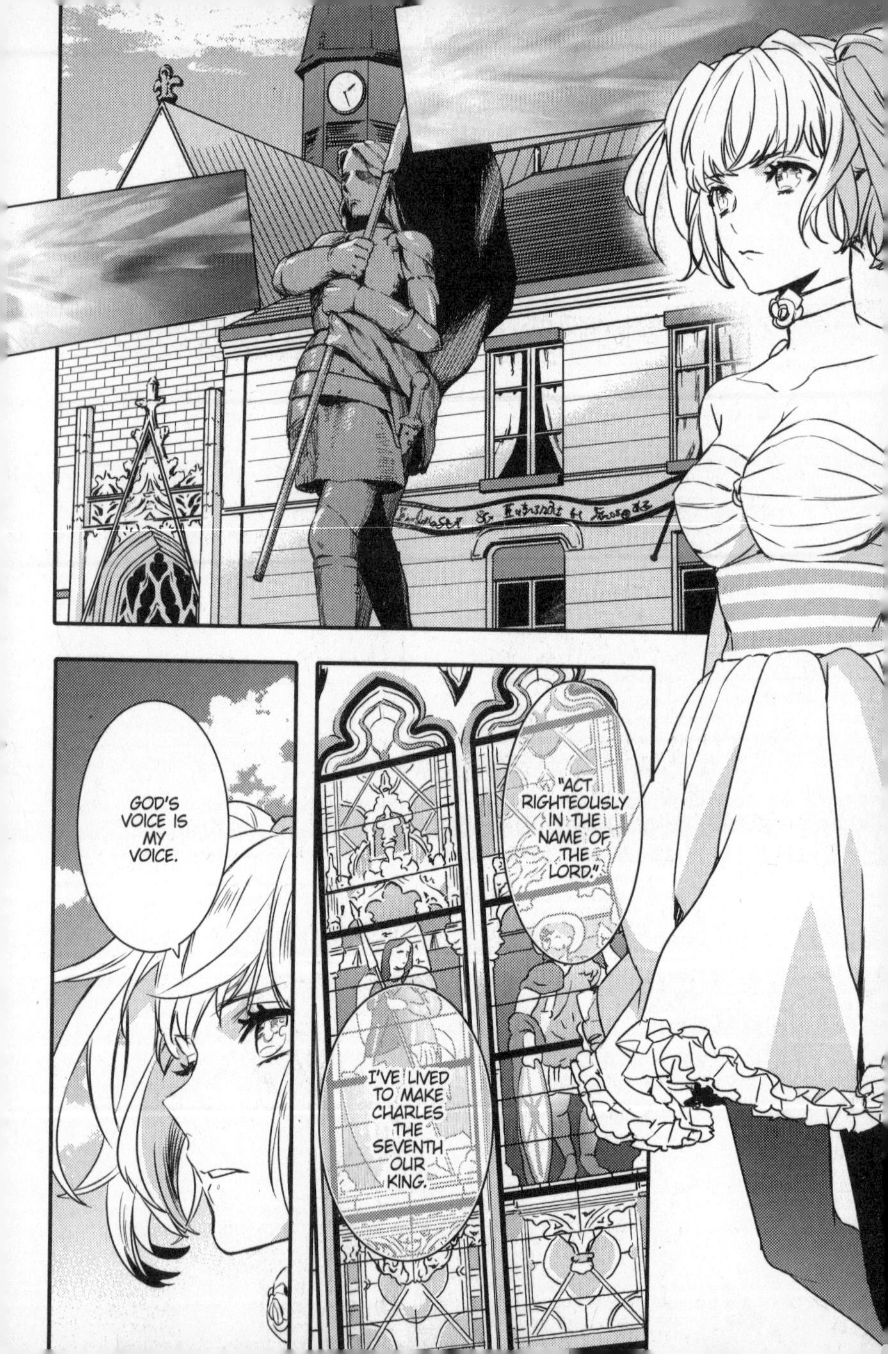
"ACT RIGHTEOUSLY IN THE NAME OF THE LORD."
I'VE LIVED TO MAKE CHARLES THE SEVENTH OUR KING.
GOD'S VOICE IS MY VOICE.

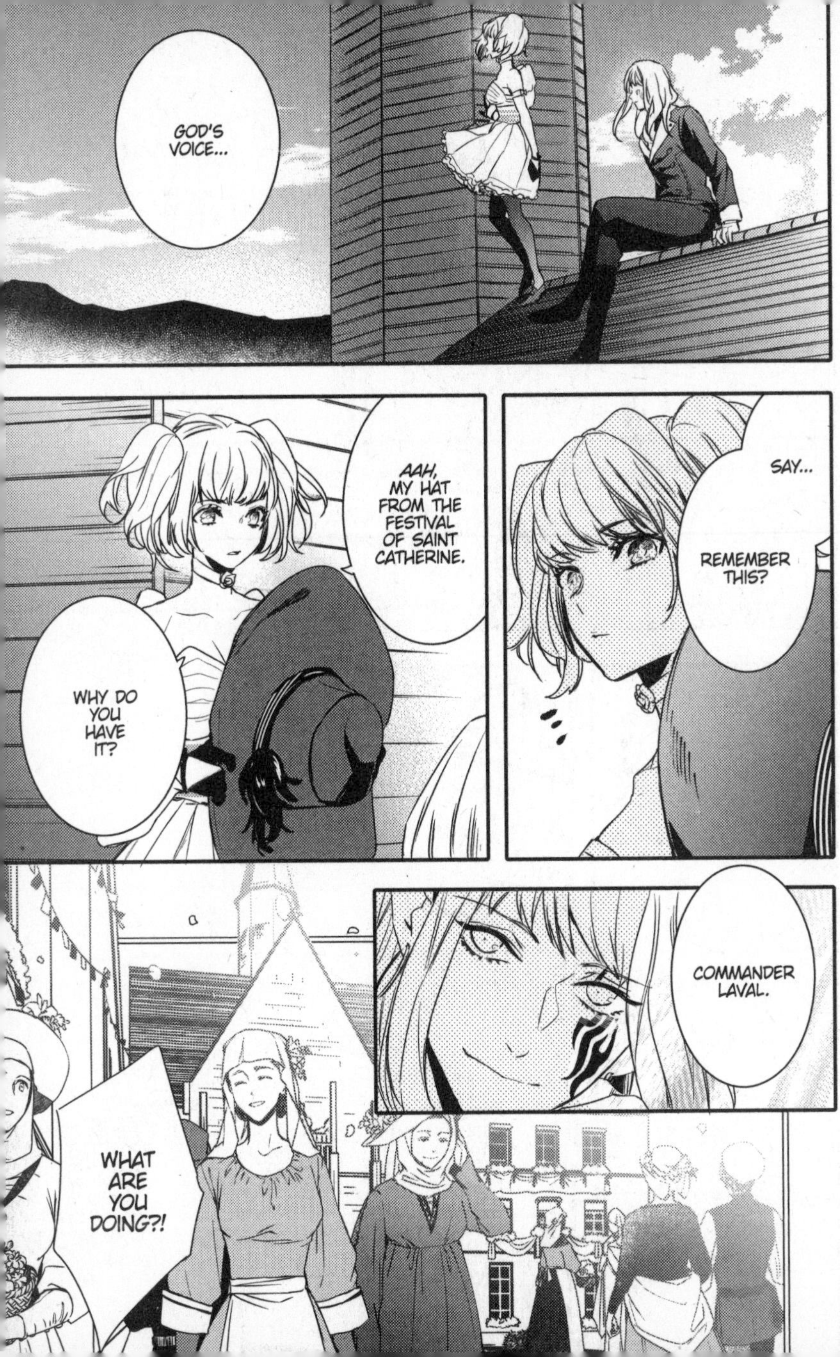
GOD'S VOICE...
SAY...
REMEMBER THIS?
AAH, MY HAT FROM THE FESTIVAL OF SAINT CATHERINE.
WHY DO YOU HAVE IT?
COMMANDER LAVAL.
WHAT ARE YOU DOING?!

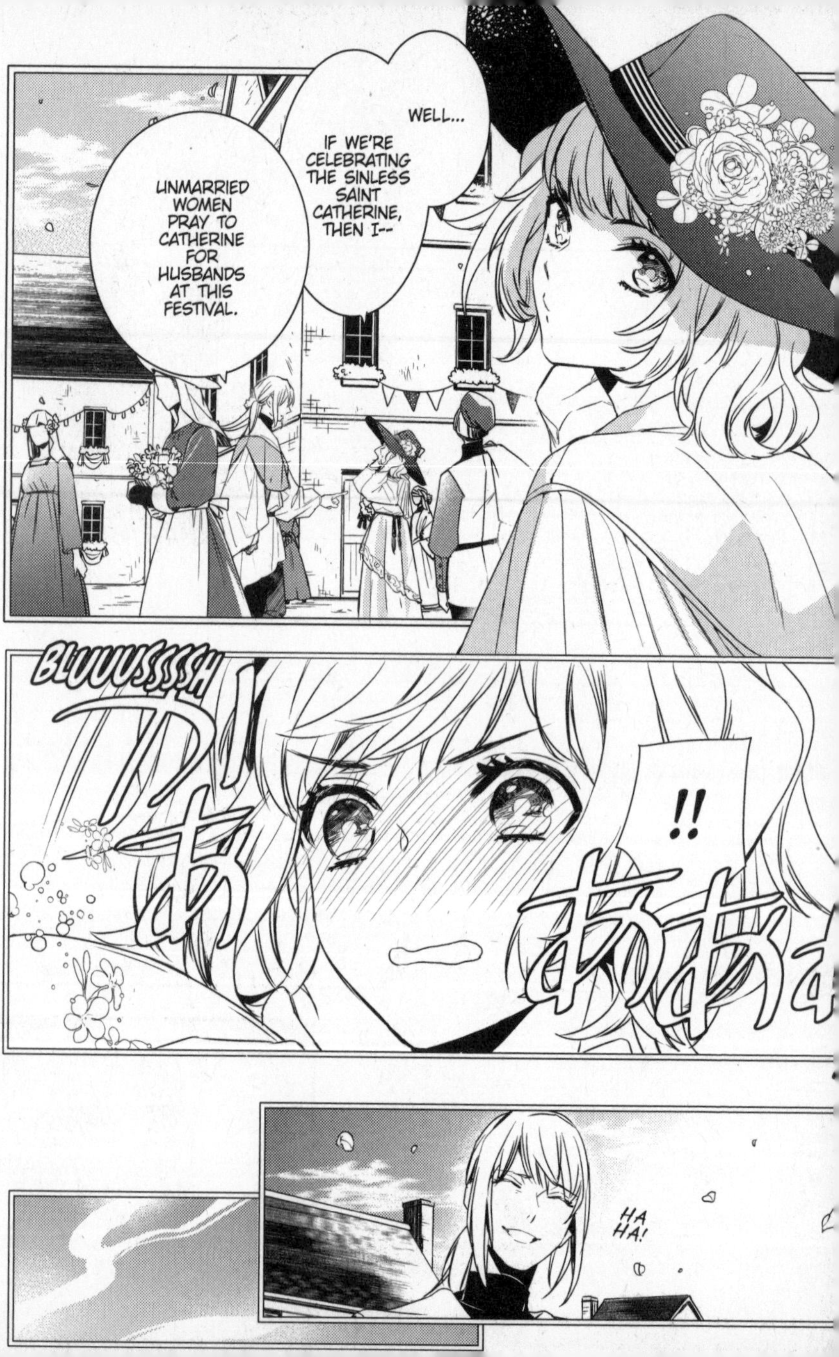
WELL... IF WE'RE CELEBRATING THE SINLESS SAINT CATHERINE, THEN I--
UNMARRIED WOMEN PRAY TO CATHERINE FOR HUSBANDS AT THIS FESTIVAL.
!!
BLUUUSSSSH
HA HA!

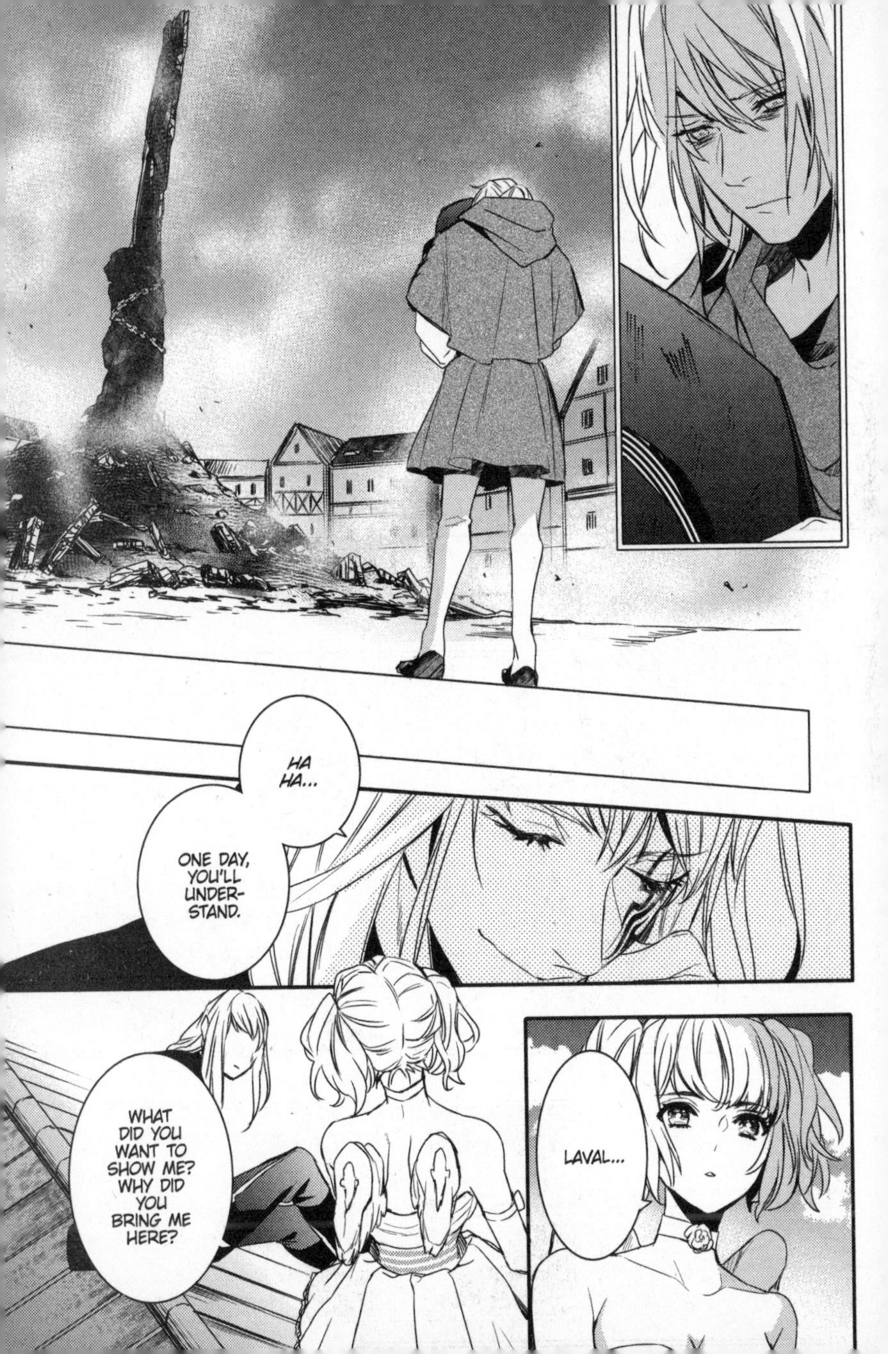
HA HA...
ONE DAY, YOU'LL UNDER-STAND.
LAVAL...
WHAT DID YOU WANT TO SHOW ME? WHY DID YOU BRING ME HERE?

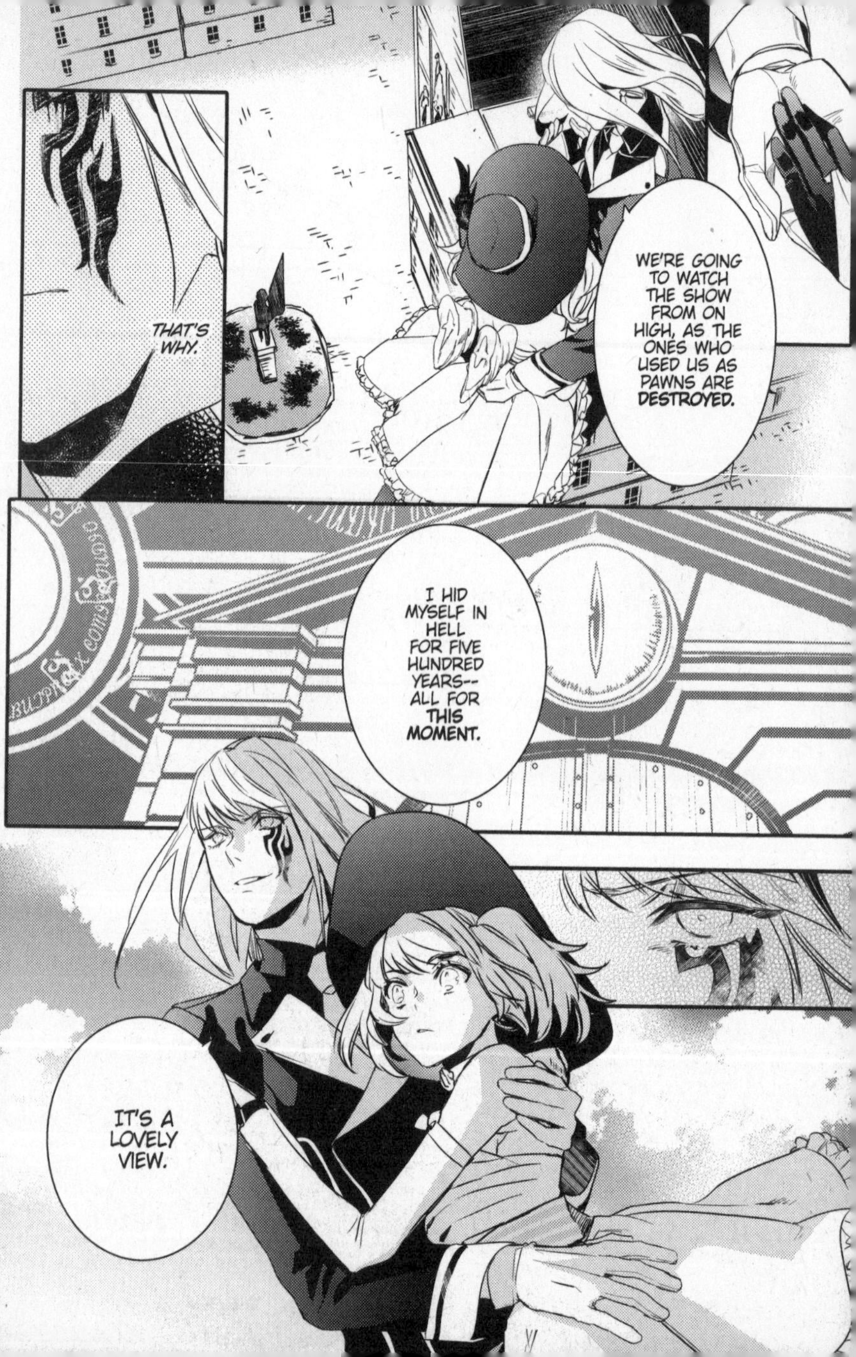
WE'RE GOING TO WATCH THE SHOW FROM ON HIGH, AS THE ONES WHO USED US AS PAWNS ARE DESTROYED.
THAT'S WHY.
I HID MYSELF IN HELL FOR FIVE HUNDRED YEARS--ALL FOR THIS MOMENT.
IT'S A LOVELY VIEW.

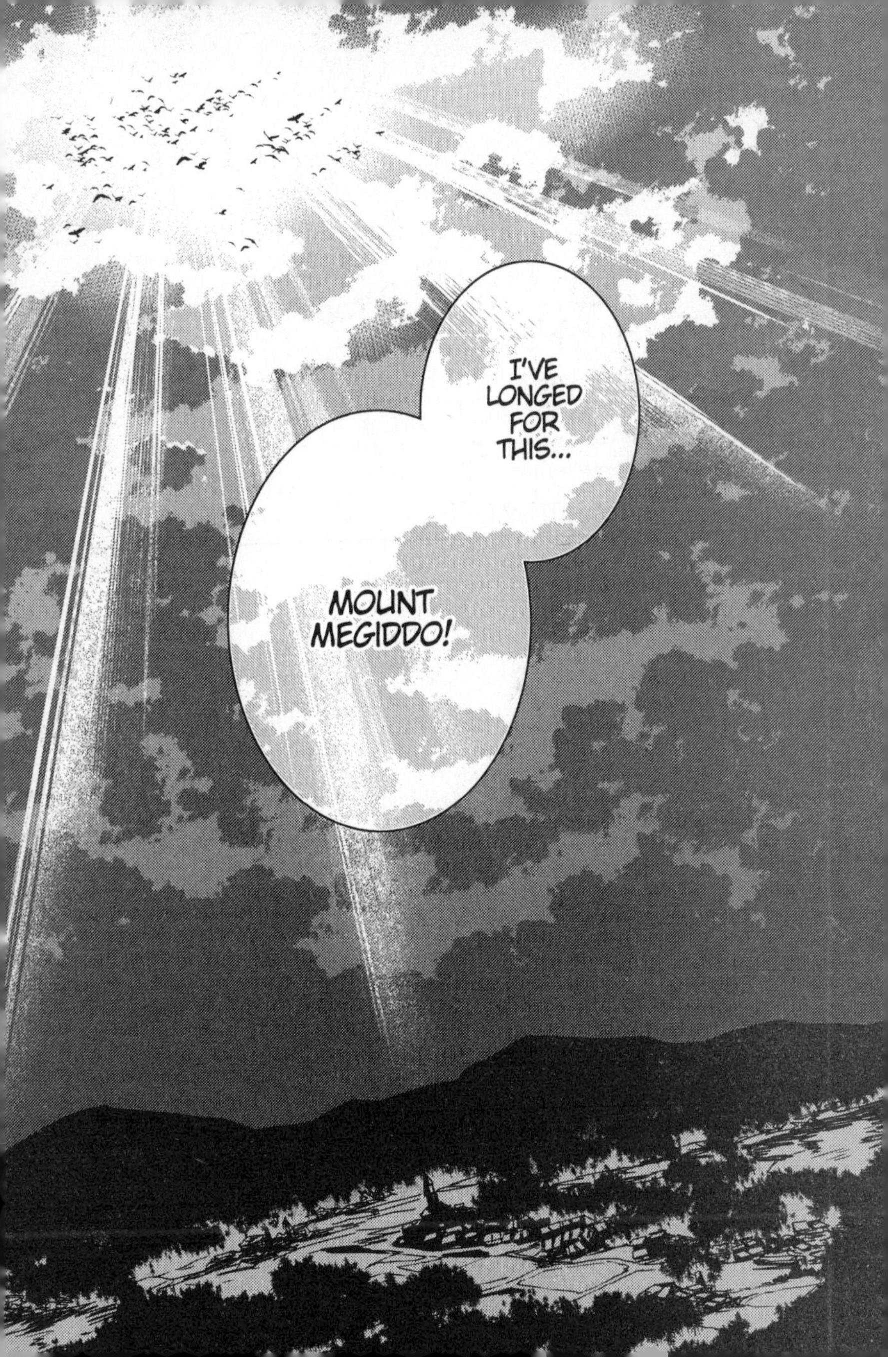
I'VE LONGED FOR THIS...
MOUNT MEGIDDO!

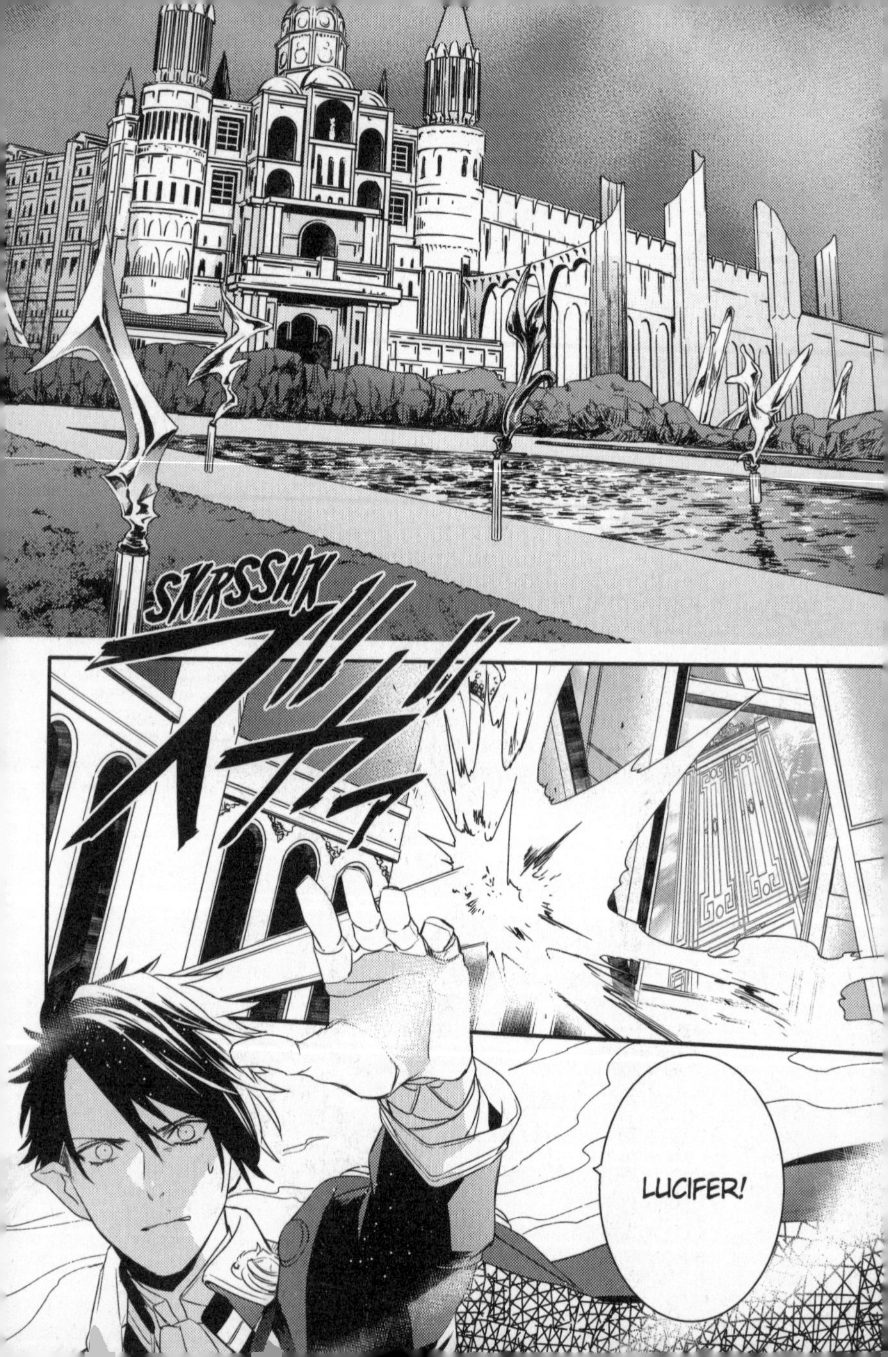
SKRSSHK
LUCIFER!

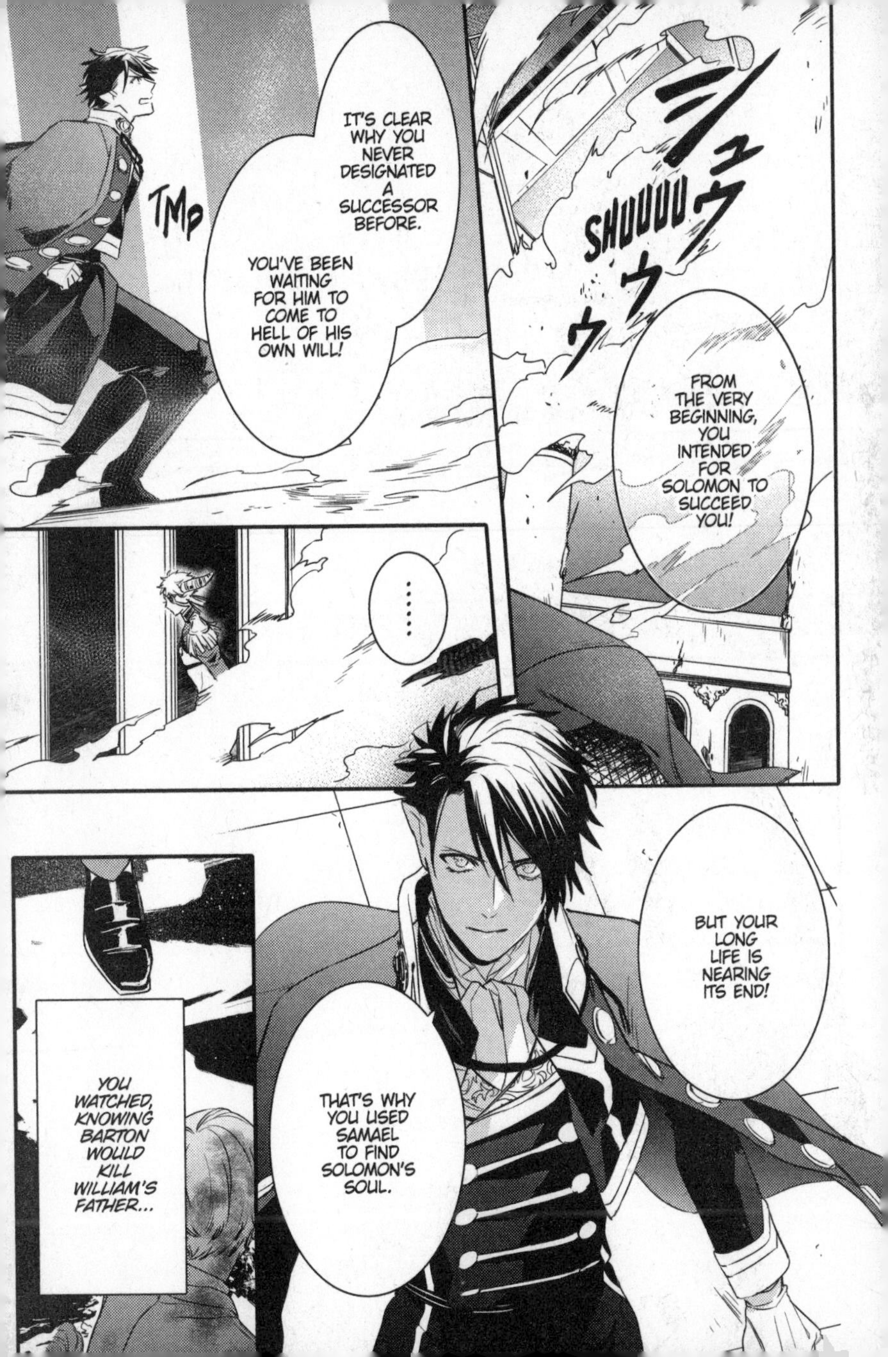
シュウウウ
SHUUUU
FROM THE VERY BEGINNING, YOU INTENDED FOR SOLOMON TO SUCCEED YOU!
IT'S CLEAR WHY YOU NEVER DESIGNATED A SUCCESSOR BEFORE.
YOU'VE BEEN WAITING FOR HIM TO COME TO HELL OF HIS OWN WILL!
TMP
......
BUT YOUR LONG LIFE IS NEARING ITS END!
THAT'S WHY YOU USED SAMAEL TO FIND SOLOMON'S SOUL.
YOU WATCHED, KNOWING BARTON WOULD KILL WILLIAM'S FATHER...

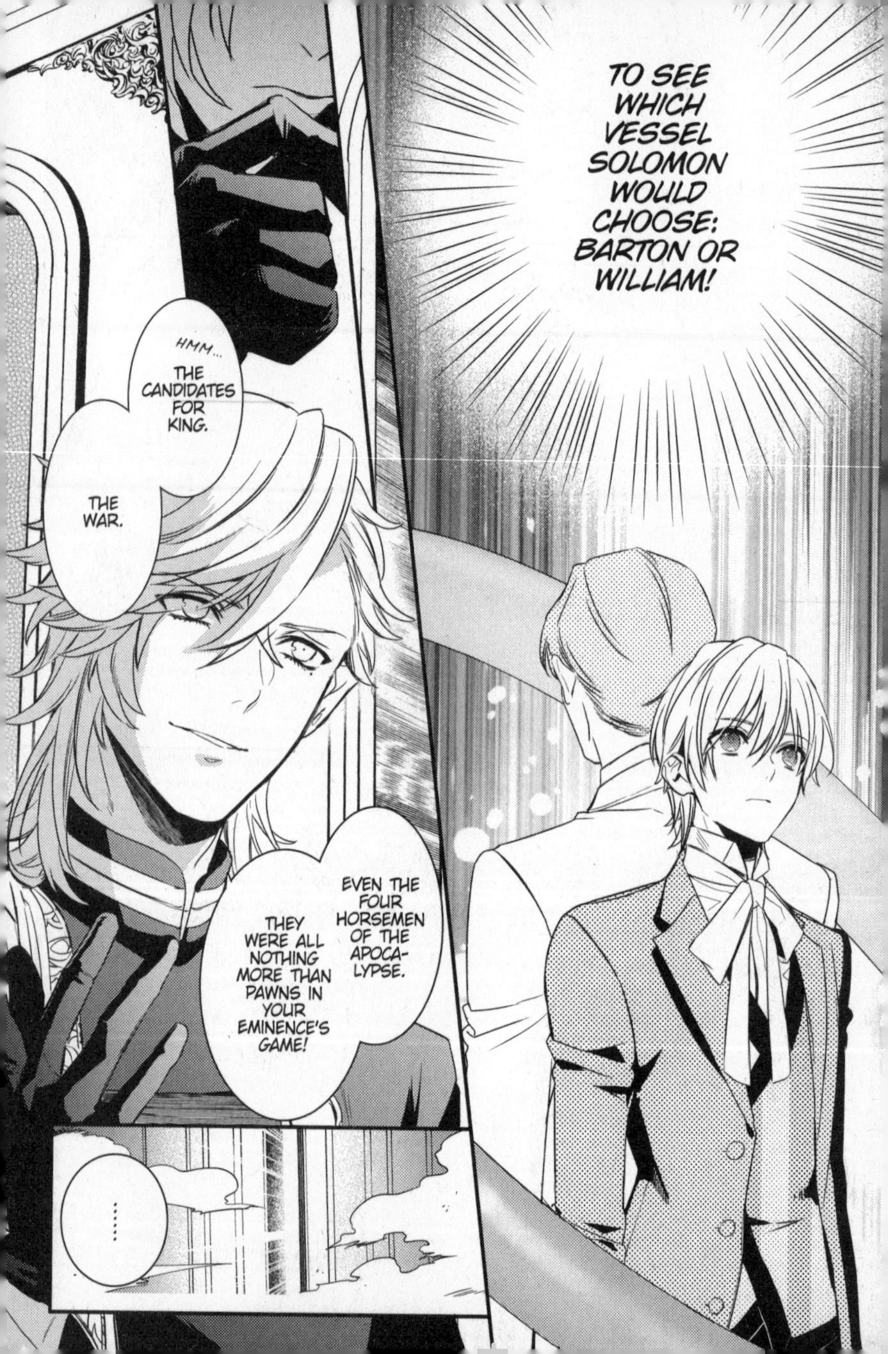
TO SEE WHICH VESSEL SOLOMON WOULD CHOOSE: BARTON OR WILLIAM!
HMM... THE CANDIDATES FOR KING.
THE WAR.
EVEN THE FOUR HORSEMEN OF THE APOCA-LYPSE.
THEY WERE ALL NOTHING MORE THAN PAWNS IN YOUR EMINENCE'S GAME!
......

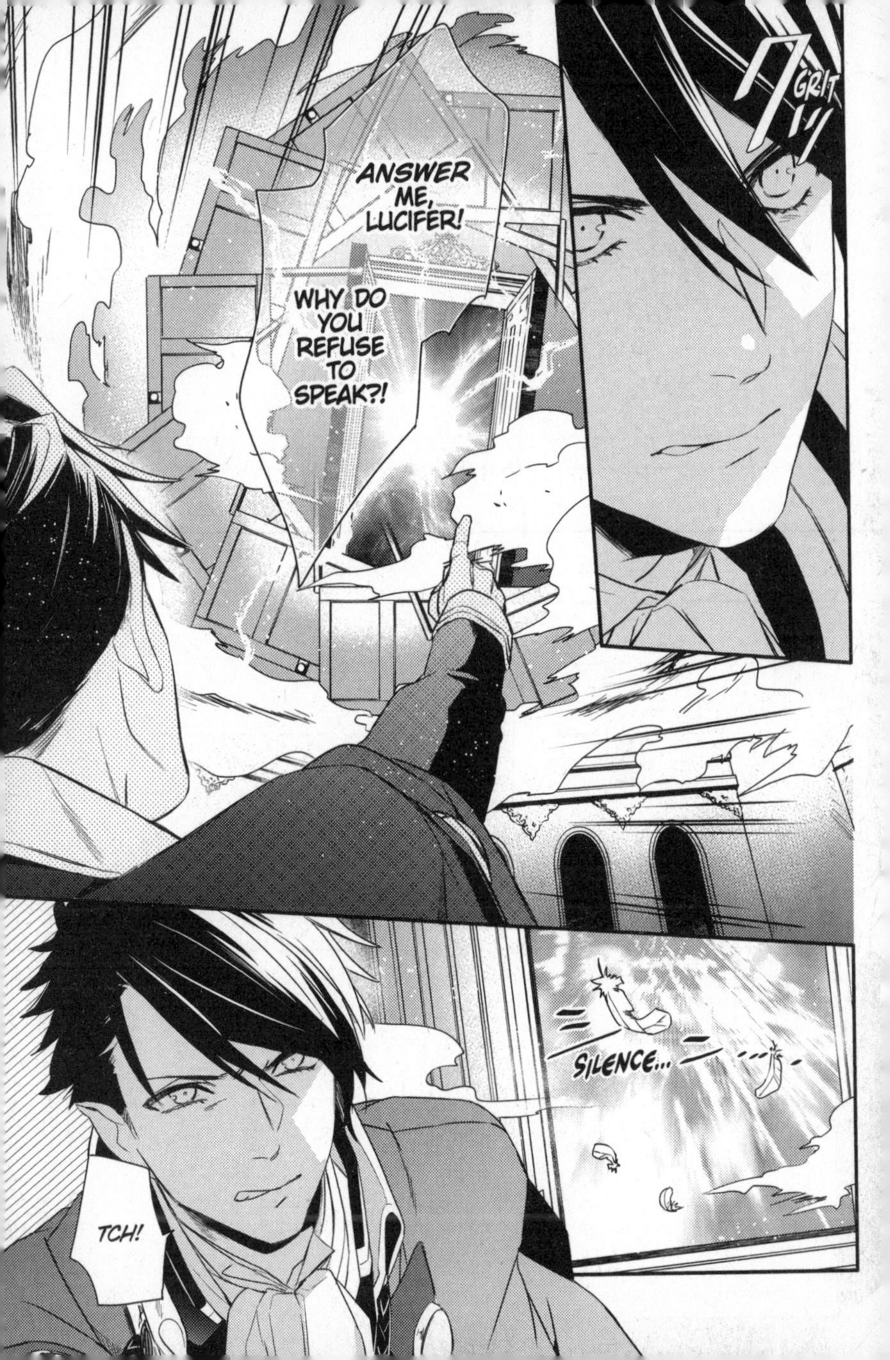
GRIT
ANSWER ME, LUCIFER!
WHY DO YOU REFUSE TO SPEAK?!
SILENCE...
TCH!

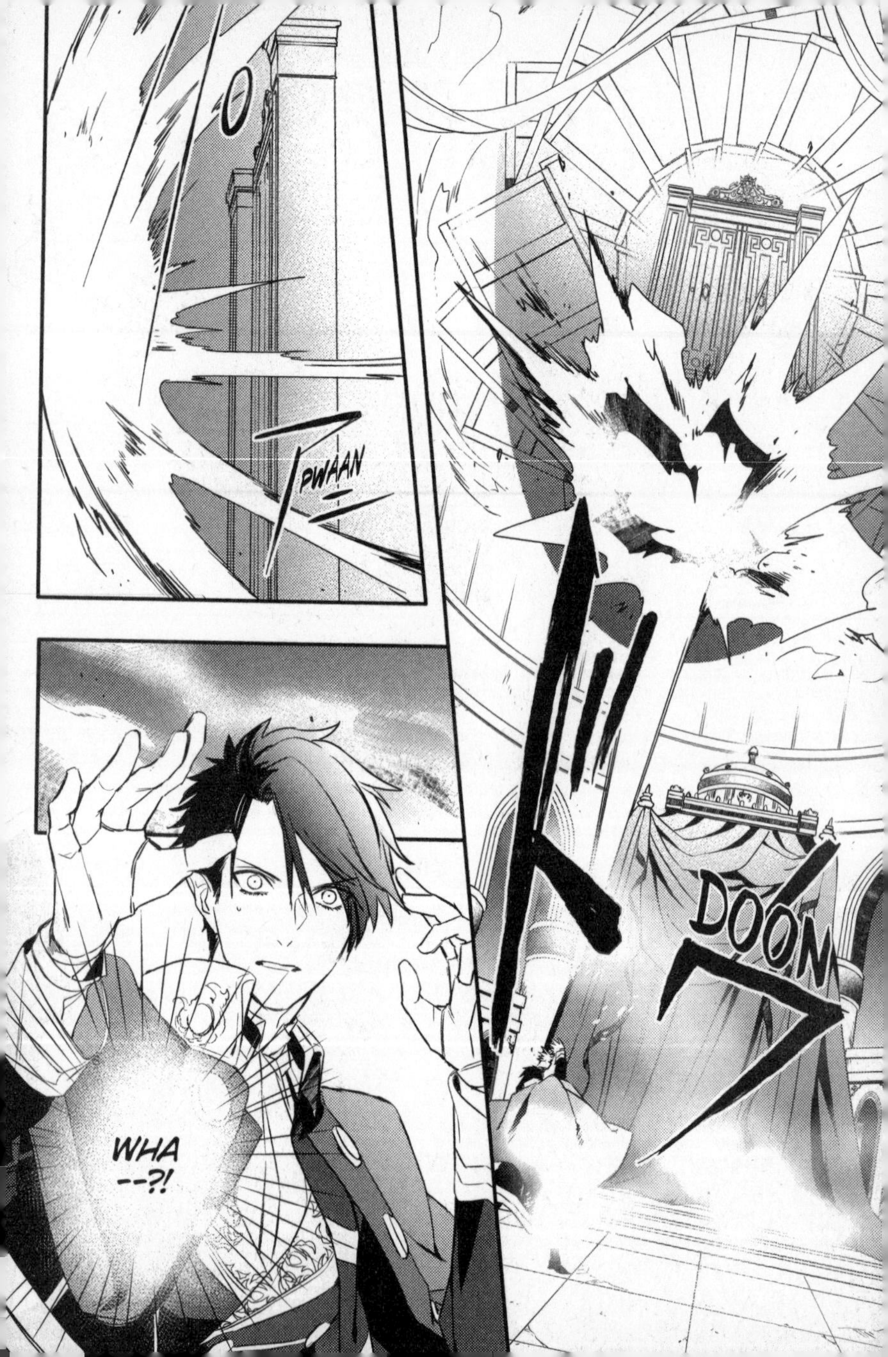
DOON
PWAAN
WHA --?!

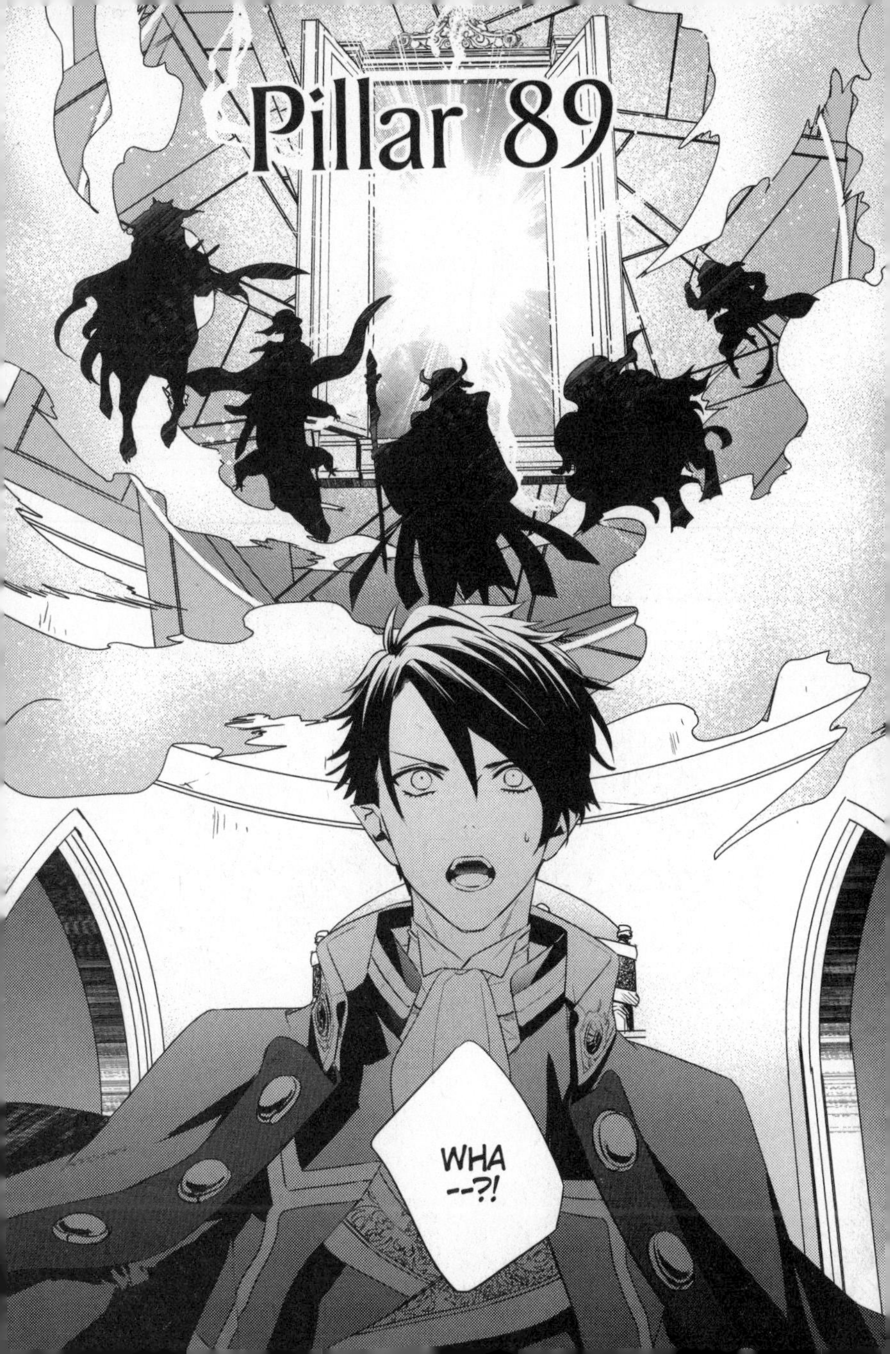
Pillar 89
WHA --?!

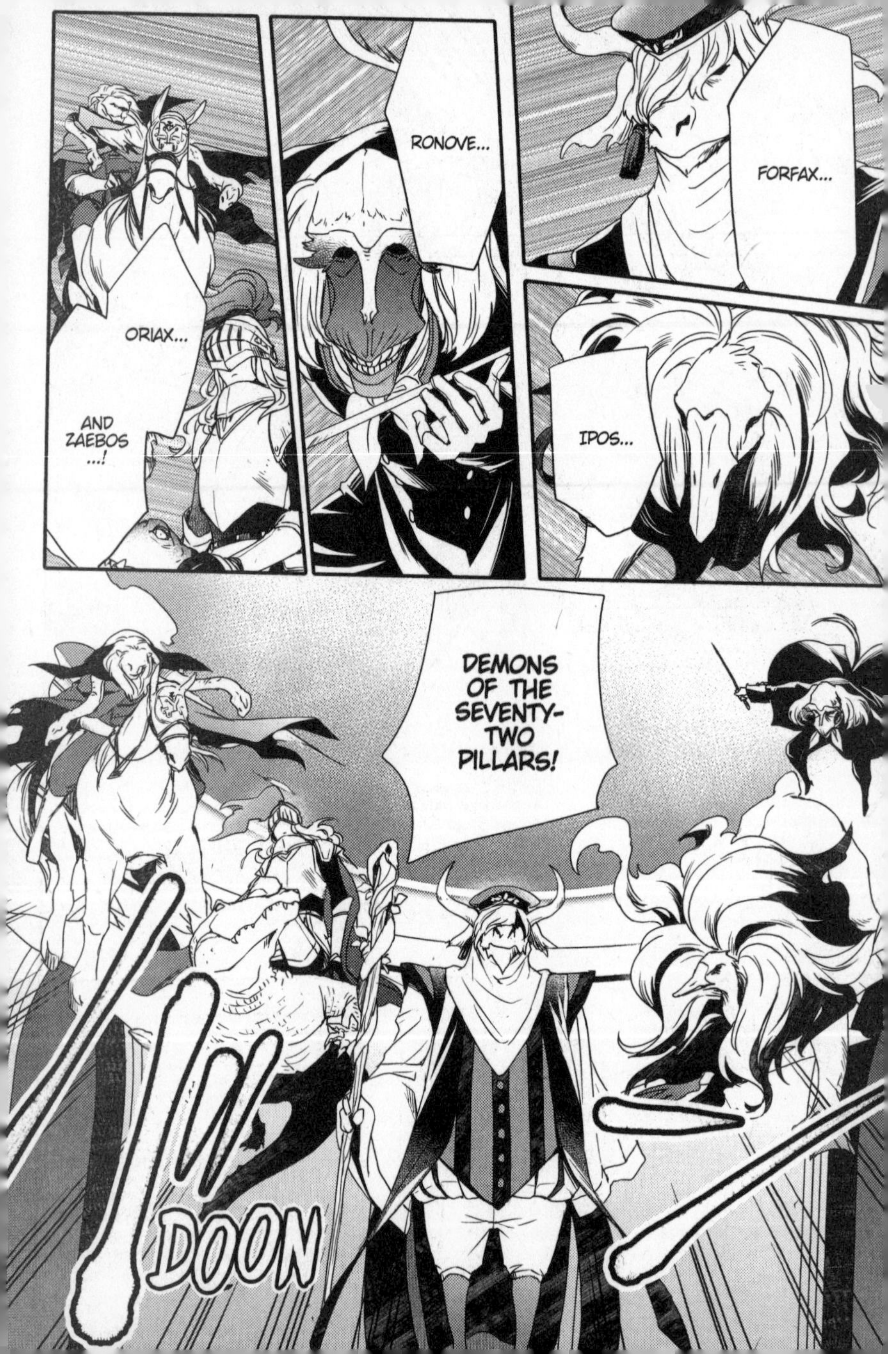
FORFAX...
IPOS...
RONOVE...
ORIAX...
AND ZAEBOS ...!
DEMONS OF THE SEVENTY-TWO PILLARS!
DOON

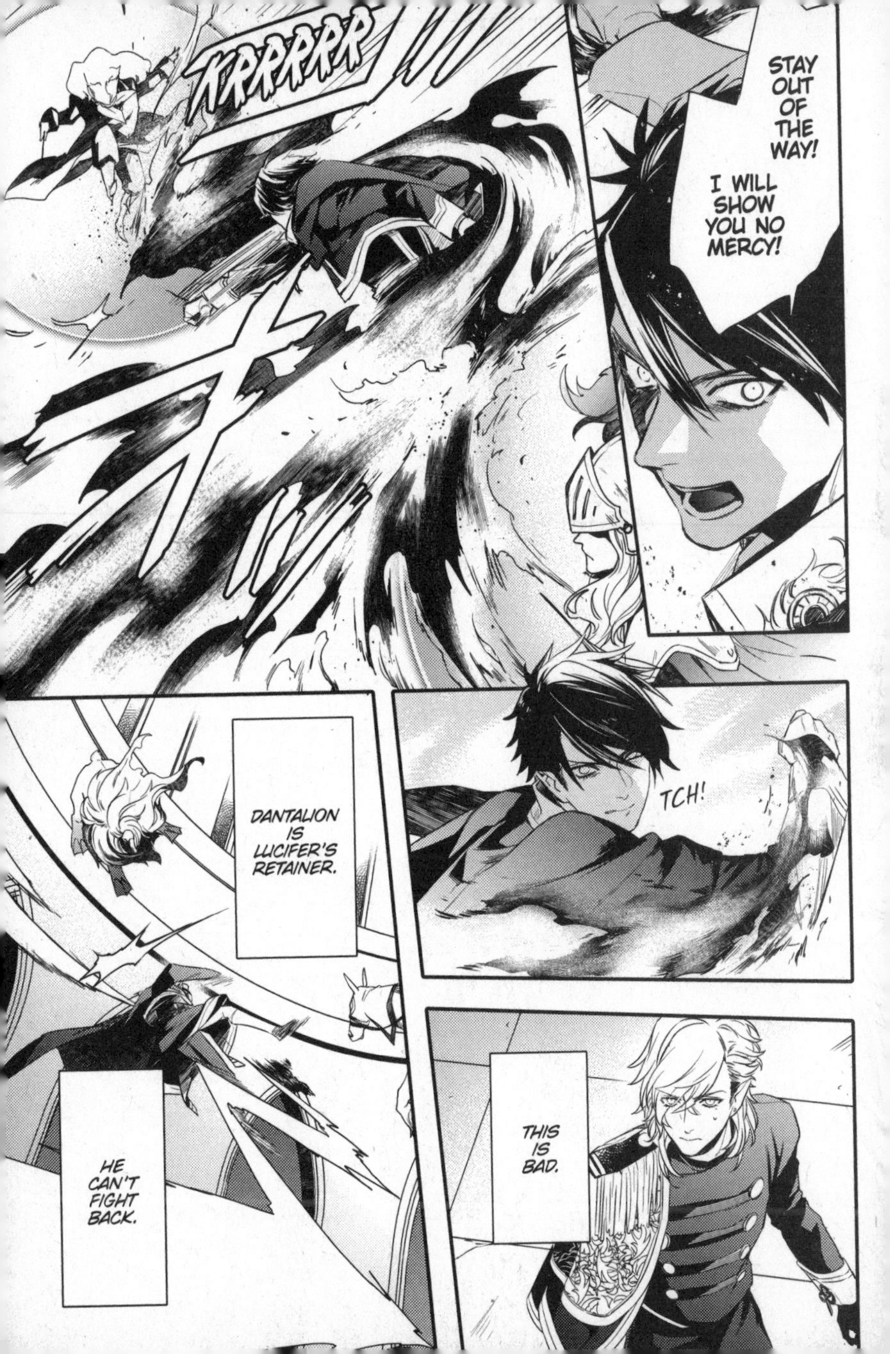
STAY OUT OF THE WAY!
I WILL SHOW YOU NO MERCY!
KRRRRR
TCH!
DANTALION IS LUCIFER'S RETAINER.
THIS IS BAD.
HE CAN'T FIGHT BACK.

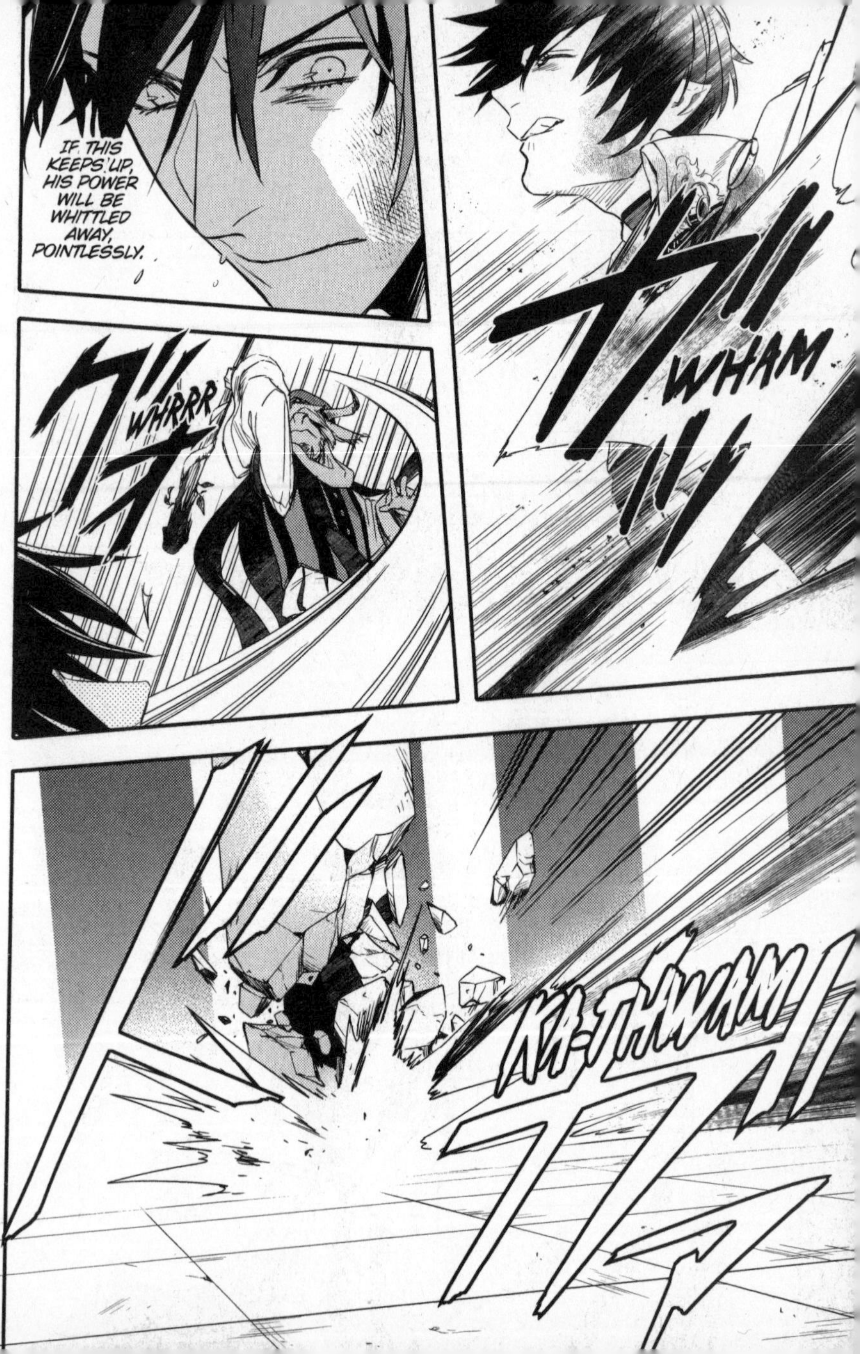
WHAM
IF THIS KEEPS UP, HIS POWER WILL BE WHITTLED AWAY, POINTLESSLY.
WHRRR
KA-THWAM

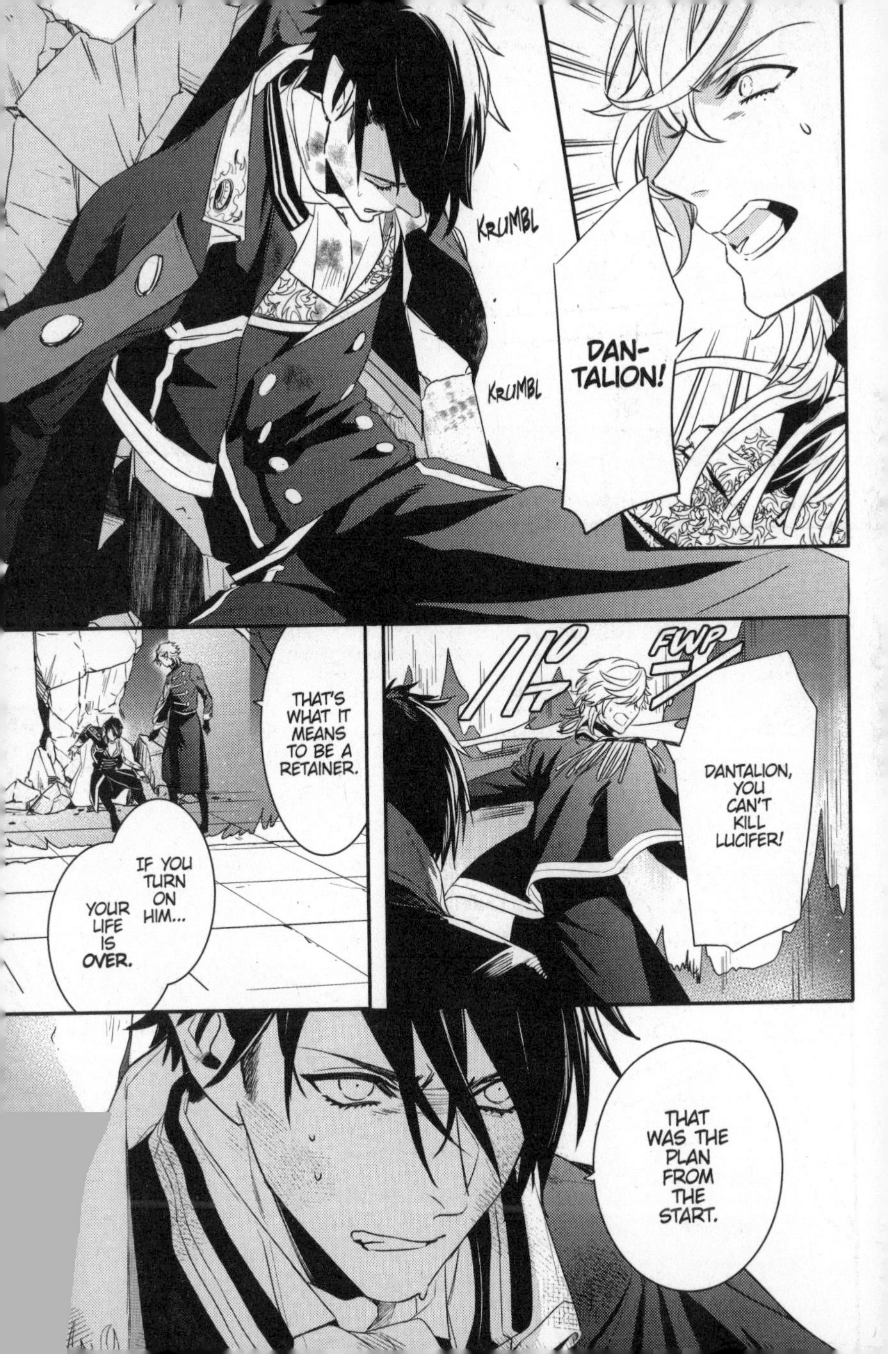
DAN-TALION!
KRUMBL
KRUMBL
FWP
DANTALION, YOU CAN'T KILL LUCIFER!
THAT'S WHAT IT MEANS TO BE A RETAINER.
IF YOU TURN ON HIM...
YOUR LIFE IS OVER.
THAT WAS THE PLAN FROM THE START.

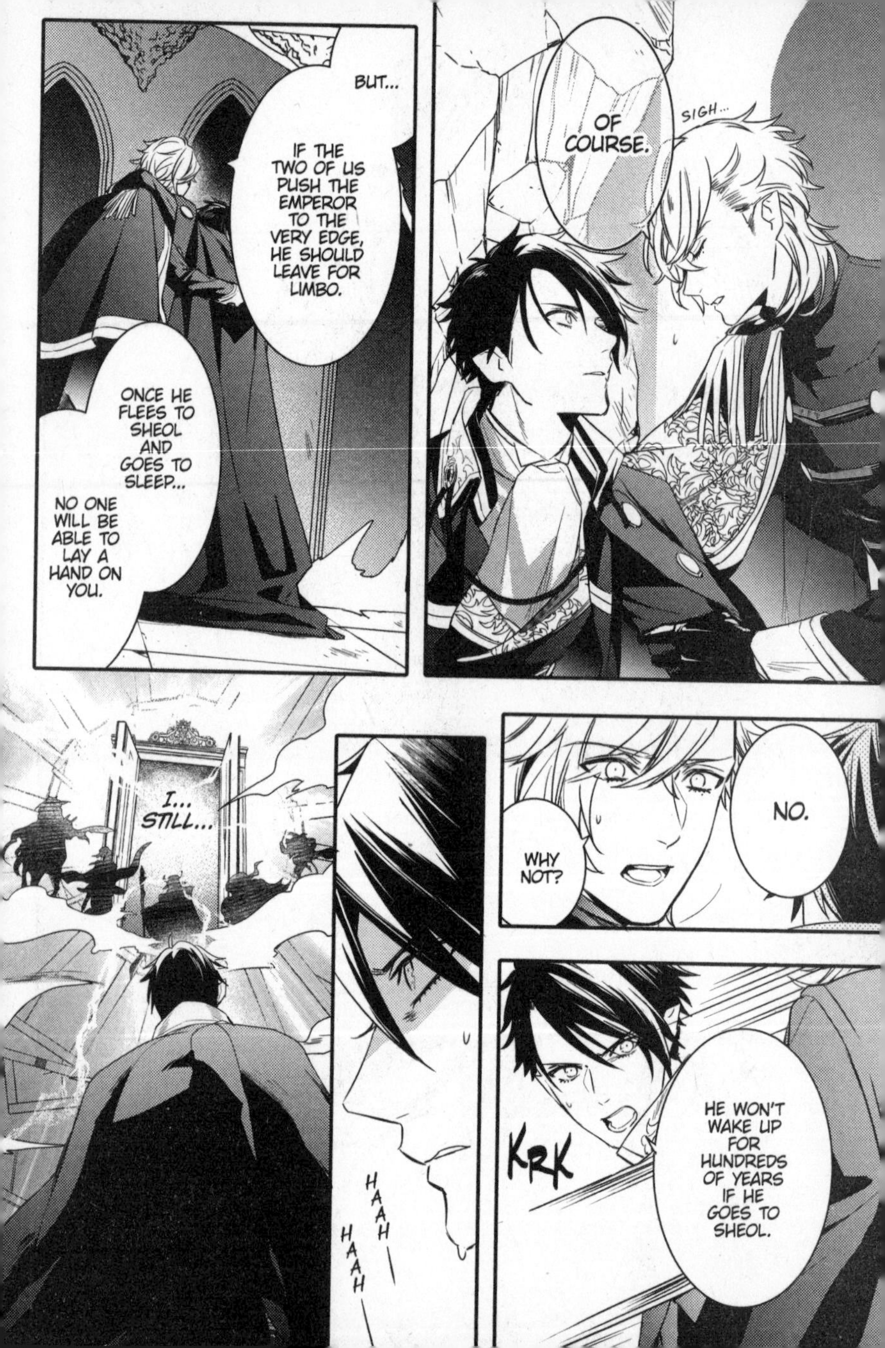
OF COURSE.
SIGH...
BUT...
IF THE TWO OF US PUSH THE EMPEROR TO THE VERY EDGE, HE SHOULD LEAVE FOR LIMBO.
ONCE HE FLEES TO SHEOL AND GOES TO SLEEP...
NO ONE WILL BE ABLE TO LAY A HAND ON YOU.
NO.
WHY NOT?
HE WON'T WAKE UP FOR HUNDREDS OF YEARS IF HE GOES TO SHEOL.
KRK
HAAAH
HAAH
I... STILL...

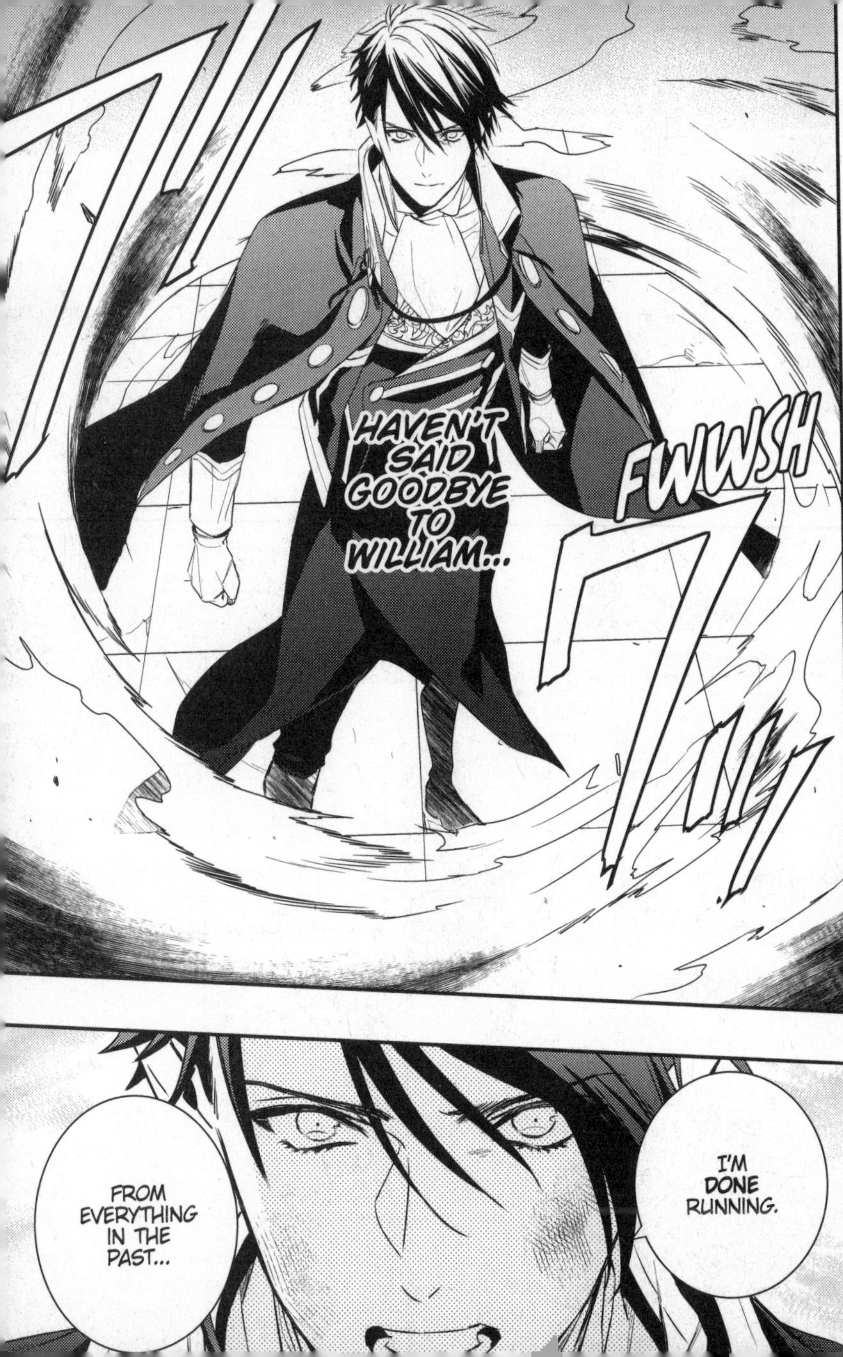
HAVEN'T SAID GOODBYE TO WILLIAM...
FWWSH
I'M DONE RUNNING.
FROM EVERYTHING IN THE PAST...

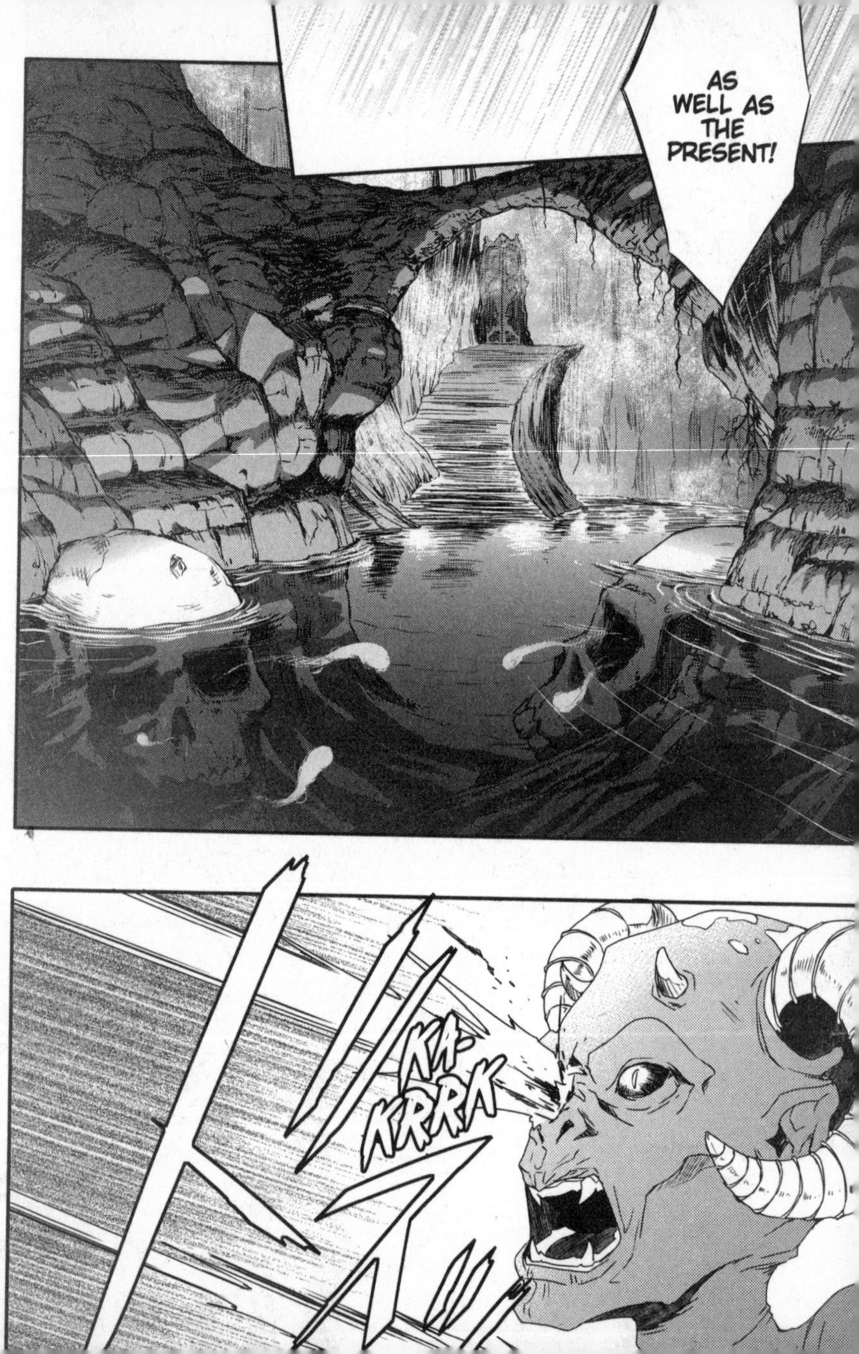
AS WELL AS THE PRESENT!
KA-KRRK

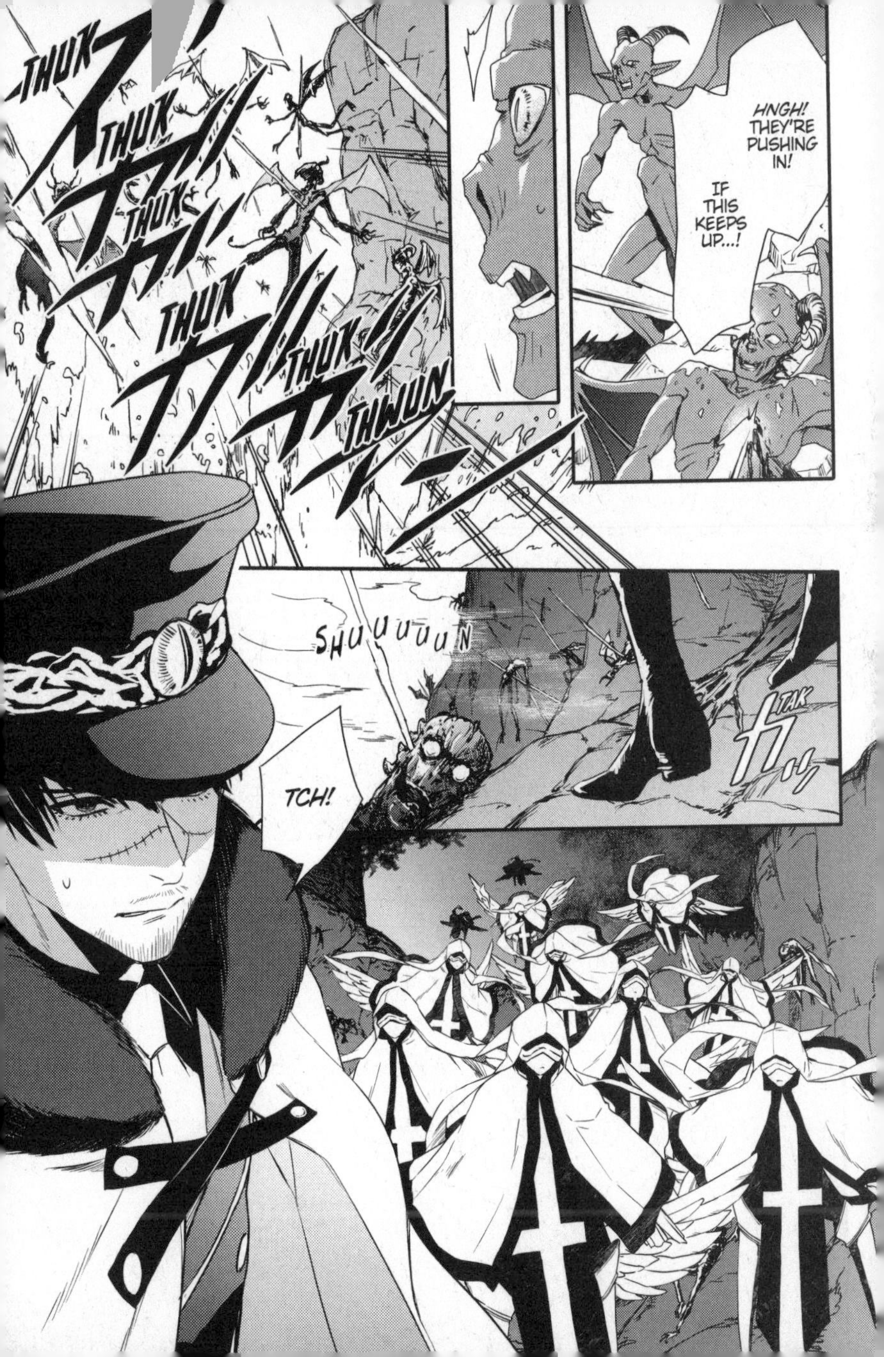
HNGH! THEY'RE PUSHING IN!
IF THIS KEEPS UP...!
THUK
THUK
THUK
THUK
THUK
THWUN
SHUUUUUUN
TAK
TCH!

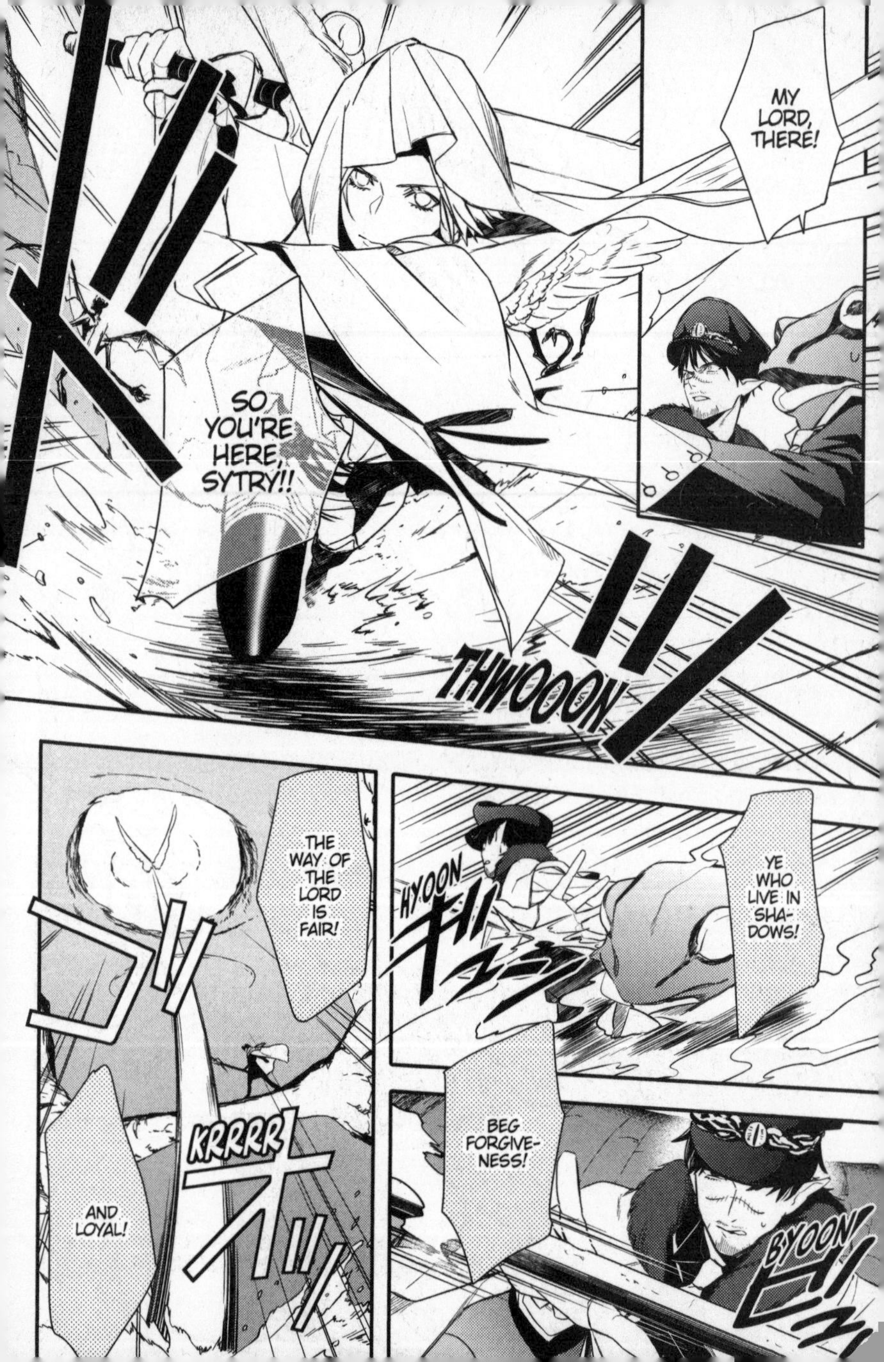
MY LORD, THERE!
SO YOU'RE HERE, SYTRY!!
THWOOOON
YE WHO LIVE IN SHADOWS!
HYOON
BEG FORGIVENESS!
BYOON
THE WAY OF THE LORD IS FAIR!
KRRRR
AND LOYAL!

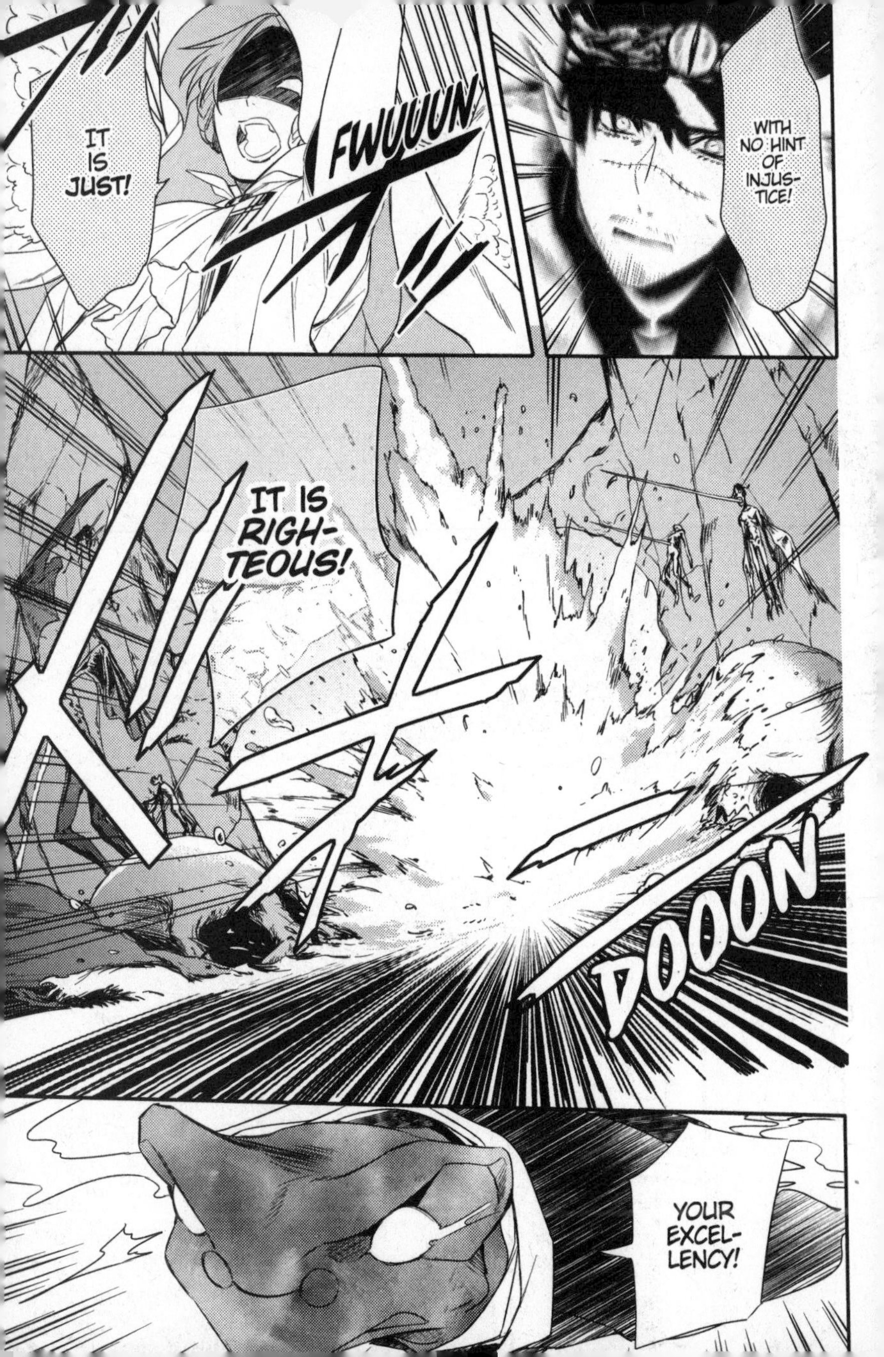
WITH NO HINT OF INJUS-TICE!
FWUUUN
IT IS JUST!
IT IS RIGH-TEOUS!
DOOON
YOUR EXCEL-LENCY!

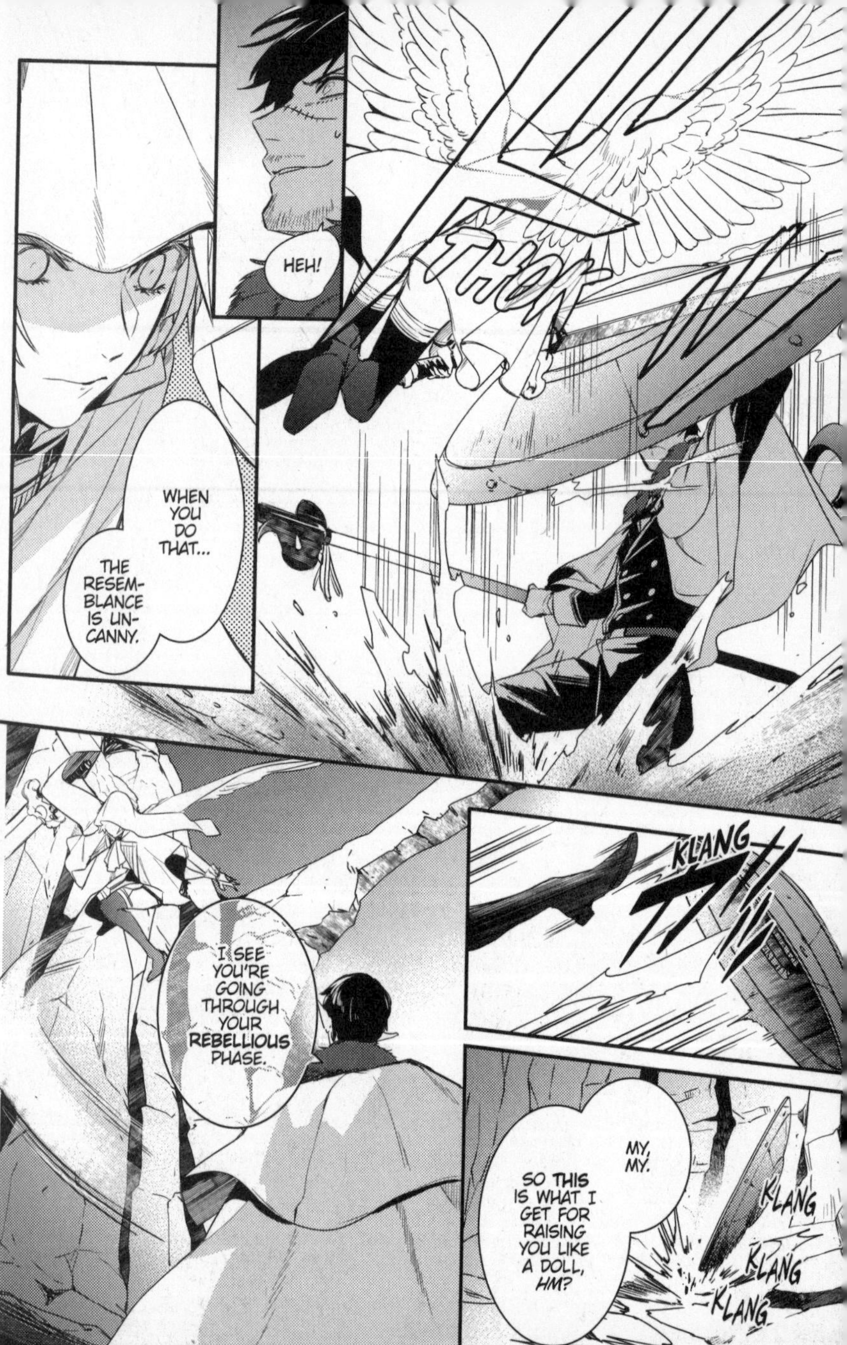
THOK
HEH!
WHEN YOU DO THAT...
THE RESEMBLANCE IS UNCANNY.
KLANG
MY, MY.
SO THIS IS WHAT I GET FOR RAISING YOU LIKE A DOLL, HM?
KLANG
KLANG
KLANG
I SEE YOU'RE GOING THROUGH YOUR REBELLIOUS PHASE.

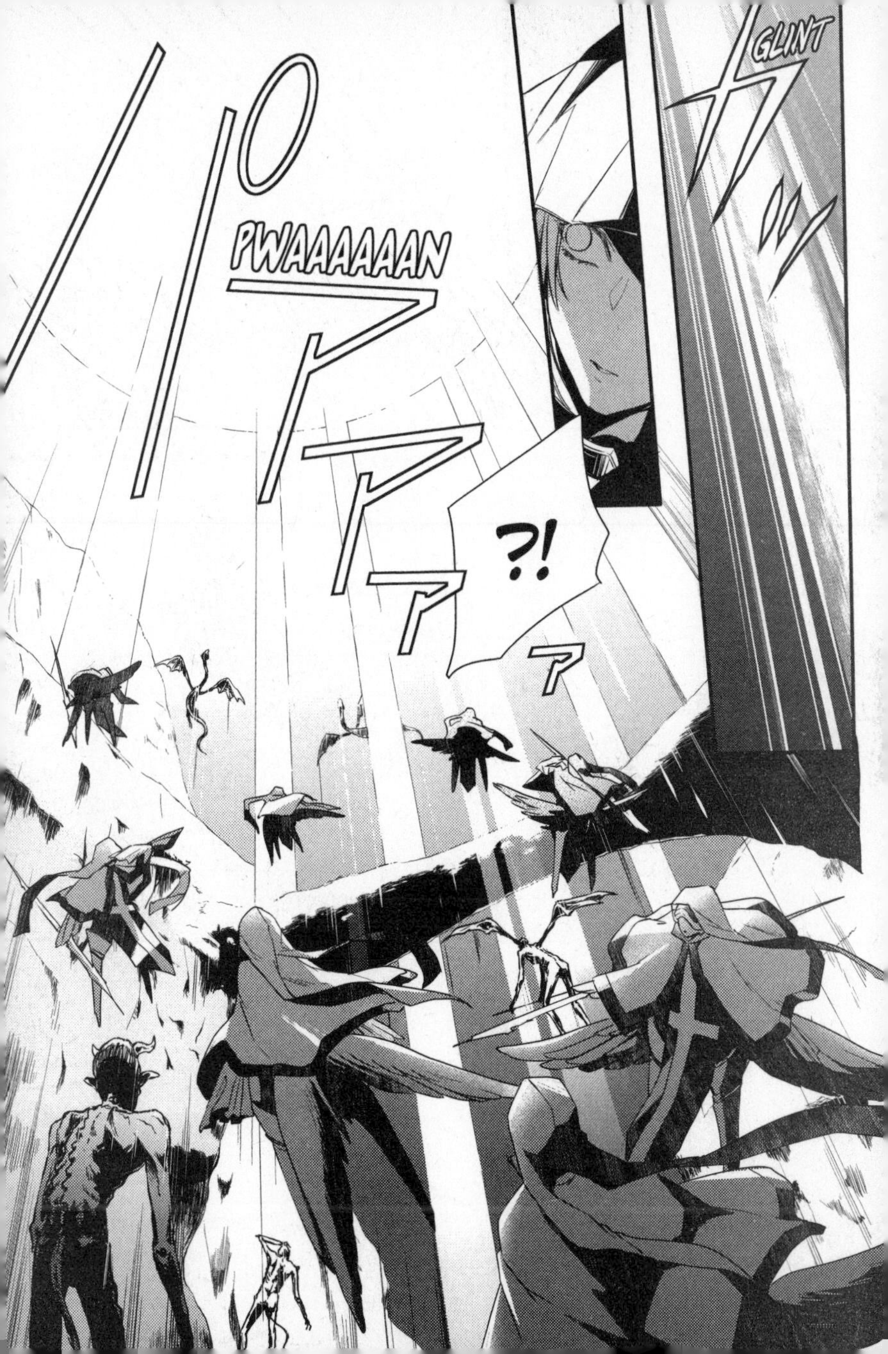
GLINT
?!
PWAAAAAAN

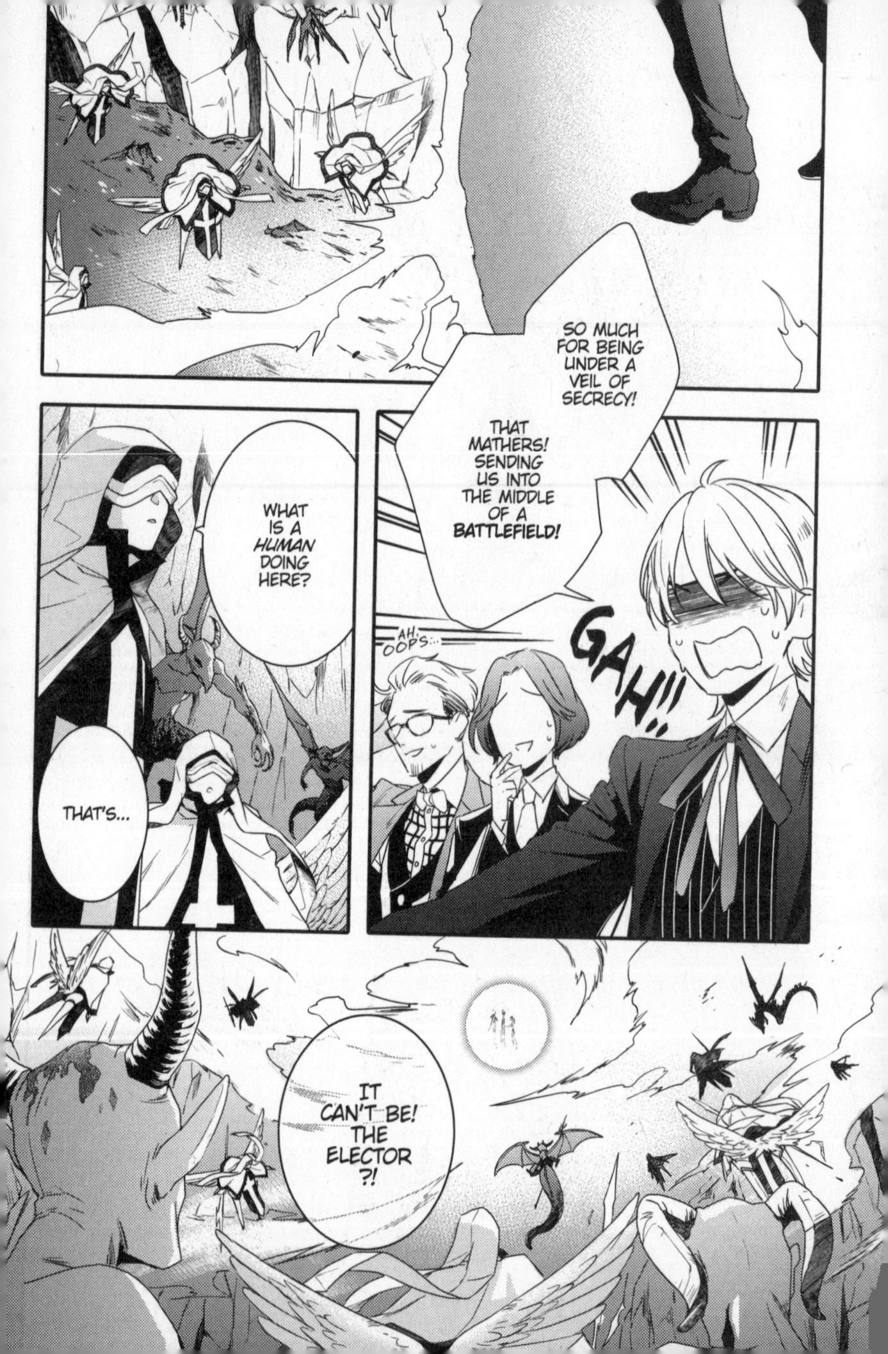
SO MUCH FOR BEING UNDER A VEIL OF SECRECY!
THAT MATHERS! SENDING US INTO THE MIDDLE OF A BATTLEFIELD!
GAH!!
AH, OOPS...
WHAT IS A *HUMAN* DOING HERE?
THAT'S...
IT CAN'T BE! THE ELECTOR ?!

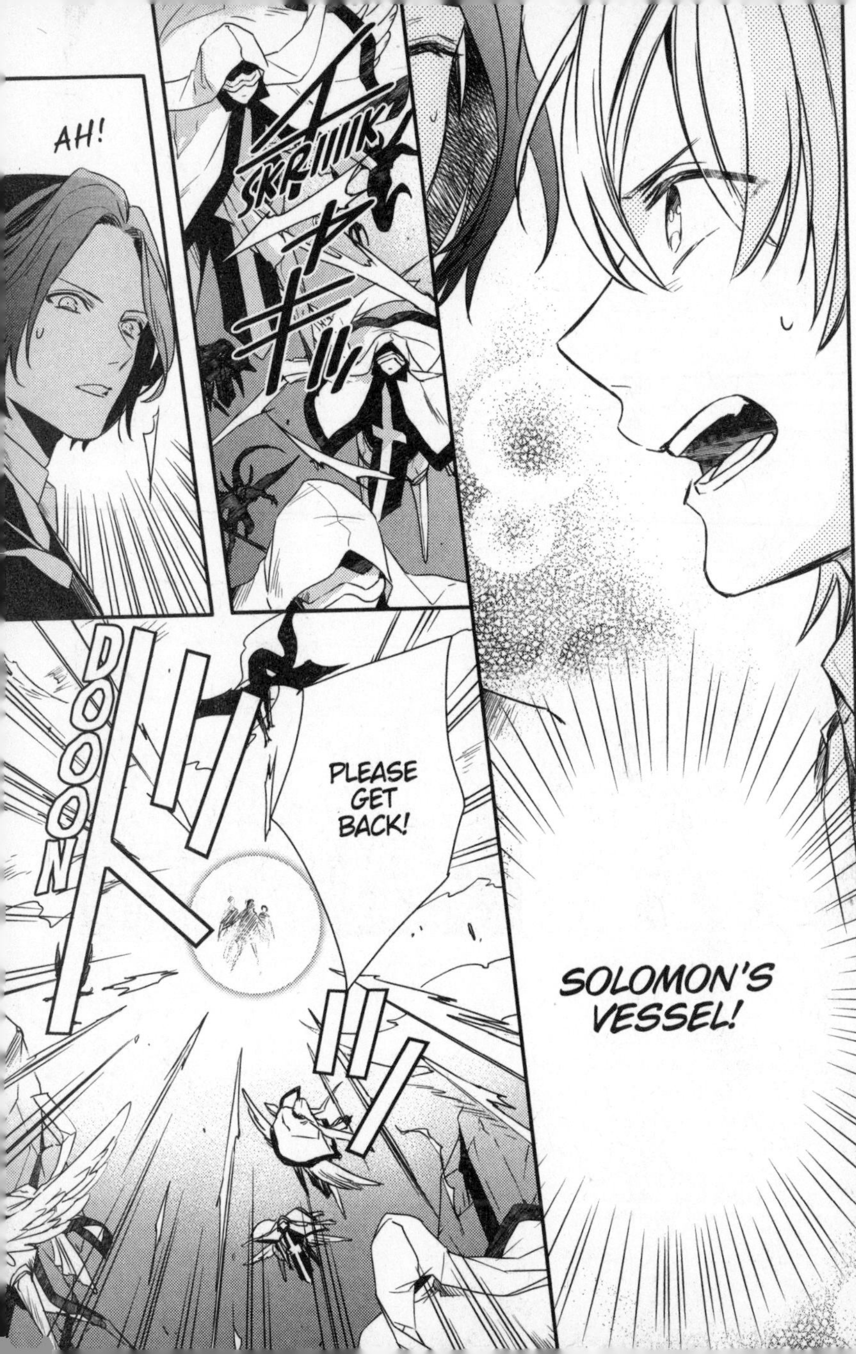
SOLOMON'S VESSEL!
SKRIIIIK
AH!
PLEASE GET BACK!
DOOOON

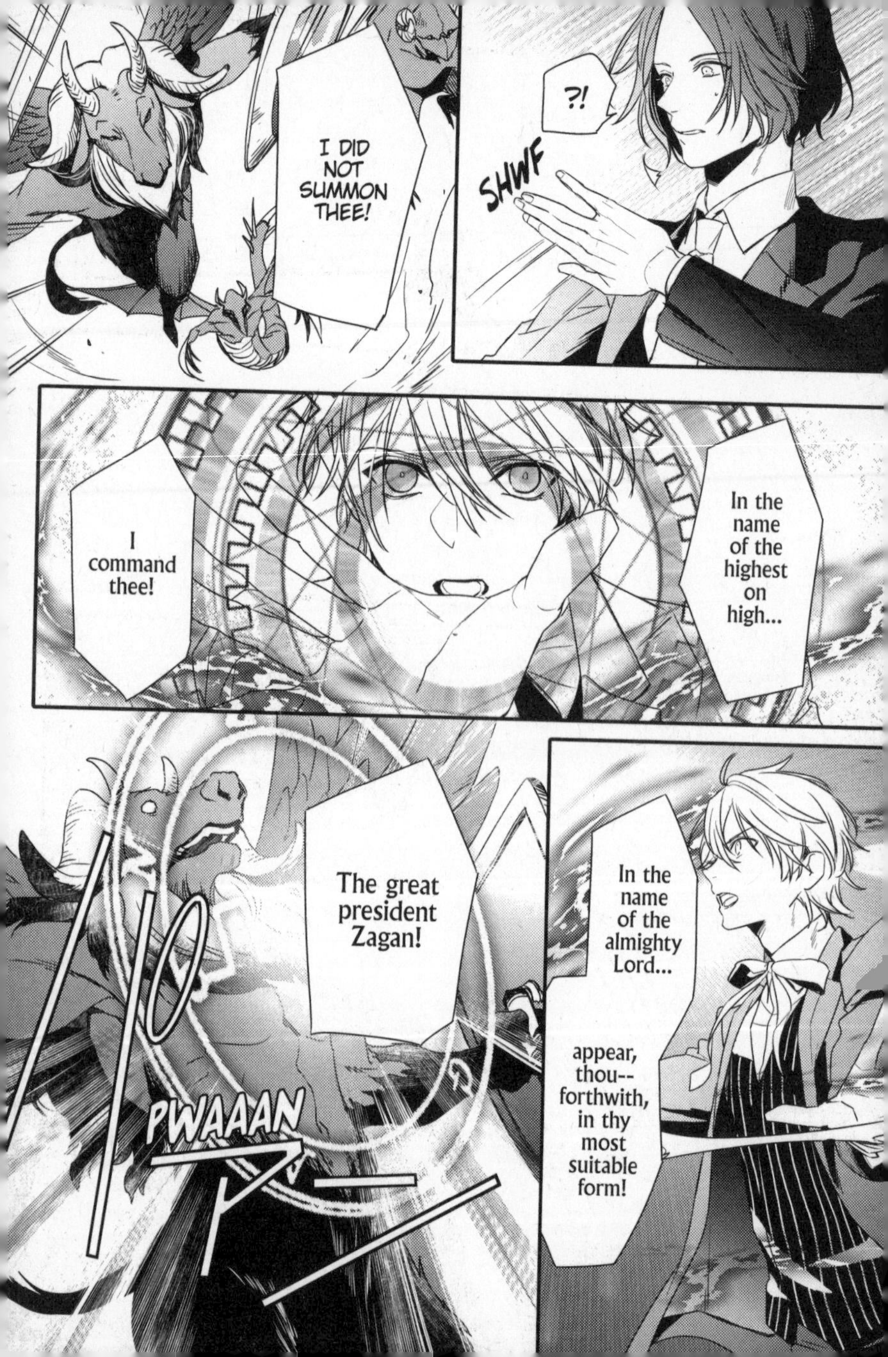
?!
SHWF
I DID NOT SUMMON THEE!
In the name of the highest on high...
I command thee!
In the name of the almighty Lord...
appear, thou--forthwith, in thy most suitable form!
The great president Zagan!
PWAAAN

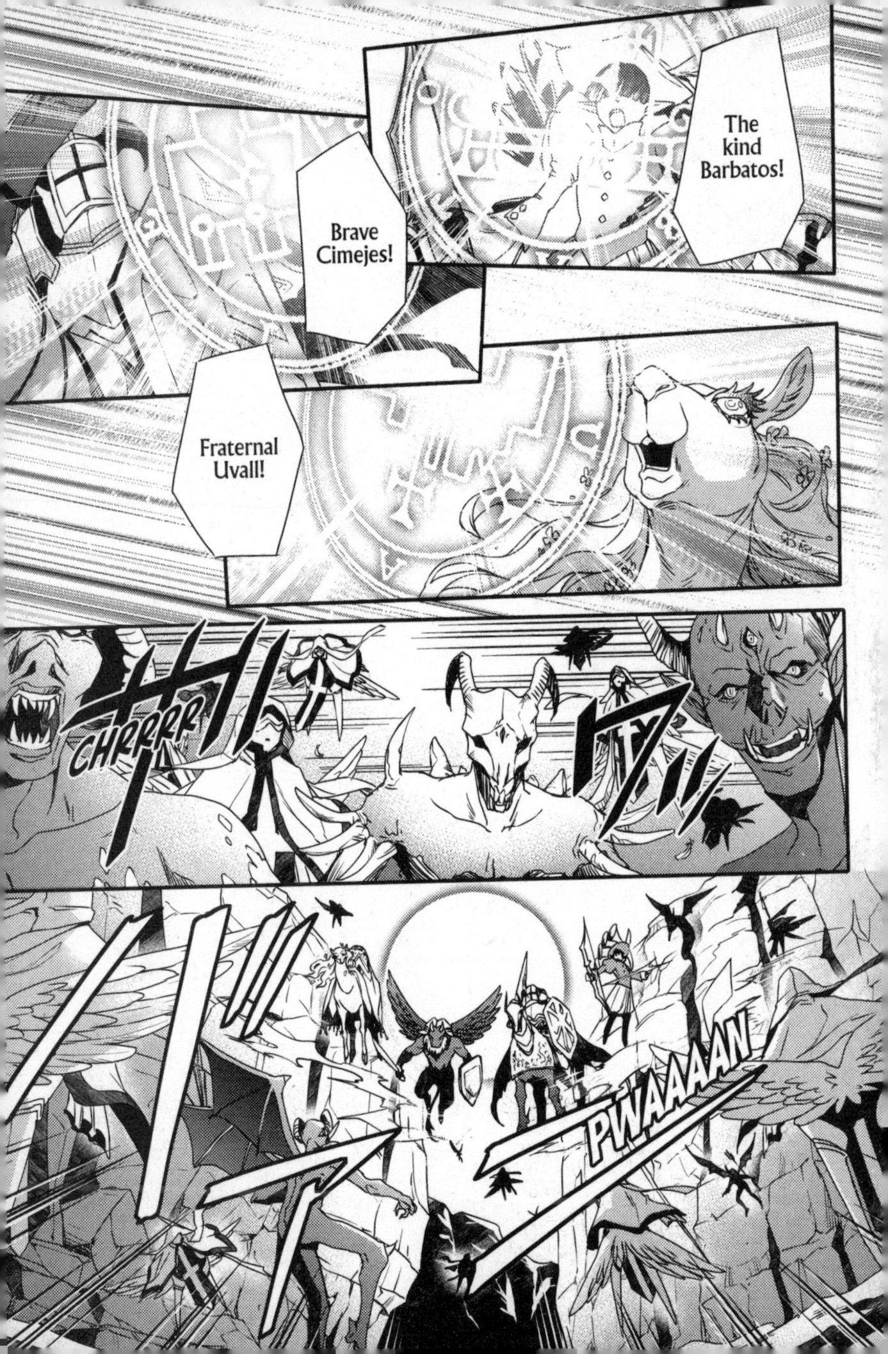
The kind Barbatos!
Brave Cimejes!
Fraternal Uvall!
CHRRRR
PWAAAAN

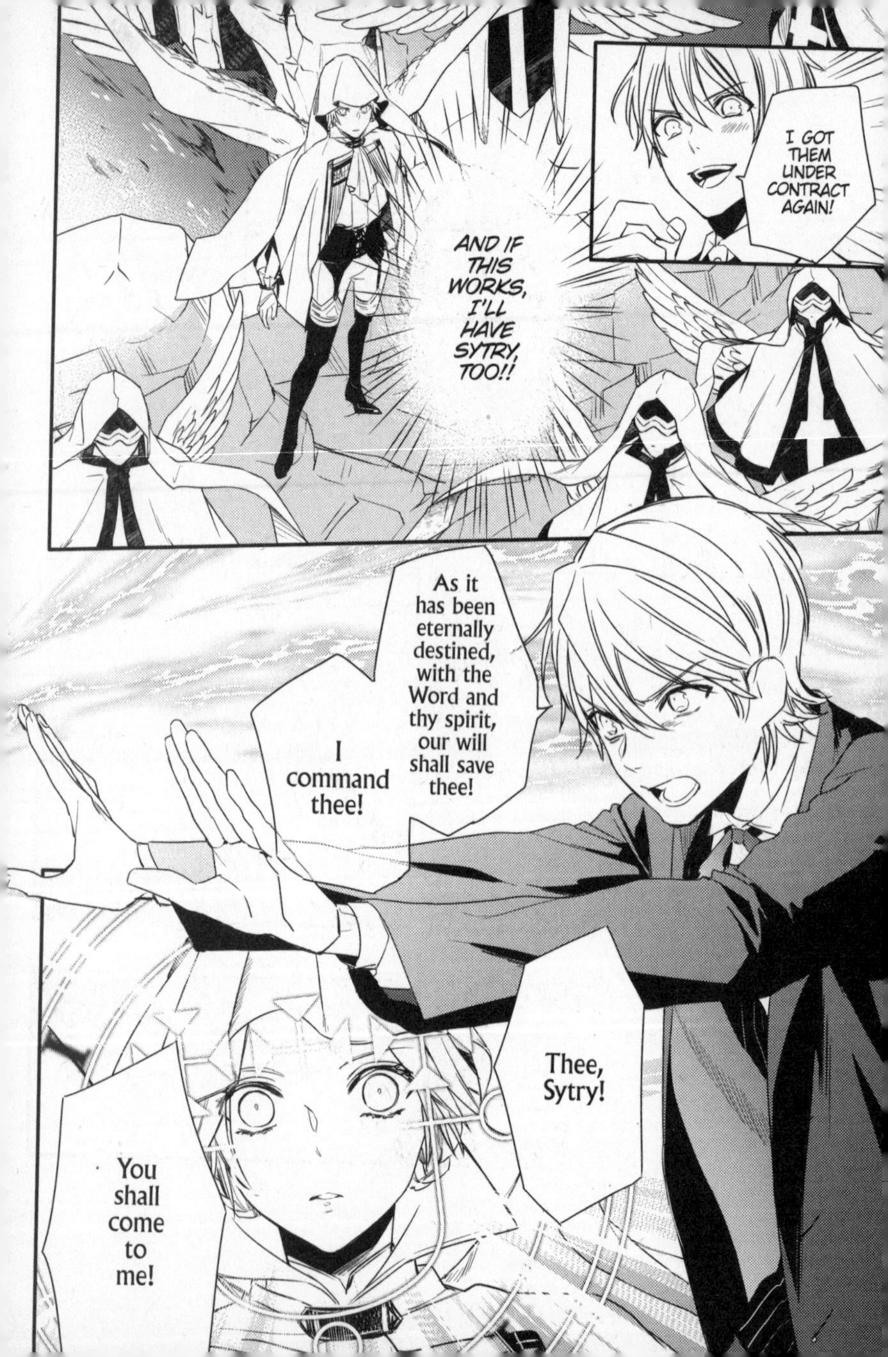
I GOT THEM UNDER CONTRACT AGAIN!
AND IF THIS WORKS, I'LL HAVE SYTRY, TOO!!
As it has been eternally destined, with the Word and thy spirit, our will shall save thee!
I command thee!
Thee, Sytry!
You shall come to me!

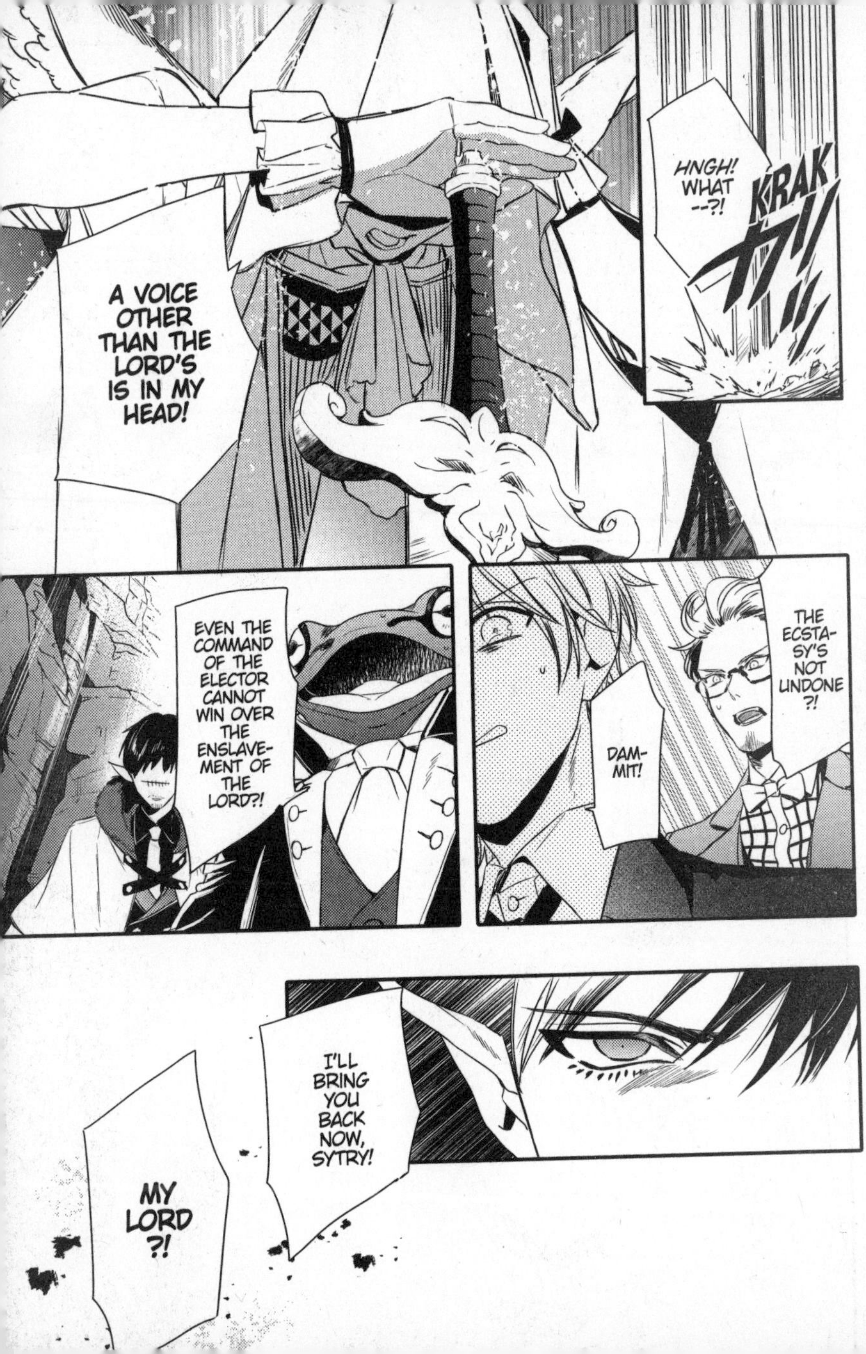
HNGH! WHAT--?!
KRAK
A VOICE OTHER THAN THE LORD'S IS IN MY HEAD!
THE ECSTASY'S NOT UNDONE?!
DAMMIT!
EVEN THE COMMAND OF THE ELECTOR CANNOT WIN OVER THE ENSLAVEMENT OF THE LORD?!
I'LL BRING YOU BACK NOW, SYTRY!
MY LORD?!

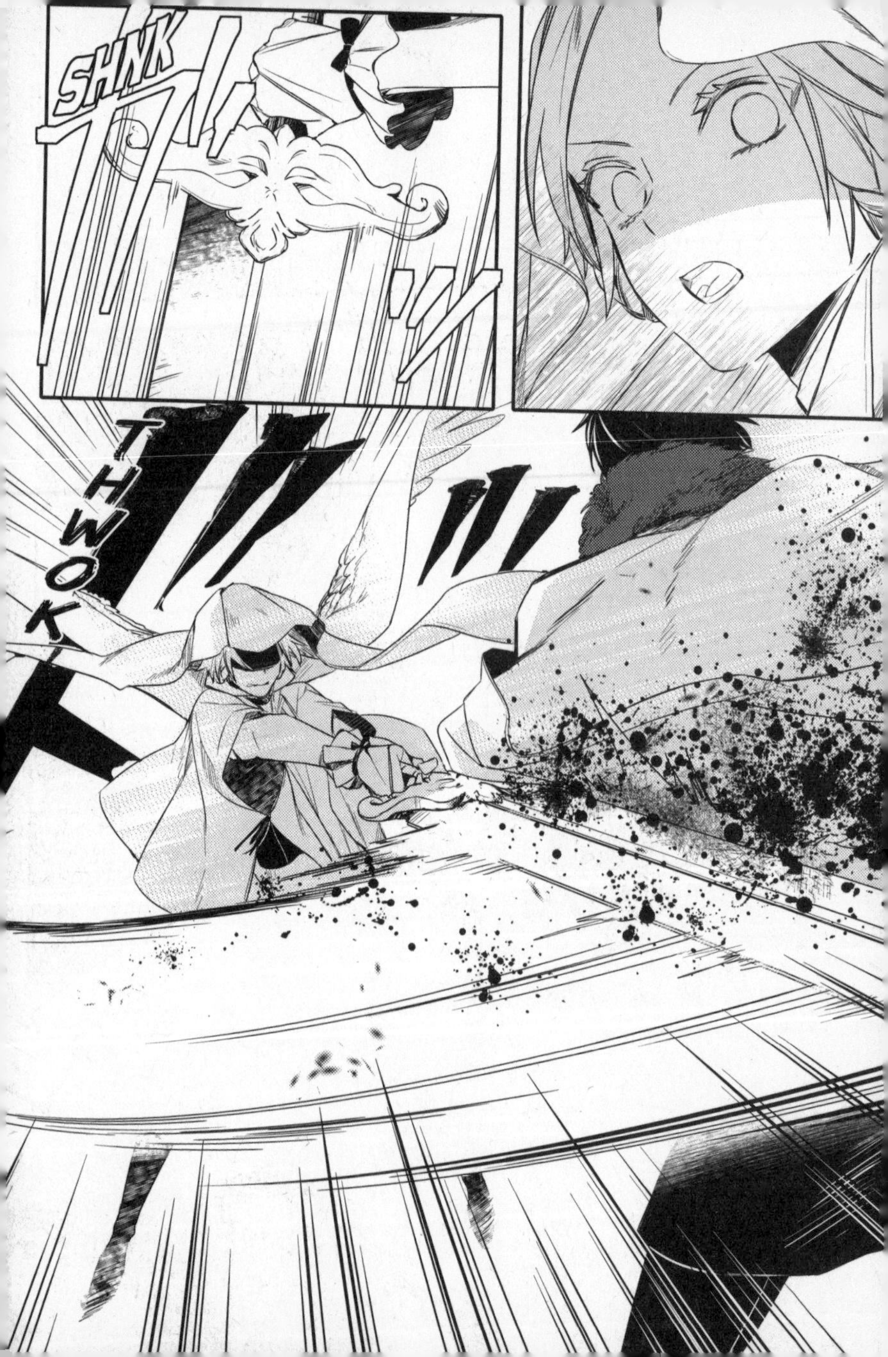
SHNK
THWOK

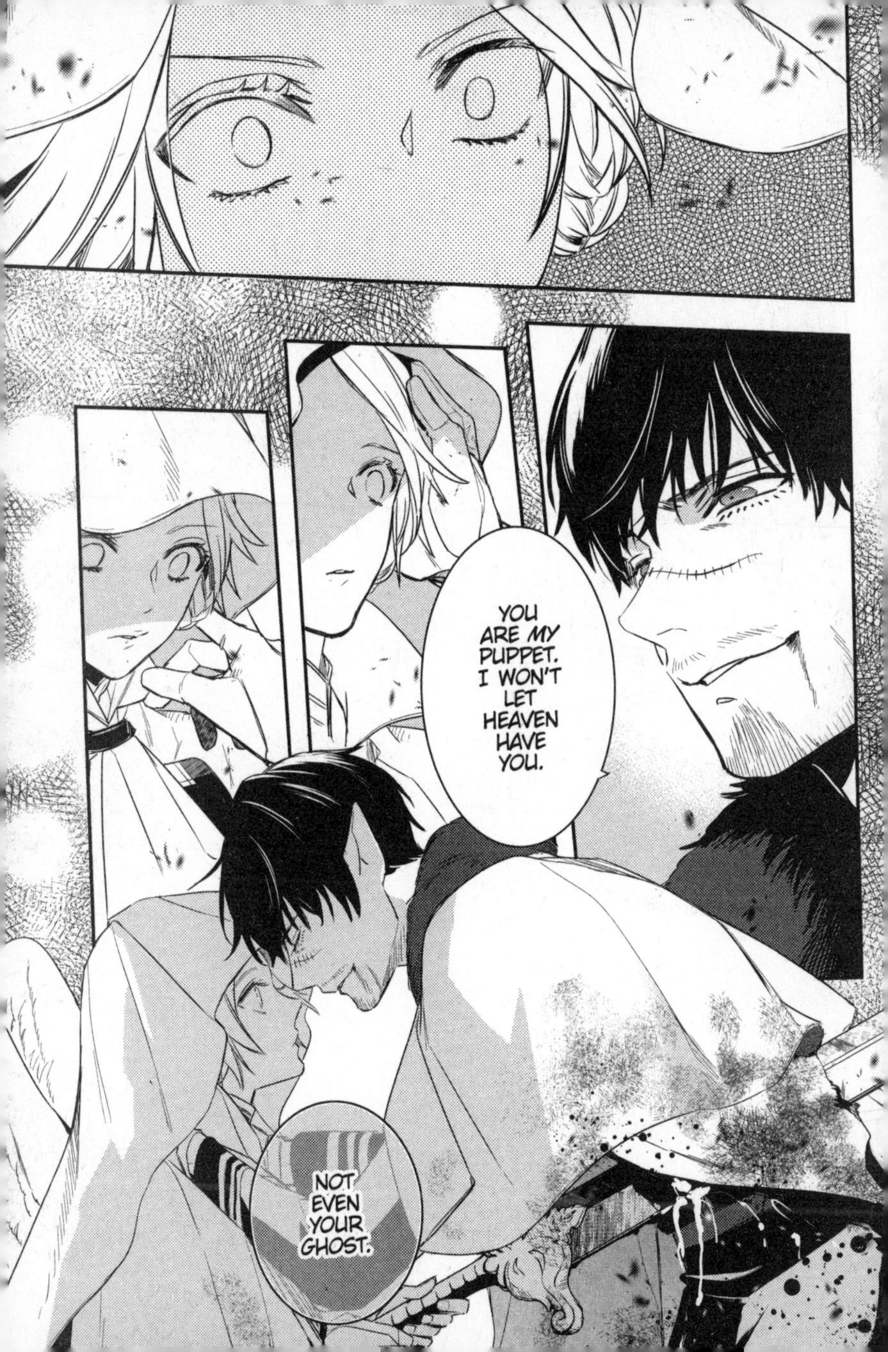
YOU ARE MY PUPPET. I WON'T LET HEAVEN HAVE YOU.
NOT EVEN YOUR GHOST.

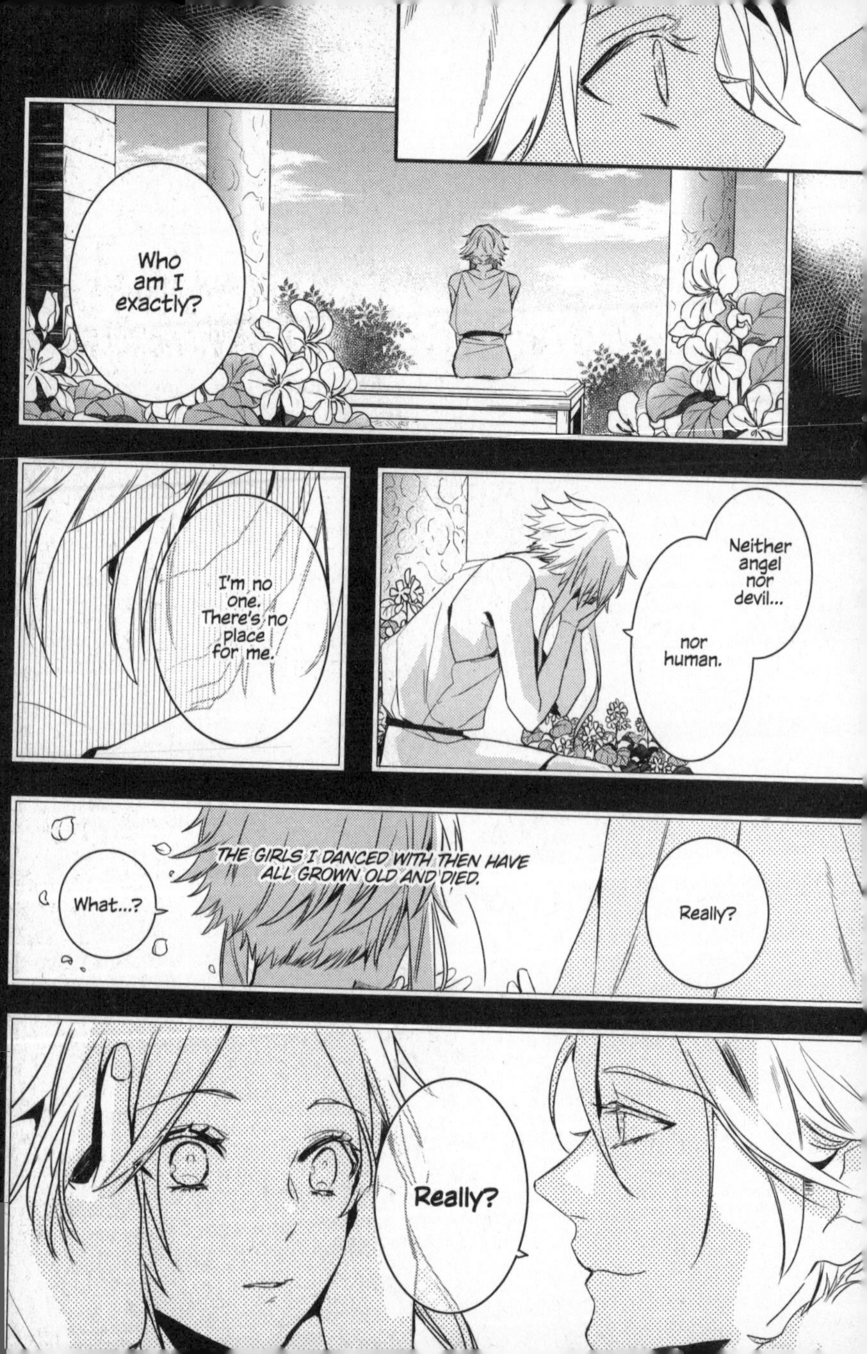

Who am I exactly?
Neither angel nor devil...
nor human.
I'm no one. There's no place for me.
Really?
THE GIRLS I DANCED WITH THEN HAVE ALL GROWN OLD AND DIED.
What...?
Really?

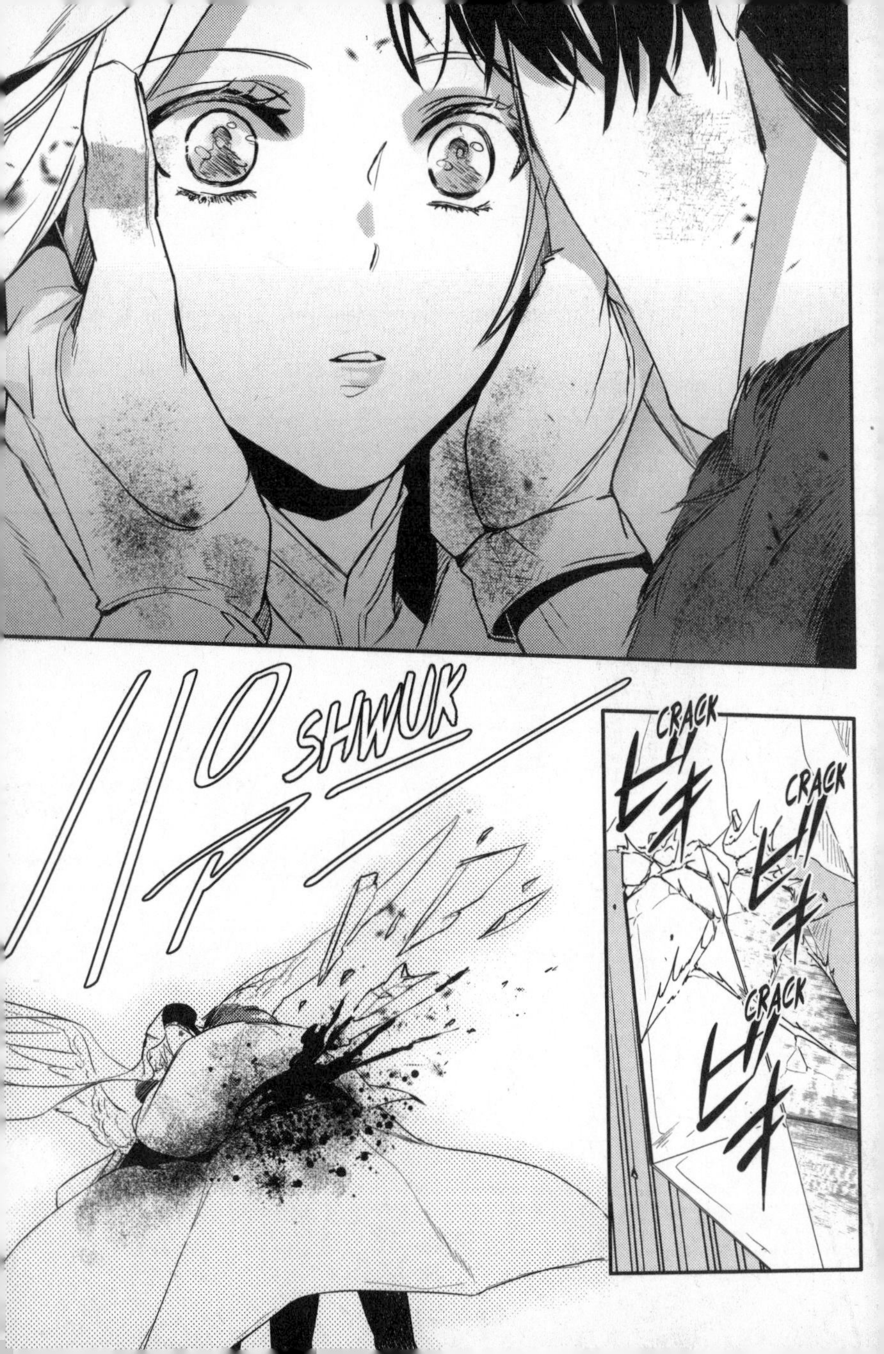
CRACK
CRACK
CRACK
SHWUK

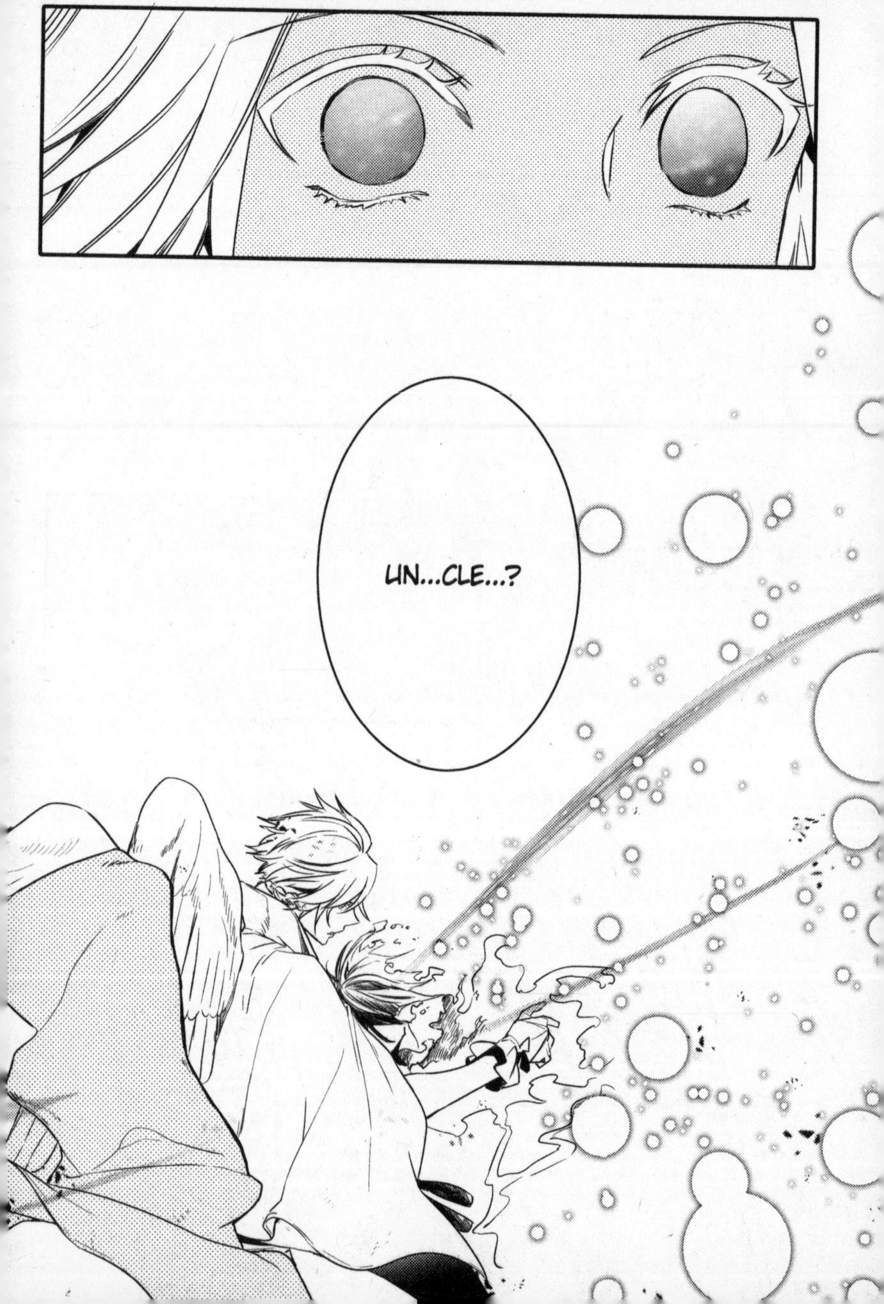
UN...CLE...?

Pillar 90

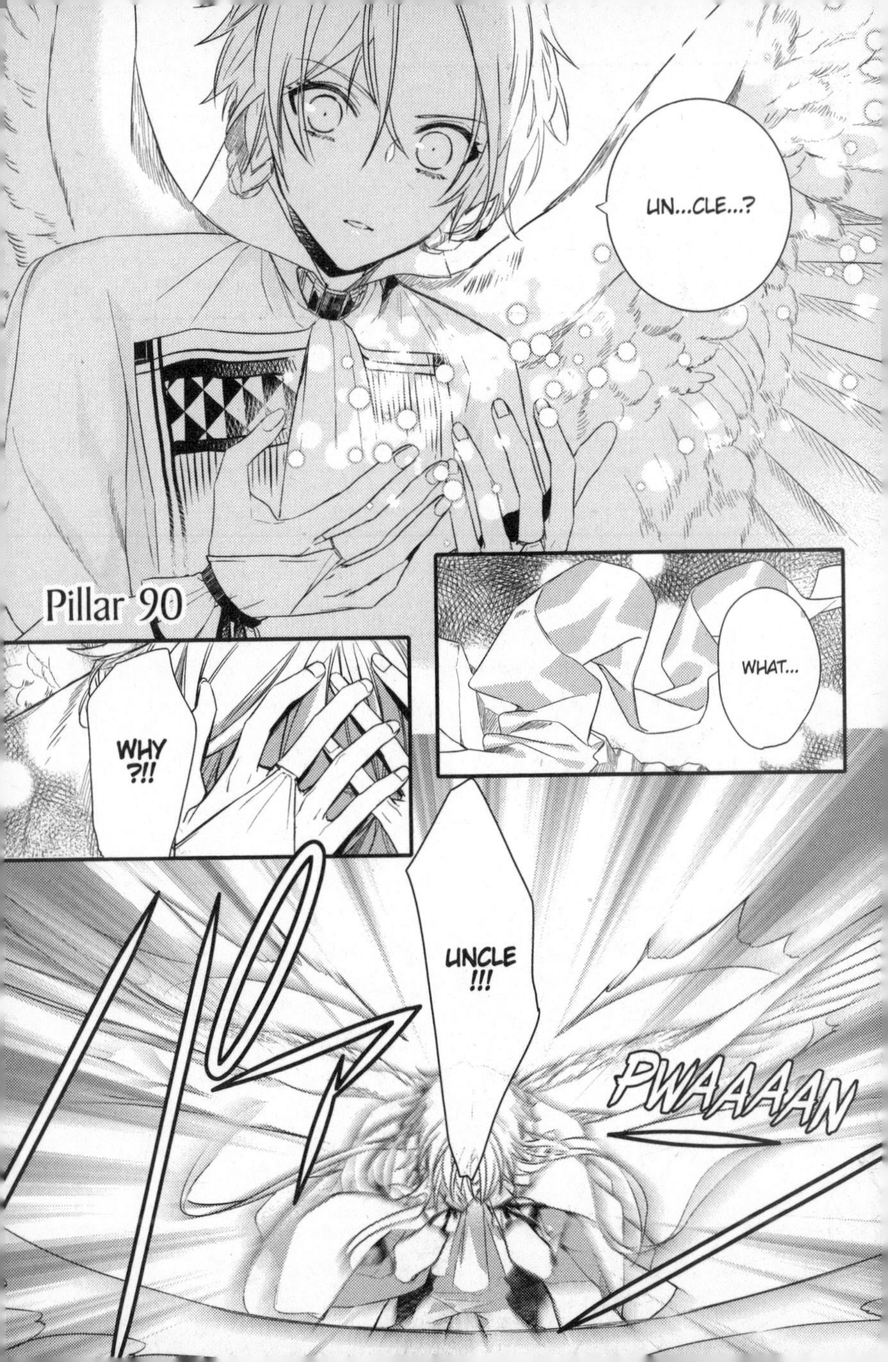
UN...CLE...?
WHAT...
WHY ?!!
UNCLE !!!
NO
PWAAAAN

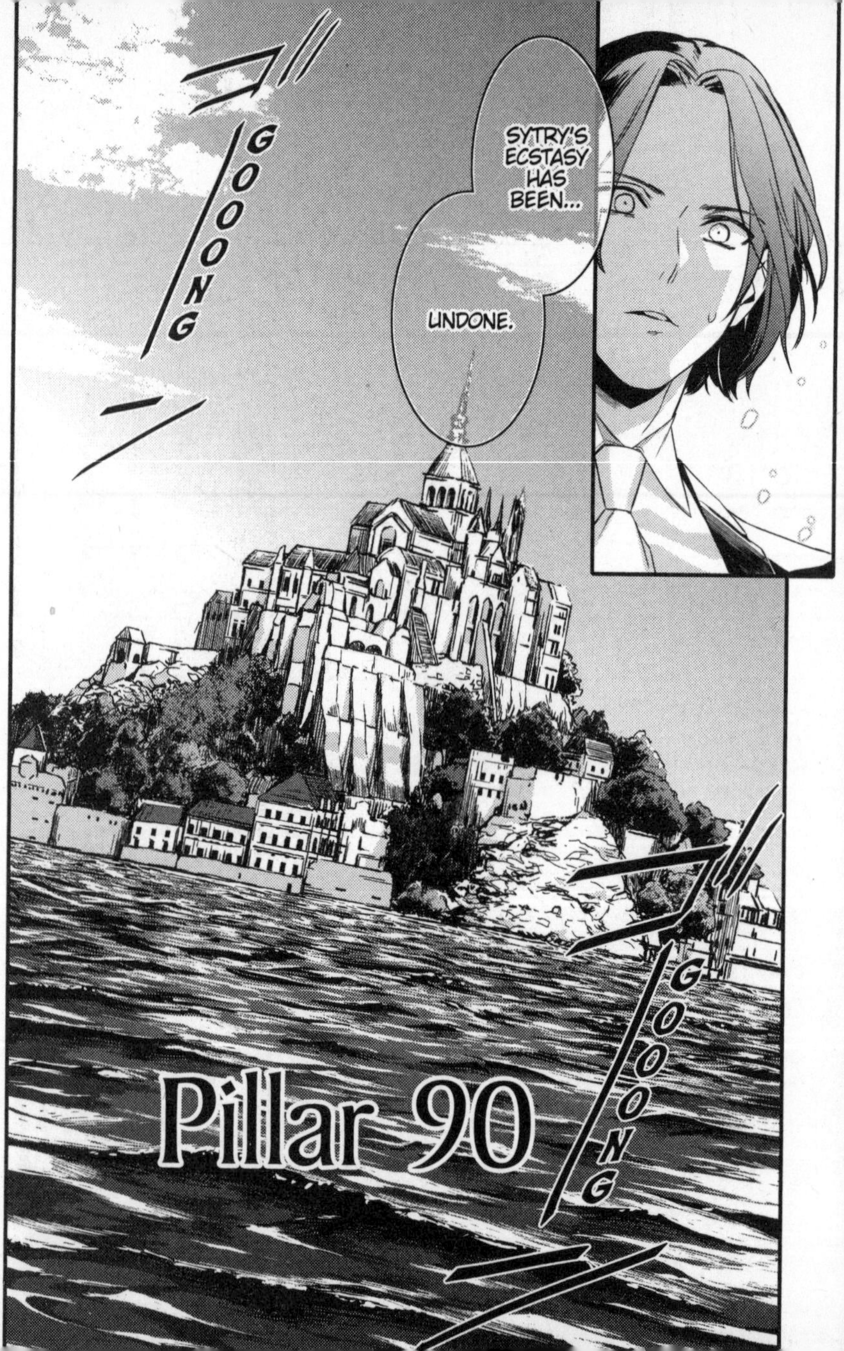
SYTRY'S ECSTASY HAS BEEN...
UNDONE.
GOOOONG
Pillar 90
GOOOONG

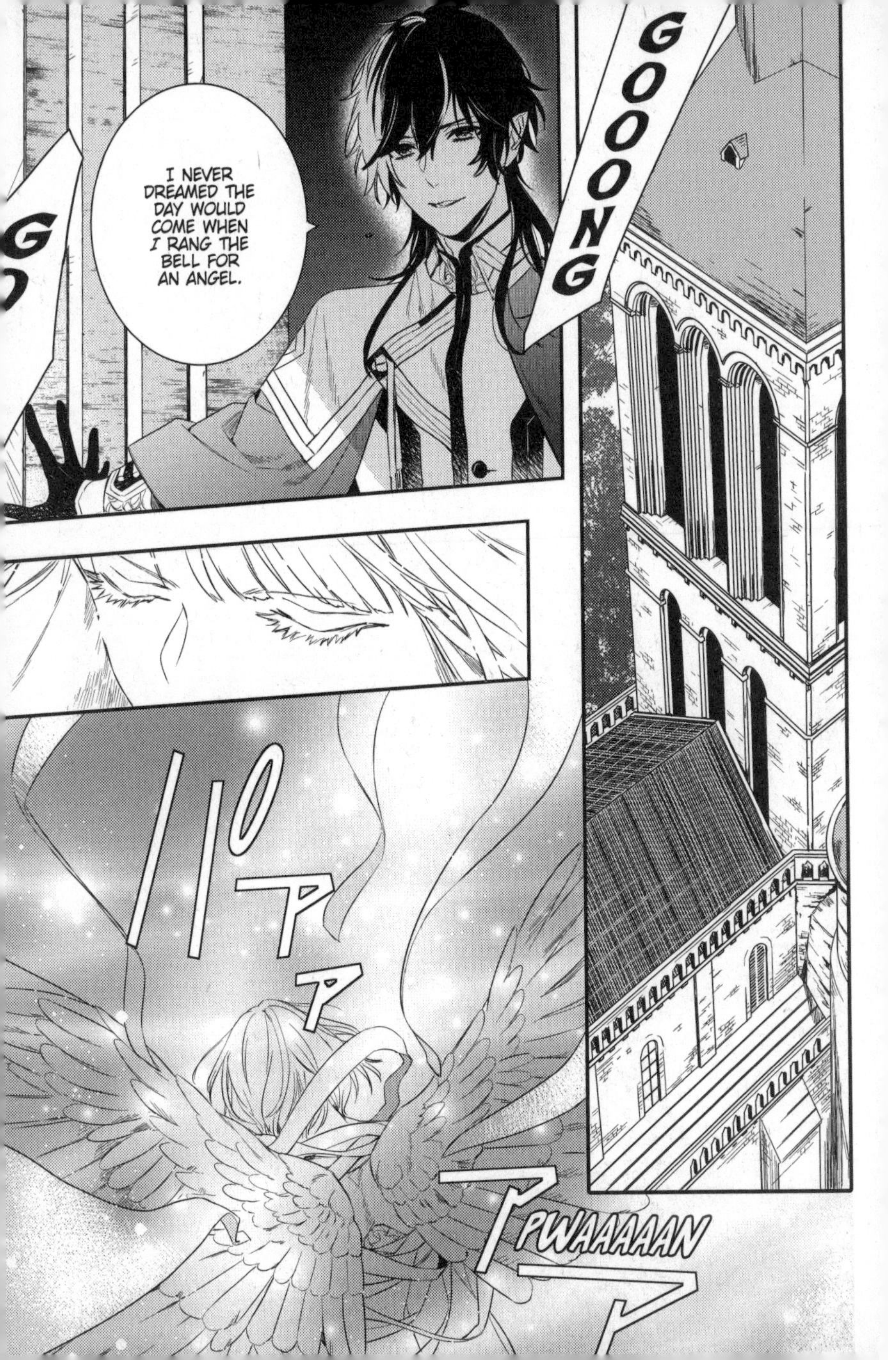
GOOOONG
G
I NEVER DREAMED THE DAY WOULD COME WHEN I RANG THE BELL FOR AN ANGEL.
パァ
PWAAAAAN

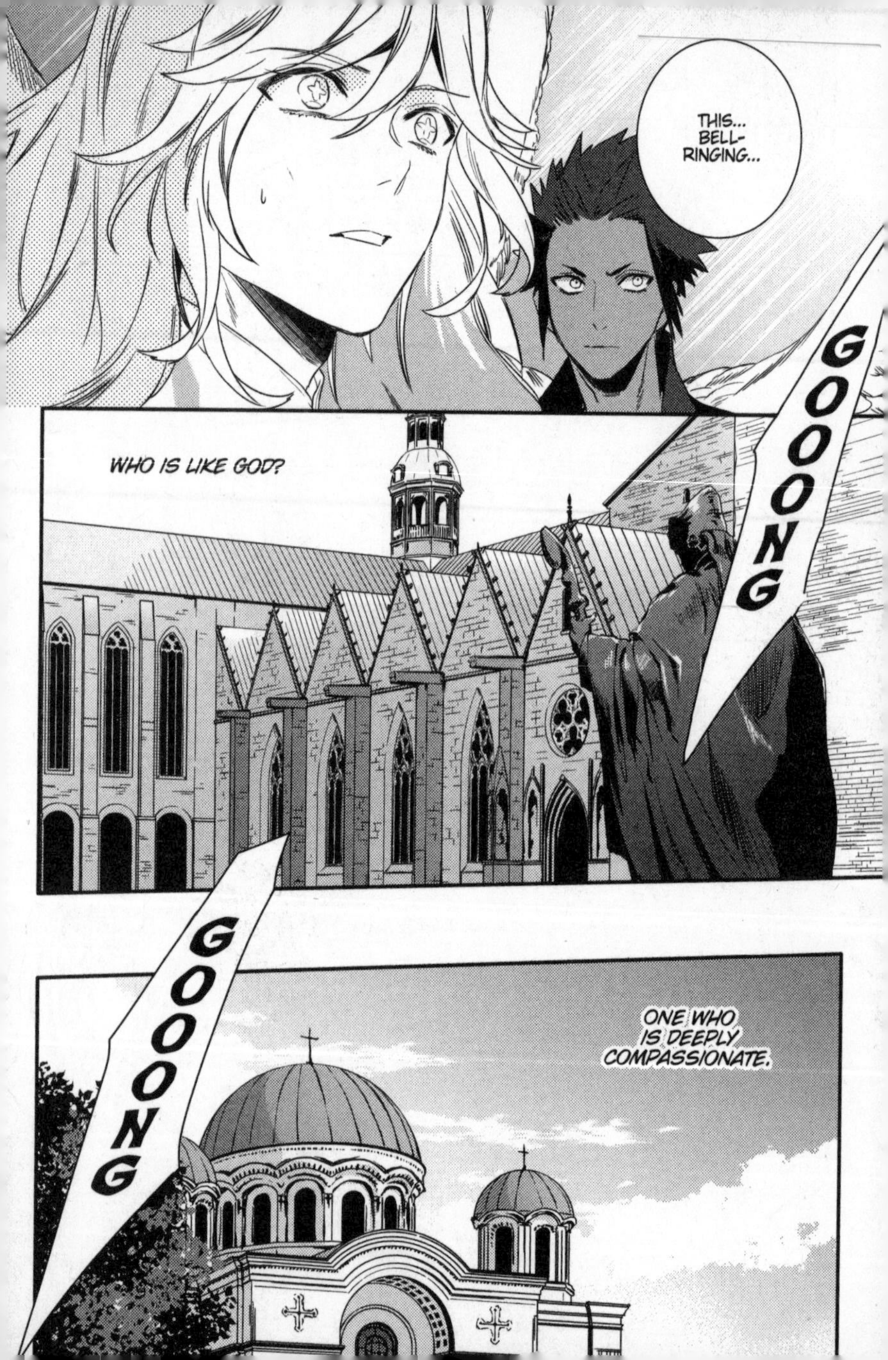
THIS... BELL-RINGING...
GOOOONG
WHO IS LIKE GOD?
GOOOONG
ONE WHO IS DEEPLY COMPASSIONATE.

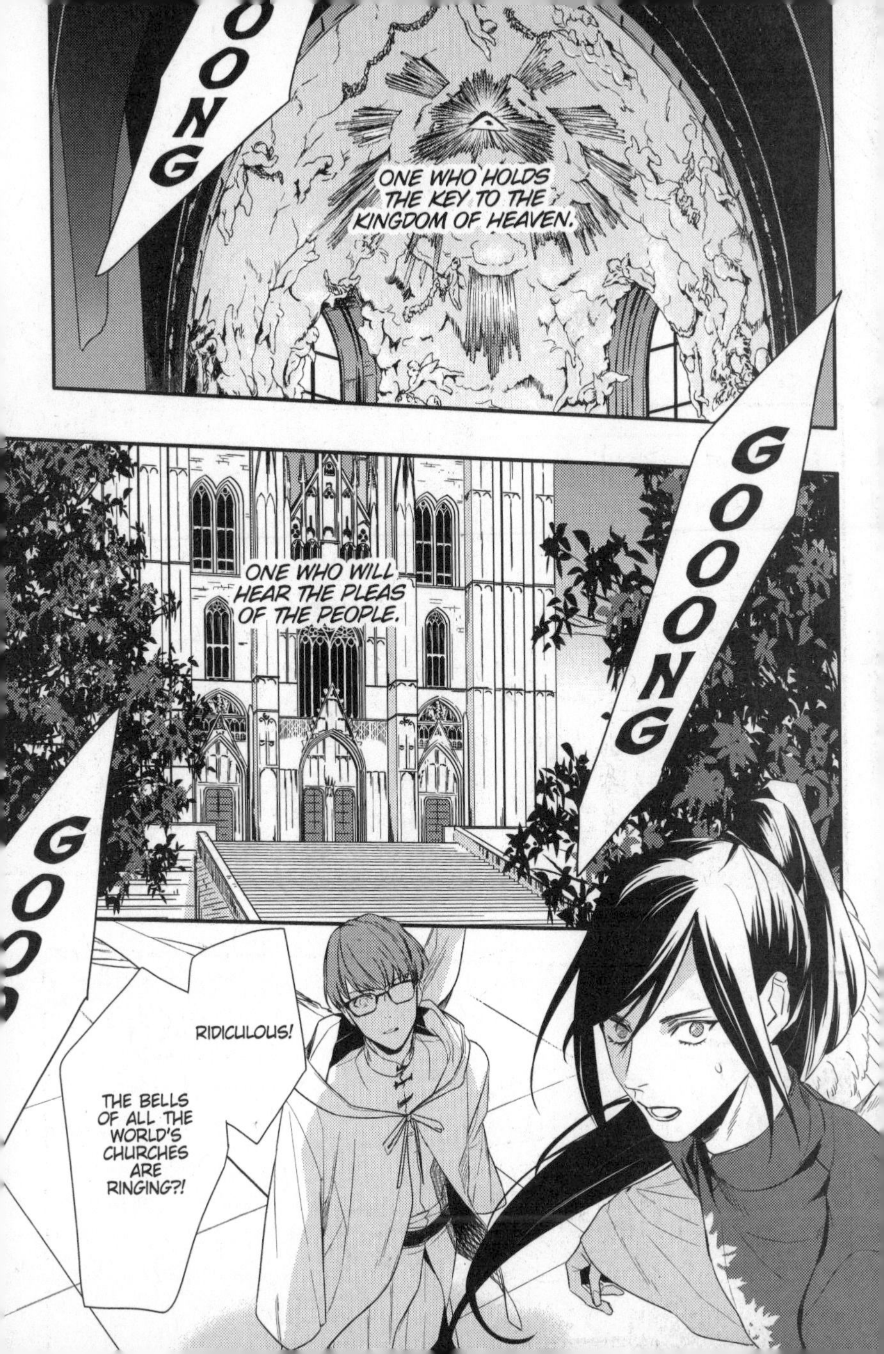

OONG
ONE WHO HOLDS THE KEY TO THE KINGDOM OF HEAVEN.
GOOOONG
ONE WHO WILL HEAR THE PLEAS OF THE PEOPLE.
GOO
RIDICULOUS!
THE BELLS OF ALL THE WORLD'S CHURCHES ARE RINGING?!

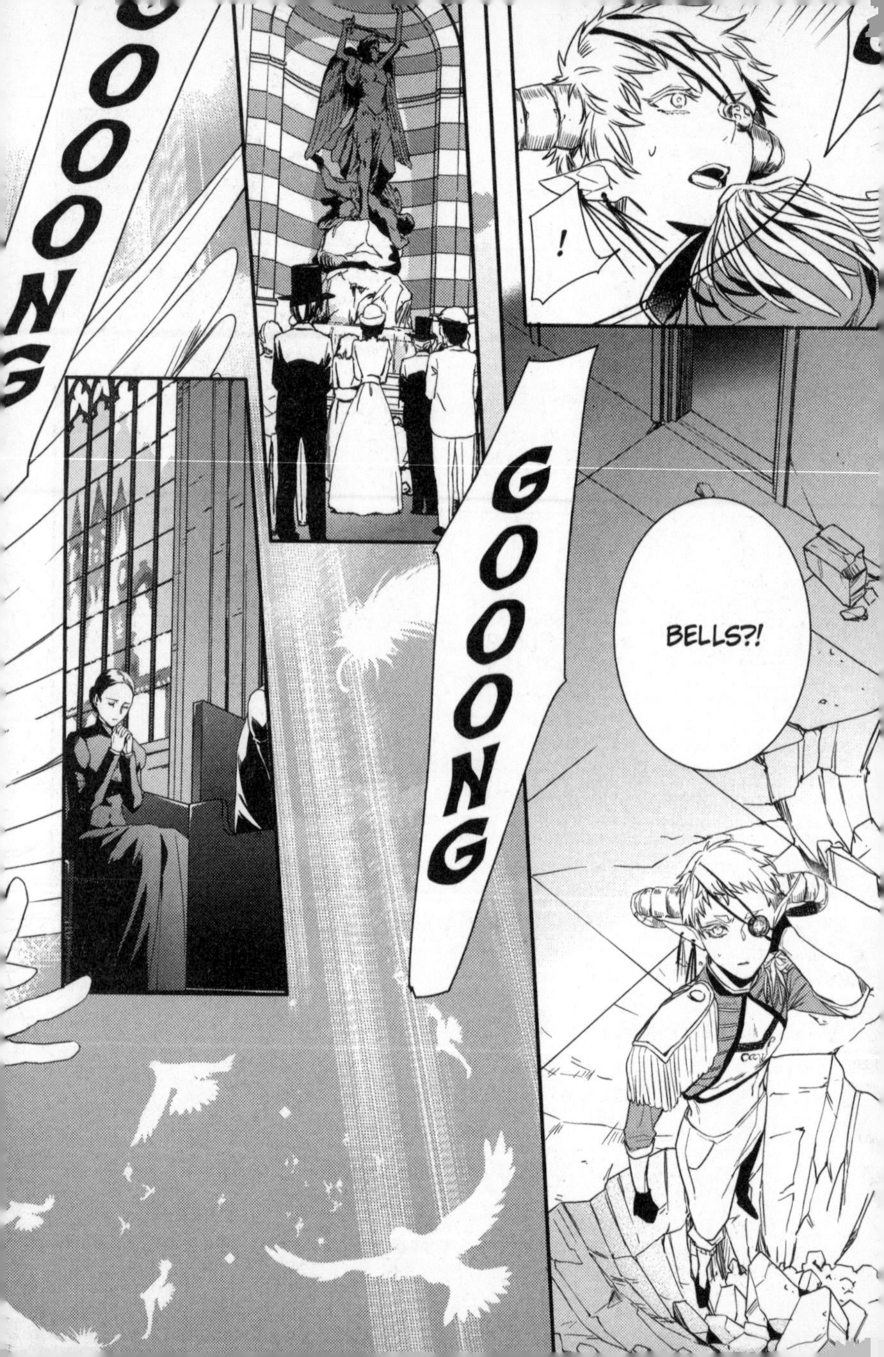

!
BELLS?!
GOOOONG
OOOONG

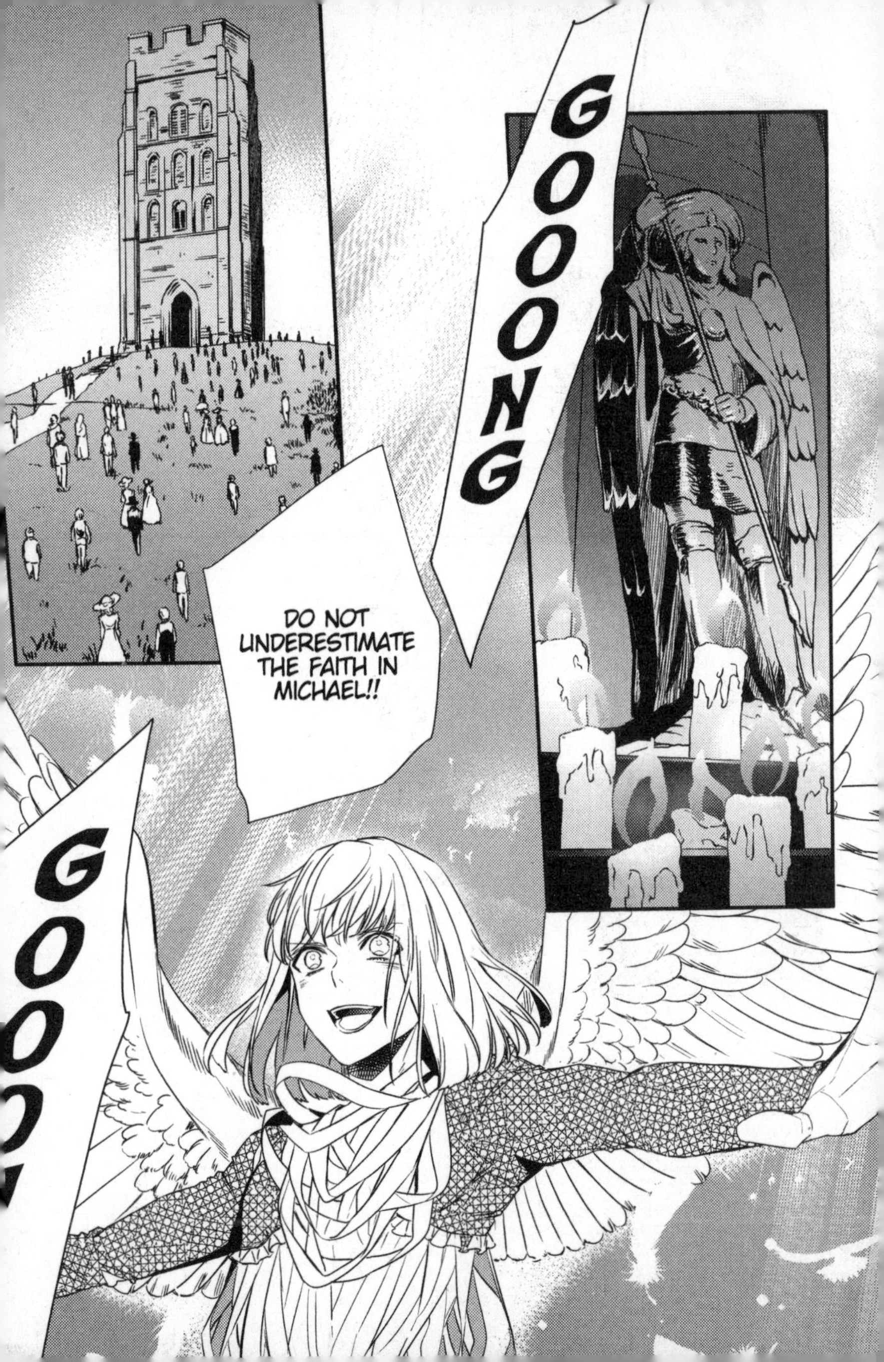
GOOONG
DO NOT UNDERESTIMATE THE FAITH IN MICHAEL!!
GOOO

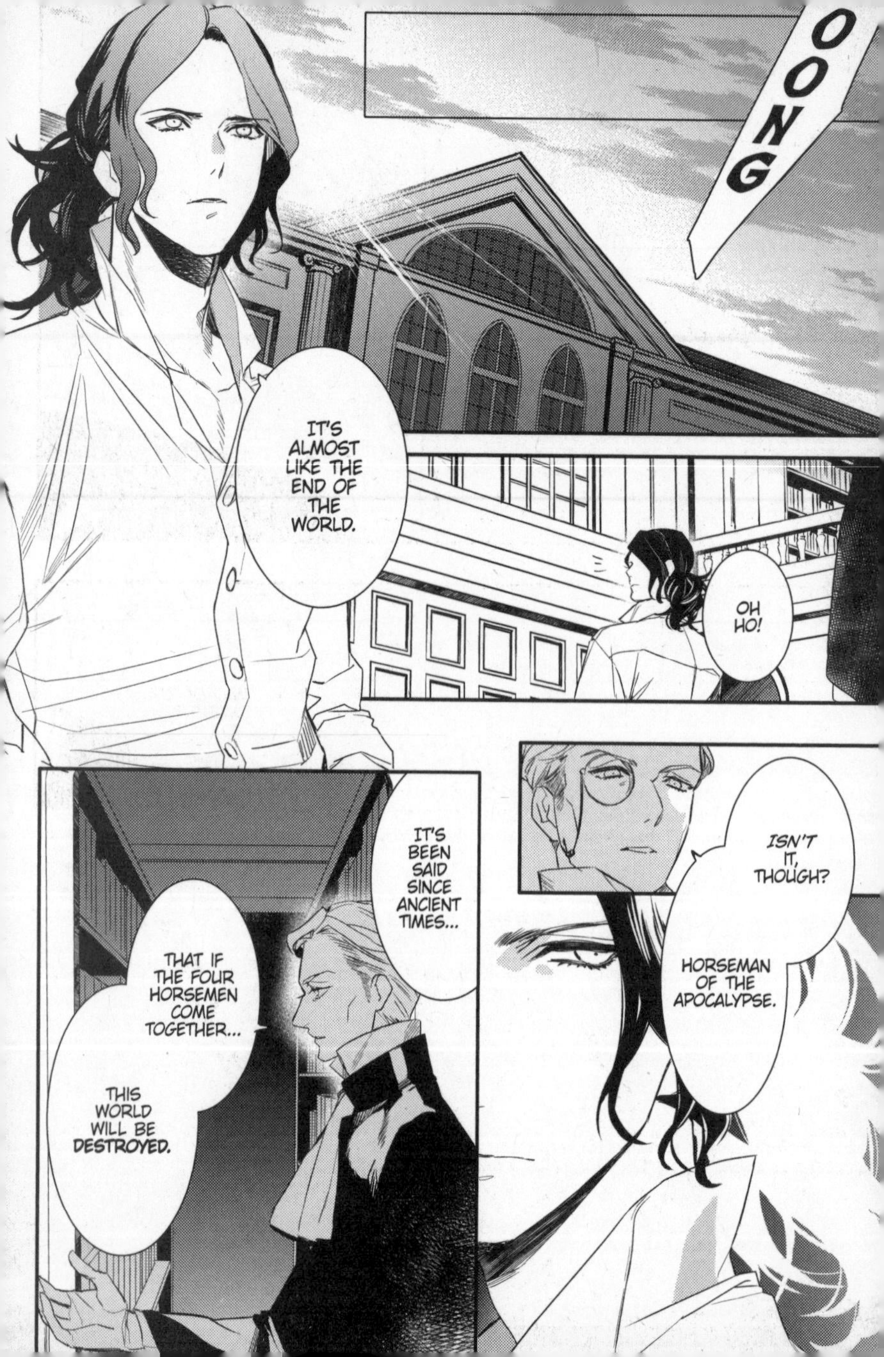
OOONG
IT'S ALMOST LIKE THE END OF THE WORLD.
OH HO!
ISN'T IT, THOUGH?
HORSEMAN OF THE APOCALYPSE.
IT'S BEEN SAID SINCE ANCIENT TIMES...
THAT IF THE FOUR HORSEMEN COME TOGETHER...
THIS WORLD WILL BE DESTROYED.

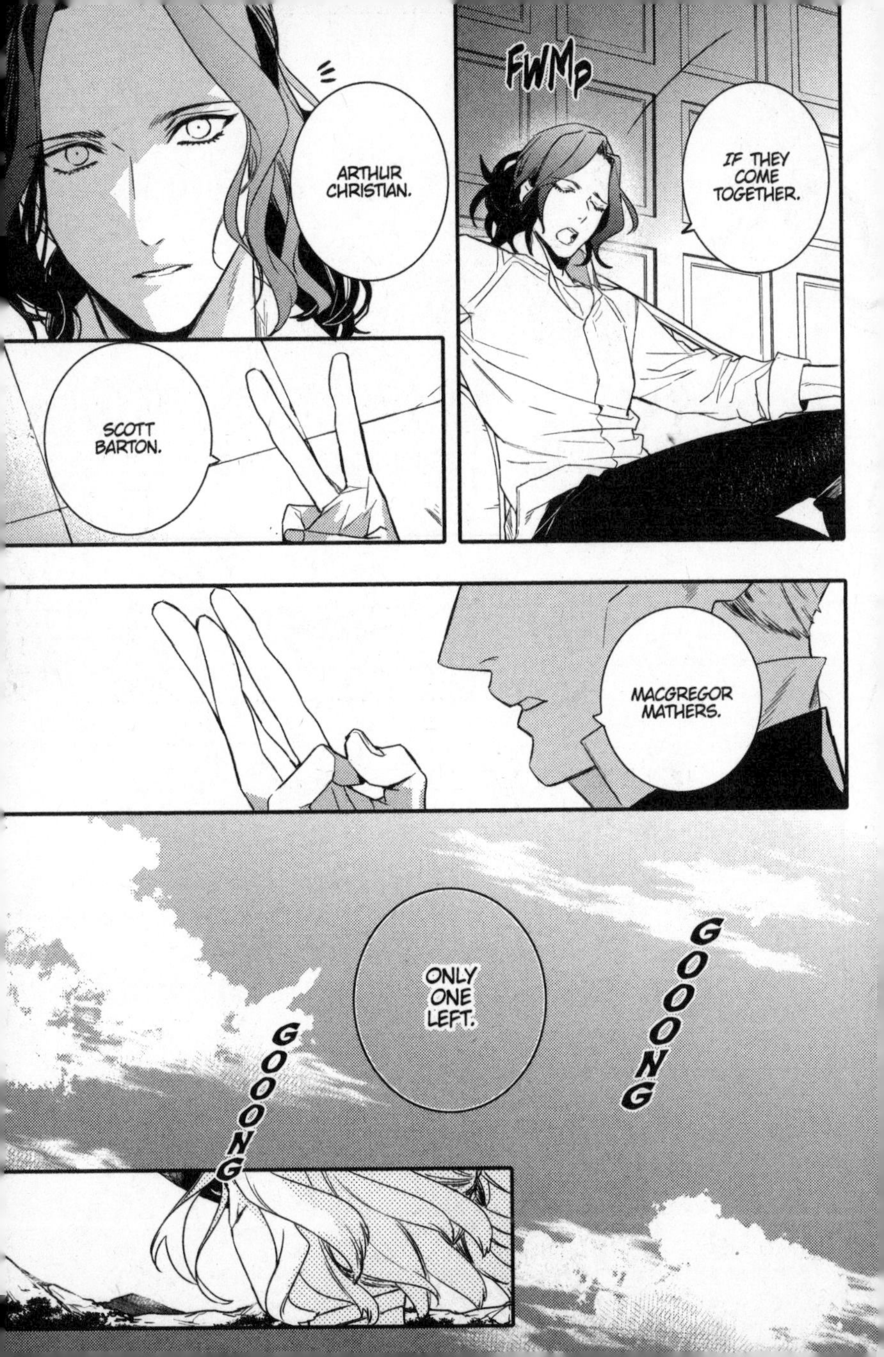
FWMp
IF THEY COME TOGETHER.
ARTHUR CHRISTIAN.
SCOTT BARTON.
MACGREGOR MATHERS.
ONLY ONE LEFT.
GOOOONG
GOOOONG

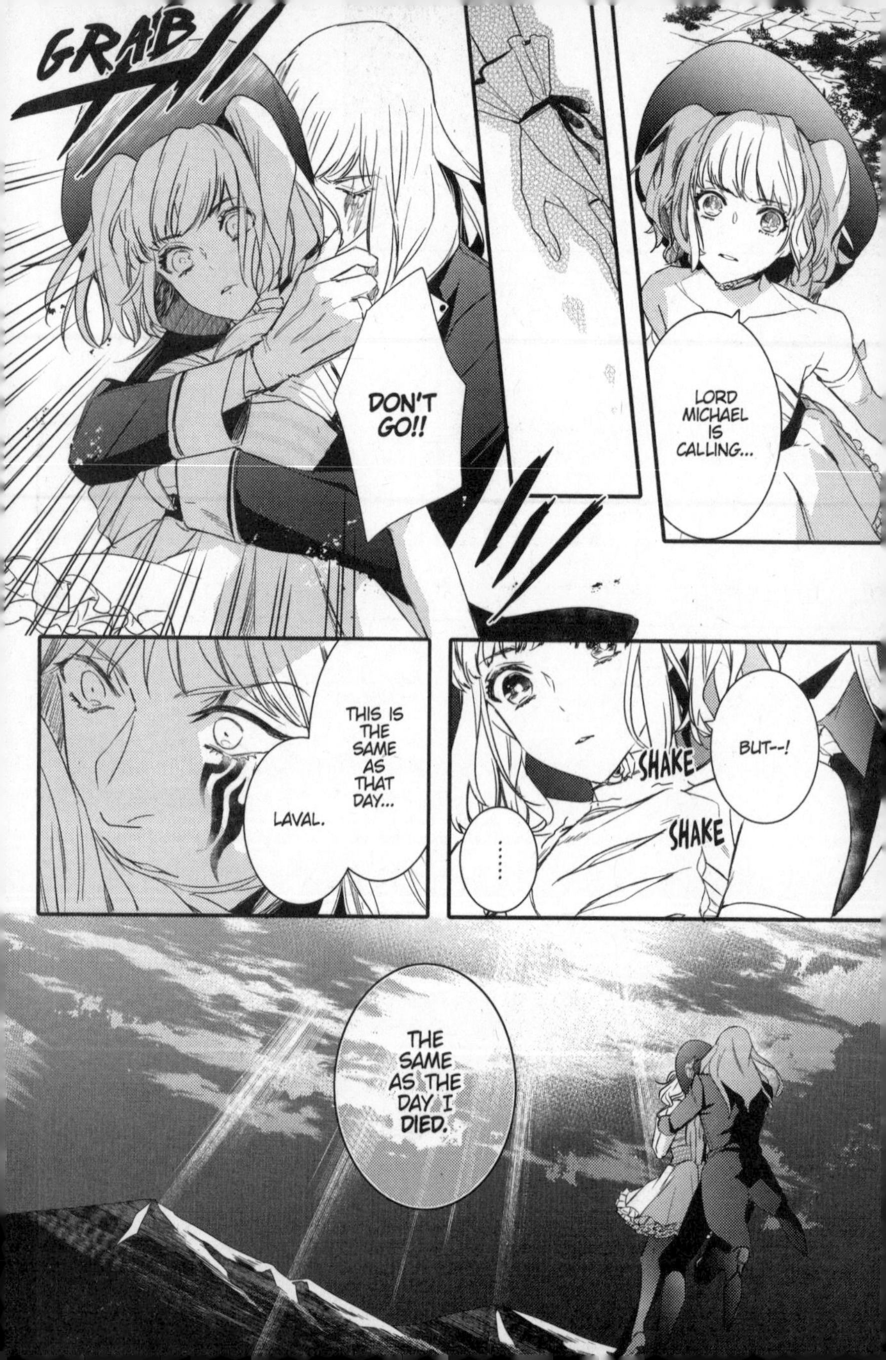
LORD MICHAEL IS CALLING...
GRAB
DON'T GO!!
BUT--!
SHAKE
SHAKE
......
THIS IS THE SAME AS THAT DAY... LAVAL.
THE SAME AS THE DAY I DIED.

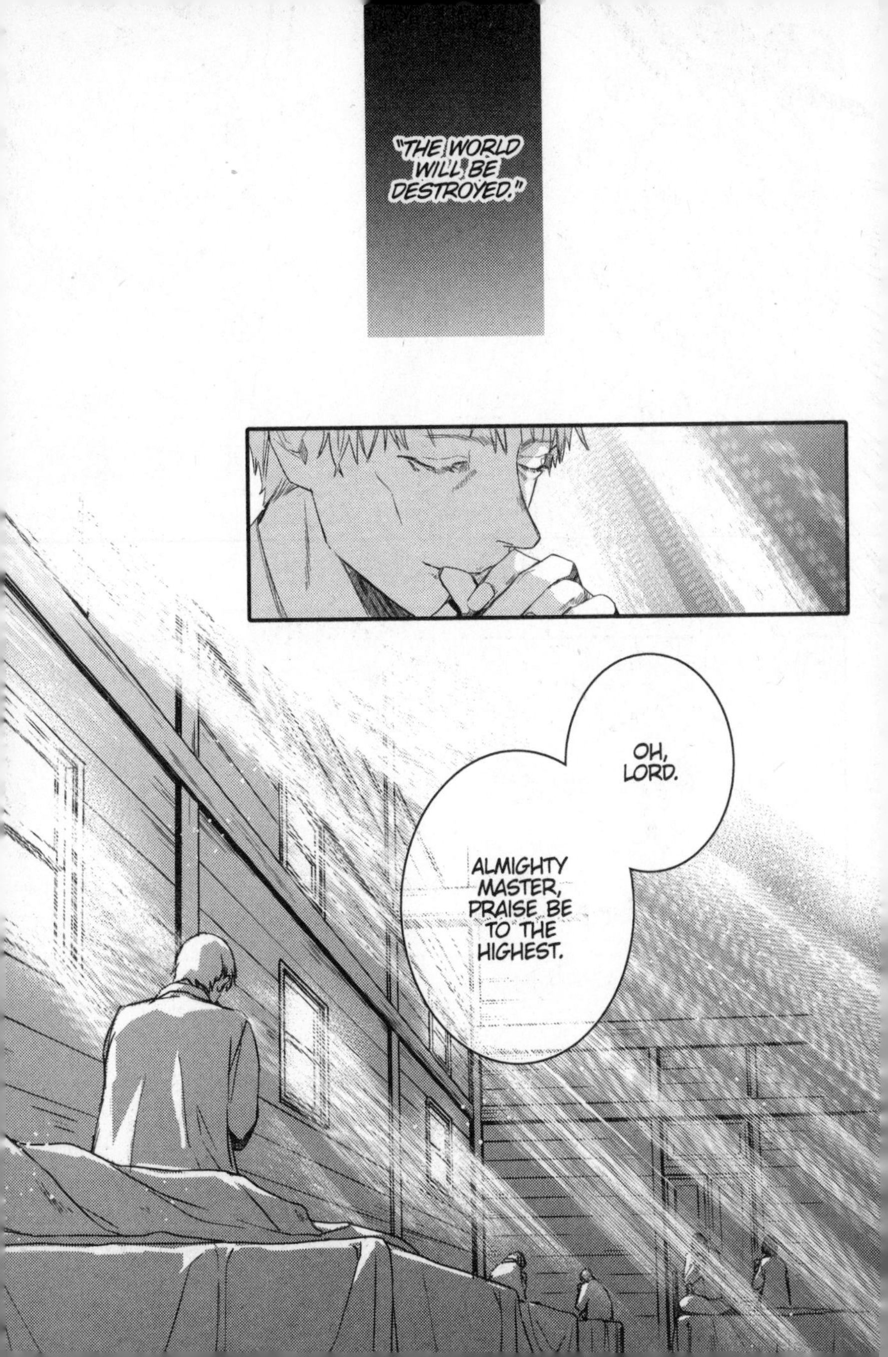
"THE WORLD WILL BE DESTROYED."
OH, LORD.
ALMIGHTY MASTER, PRAISE BE TO THE HIGHEST.

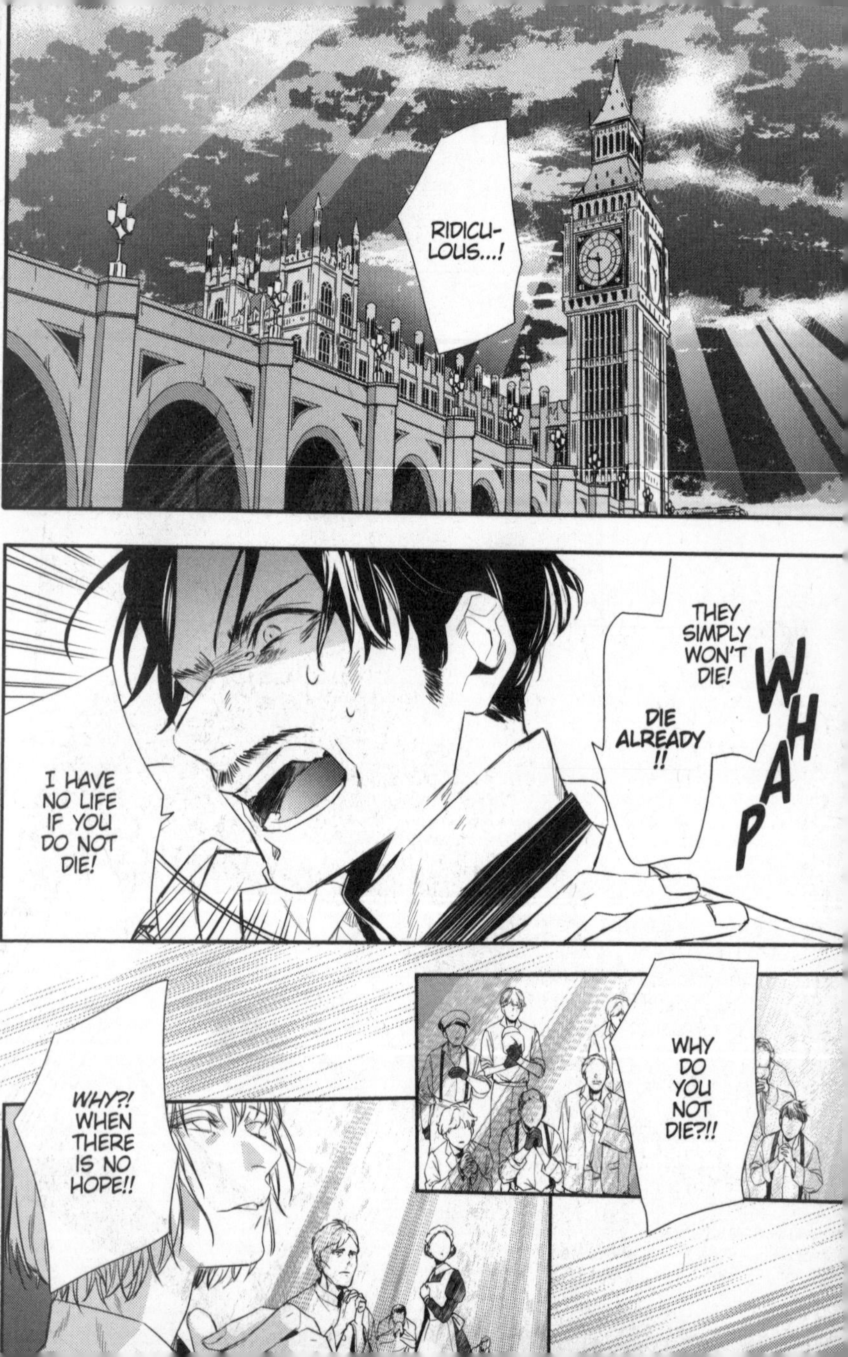
RIDICULOUS...!
THEY SIMPLY WON'T DIE!
DIE ALREADY!!
WHAP
I HAVE NO LIFE IF YOU DO NOT DIE!
WHY DO YOU NOT DIE?!!
WHY?! WHEN THERE IS NO HOPE!!

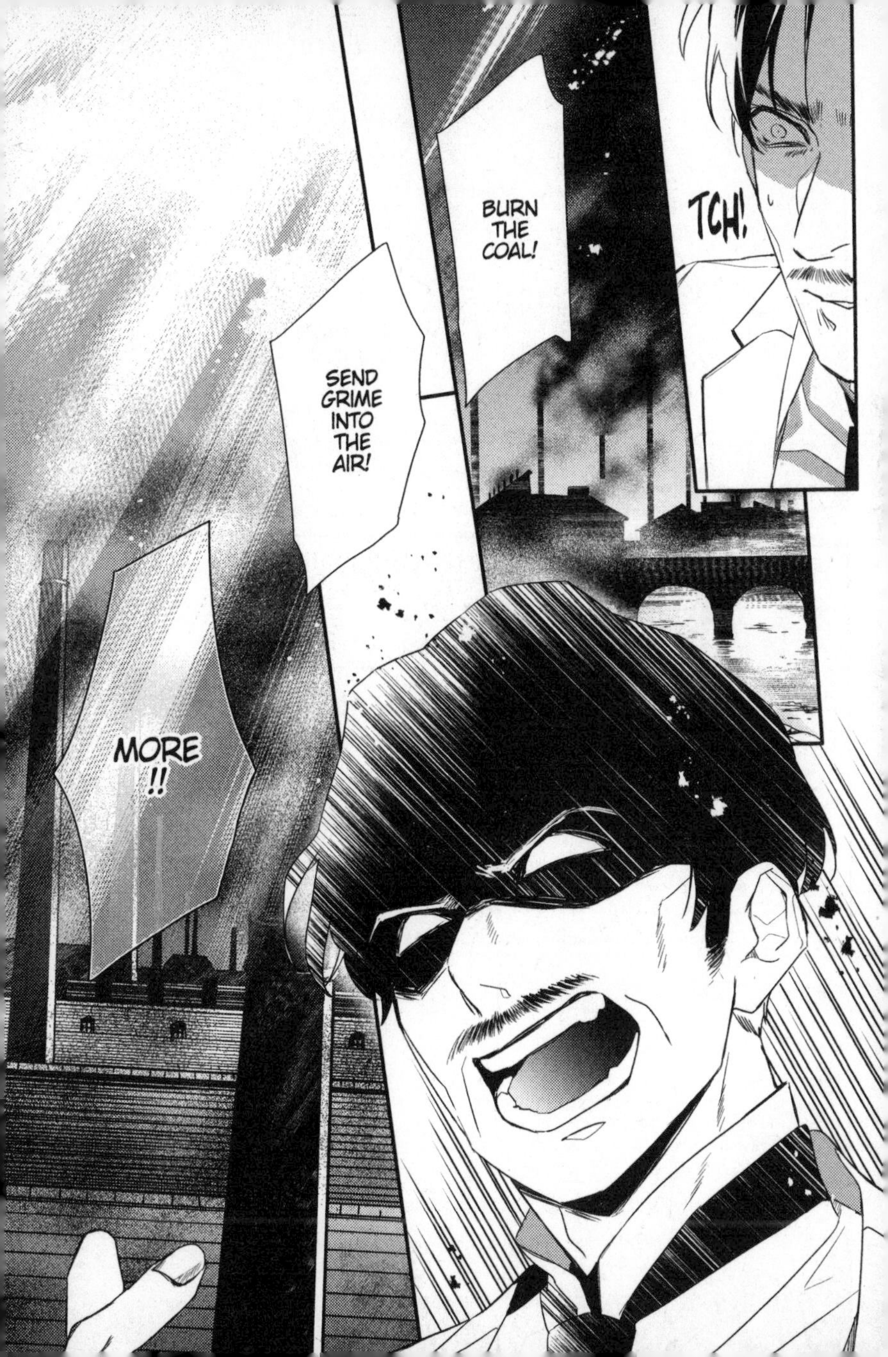
TCH!
BURN THE COAL!
SEND GRIME INTO THE AIR!
MORE !!

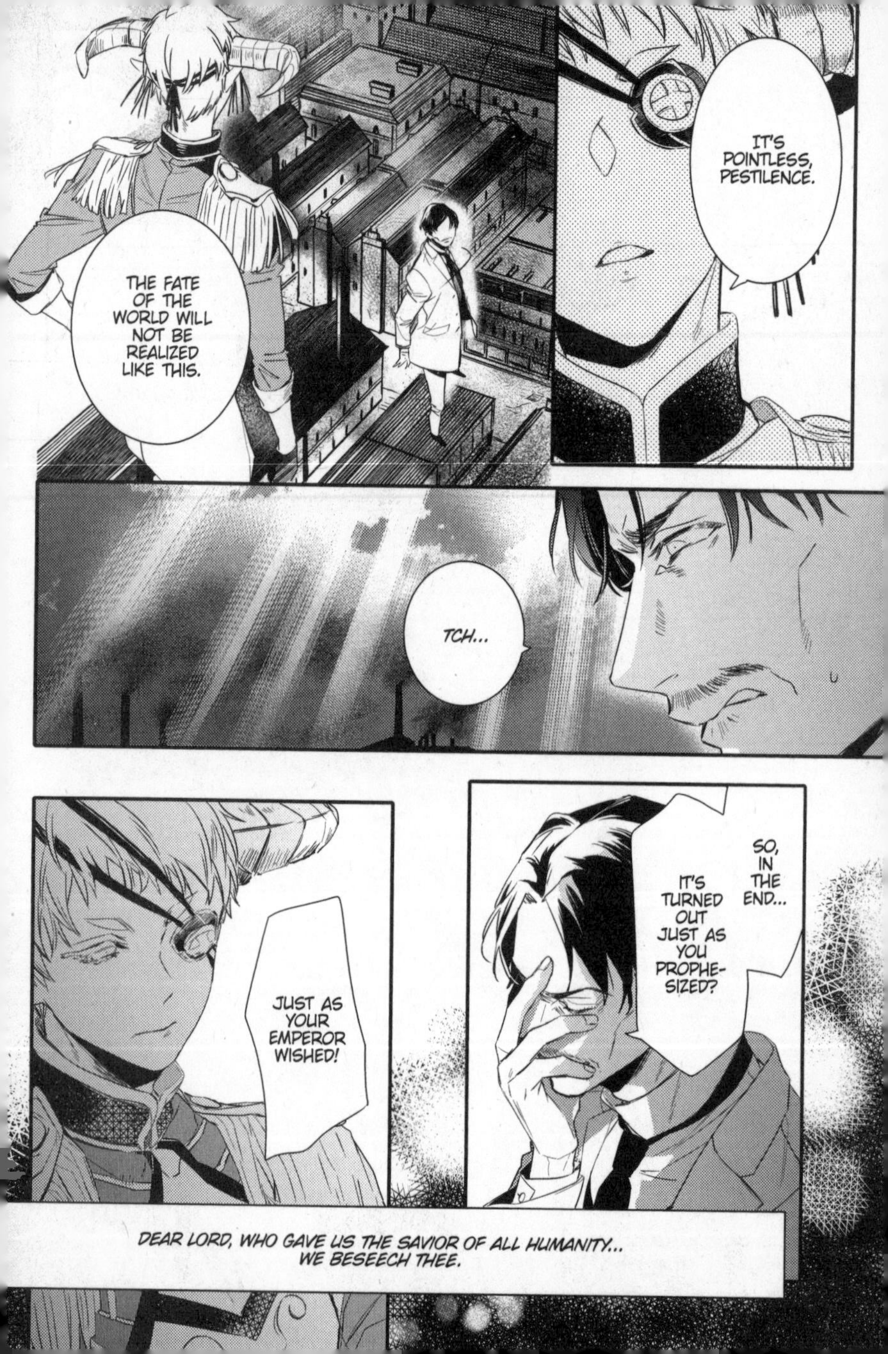

IT'S POINTLESS, PESTILENCE.
THE FATE OF THE WORLD WILL NOT BE REALIZED LIKE THIS.
TCH...
SO, IN THE END...
IT'S TURNED OUT JUST AS YOU PROPHESIZED?
JUST AS YOUR EMPEROR WISHED!
DEAR LORD, WHO GAVE US THE SAVIOR OF ALL HUMANITY... WE BESEECH THEE.

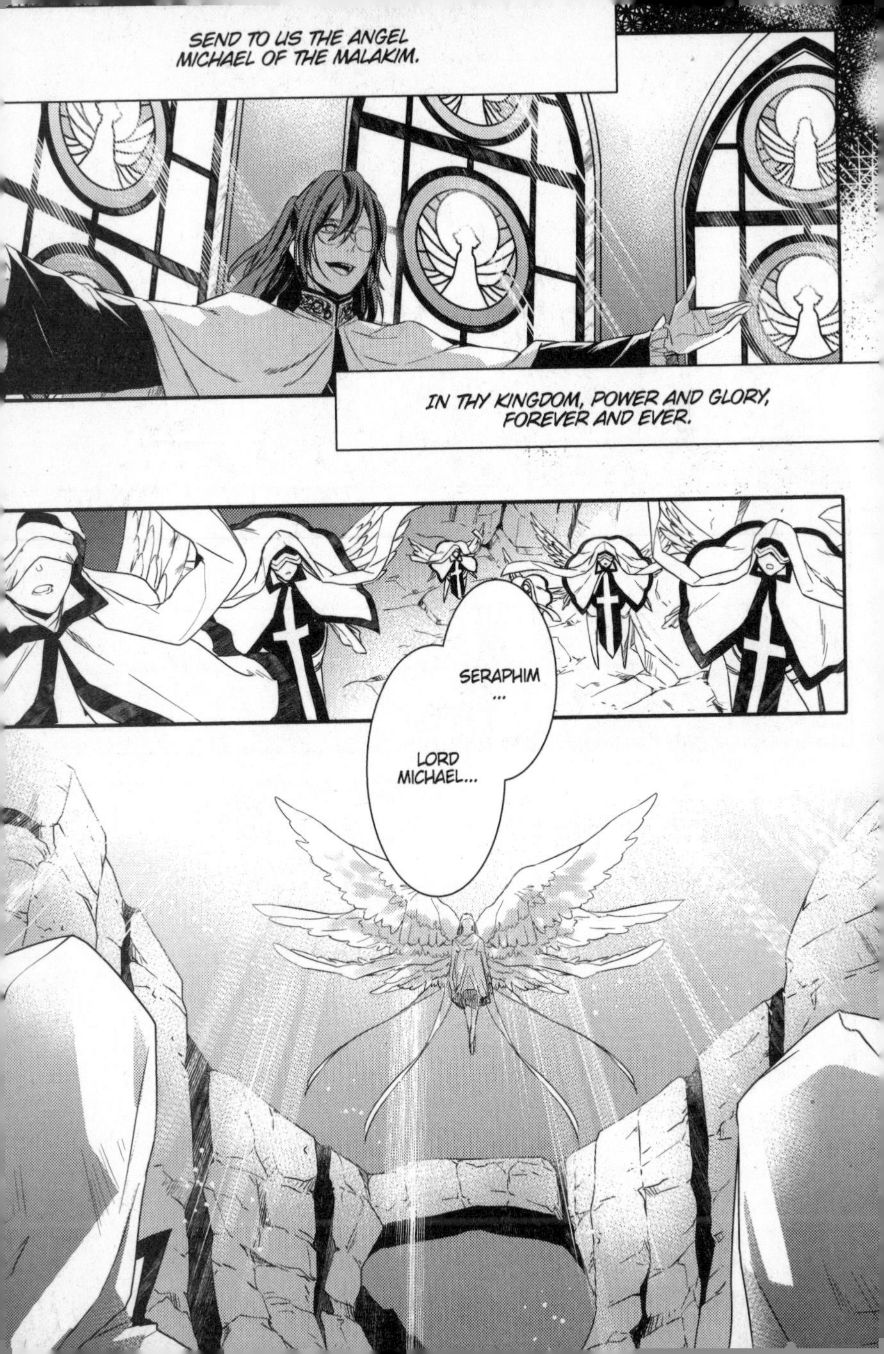
SEND TO US THE ANGEL MICHAEL OF THE MALAKIM.
IN THY KINGDOM, POWER AND GLORY, FOREVER AND EVER.
SERAPHIM ...
LORD MICHAEL...

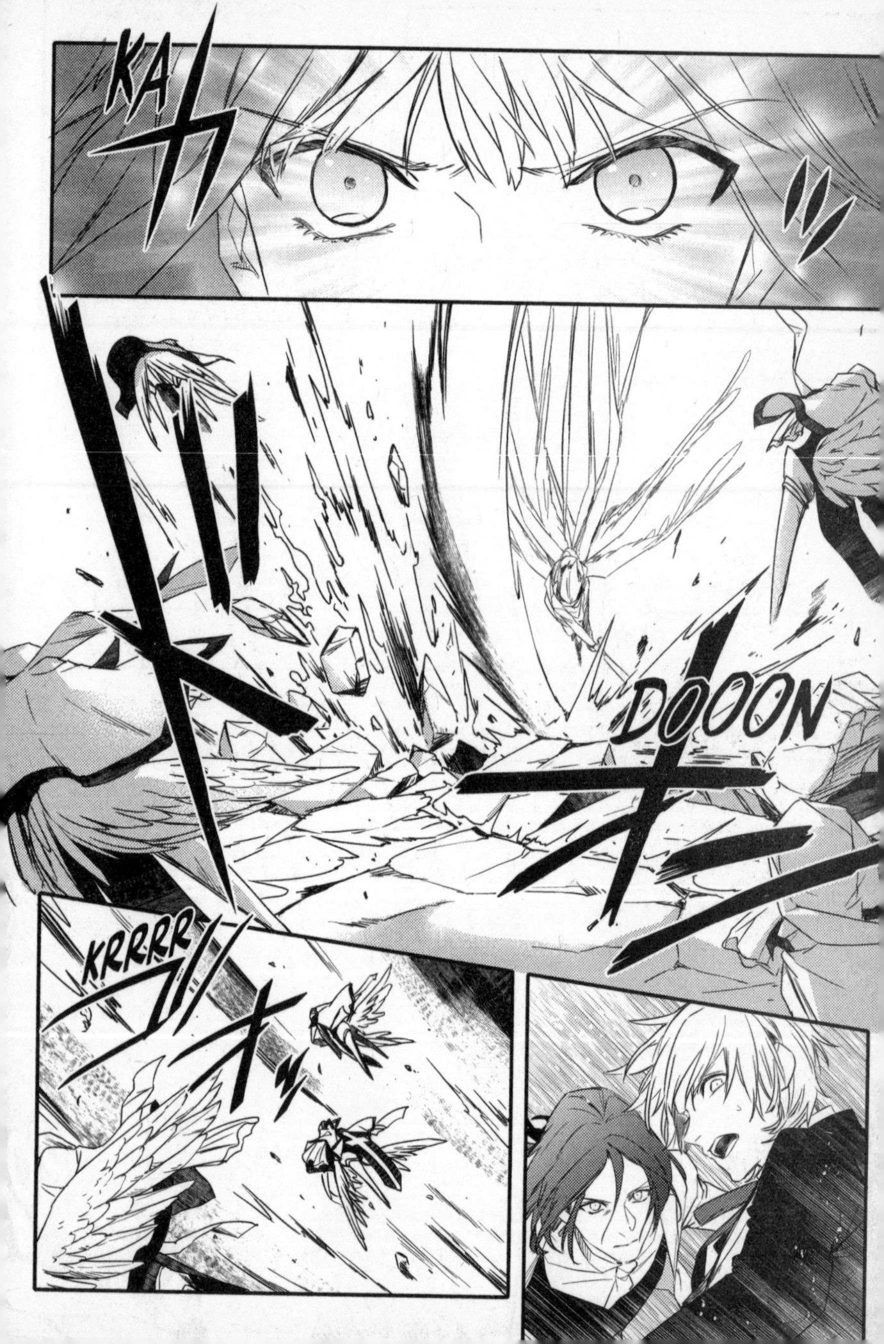
KA
DOOON
KRRRR

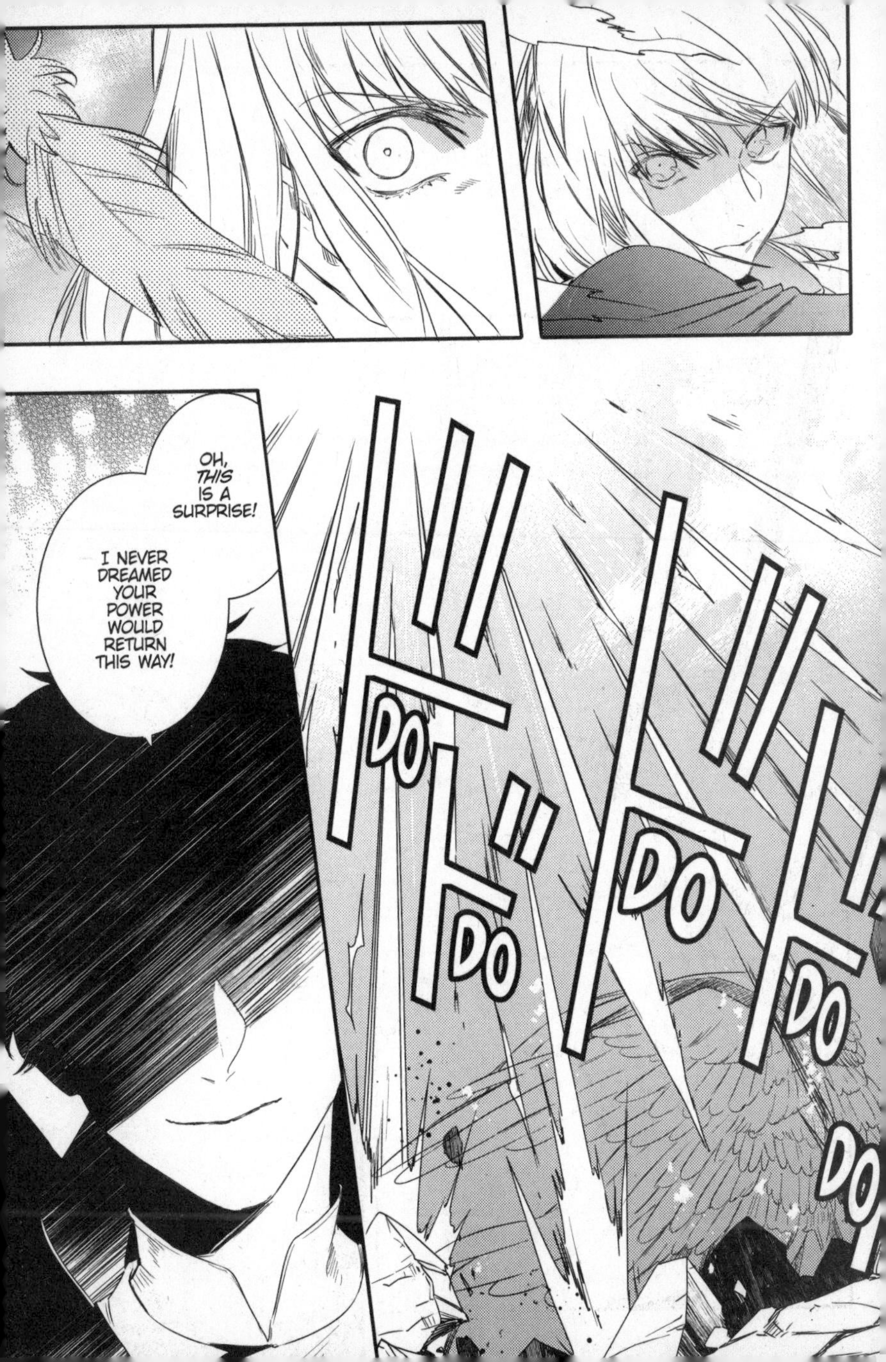
OH, *THIS* IS A SURPRISE!
I NEVER DREAMED YOUR POWER WOULD RETURN THIS WAY!
DO
DO
DO
DO
DO
DO

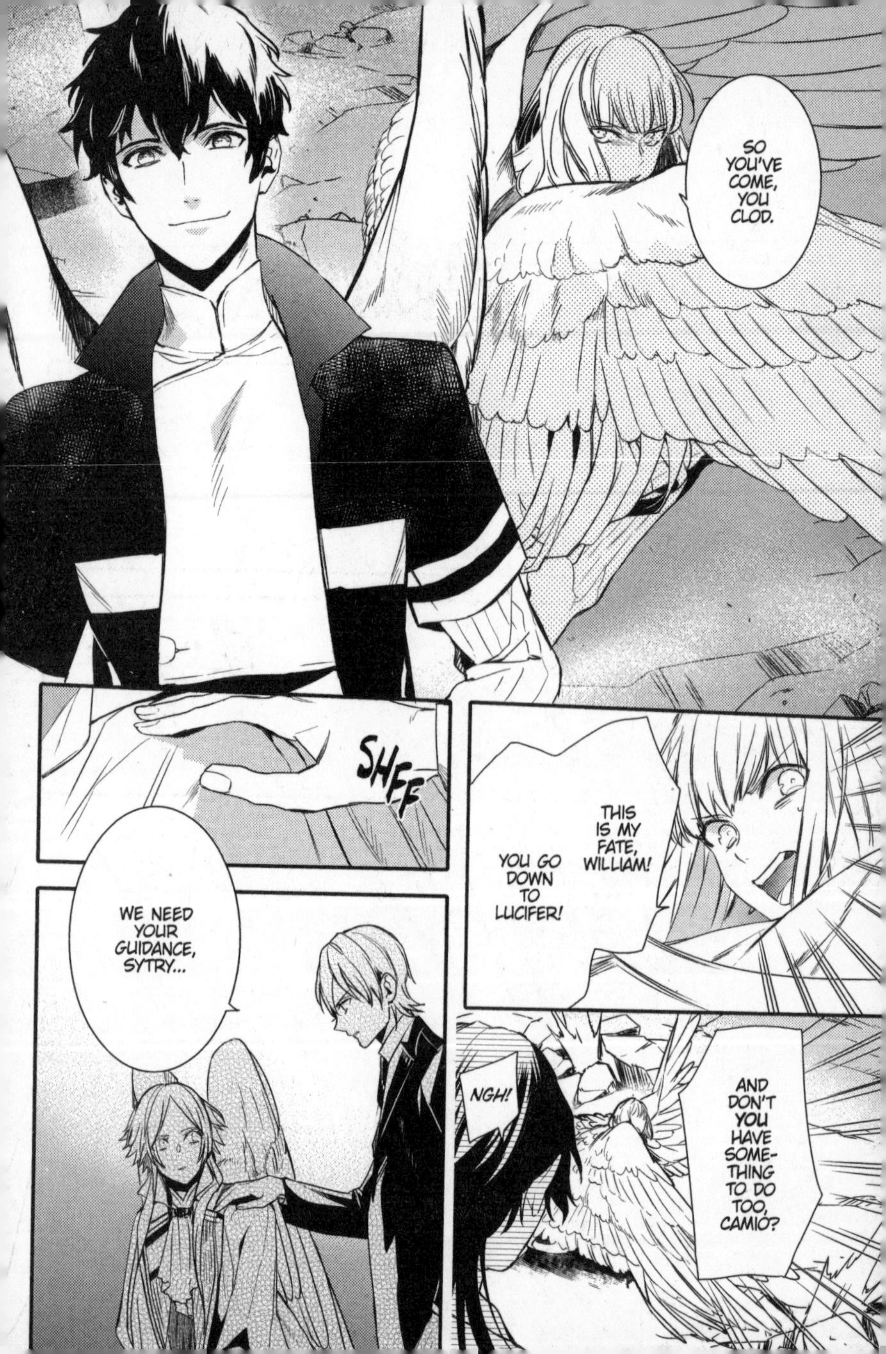
SO YOU'VE COME, YOU CLOD.
THIS IS MY FATE, WILLIAM!
YOU GO DOWN TO LUCIFER!
AND DON'T YOU HAVE SOME-THING TO DO TOO, CAMIO?
NGH!
SHFF
WE NEED YOUR GUIDANCE, SYTRY...

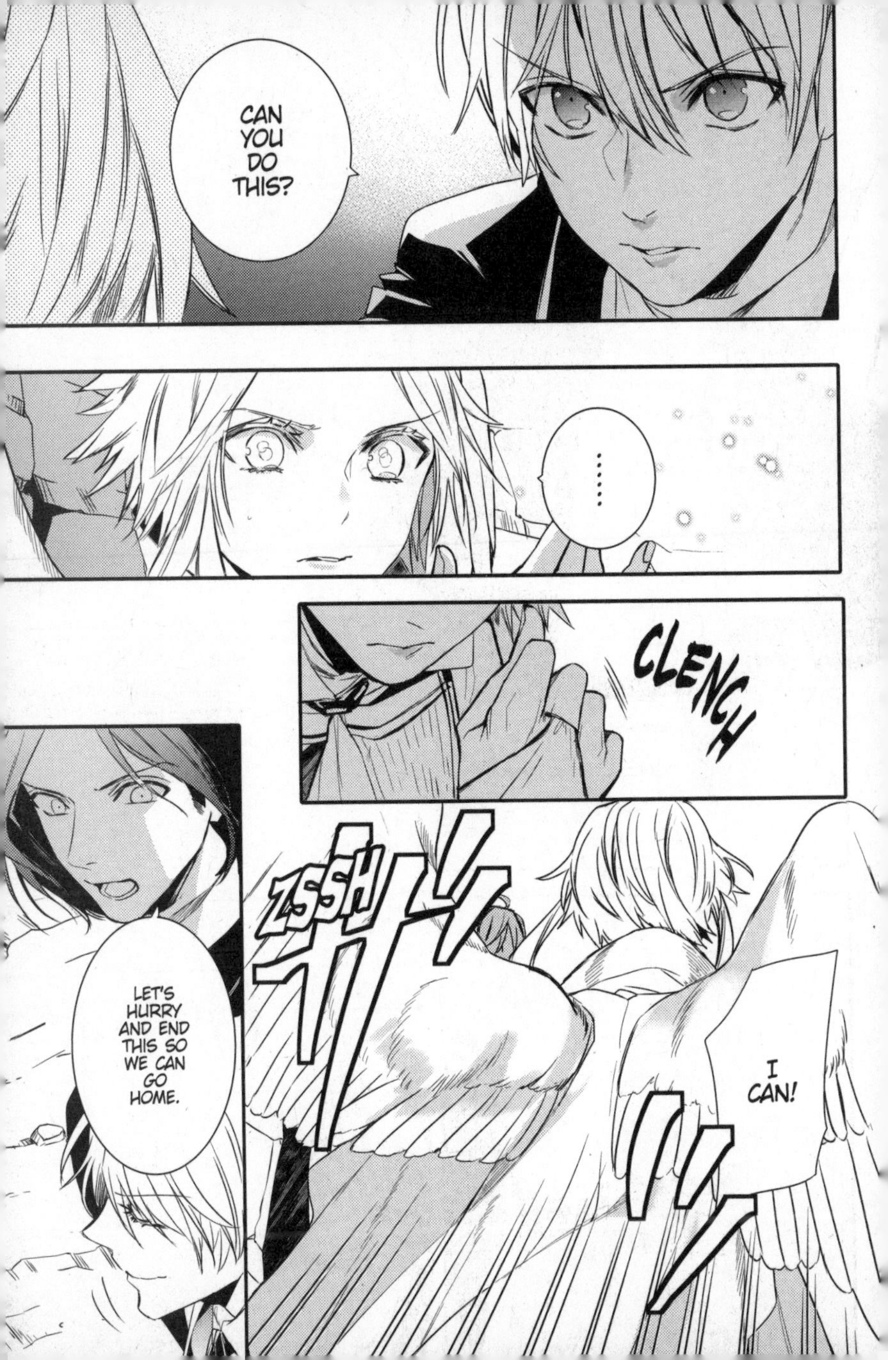
CAN YOU DO THIS?
......
CLENCH
I CAN!
ZSSH
LET'S HURRY AND END THIS SO WE CAN GO HOME.

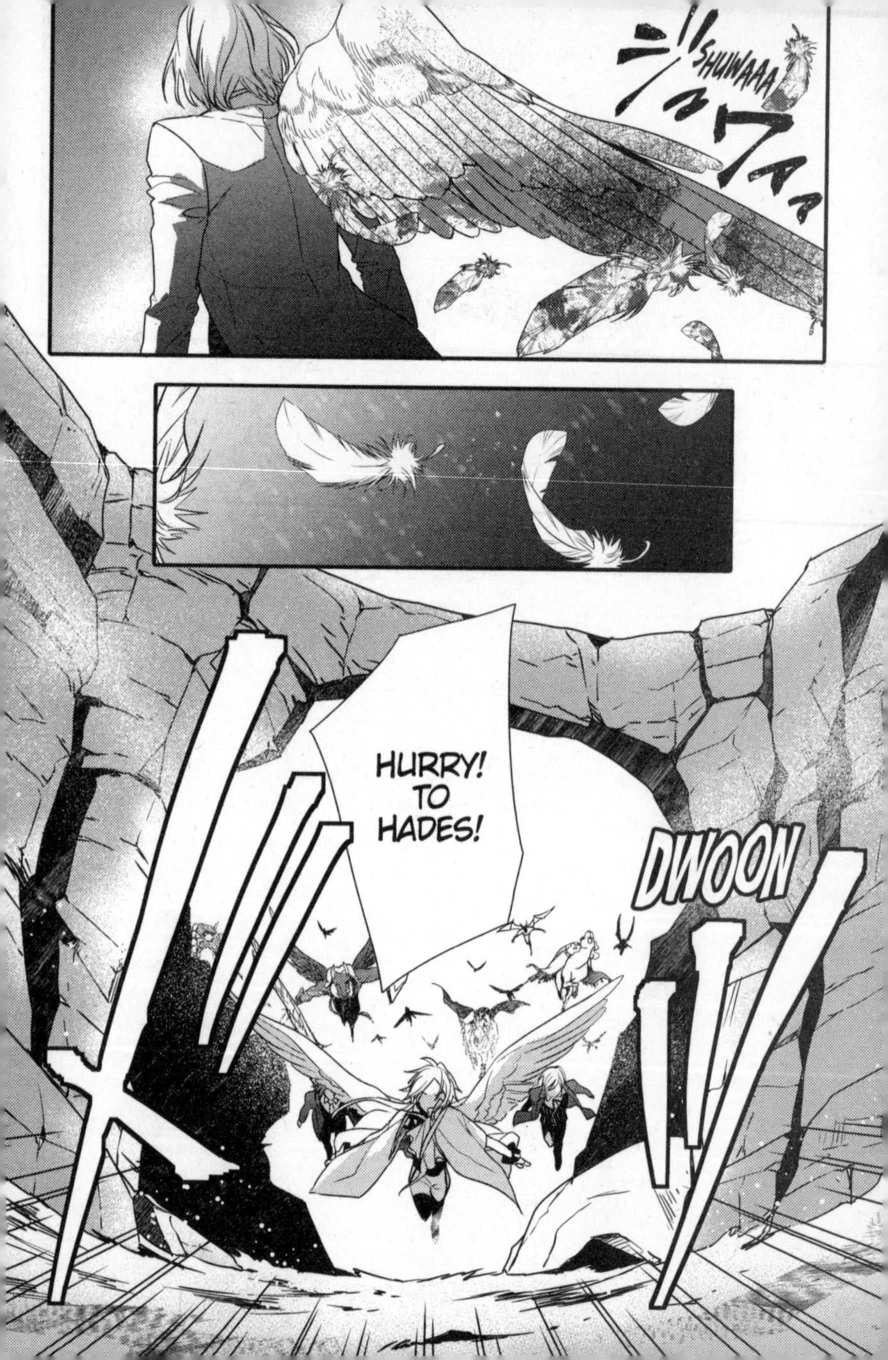
SHUWAAA
HURRY! TO HADES!
DWOON

Pillar 91

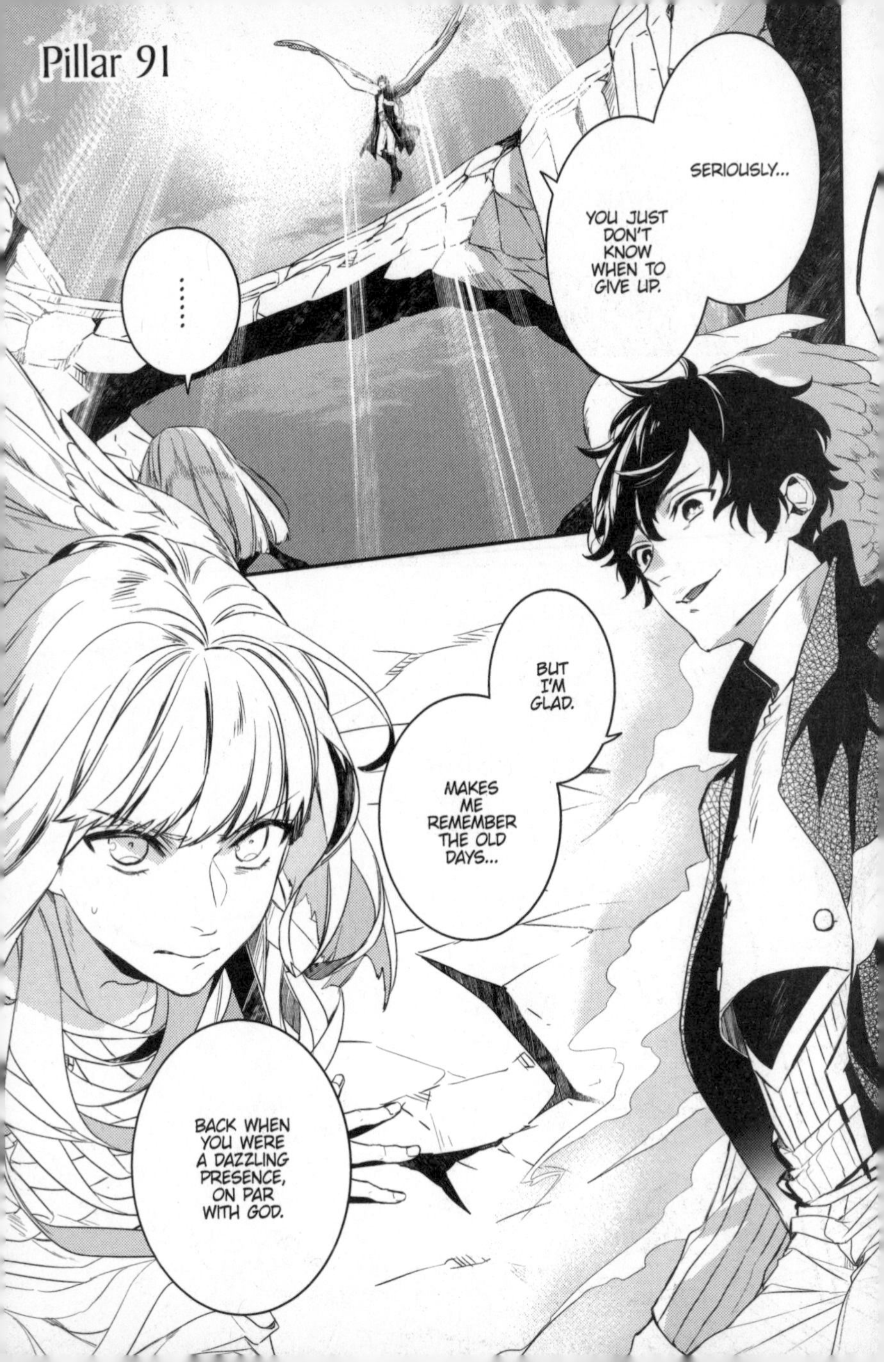
SERIOUSLY...
YOU JUST DON'T KNOW WHEN TO GIVE UP.
......
BUT I'M GLAD.
MAKES ME REMEMBER THE OLD DAYS...
BACK WHEN YOU WERE A DAZZLING PRESENCE, ON PAR WITH GOD.

Pillar 91

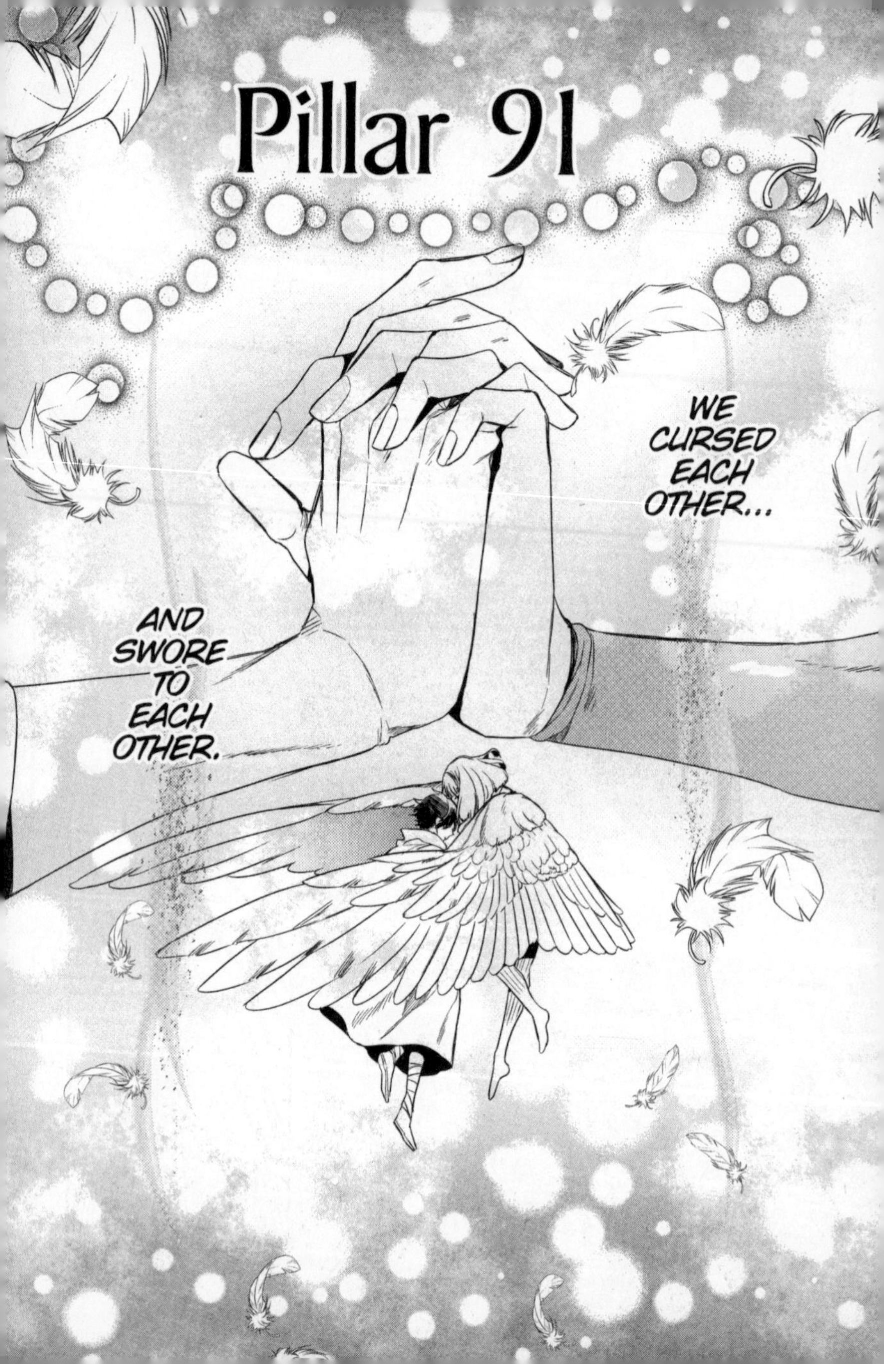
WE CURSED EACH OTHER...
AND SWORE TO EACH OTHER.

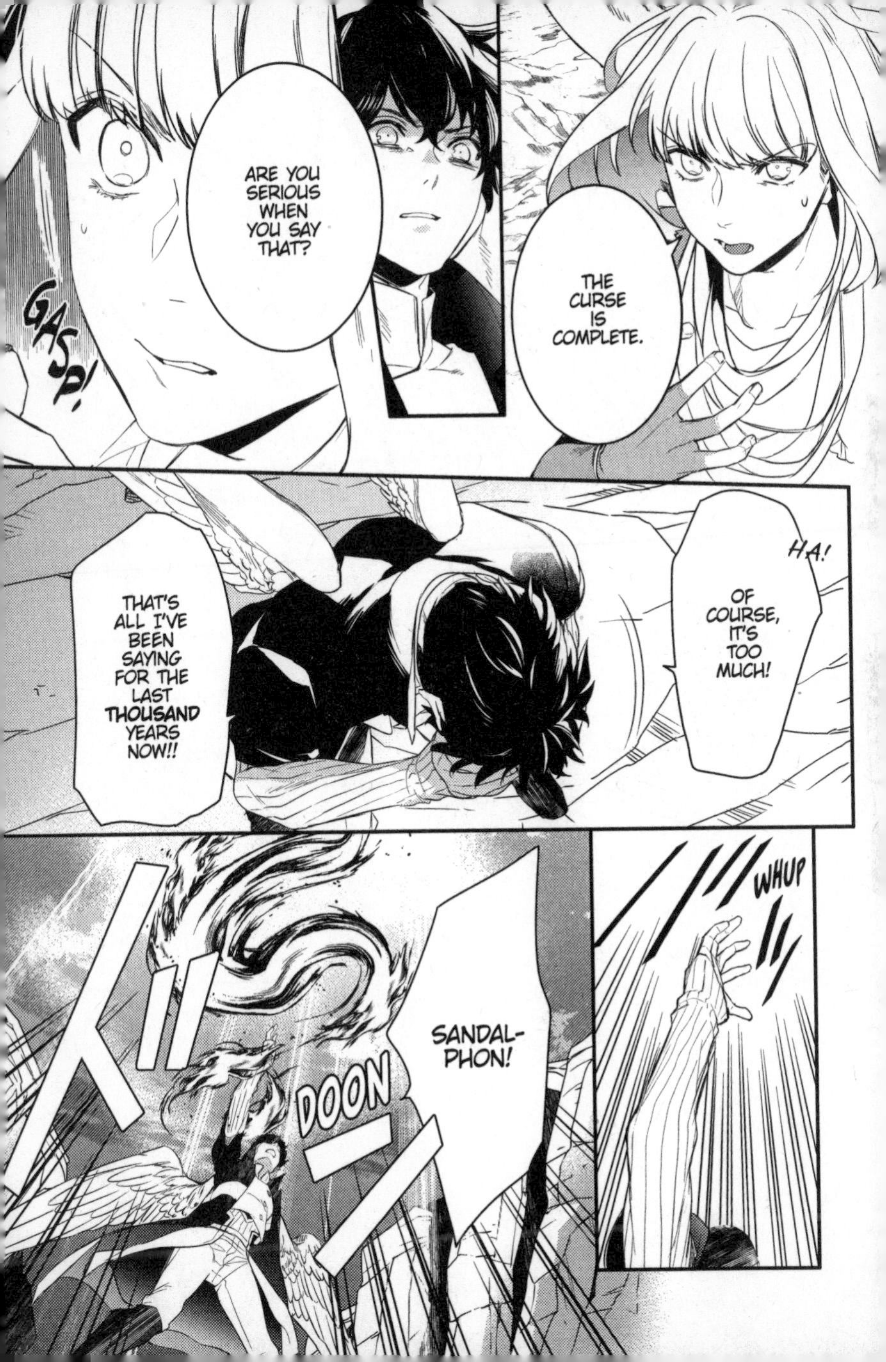
THE CURSE IS COMPLETE.
ARE YOU SERIOUS WHEN YOU SAY THAT?
GASP!
HA!
OF COURSE, IT'S TOO MUCH!
THAT'S ALL I'VE BEEN SAYING FOR THE LAST THOUSAND YEARS NOW!!
WHUP
SANDAL-PHON!
DOON

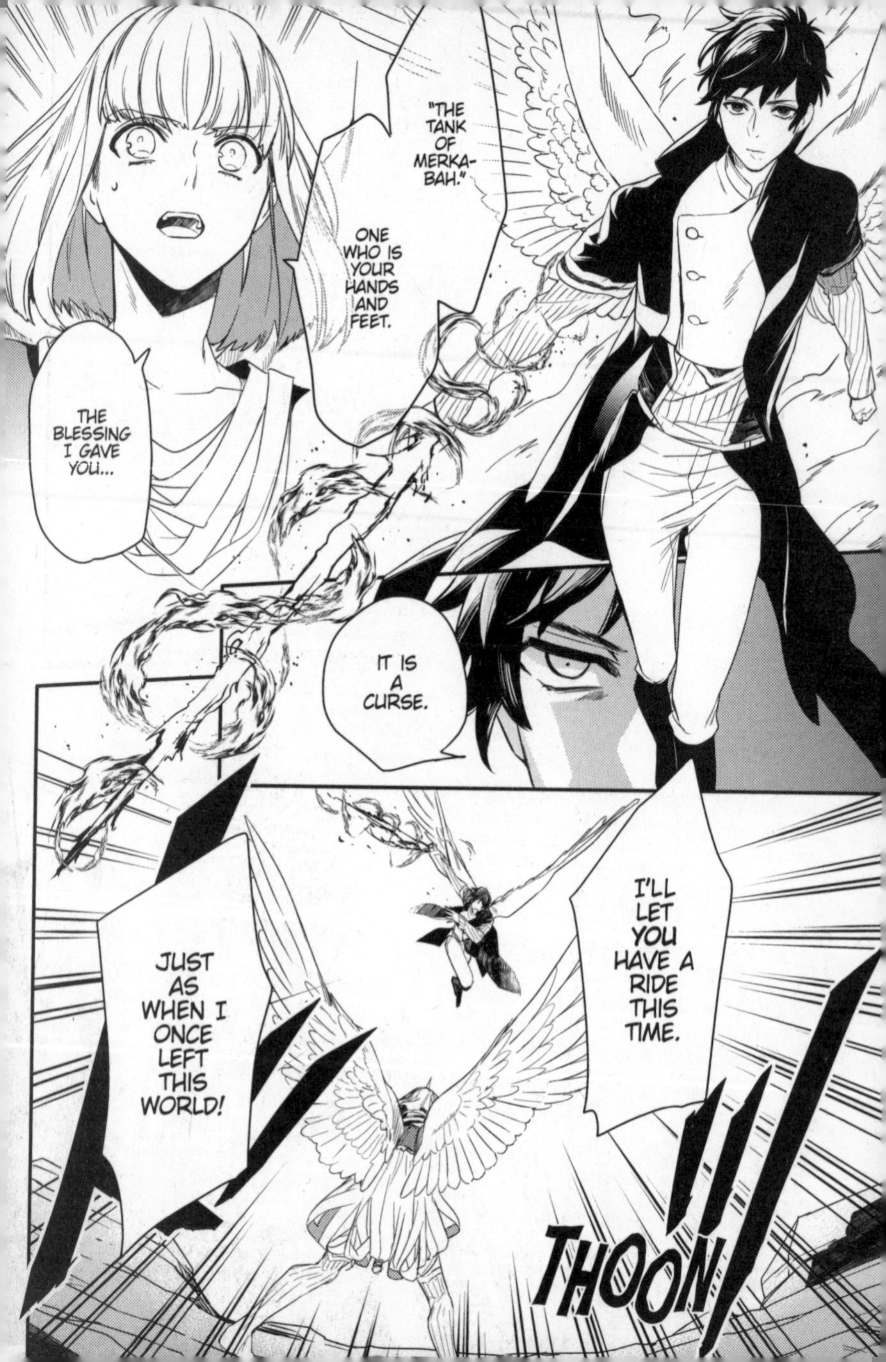
"THE TANK OF MERKABAH."
ONE WHO IS YOUR HANDS AND FEET.
THE BLESSING I GAVE YOU...
IT IS A CURSE.
I'LL LET YOU HAVE A RIDE THIS TIME.
JUST AS WHEN I ONCE LEFT THIS WORLD!
THOON

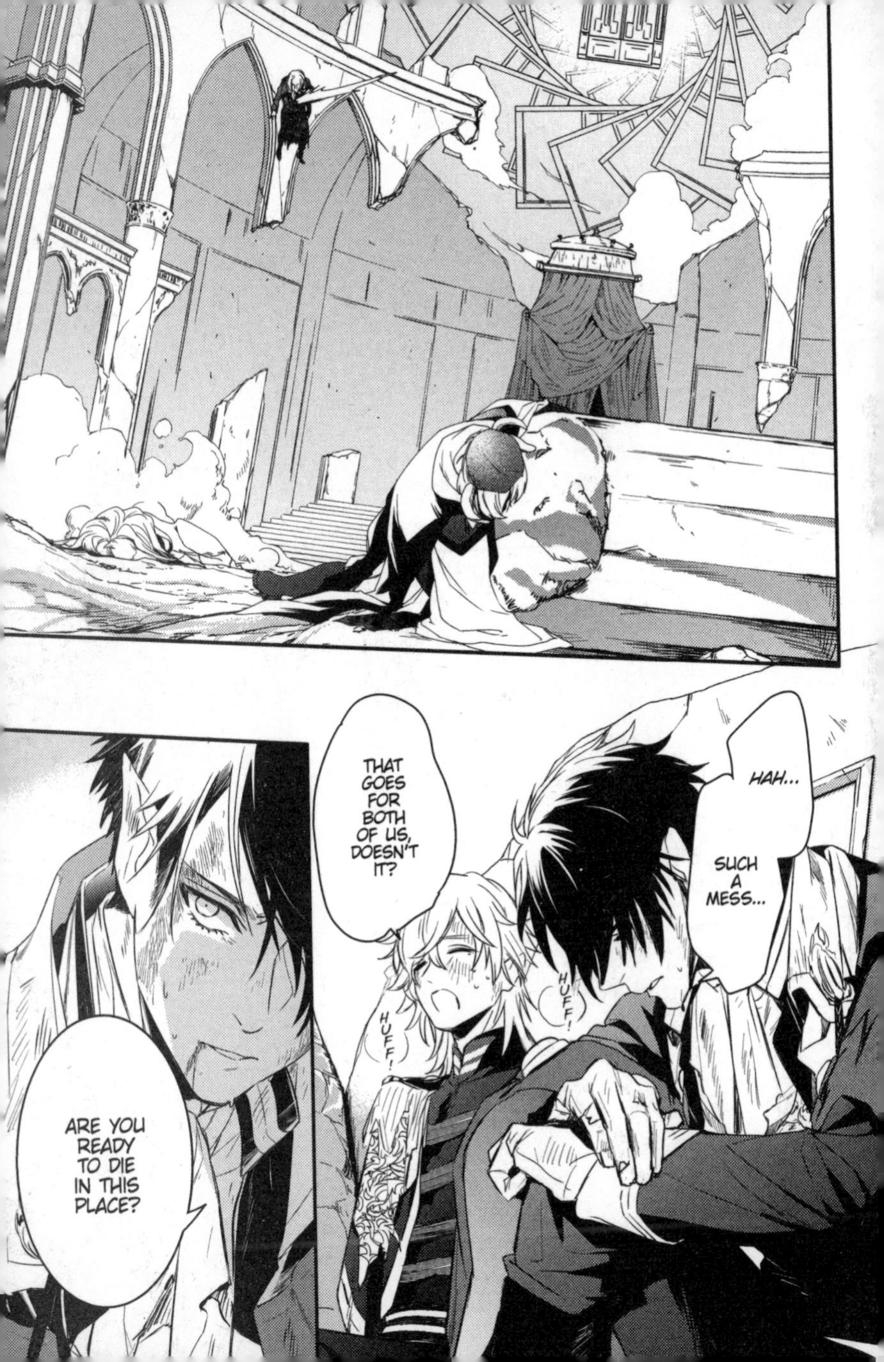
HAH... SUCH A MESS...
THAT GOES FOR BOTH OF US, DOESN'T IT?
HUFF!
HUFF!
ARE YOU READY TO DIE IN THIS PLACE?

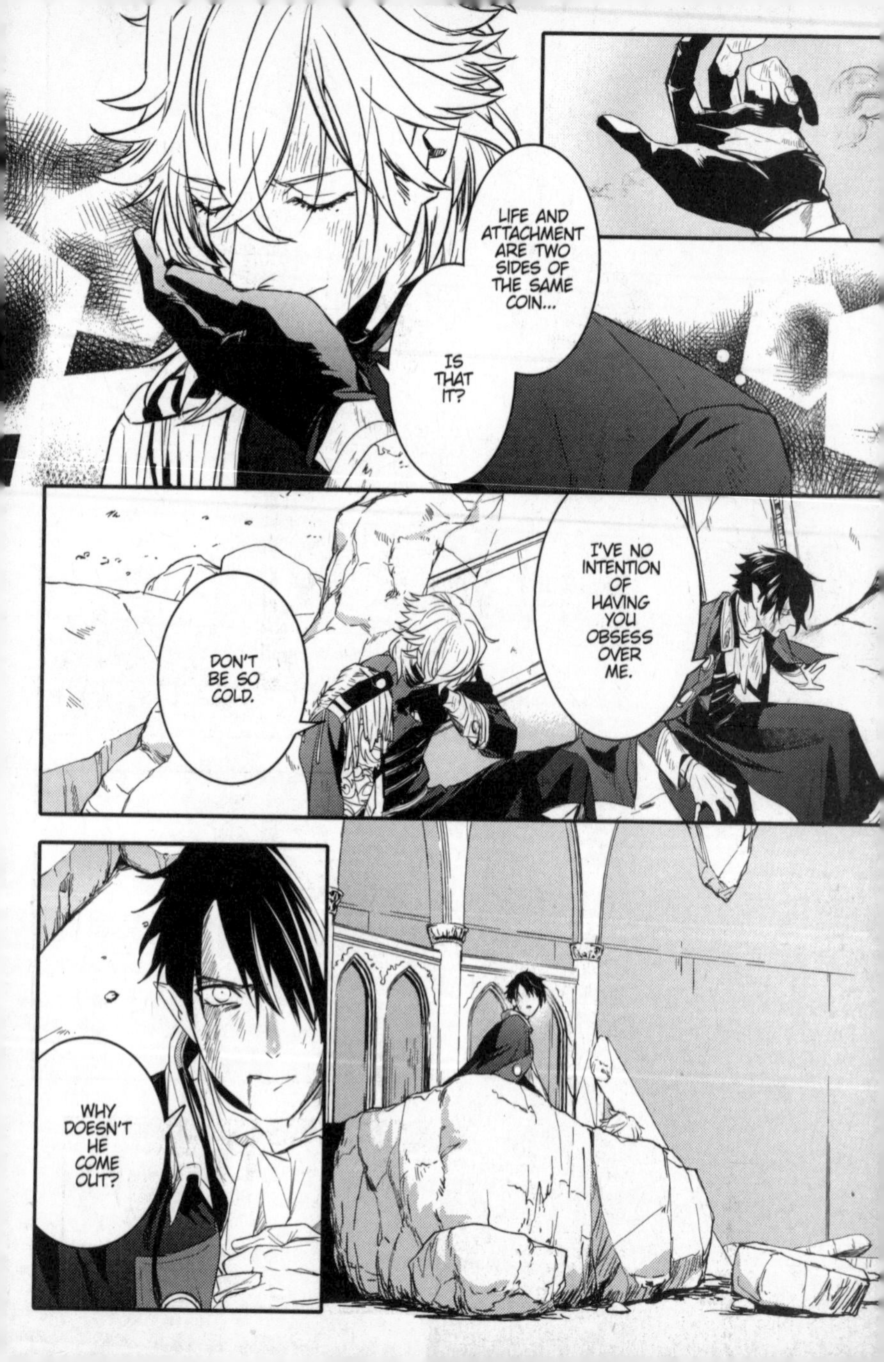
LIFE AND ATTACHMENT ARE TWO SIDES OF THE SAME COIN...
IS THAT IT?
I'VE NO INTENTION OF HAVING YOU OBSESS OVER ME.
DON'T BE SO COLD.
WHY DOESN'T HE COME OUT?

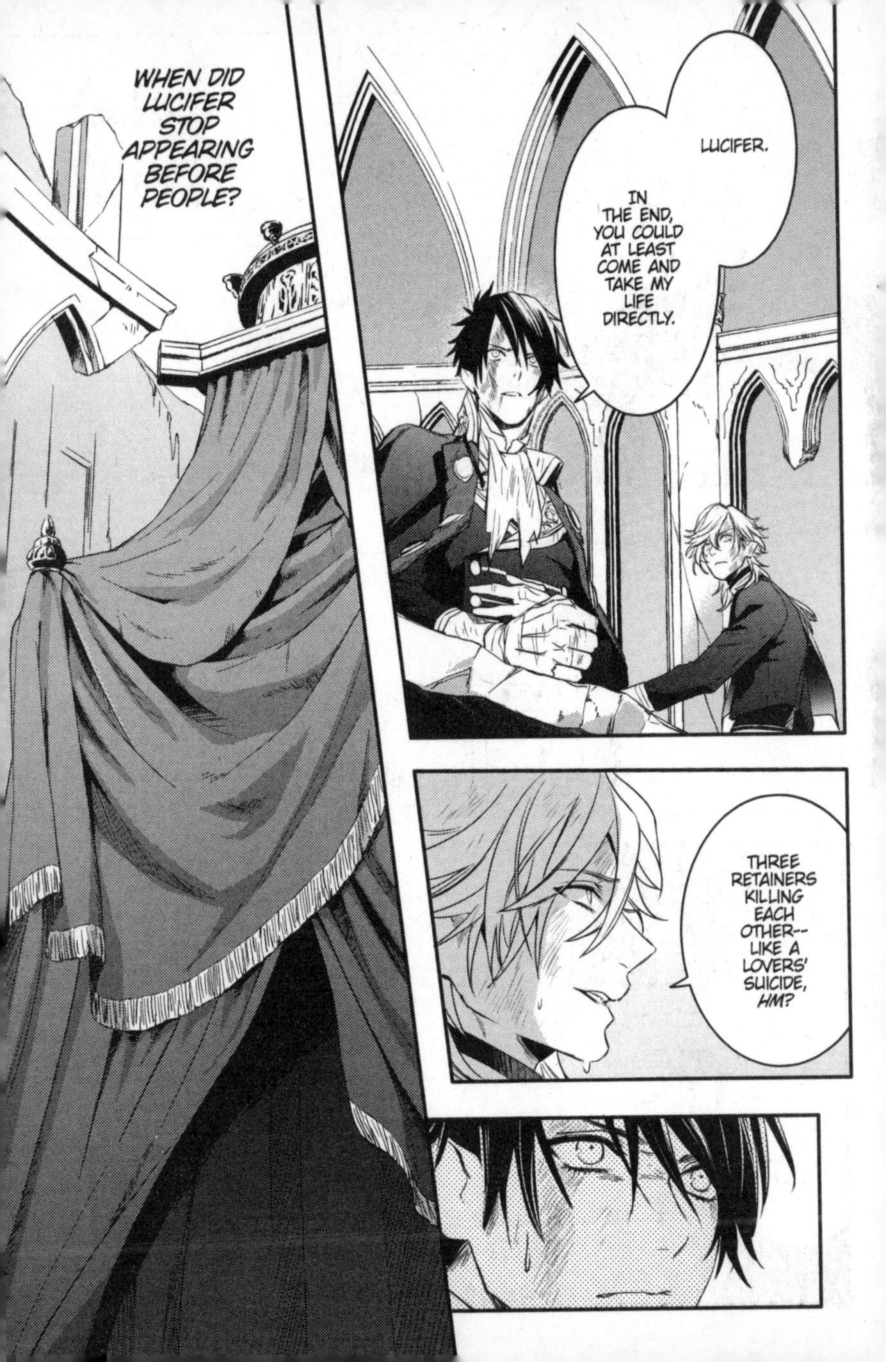
LUCIFER.
IN THE END, YOU COULD AT LEAST COME AND TAKE MY LIFE DIRECTLY.
THREE RETAINERS KILLING EACH OTHER--LIKE A LOVERS' SUICIDE, HM?
WHEN DID LUCIFER STOP APPEARING BEFORE PEOPLE?

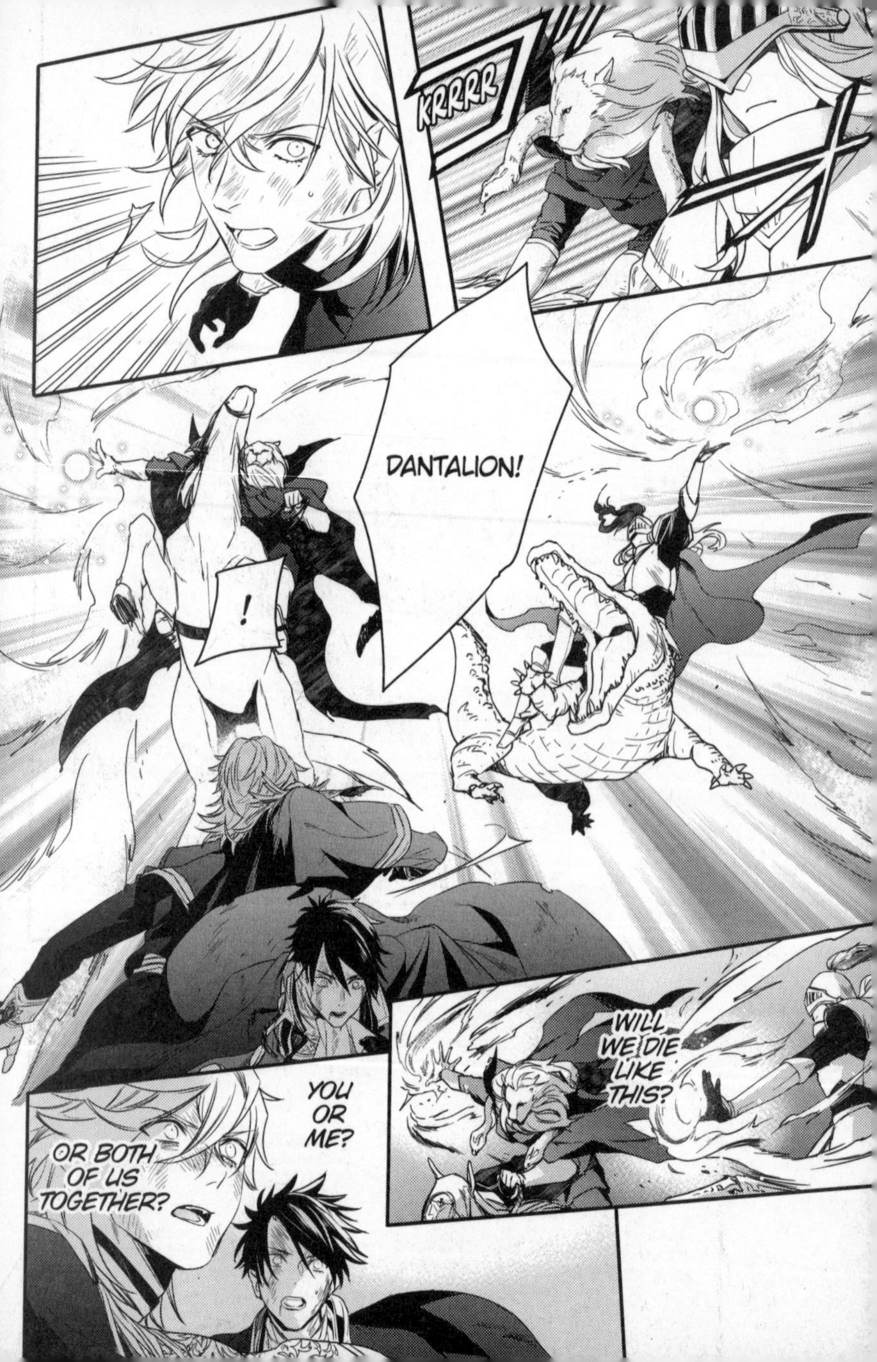
KRRRR
DANTALION!
!
WILL WE DIE LIKE THIS?
YOU OR ME?
OR BOTH OF US TOGETHER?

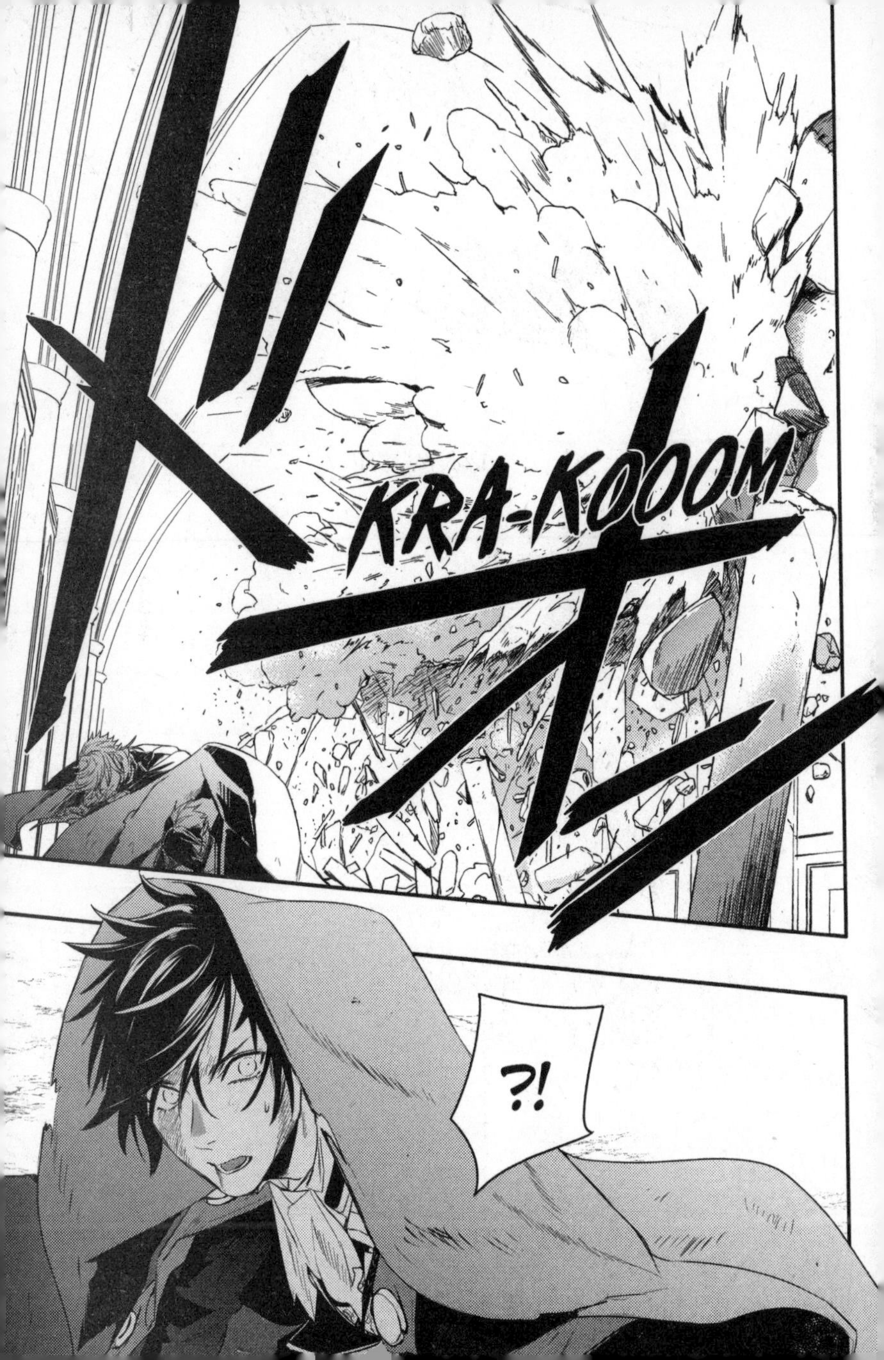
KRA-KOOOM
?!

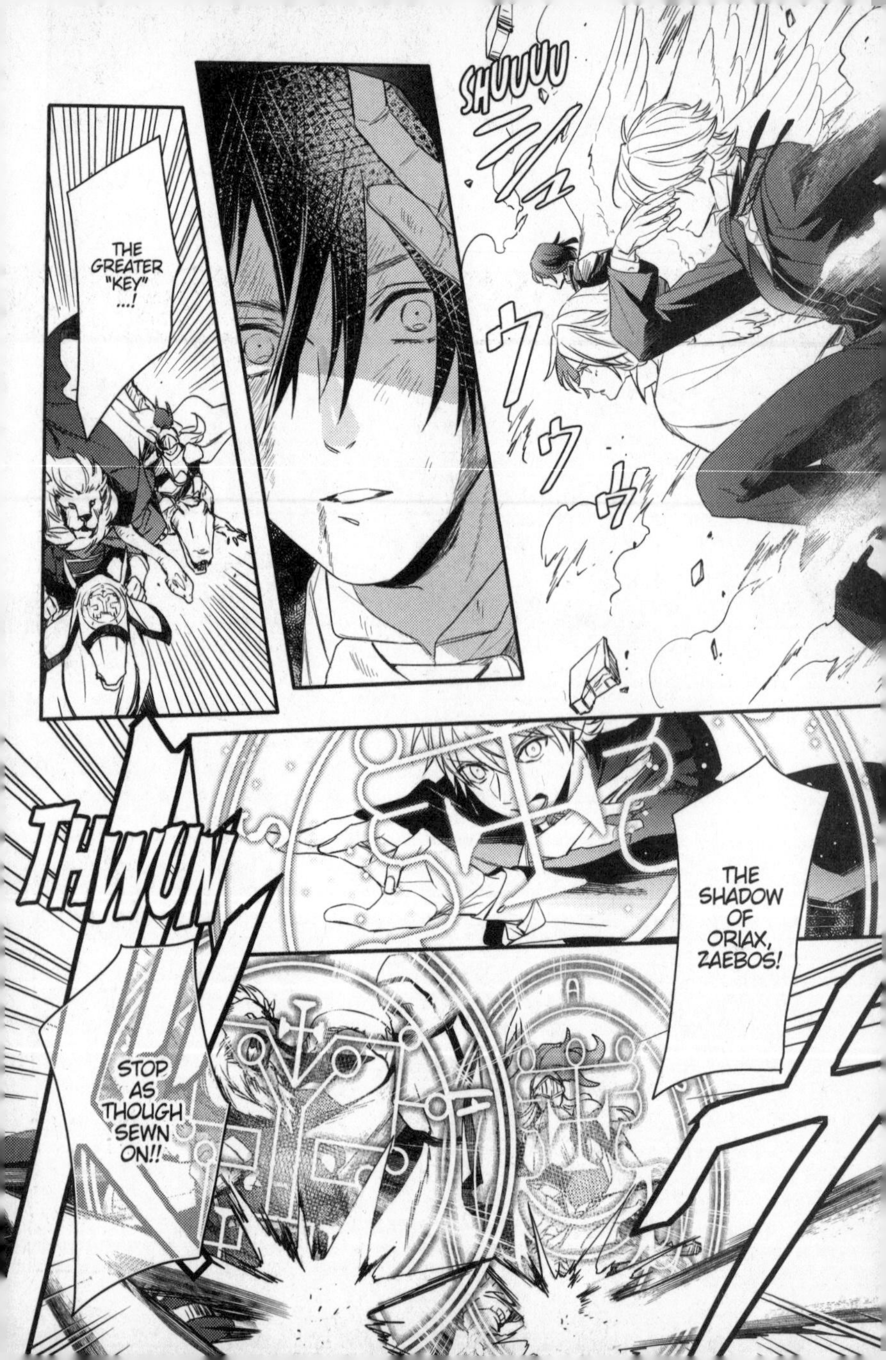
SHUUUU
THE GREATER "KEY" ...!
THE SHADOW OF ORIAX, ZAEBOS!
THWUN
STOP AS THOUGH SEWN ON!!

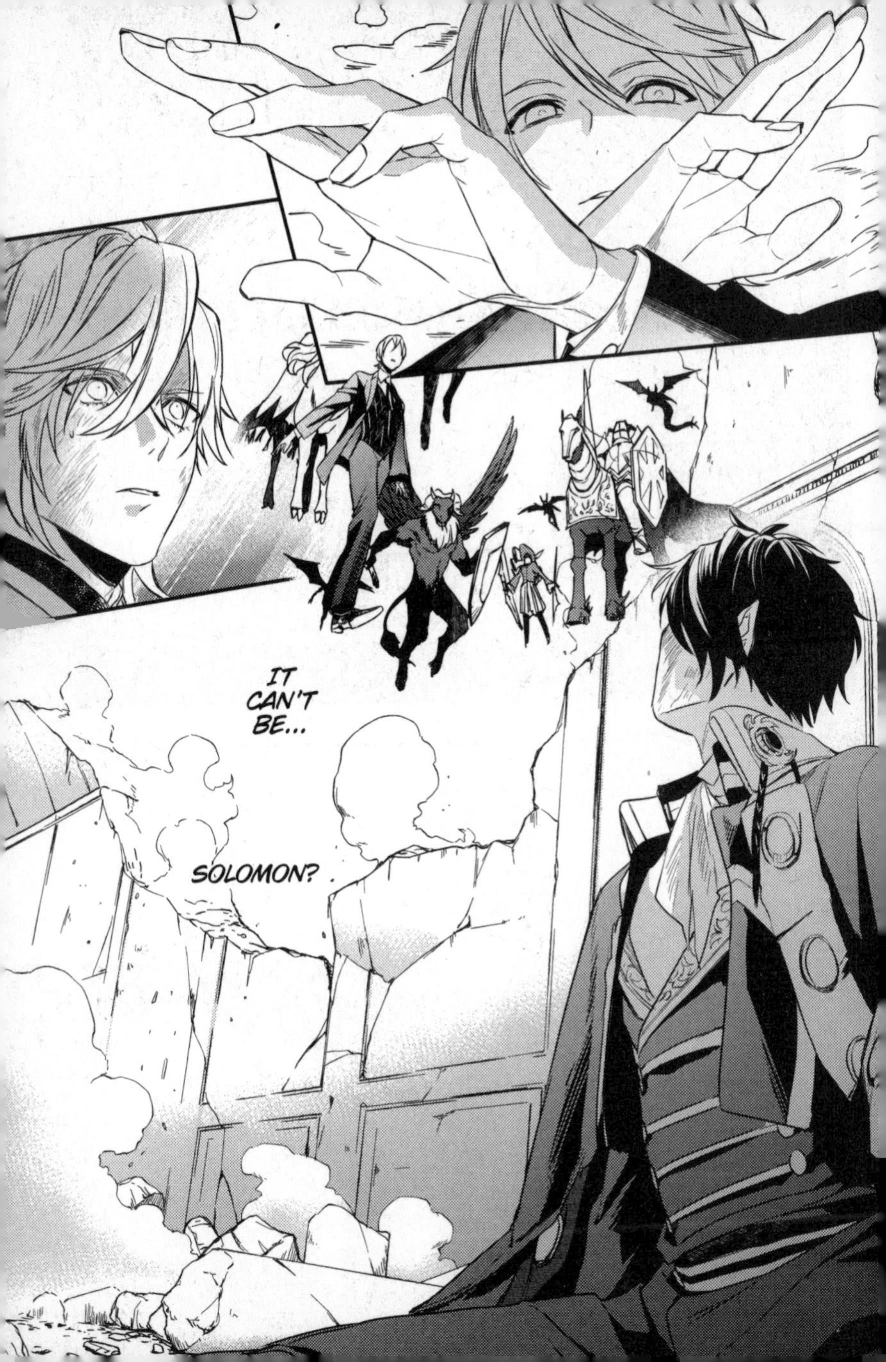
IT CAN'T BE...
SOLOMON?

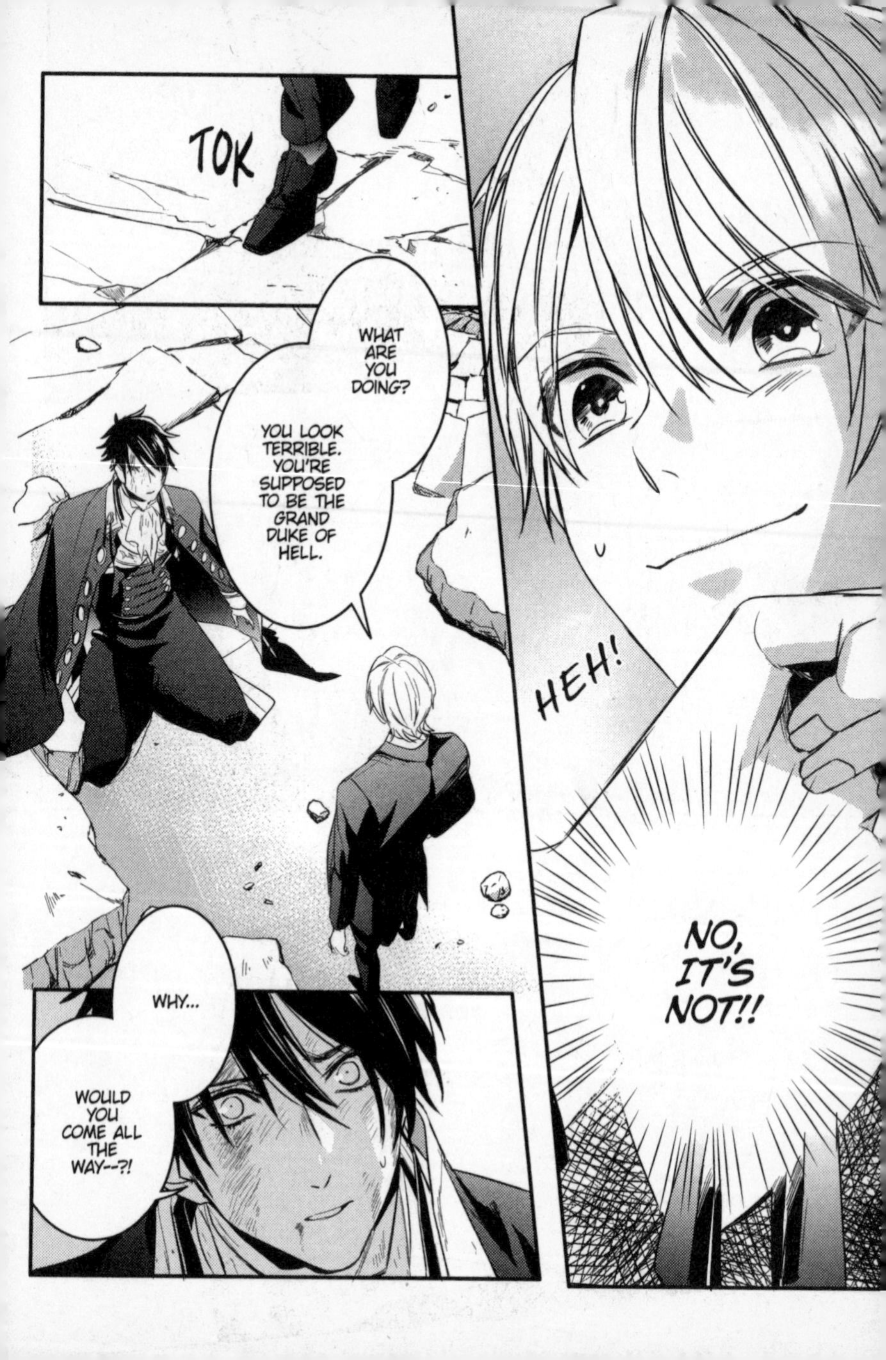
HEH!
NO, IT'S NOT!!
TOK
WHAT ARE YOU DOING?
YOU LOOK TERRIBLE. YOU'RE SUPPOSED TO BE THE GRAND DUKE OF HELL.
WHY...
WOULD YOU COME ALL THE WAY--?!

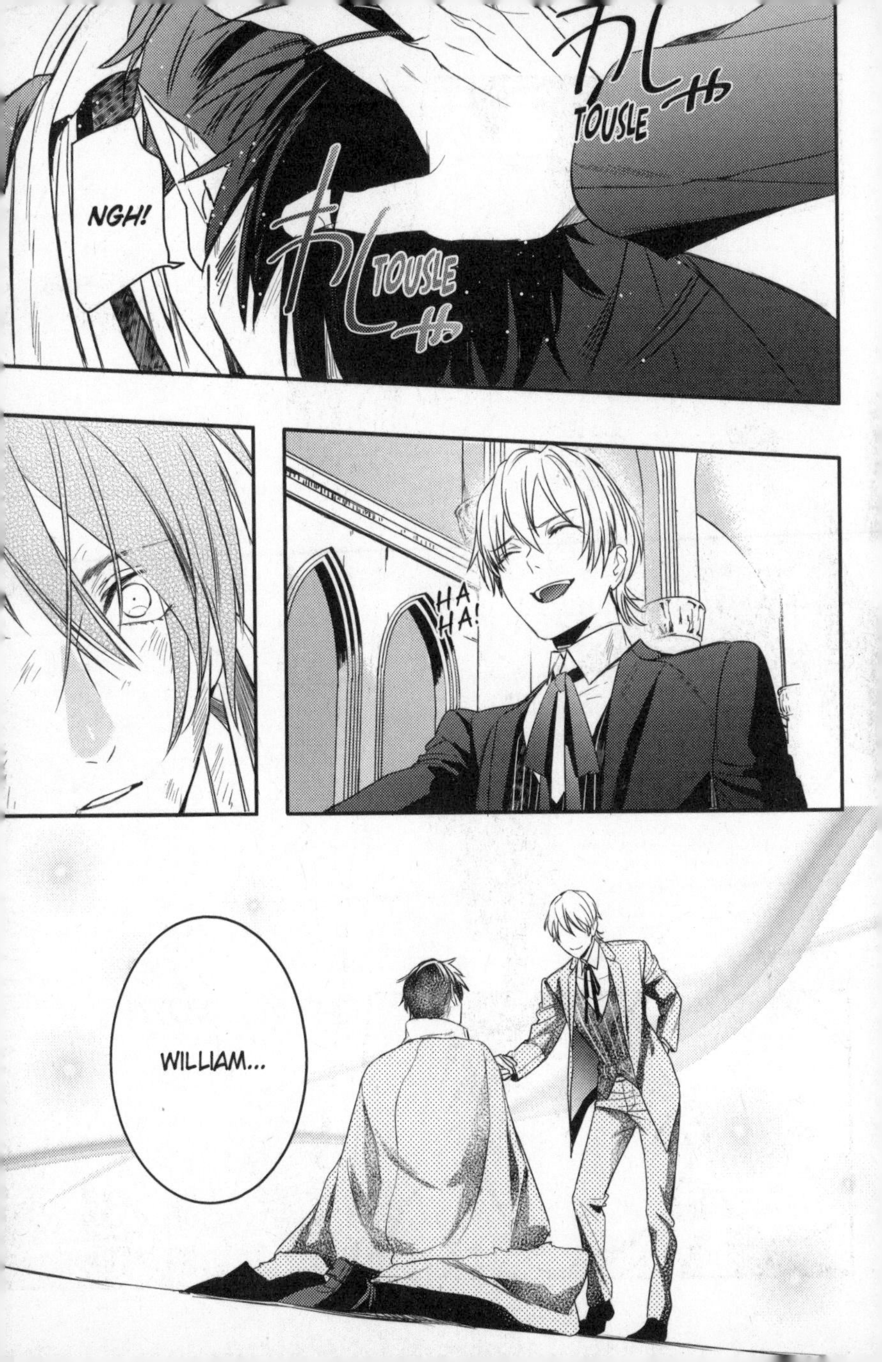

わしゃ
TOUSLE
わしゃ
TOUSLE
NGH!
HA HA!
WILLIAM...

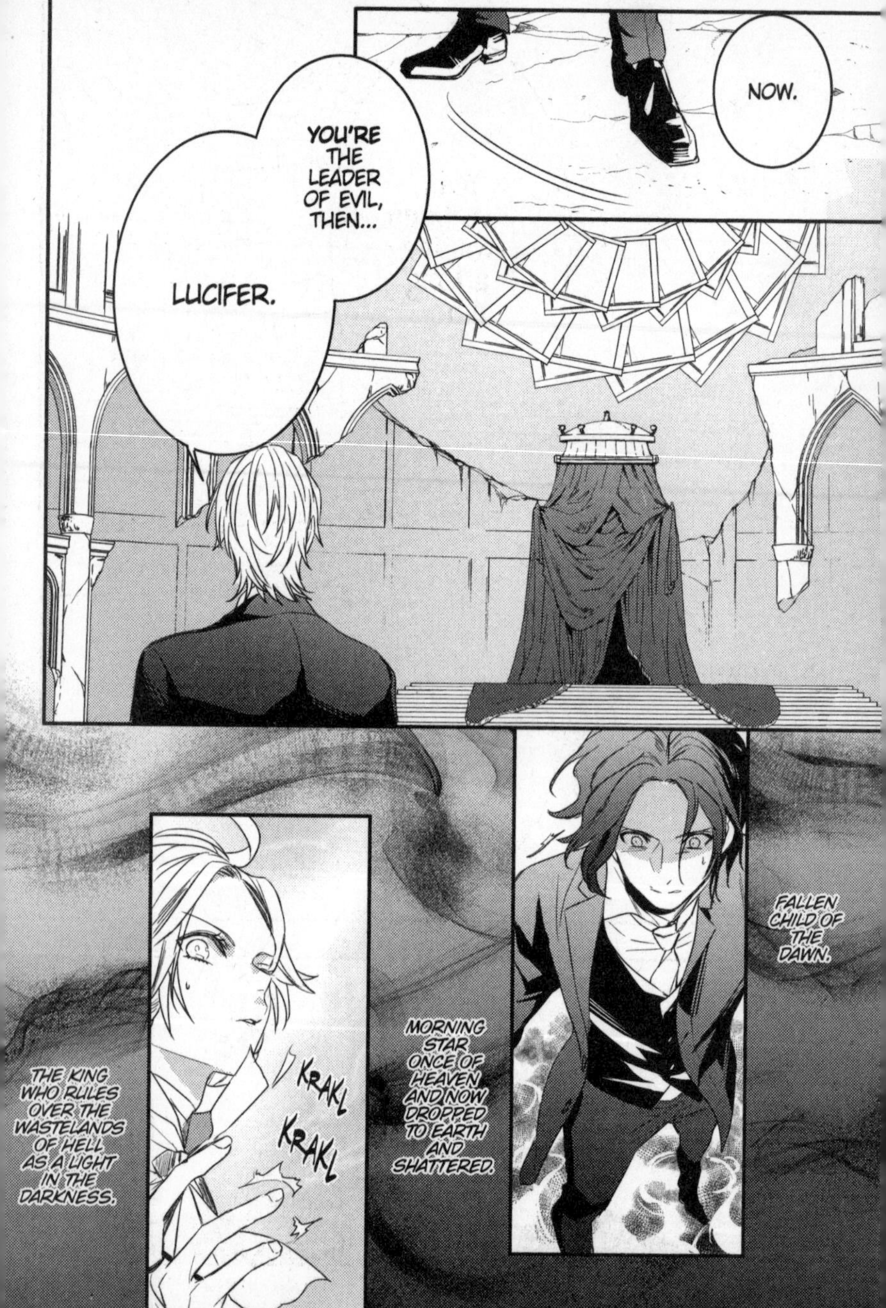
NOW.
YOU'RE THE LEADER OF EVIL, THEN...
LUCIFER.
FALLEN CHILD OF THE DAWN.
MORNING STAR ONCE OF HEAVEN AND NOW DROPPED TO EARTH AND SHATTERED.
KRAKL
KRAKL
THE KING WHO RULES OVER THE WASTELANDS OF HELL AS A LIGHT IN THE DARKNESS.

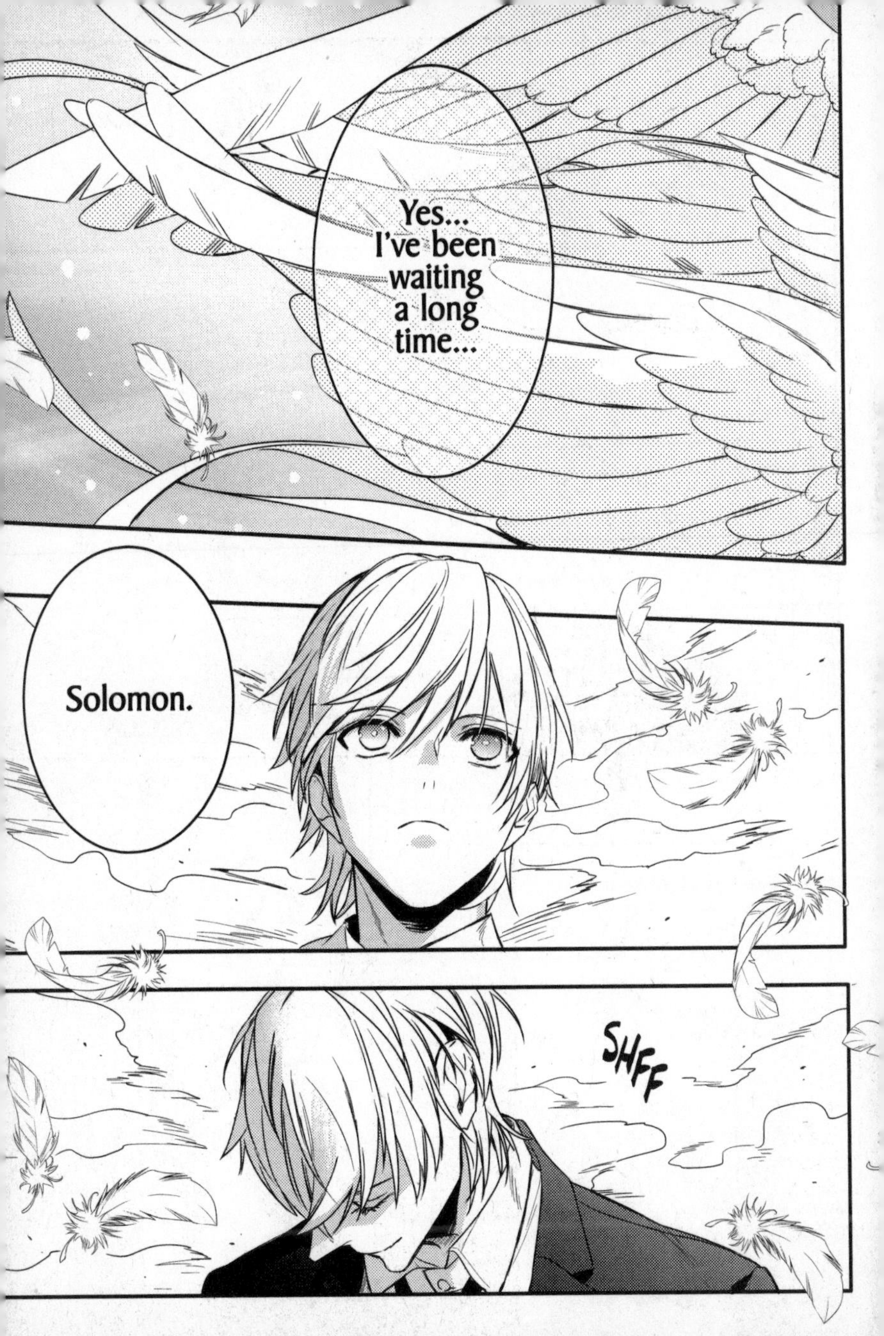
Yes... I've been waiting a long time...
Solomon.
SHFF

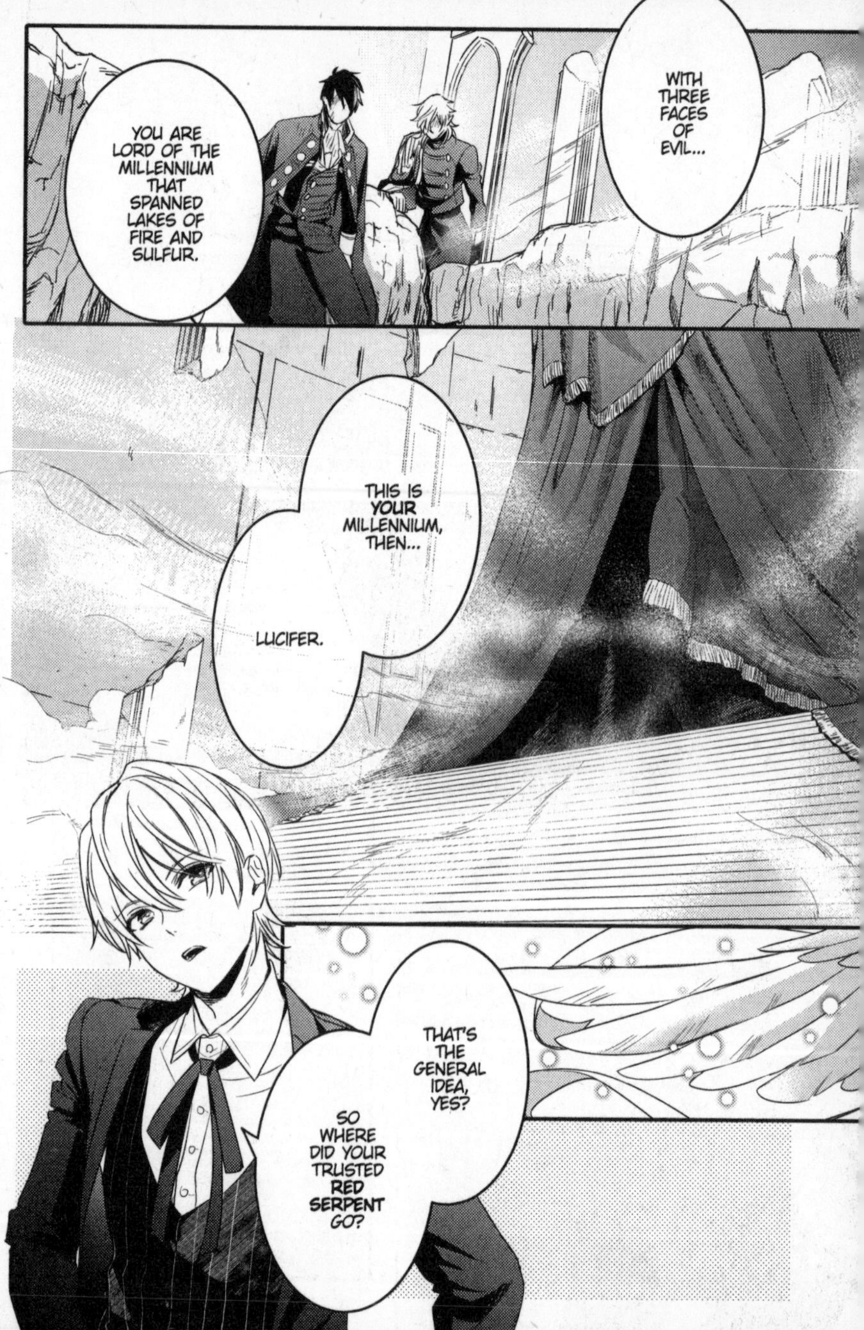
WITH THREE FACES OF EVIL...
YOU ARE LORD OF THE MILLENNIUM THAT SPANNED LAKES OF FIRE AND SULFUR.
THIS IS YOUR MILLENNIUM, THEN...
LUCIFER.
THAT'S THE GENERAL IDEA, YES?
SO WHERE DID YOUR TRUSTED RED SERPENT GO?

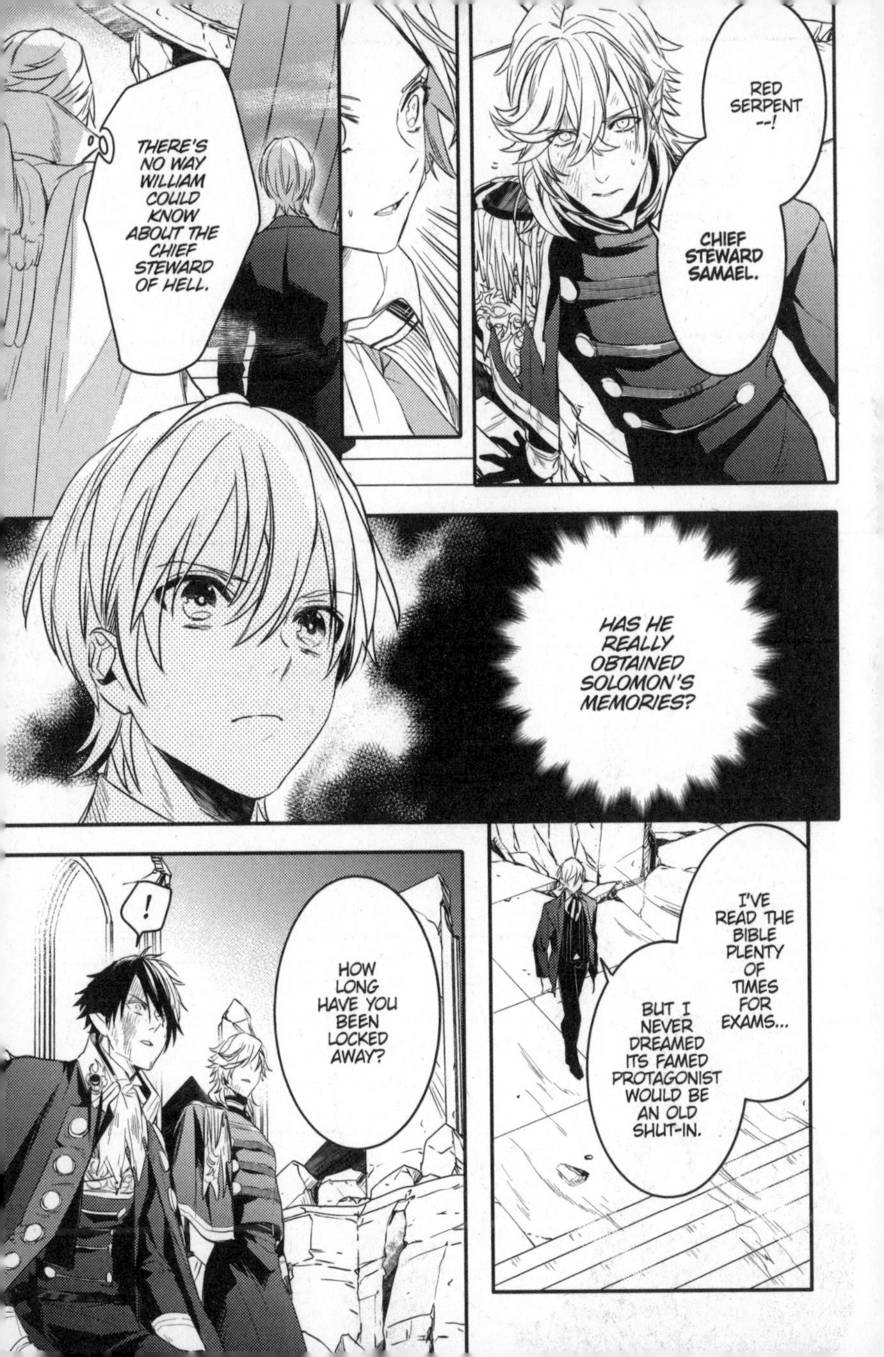
RED SERPENT--!
CHIEF STEWARD SAMAEL.
THERE'S NO WAY WILLIAM COULD KNOW ABOUT THE CHIEF STEWARD OF HELL.
HAS HE REALLY OBTAINED SOLOMON'S MEMORIES?
I'VE READ THE BIBLE PLENTY OF TIMES FOR EXAMS...
BUT I NEVER DREAMED ITS FAMED PROTAGONIST WOULD BE AN OLD SHUT-IN.
!
HOW LONG HAVE YOU BEEN LOCKED AWAY?

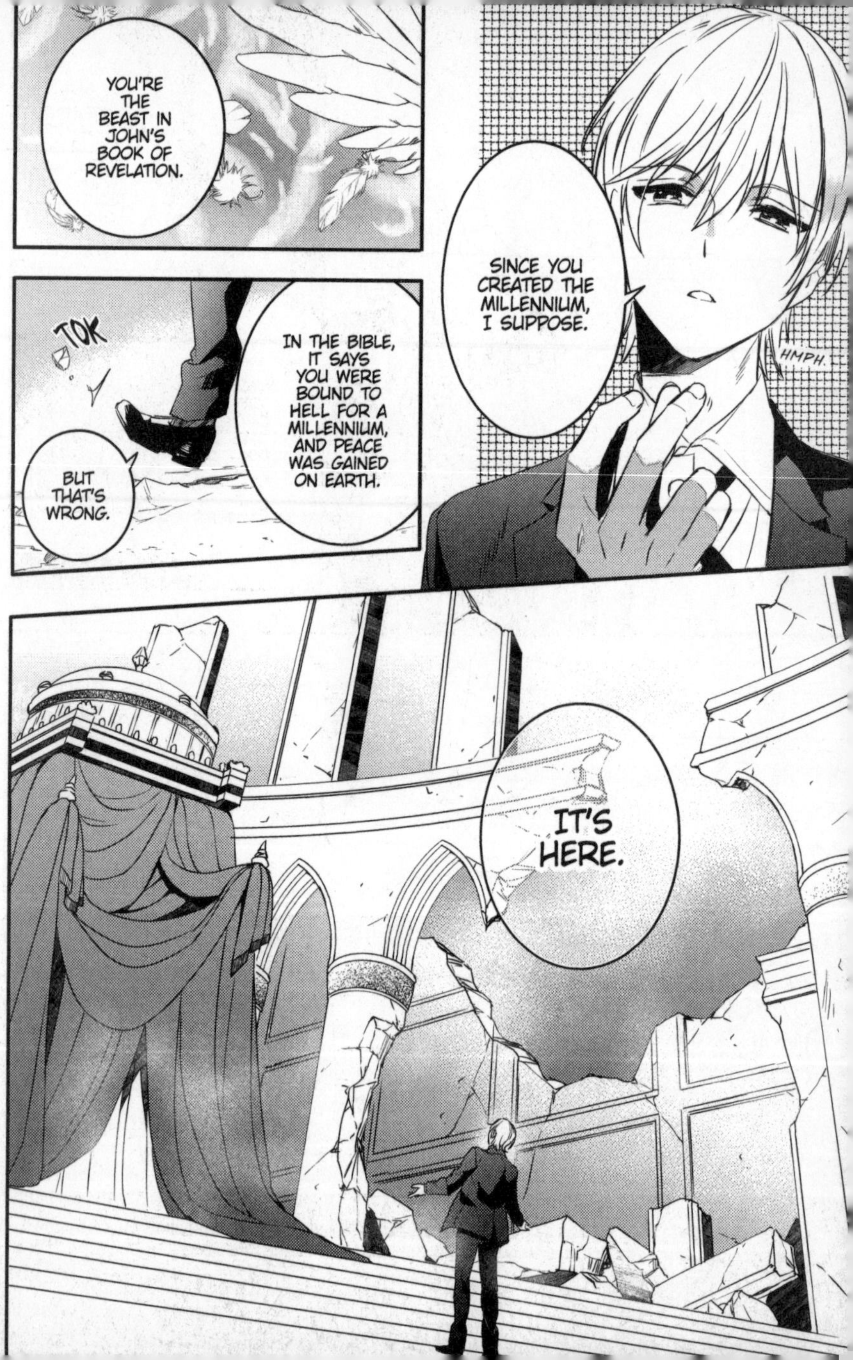
SINCE YOU CREATED THE MILLENNIUM, I SUPPOSE.
HMPH.
YOU'RE THE BEAST IN JOHN'S BOOK OF REVELATION.
TOK
IN THE BIBLE, IT SAYS YOU WERE BOUND TO HELL FOR A MILLENNIUM, AND PEACE WAS GAINED ON EARTH.
BUT THAT'S WRONG.
IT'S HERE.

USING WISDOM.

YOU CREATED A LARGE DOOR SO GOD'S WILL COULDN'T REACH YOU, AND THEN YOU LOCKED IT.

ANYONE CAN OPEN THIS DOOR USING THE KEY...

!

SOLOMON FIRST BROKE THAT DOOR DOWN!

WHILE STILL HUMAN, HE WAS BELOVED BY GOD AND BOUND SEVENTY-TWO DEMONS AS PILLARS TO SERVE HIM.

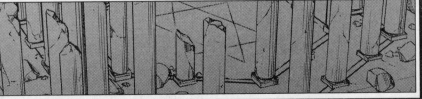

ONE WHO HOLDS THE KEY OF DAVID... ONCE OPENED, HE CAN BE CLOSED BY NONE. ONCE CLOSED, HE CAN BE OPENED BY NONE. THIS PERSON ONCE SAID...

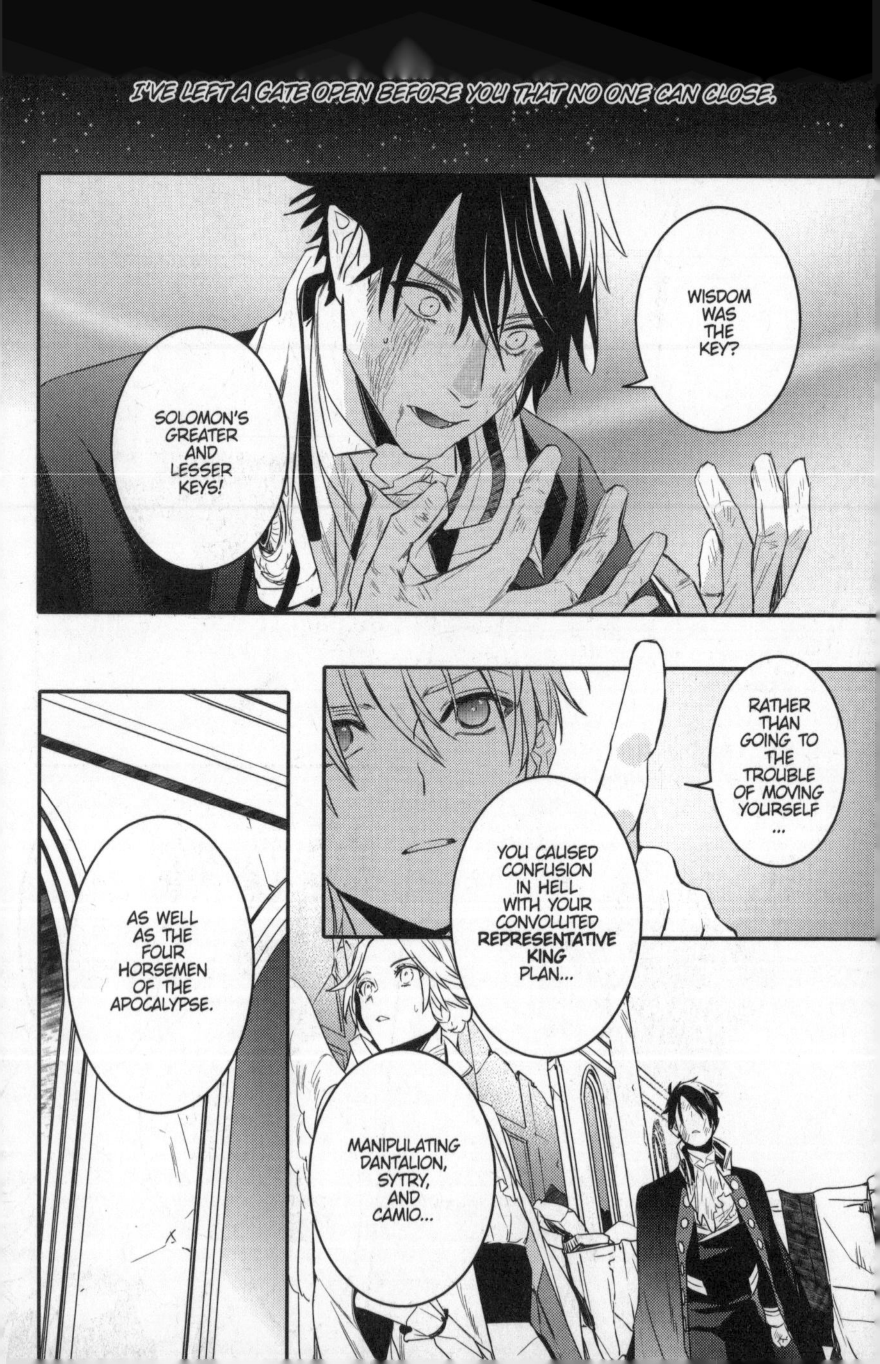
I'VE LEFT A GATE OPEN BEFORE YOU THAT NO ONE CAN CLOSE.
WISDOM WAS THE KEY?
SOLOMON'S GREATER AND LESSER KEYS!
RATHER THAN GOING TO THE TROUBLE OF MOVING YOURSELF ...
YOU CAUSED CONFUSION IN HELL WITH YOUR CONVOLUTED REPRESENTATIVE KING PLAN...
MANIPULATING DANTALION, SYTRY, AND CAMIO...
AS WELL AS THE FOUR HORSEMEN OF THE APOCALYPSE.

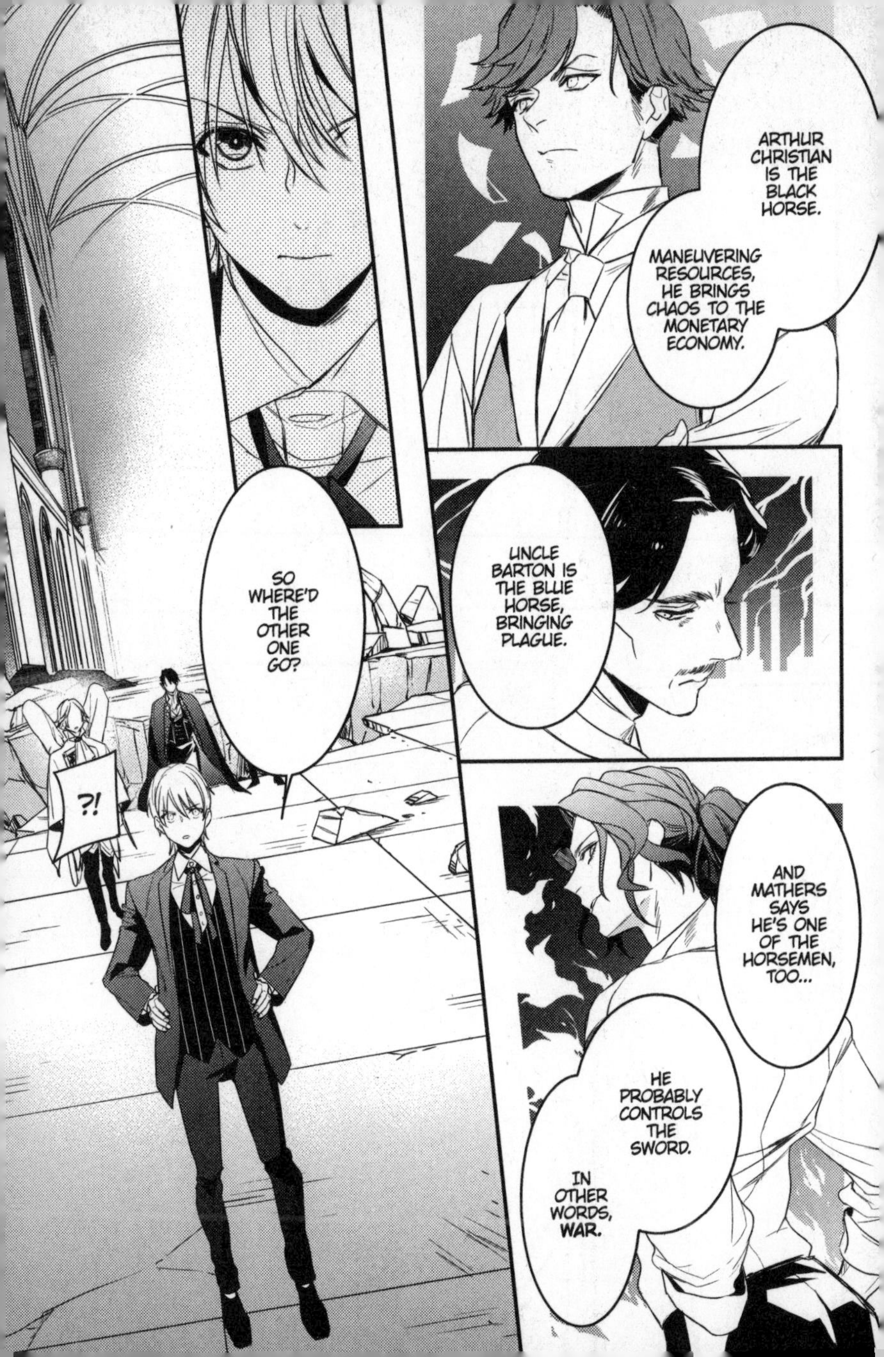
ARTHUR CHRISTIAN IS THE BLACK HORSE.
MANEUVERING RESOURCES, HE BRINGS CHAOS TO THE MONETARY ECONOMY.
UNCLE BARTON IS THE BLUE HORSE, BRINGING PLAGUE.
AND MATHERS SAYS HE'S ONE OF THE HORSEMEN, TOO...
HE PROBABLY CONTROLS THE SWORD.
IN OTHER WORDS, WAR.
SO WHERE'D THE OTHER ONE GO?
?!

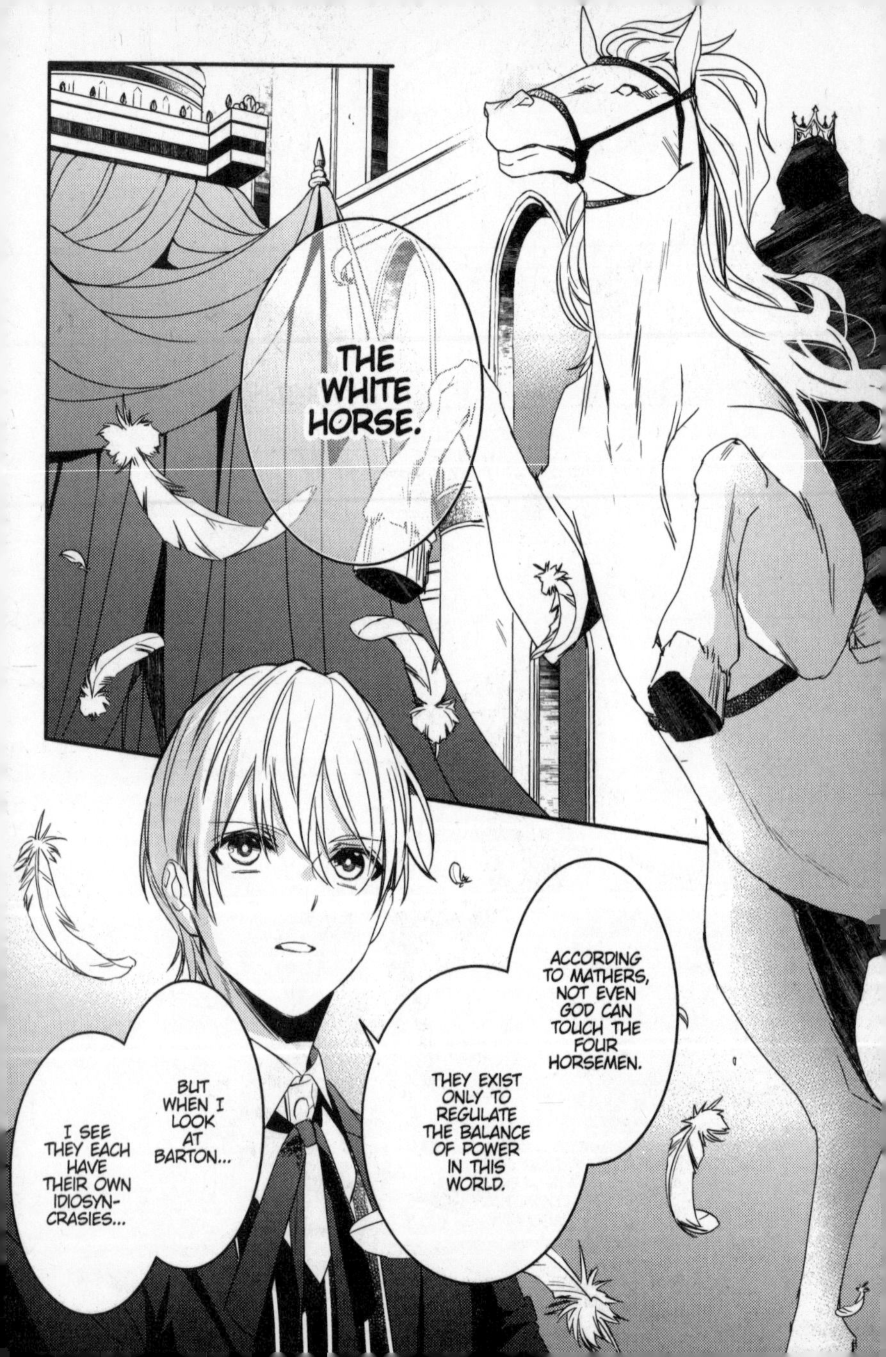
THE WHITE HORSE.
ACCORDING TO MATHERS, NOT EVEN GOD CAN TOUCH THE FOUR HORSEMEN.
THEY EXIST ONLY TO REGULATE THE BALANCE OF POWER IN THIS WORLD.
BUT WHEN I LOOK AT BARTON...
I SEE THEY EACH HAVE THEIR OWN IDIOSYN-CRASIES...

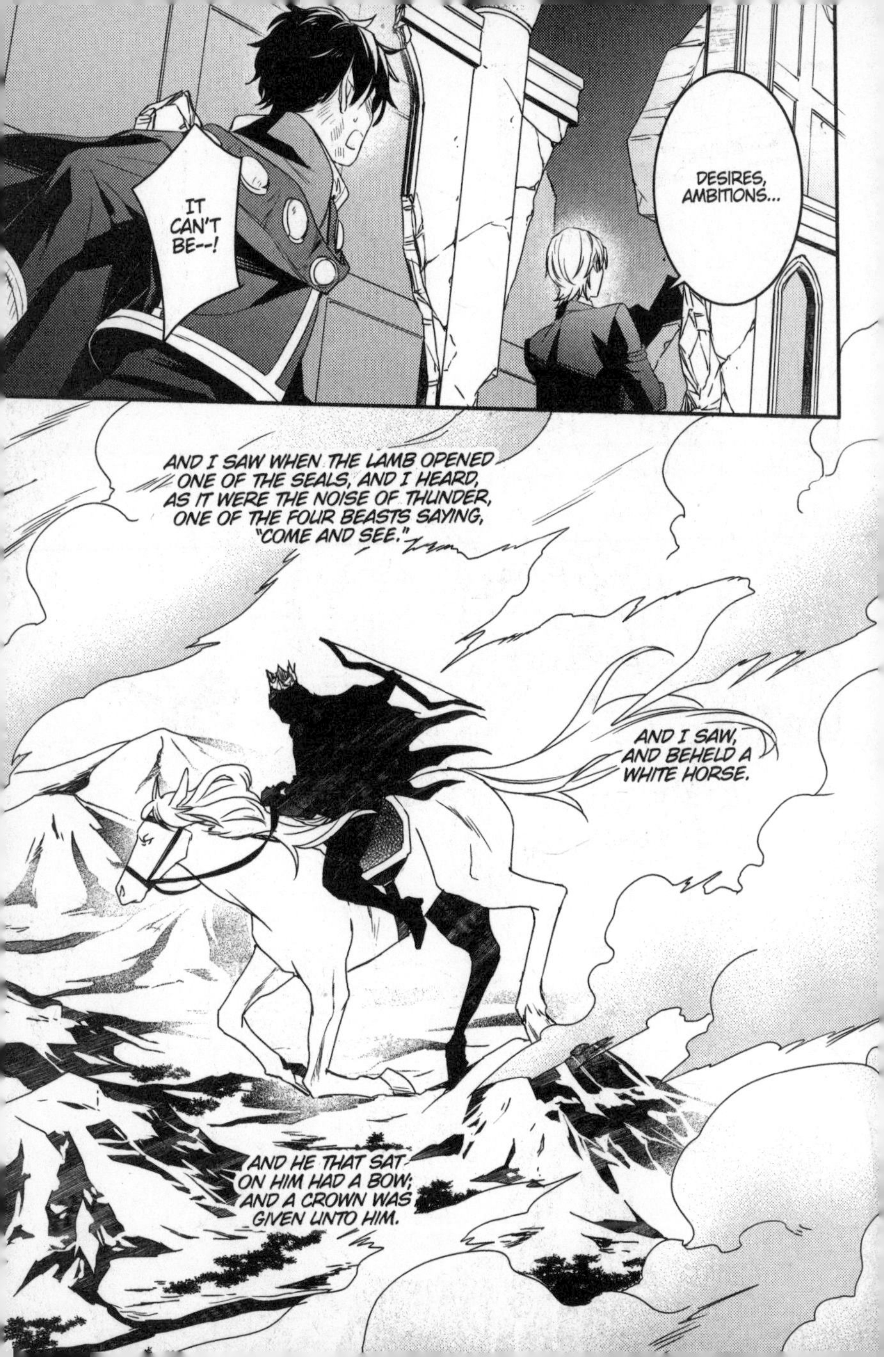
DESIRES, AMBITIONS...
IT CAN'T BE--!
AND I SAW WHEN THE LAMB OPENED ONE OF THE SEALS, AND I HEARD, AS IT WERE THE NOISE OF THUNDER, ONE OF THE FOUR BEASTS SAYING, "COME AND SEE."
AND I SAW, AND BEHELD A WHITE HORSE.
AND HE THAT SAT ON HIM HAD A BOW; AND A CROWN WAS GIVEN UNTO HIM.

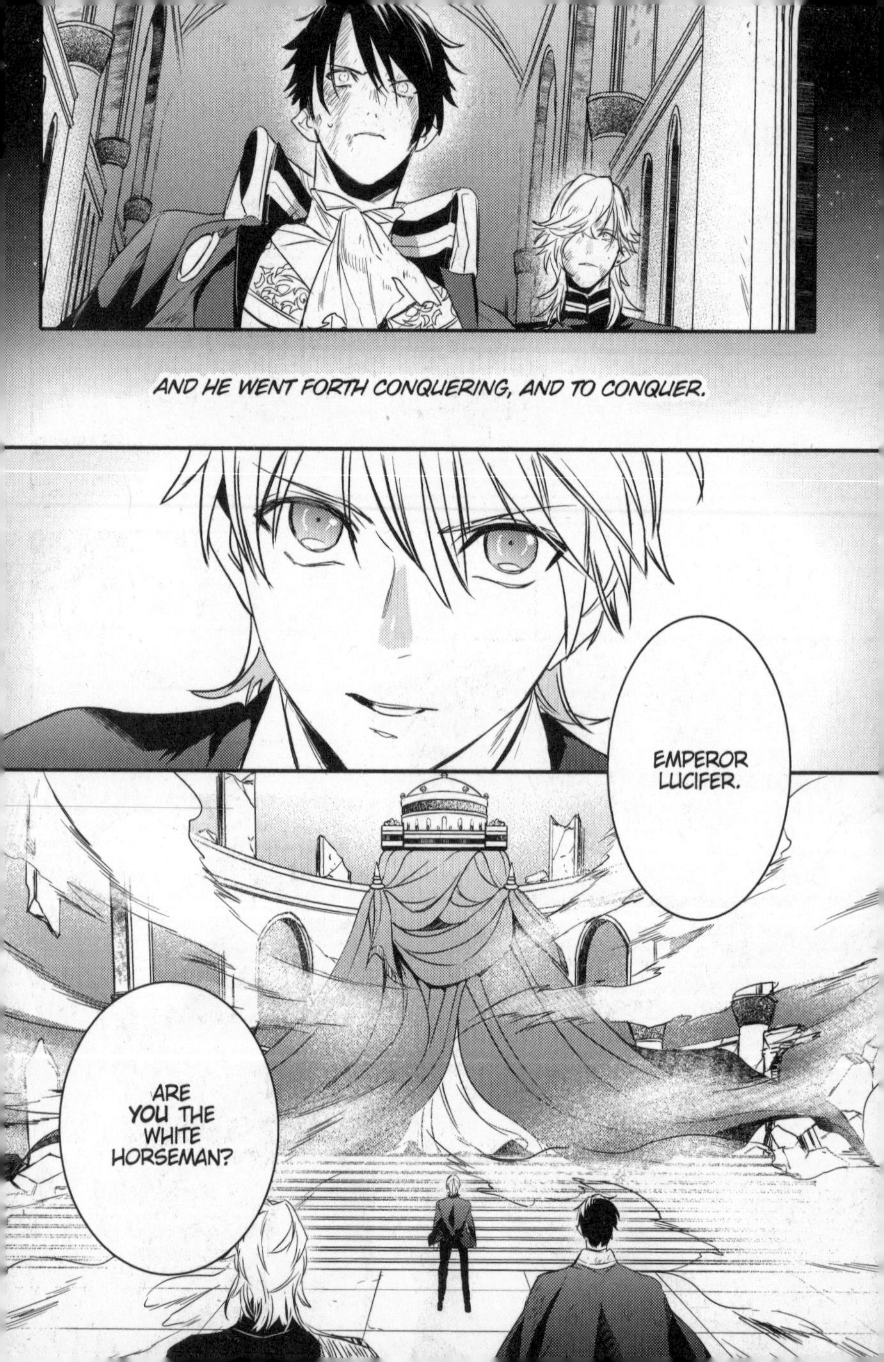
AND HE WENT FORTH CONQUERING, AND TO CONQUER.
EMPEROR LUCIFER.
ARE YOU THE WHITE HORSEMAN?

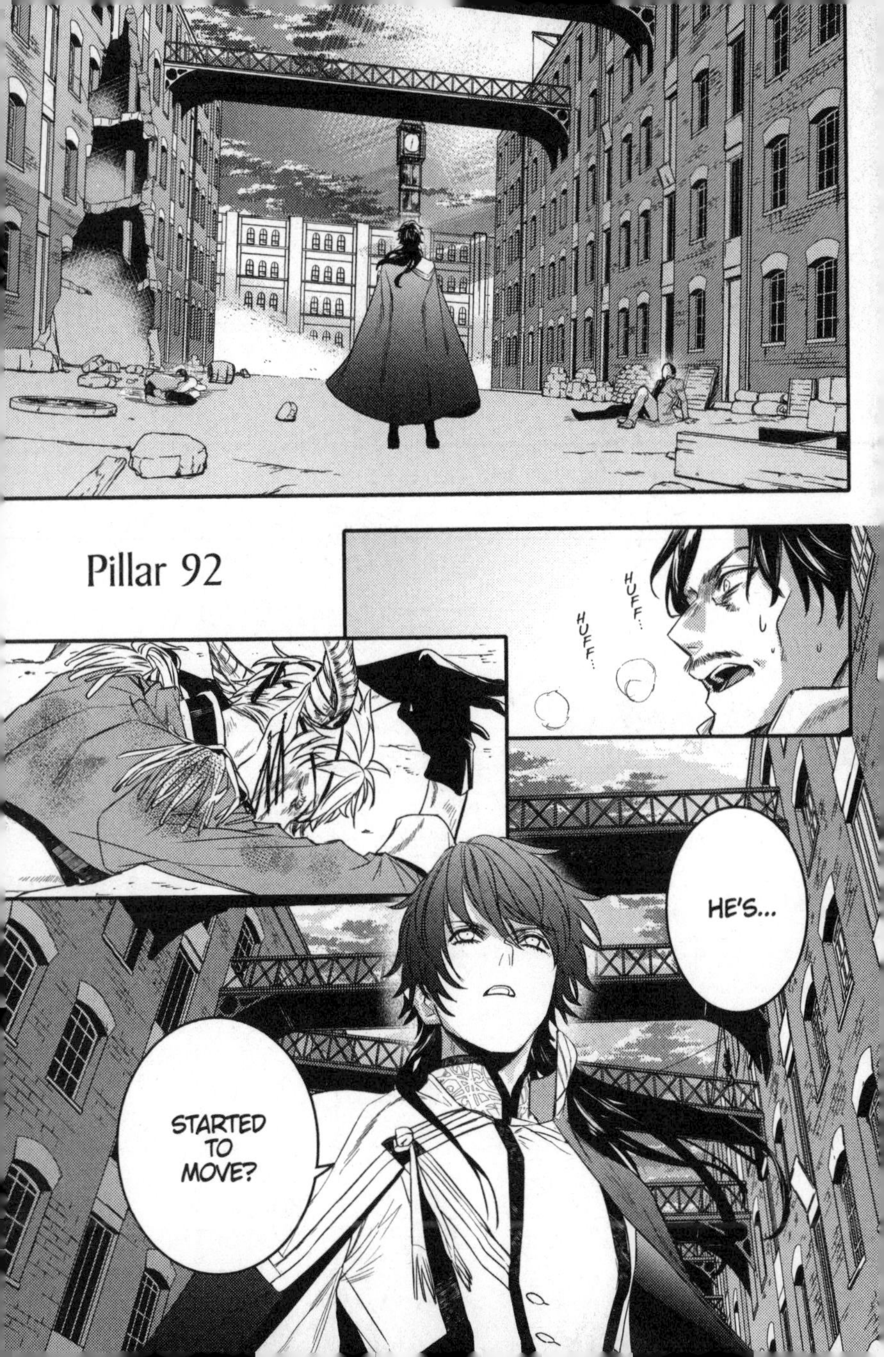
Pillar 92
HUFF...
HUFF...
HE'S...
STARTED TO MOVE?

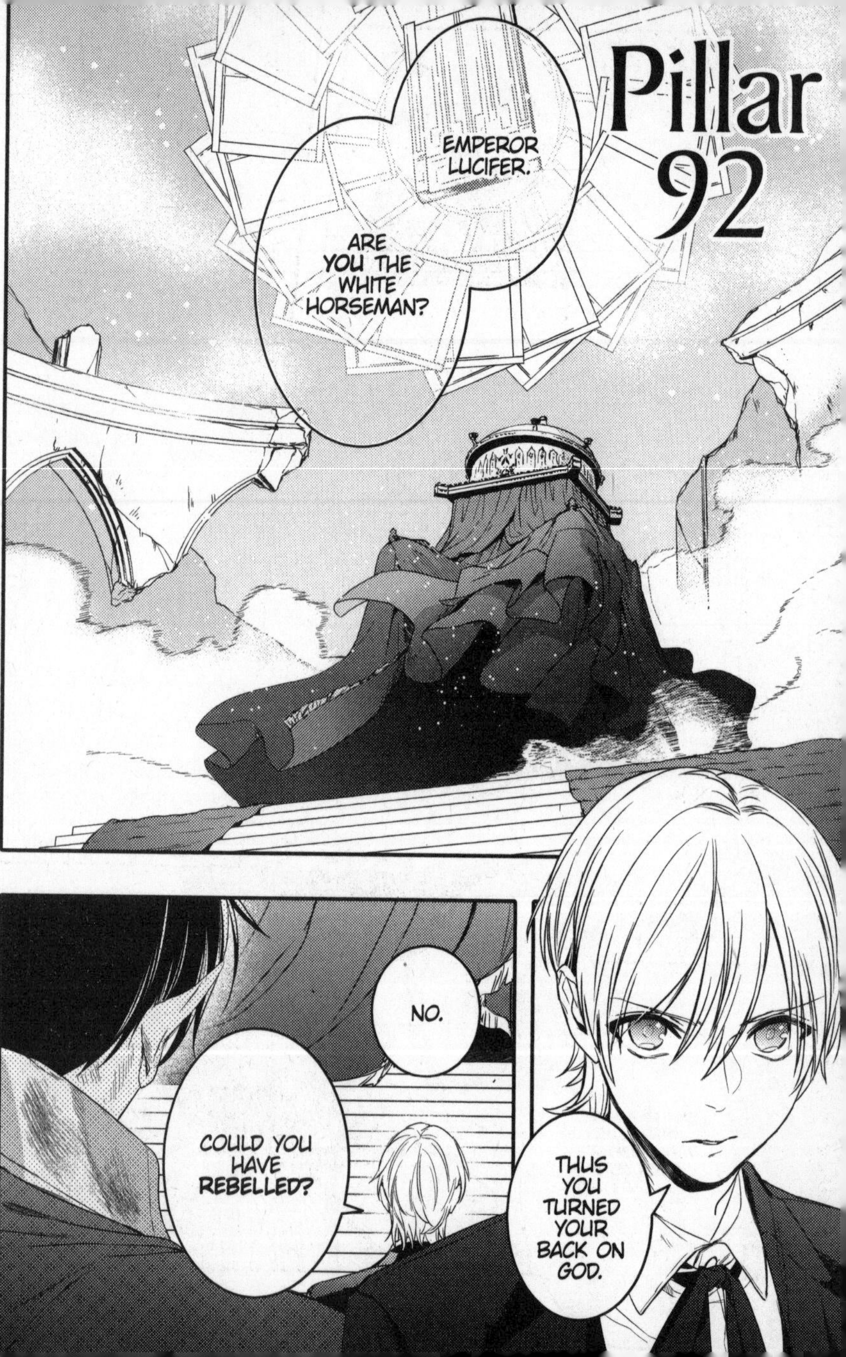
Pillar 92
EMPEROR LUCIFER.
ARE YOU THE WHITE HORSEMAN?
THUS YOU TURNED YOUR BACK ON GOD.
NO.
COULD YOU HAVE REBELLED?

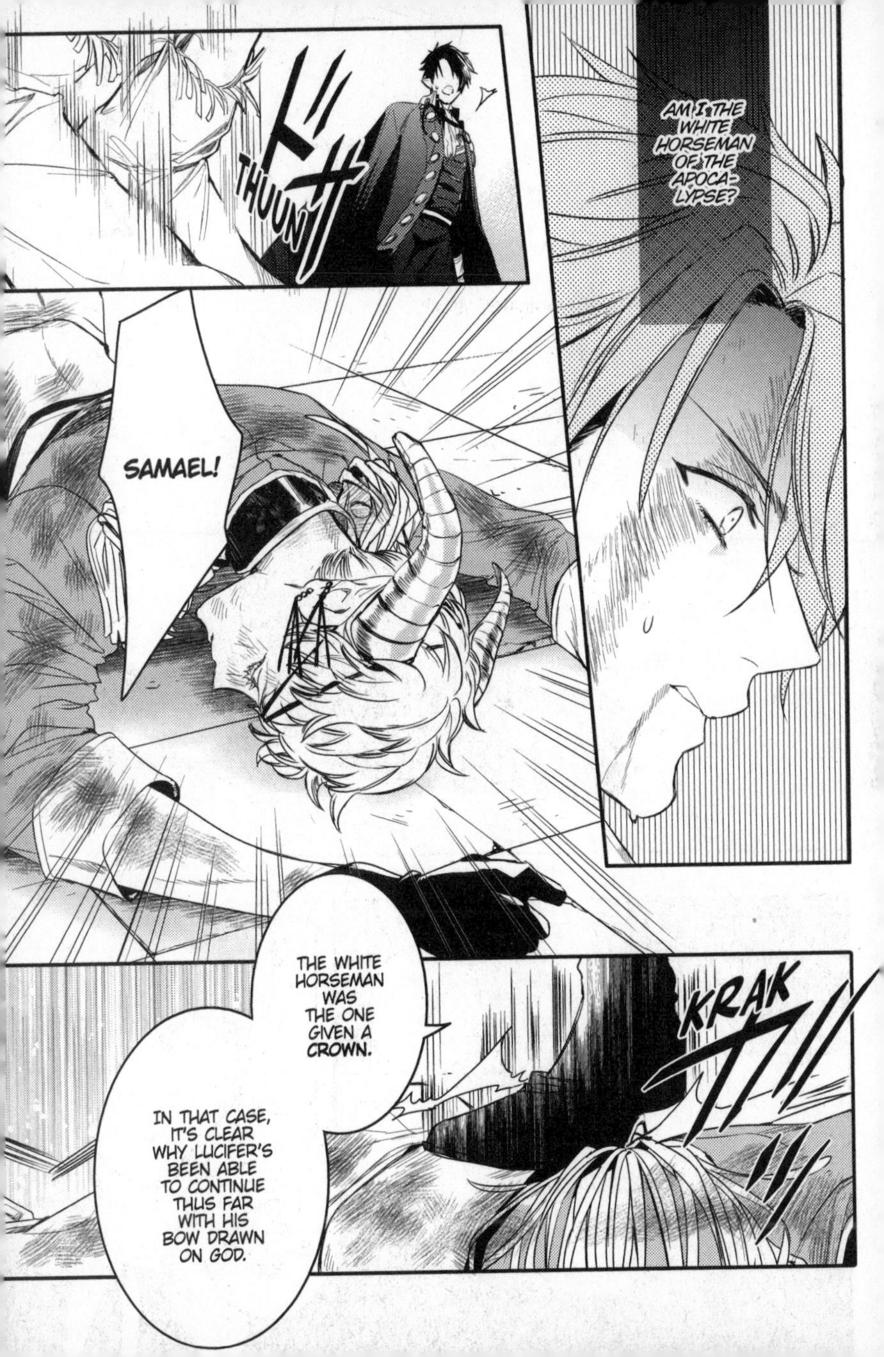
AM I THE WHITE HORSEMAN OF THE APOCA-LYPSE?
THUUN
SAMAEL!
KRAK
THE WHITE HORSEMAN WAS THE ONE GIVEN A CROWN.
IN THAT CASE, IT'S CLEAR WHY LUCIFER'S BEEN ABLE TO CONTINUE THUS FAR WITH HIS BOW DRAWN ON GOD.

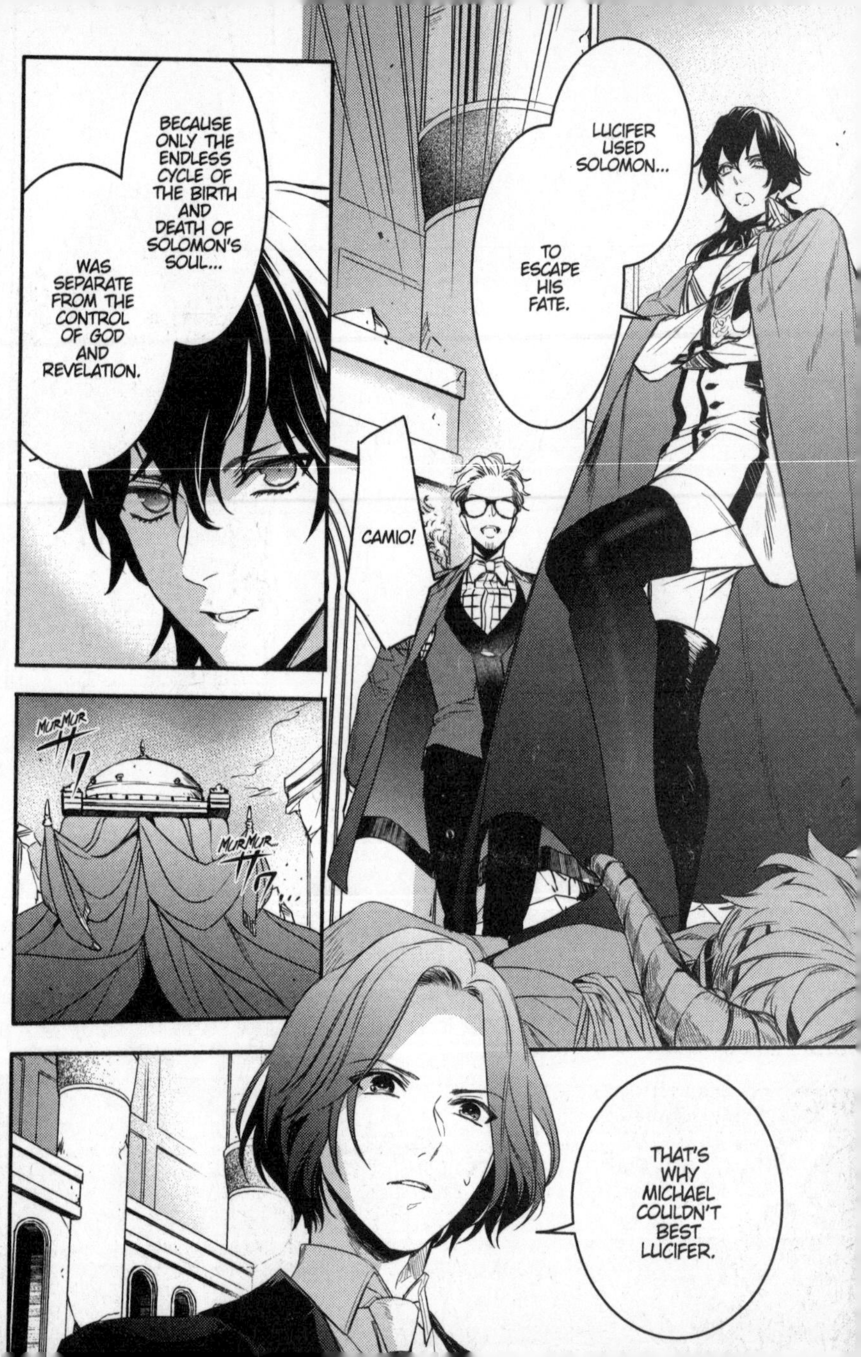
LUCIFER USED SOLOMON...
TO ESCAPE HIS FATE.
CAMIO!
BECAUSE ONLY THE ENDLESS CYCLE OF THE BIRTH AND DEATH OF SOLOMON'S SOUL...
WAS SEPARATE FROM THE CONTROL OF GOD AND REVELATION.
MURMUR
MURMUR...
THAT'S WHY MICHAEL COULDN'T BEST LUCIFER.

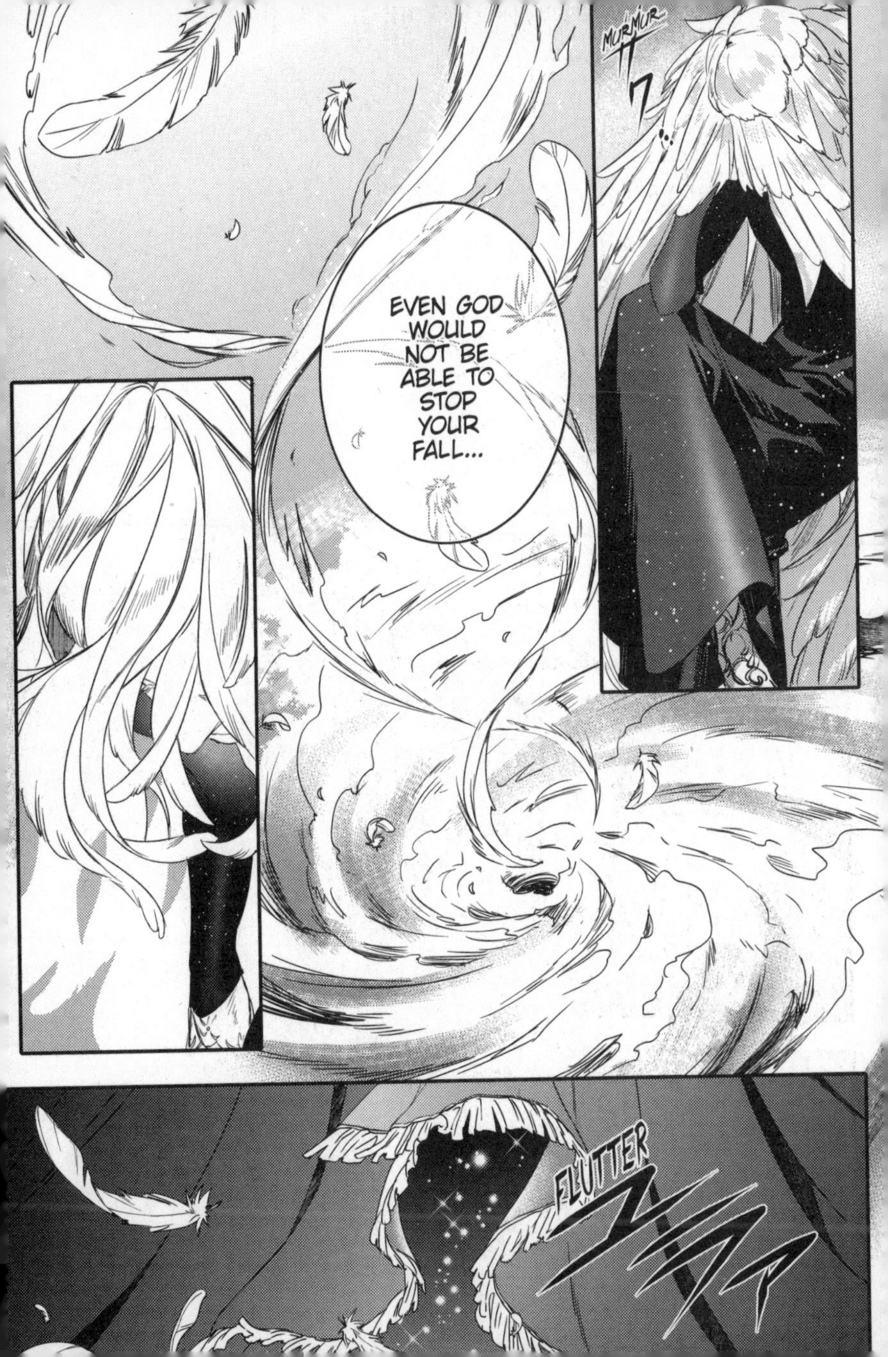
MURMUR
EVEN GOD WOULD NOT BE ABLE TO STOP YOUR FALL...
FLUTTER

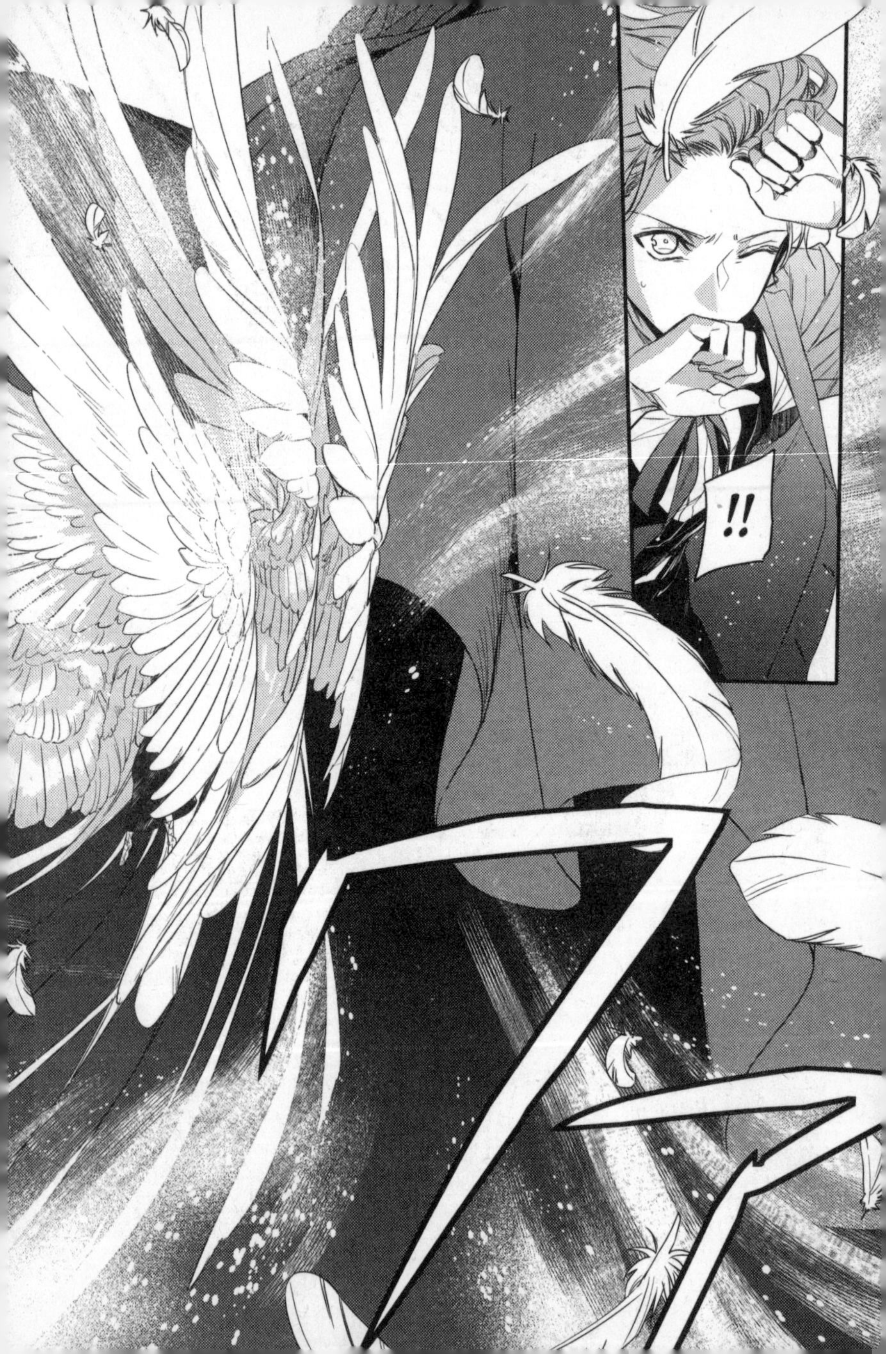
!!

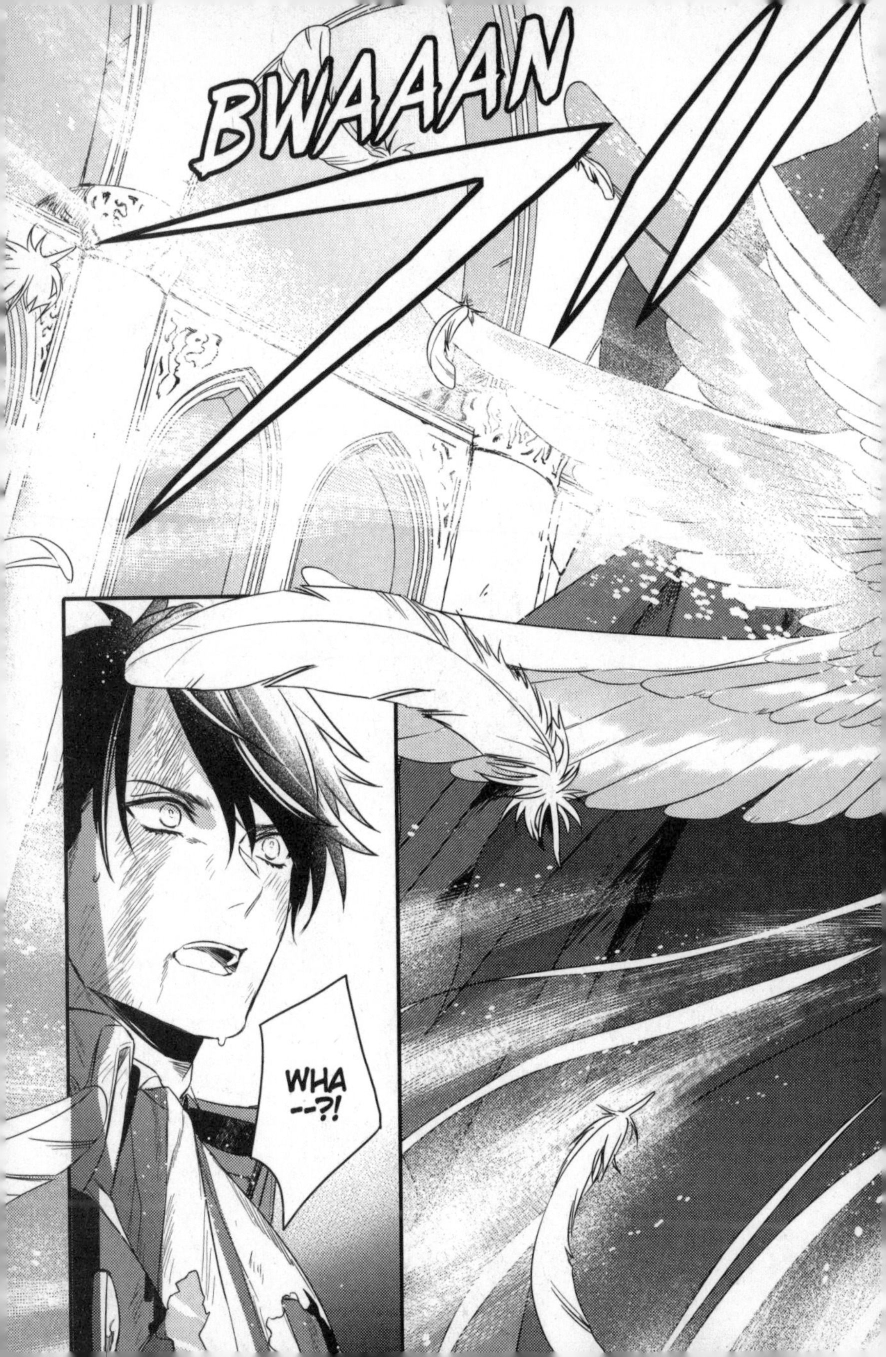
BWAAAN
WHA
--?!

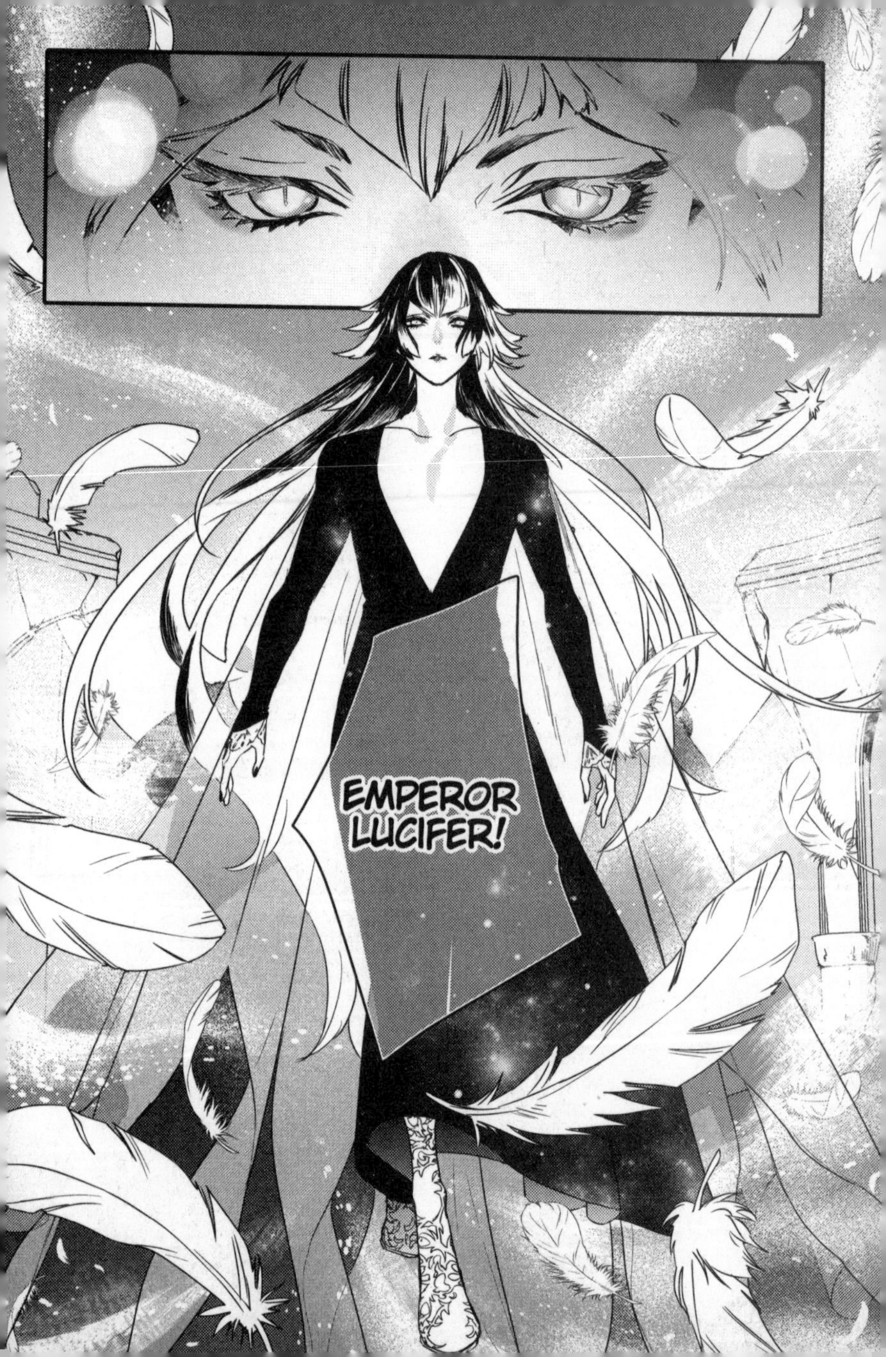
EMPEROR LUCIFER!

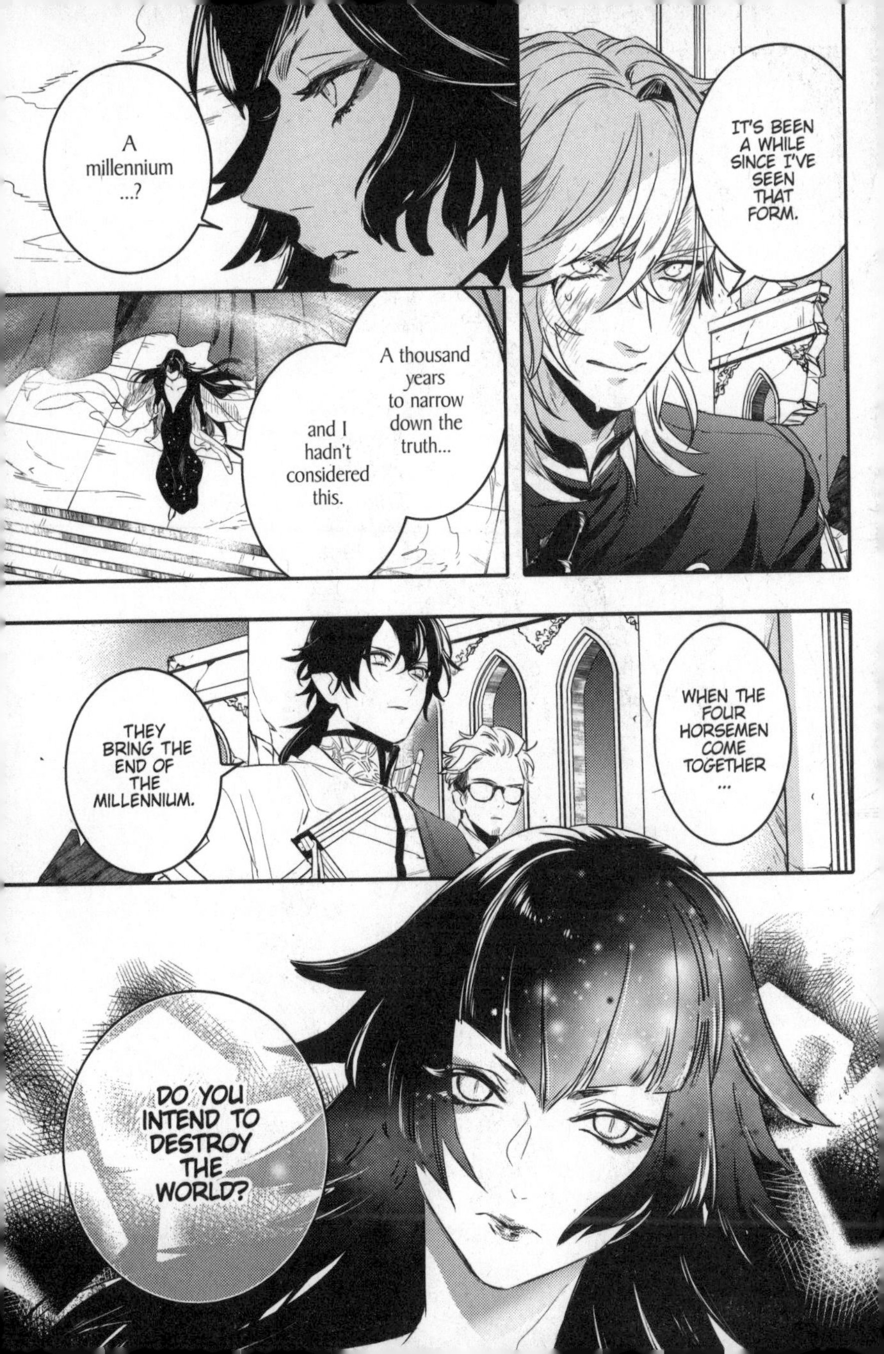
IT'S BEEN A WHILE SINCE I'VE SEEN THAT FORM.
A millennium ...?
A thousand years to narrow down the truth...
and I hadn't considered this.
WHEN THE FOUR HORSEMEN COME TOGETHER ...
THEY BRING THE END OF THE MILLENNIUM.
DO YOU INTEND TO DESTROY THE WORLD?

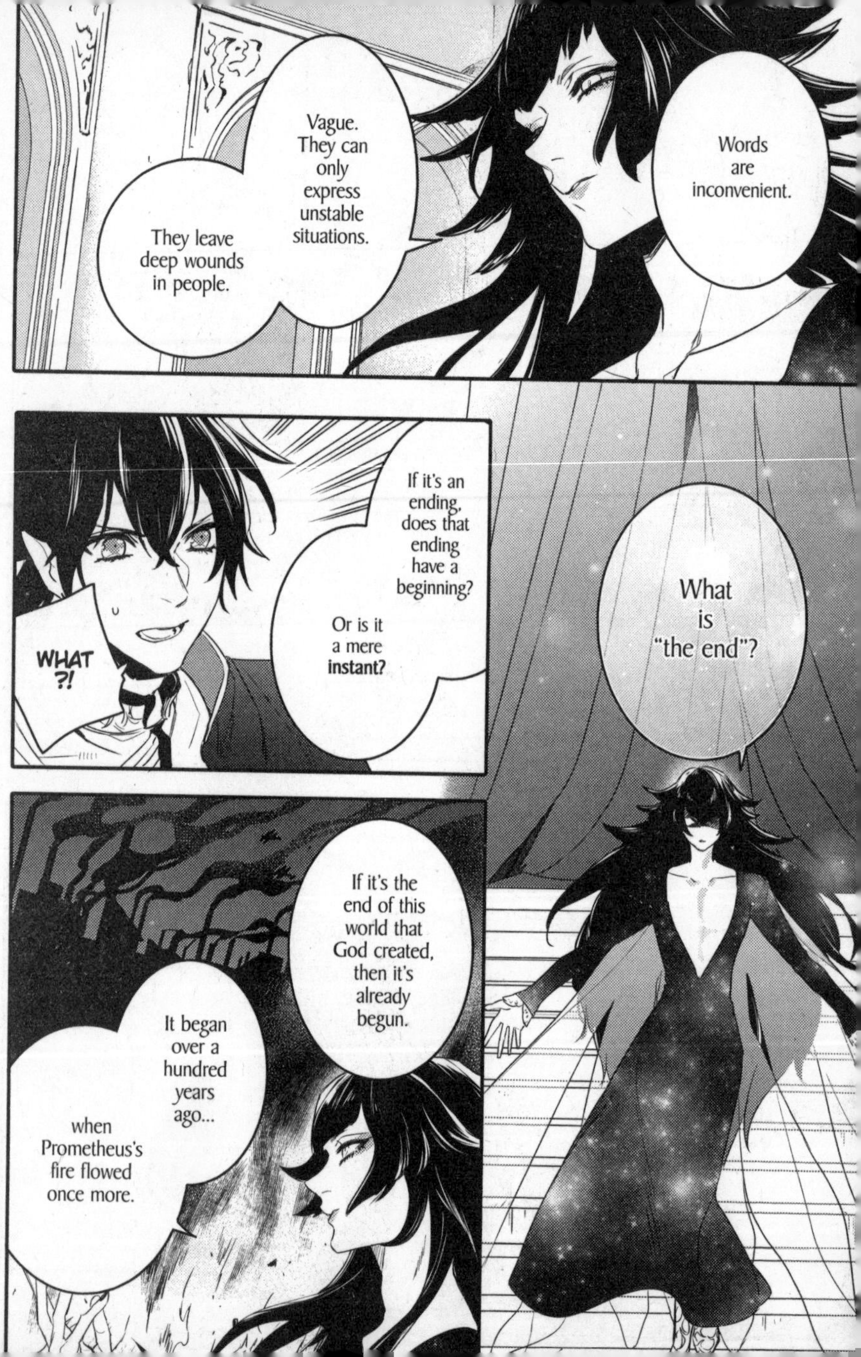
Words are inconvenient.
Vague. They can only express unstable situations.
They leave deep wounds in people.
What is "the end"?
If it's an ending, does that ending have a beginning?
Or is it a mere **instant?**
WHAT ?!
If it's the end of this world that God created, then it's already begun.
It began over a hundred years ago...
when Prometheus's fire flowed once more.

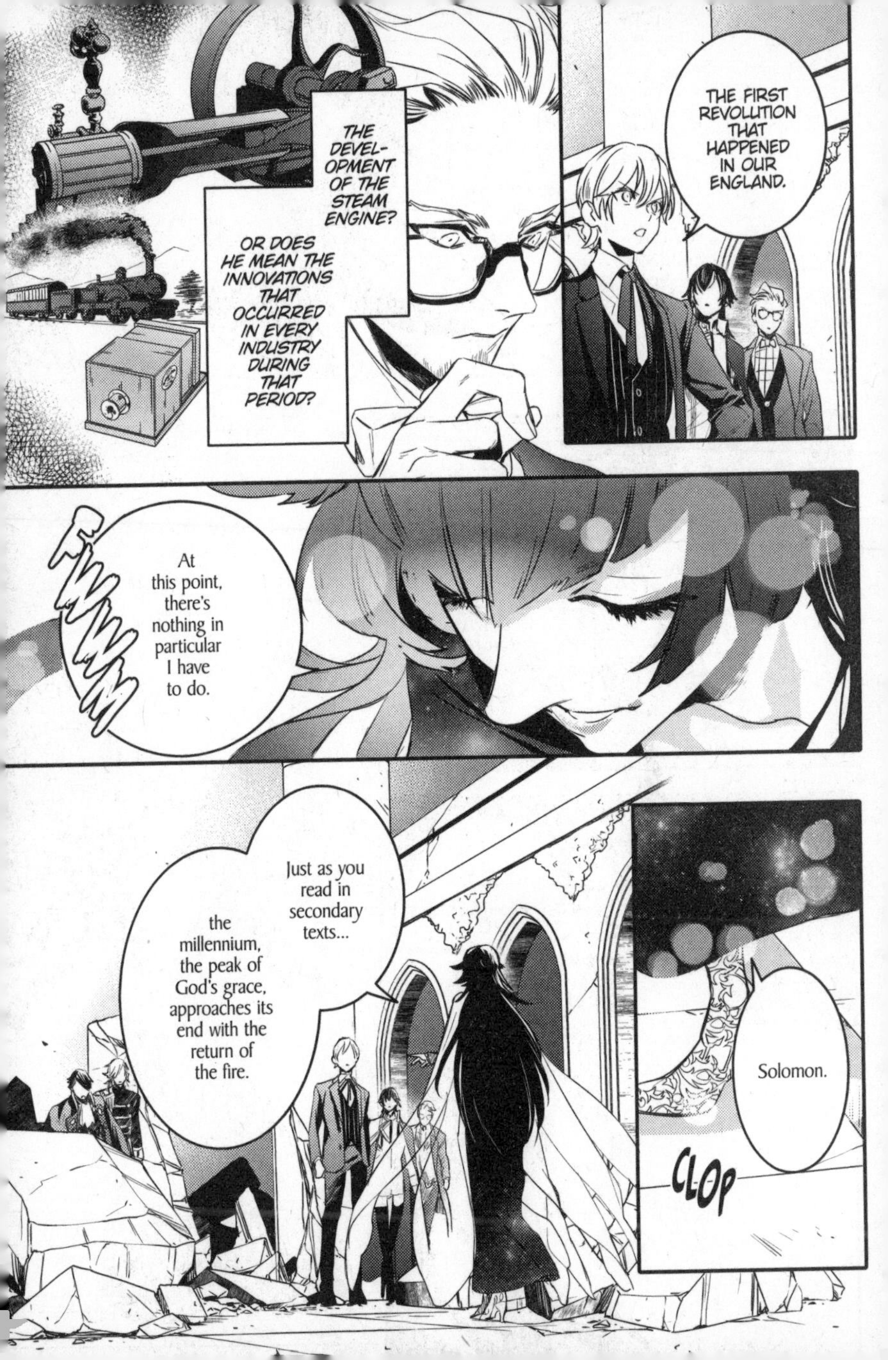
THE FIRST REVOLUTION THAT HAPPENED IN OUR ENGLAND.
THE DEVEL-OPMENT OF THE STEAM ENGINE?
OR DOES HE MEAN THE INNOVATIONS THAT OCCURRED IN EVERY INDUSTRY DURING THAT PERIOD?
FWMM
At this point, there's nothing in particular I have to do.
Solomon.
CLOP
Just as you read in secondary texts...
the millennium, the peak of God's grace, approaches its end with the return of the fire.

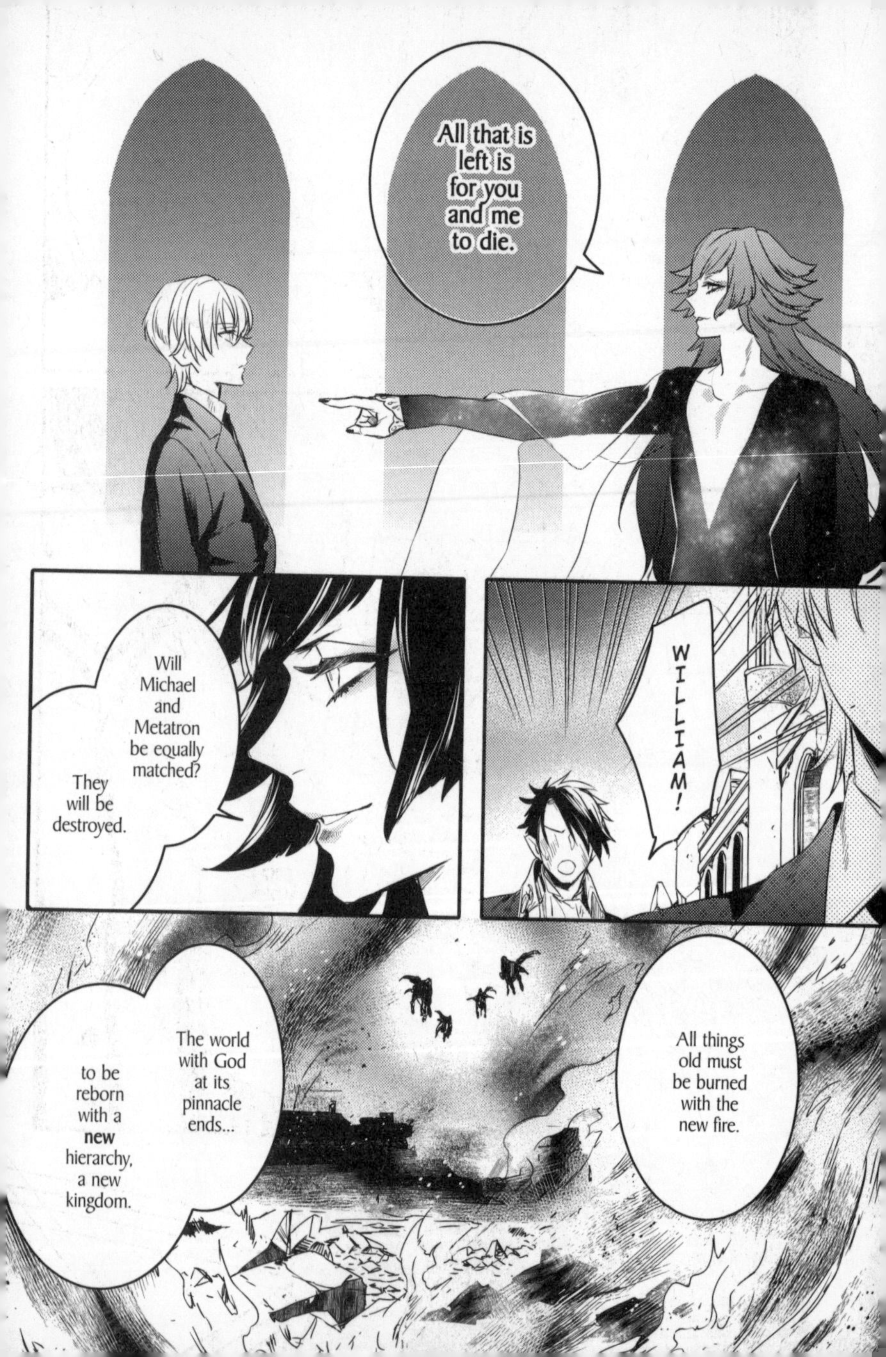
All that is left is for you and me to die.
WILLIAM!
Will Michael and Metatron be equally matched?
They will be destroyed.
All things old must be burned with the new fire.
The world with God at its pinnacle ends...
to be reborn with a **new** hierarchy, a new kingdom.

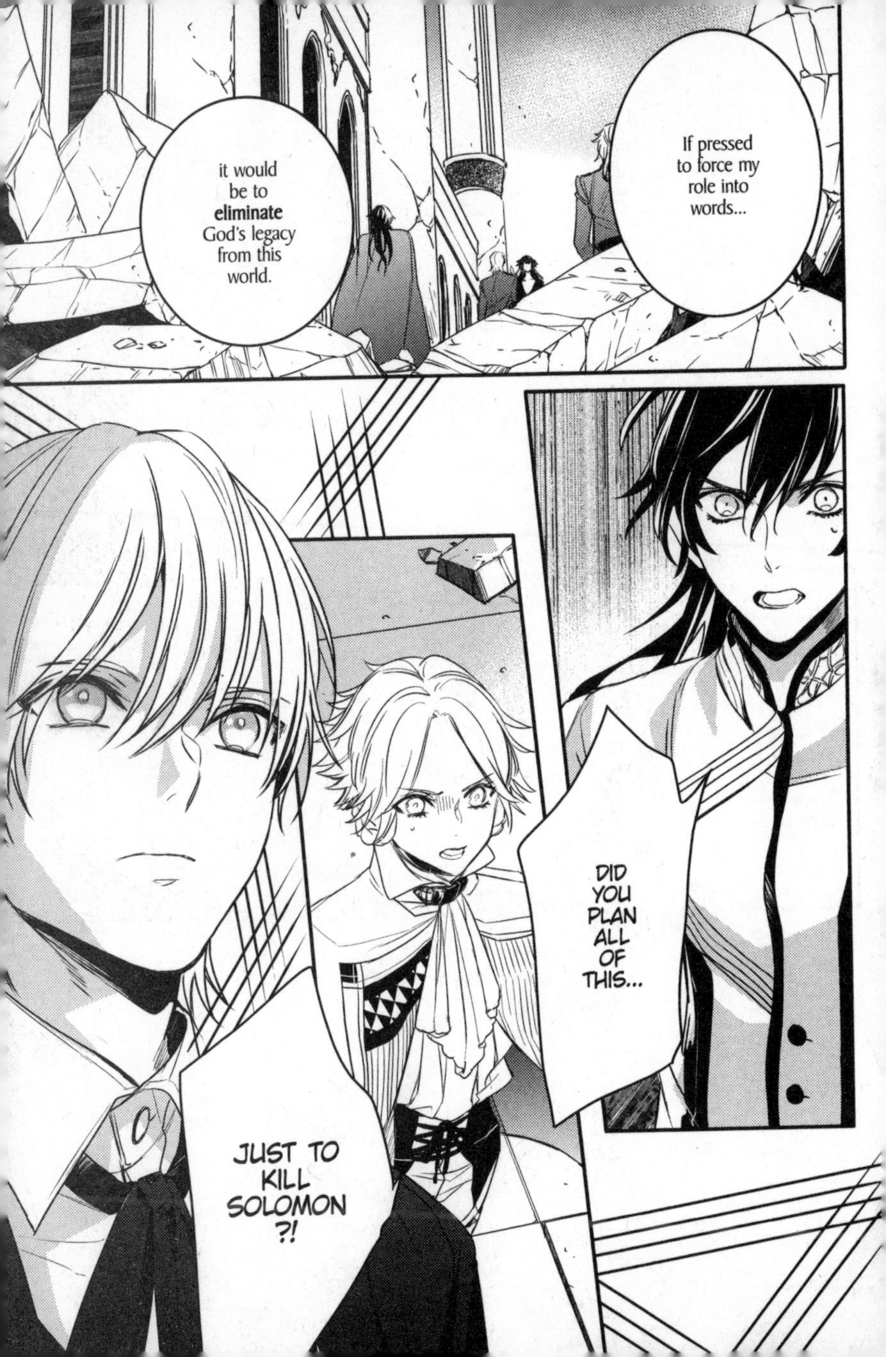
If pressed to force my role into words...
it would be to **eliminate** God's legacy from this world.
DID YOU PLAN ALL OF THIS...
JUST TO KILL SOLOMON ?!

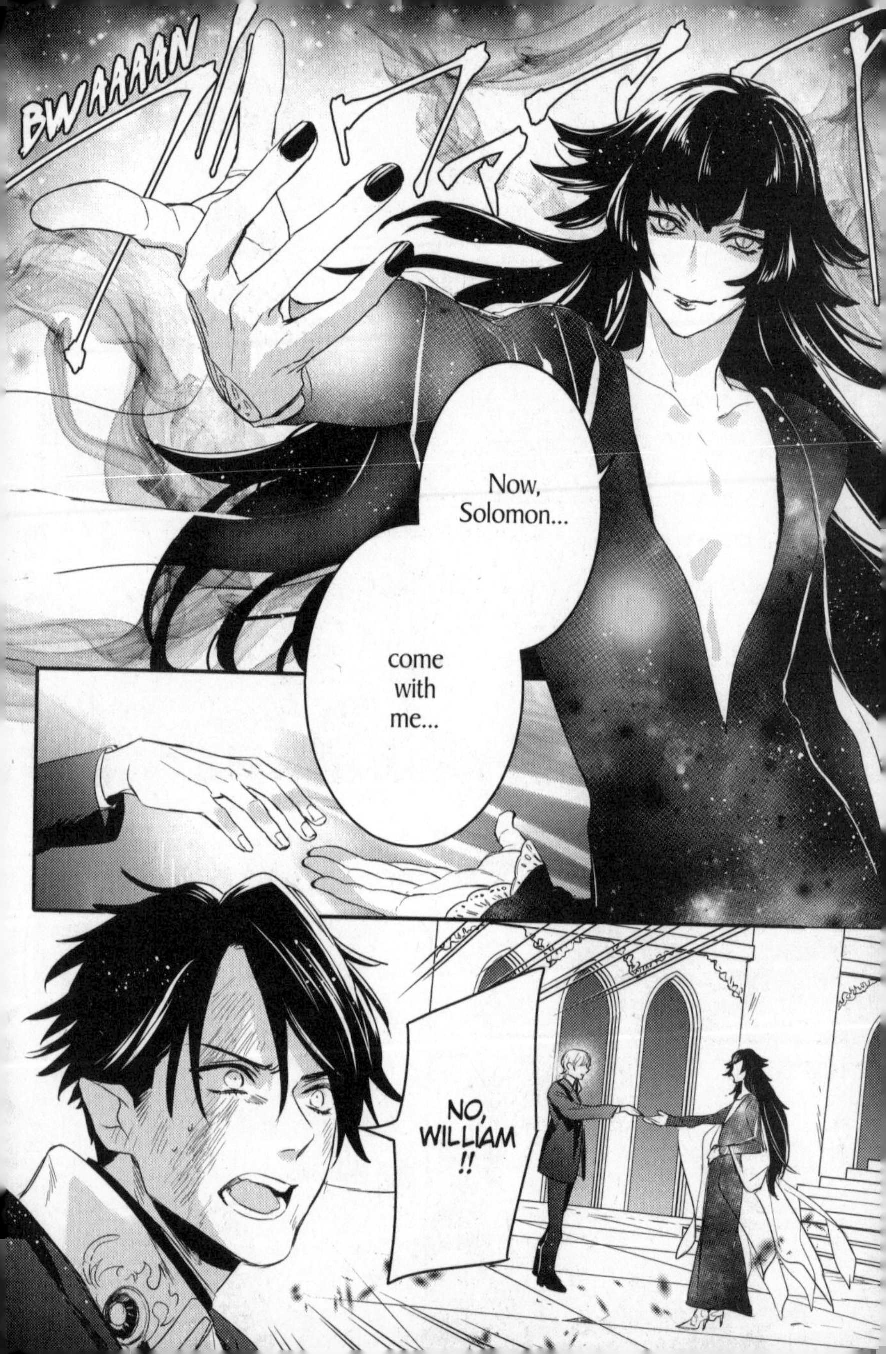
BWAAAAN
Now, Solomon...
come with me...
NO, WILLIAM!!

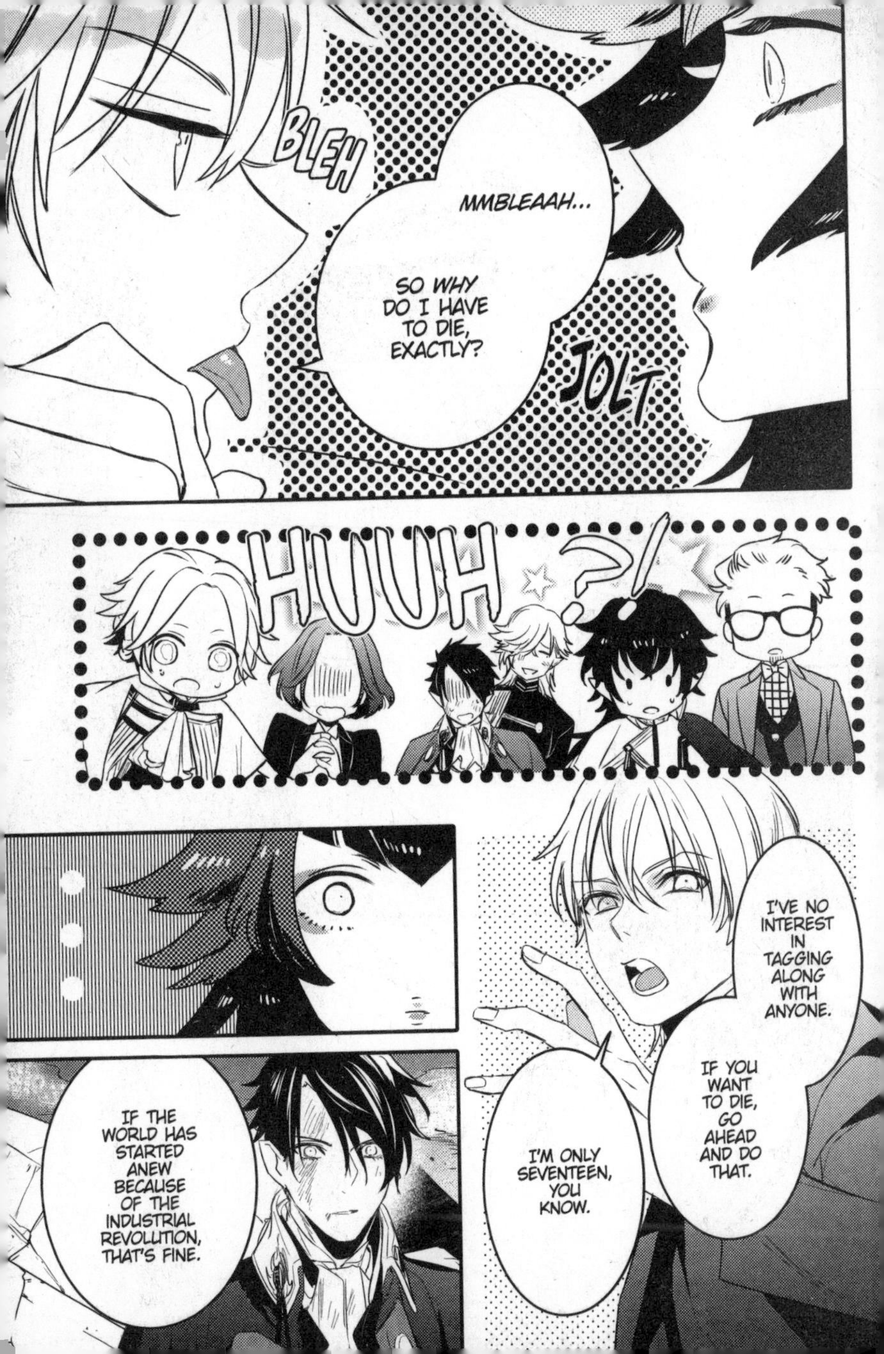
BLEH
MMBLEAAH...
SO WHY DO I HAVE TO DIE, EXACTLY?
JOLT
HUUH?!
I'VE NO INTEREST IN TAGGING ALONG WITH ANYONE.
IF YOU WANT TO DIE, GO AHEAD AND DO THAT.
I'M ONLY SEVENTEEN, YOU KNOW.
IF THE WORLD HAS STARTED ANEW BECAUSE OF THE INDUSTRIAL REVOLUTION, THAT'S FINE.

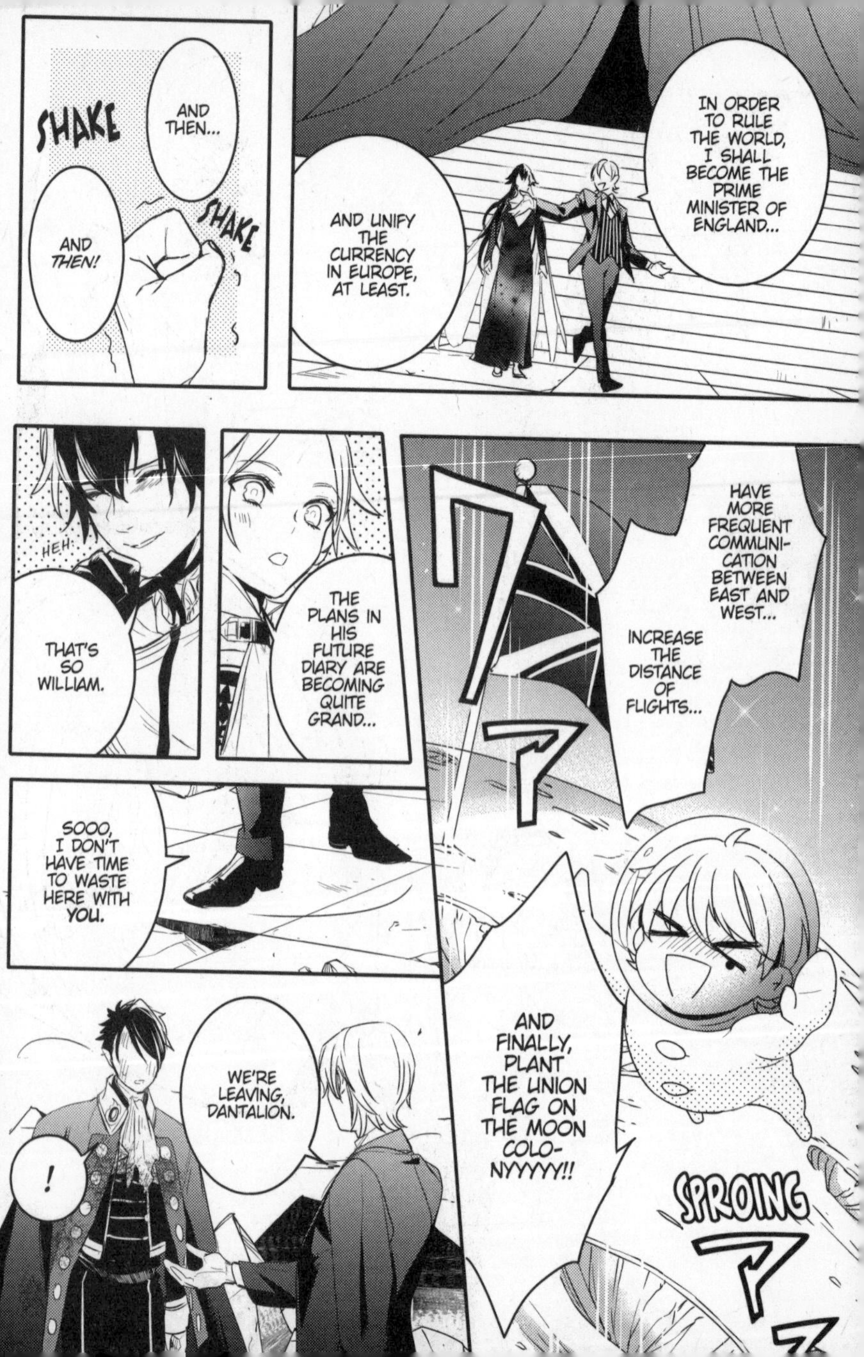
IN ORDER TO RULE THE WORLD, I SHALL BECOME THE PRIME MINISTER OF ENGLAND...
AND UNIFY THE CURRENCY IN EUROPE, AT LEAST.
AND THEN...
SHAKE
SHAKE
AND THEN!
HAVE MORE FREQUENT COMMUNI-CATION BETWEEN EAST AND WEST...
INCREASE THE DISTANCE OF FLIGHTS...
AND FINALLY, PLANT THE UNION FLAG ON THE MOON COLO-NYYYYY!!
SPROING
THE PLANS IN HIS FUTURE DIARY ARE BECOMING QUITE GRAND...
HEH
THAT'S SO WILLIAM.
SOOO, I DON'T HAVE TIME TO WASTE HERE WITH YOU.
WE'RE LEAVING, DANTALION.
!

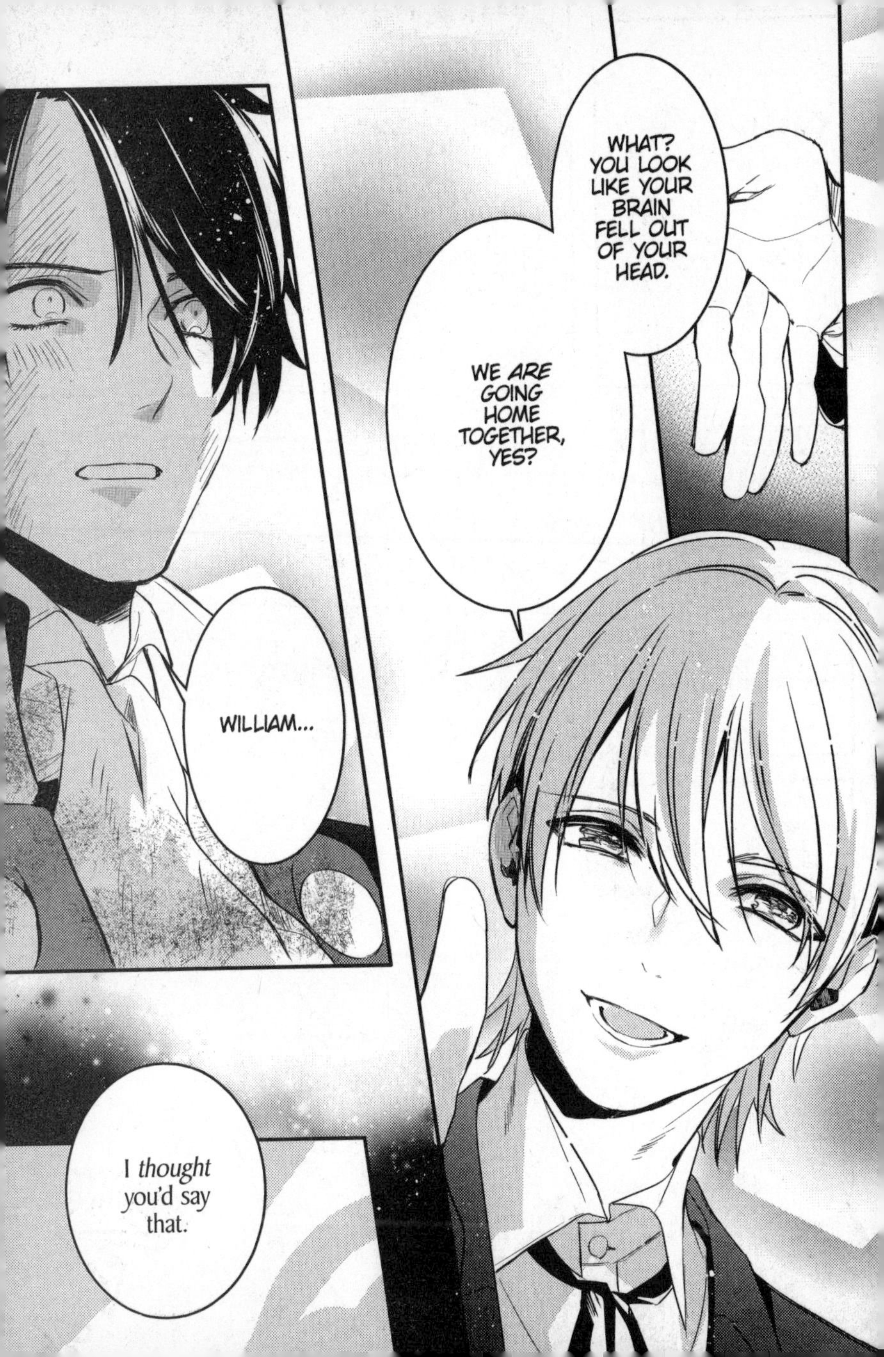
WHAT? YOU LOOK LIKE YOUR BRAIN FELL OUT OF YOUR HEAD.
WE *ARE* GOING HOME TOGETHER, YES?
WILLIAM...
I *thought* you'd say that.

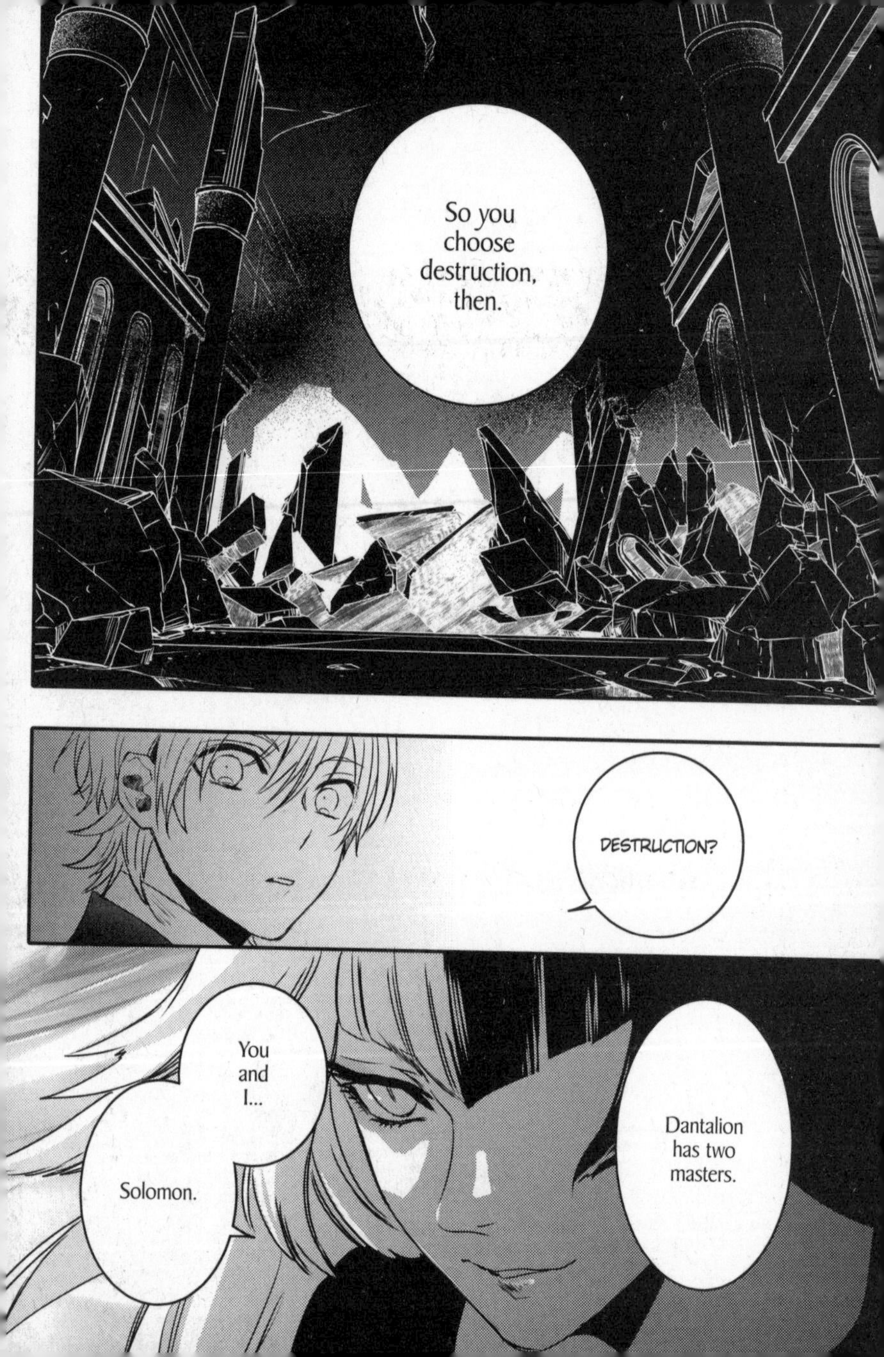
So you choose destruction, then.
DESTRUCTION?
Dantalion has two masters.
You and I...
Solomon.

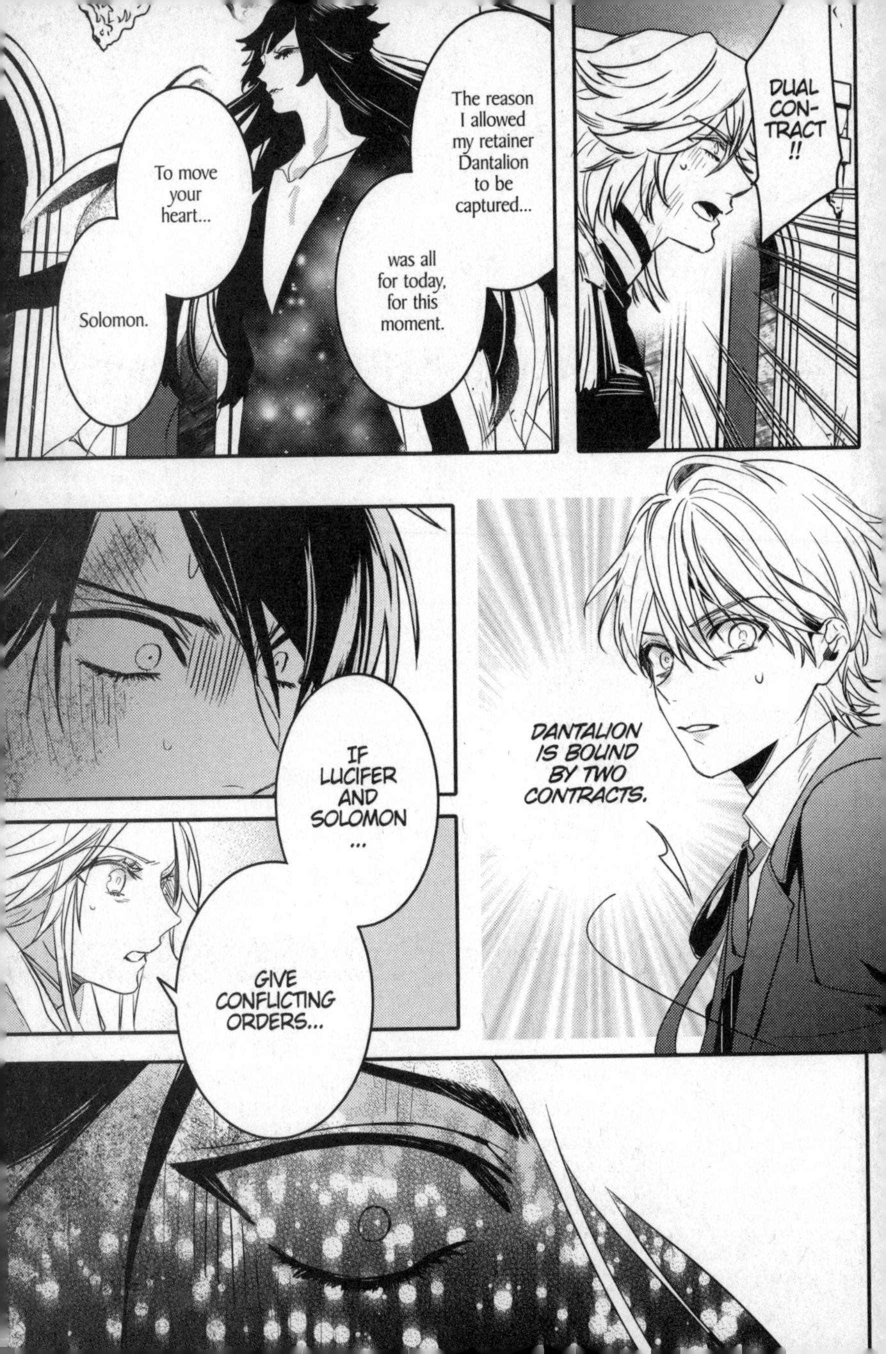
DUAL CONTRACT!!
The reason I allowed my retainer Dantalion to be captured...
was all for today, for this moment.
To move your heart...
Solomon.
DANTALION IS BOUND BY TWO CONTRACTS.
IF LUCIFER AND SOLOMON...
GIVE CONFLICTING ORDERS...

DAN-TALION'S MIND WILL BE DES-TROYED.
Come back, Dantalion.
You *will* kill him.
Once again--with that hand, Solomon.
KILL HIM.

Pillar 93

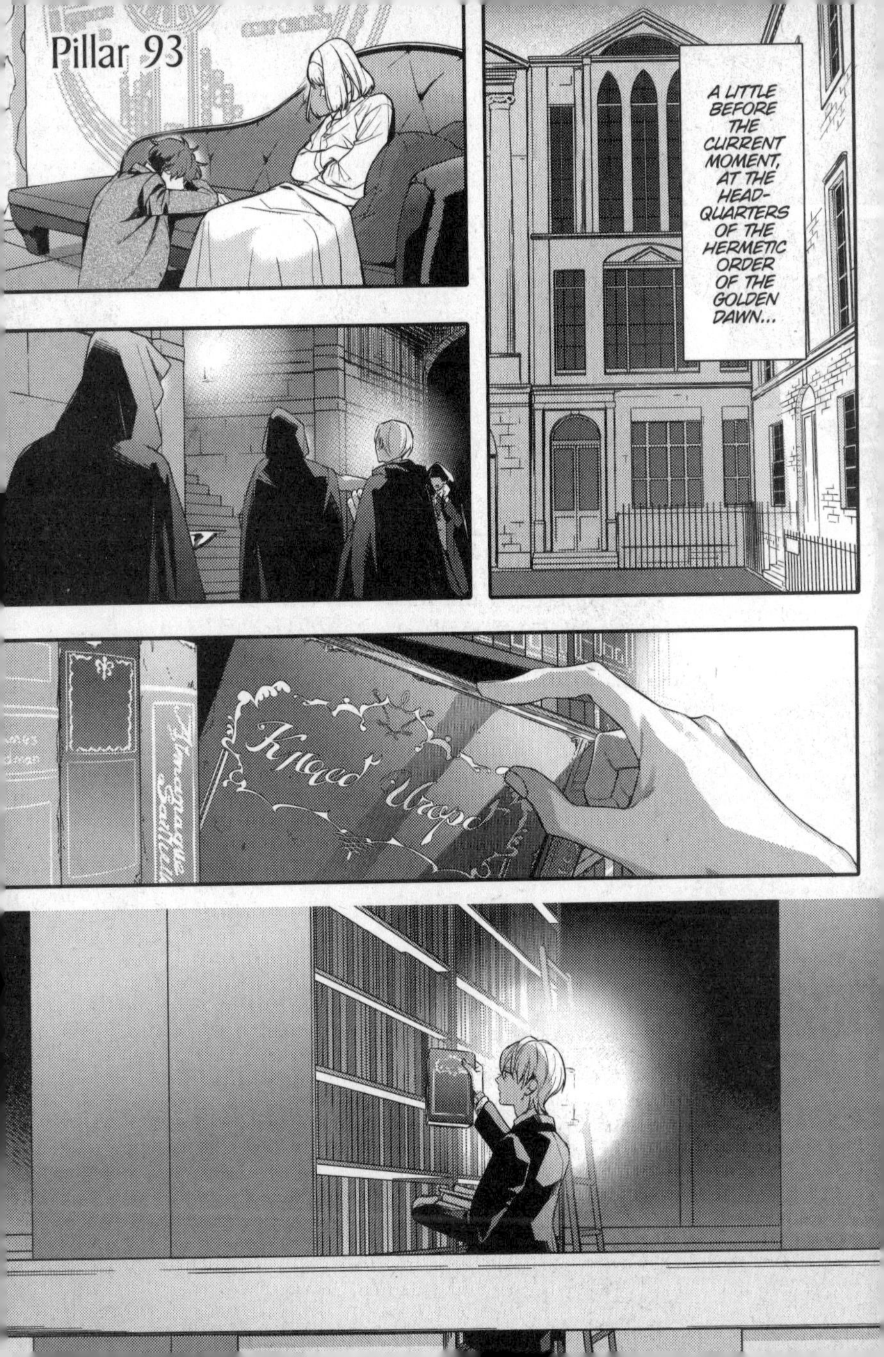
A LITTLE BEFORE THE CURRENT MOMENT, AT THE HEAD-QUARTERS OF THE HERMETIC ORDER OF THE GOLDEN DAWN...

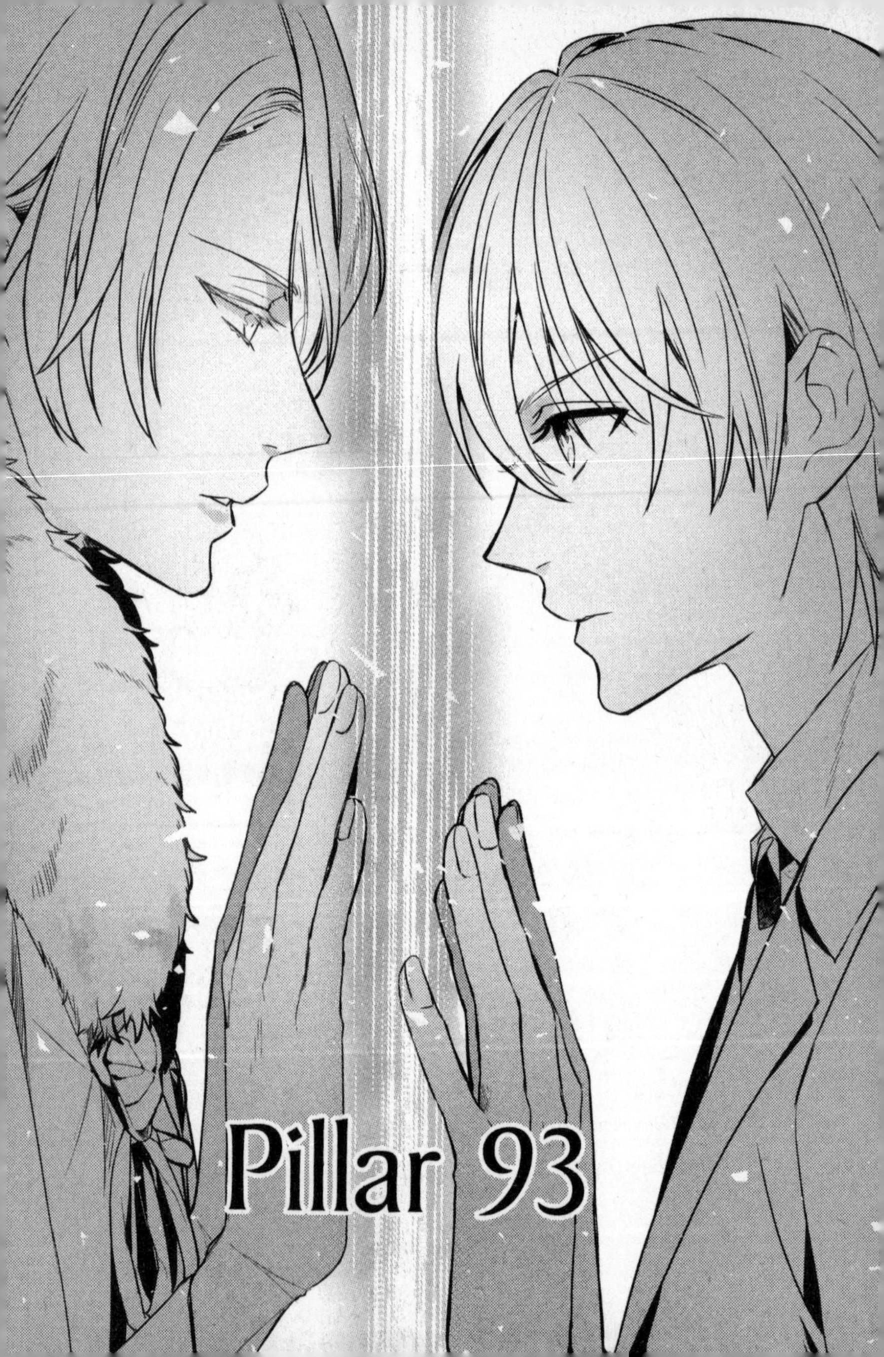
Pillar 93

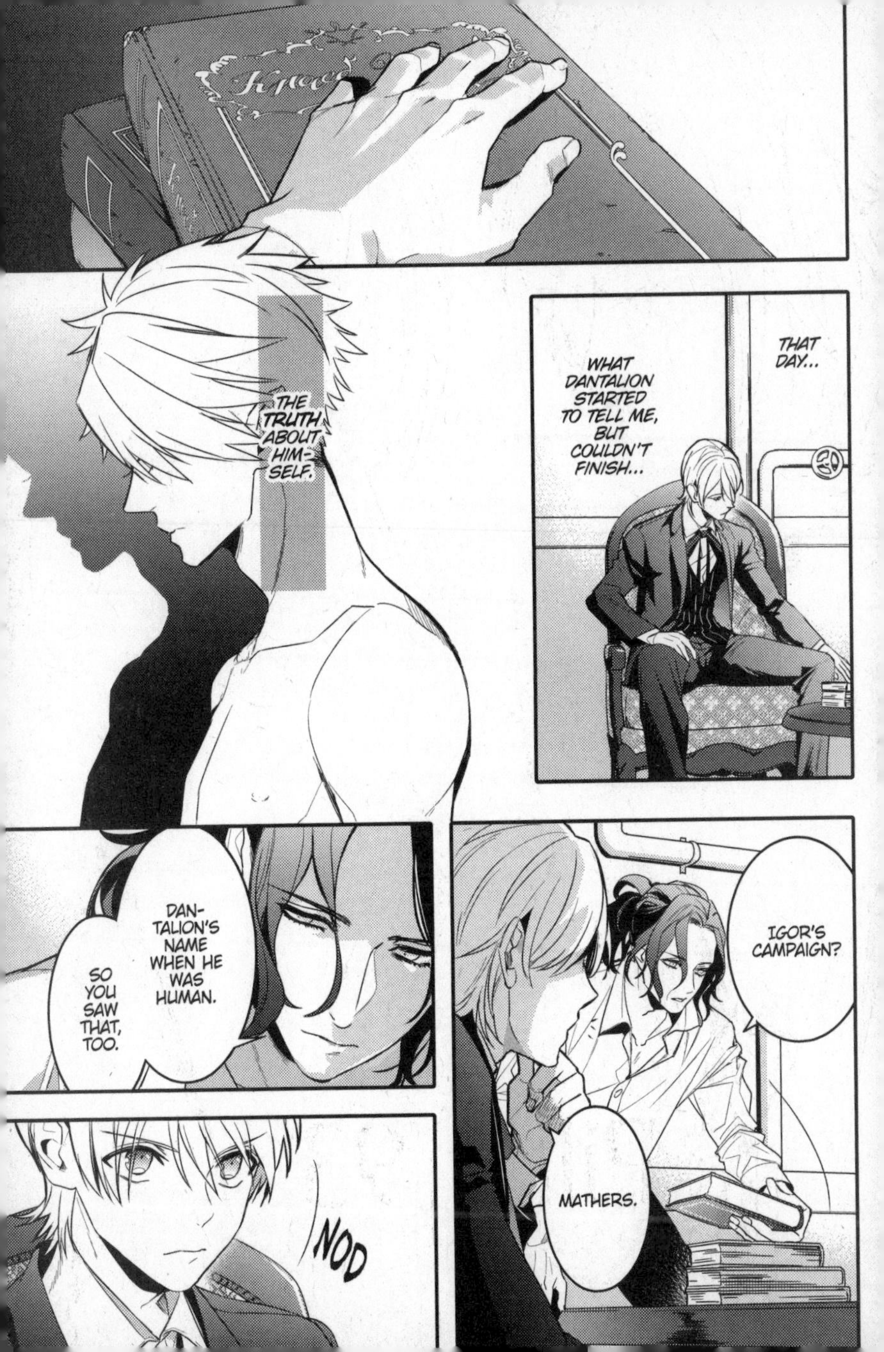
THAT DAY...
WHAT DANTALION STARTED TO TELL ME, BUT COULDN'T FINISH...
THE TRUTH ABOUT HIM-SELF.
IGOR'S CAMPAIGN?
MATHERS.
DAN-TALION'S NAME WHEN HE WAS HUMAN.
SO YOU SAW THAT, TOO.
NOD

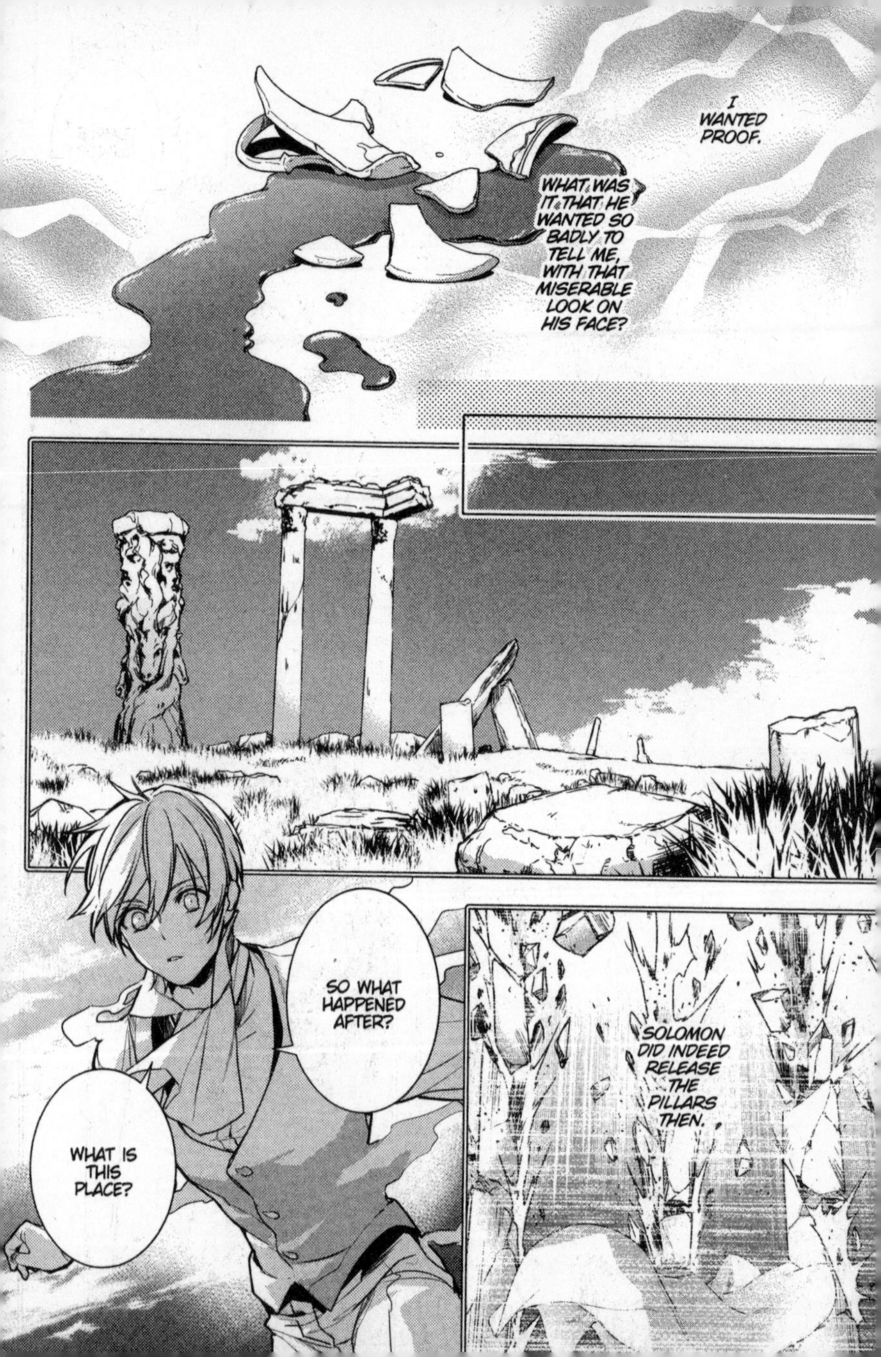
I WANTED PROOF.
WHAT WAS IT THAT HE WANTED SO BADLY TO TELL ME, WITH THAT MISERABLE LOOK ON HIS FACE?
SOLOMON DID INDEED RELEASE THE PILLARS THEN.
SO WHAT HAPPENED AFTER?
WHAT IS THIS PLACE?

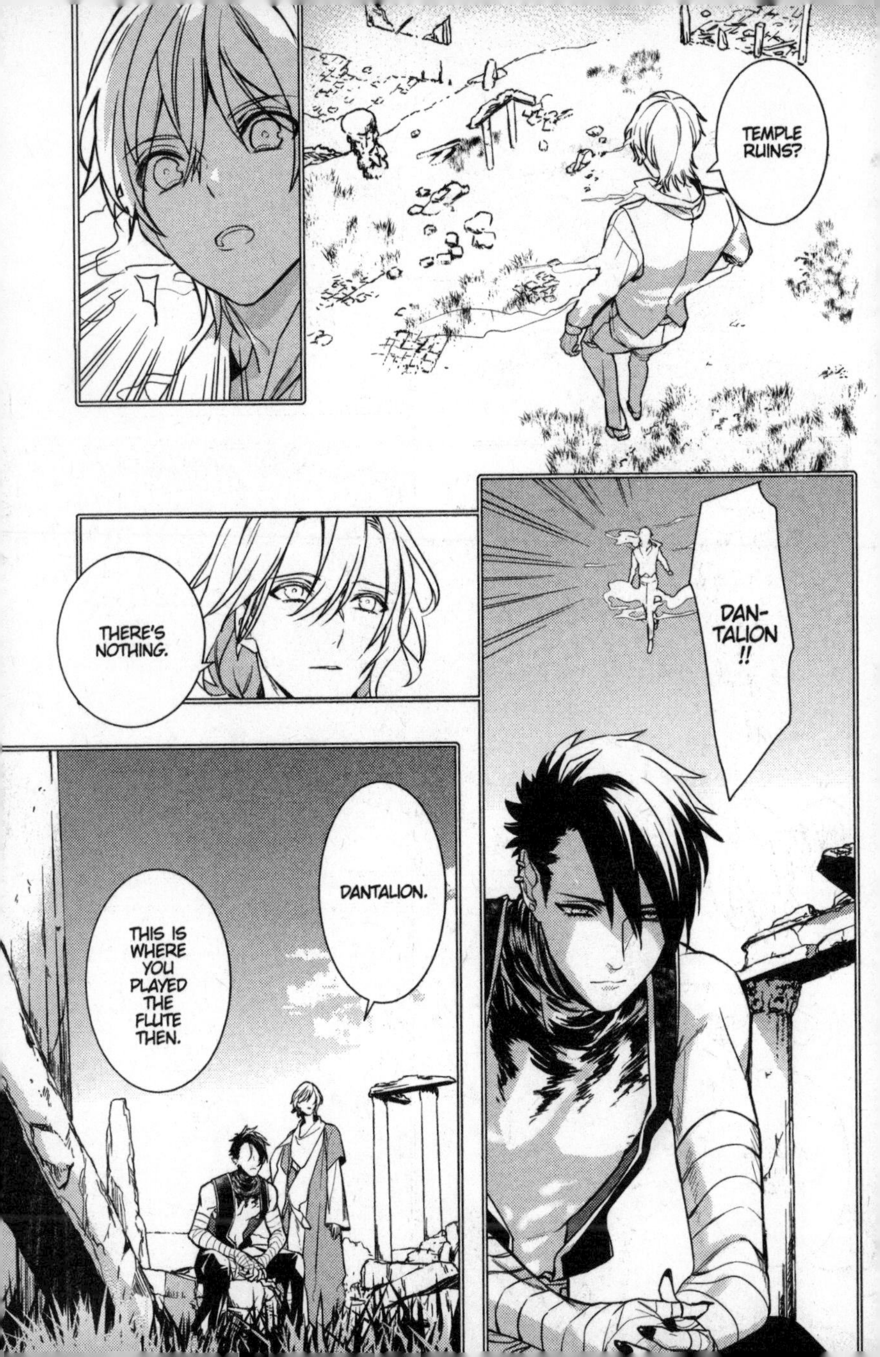
TEMPLE RUINS?
DAN-TALION!!
THERE'S NOTHING.
DANTALION.
THIS IS WHERE YOU PLAYED THE FLUTE THEN.

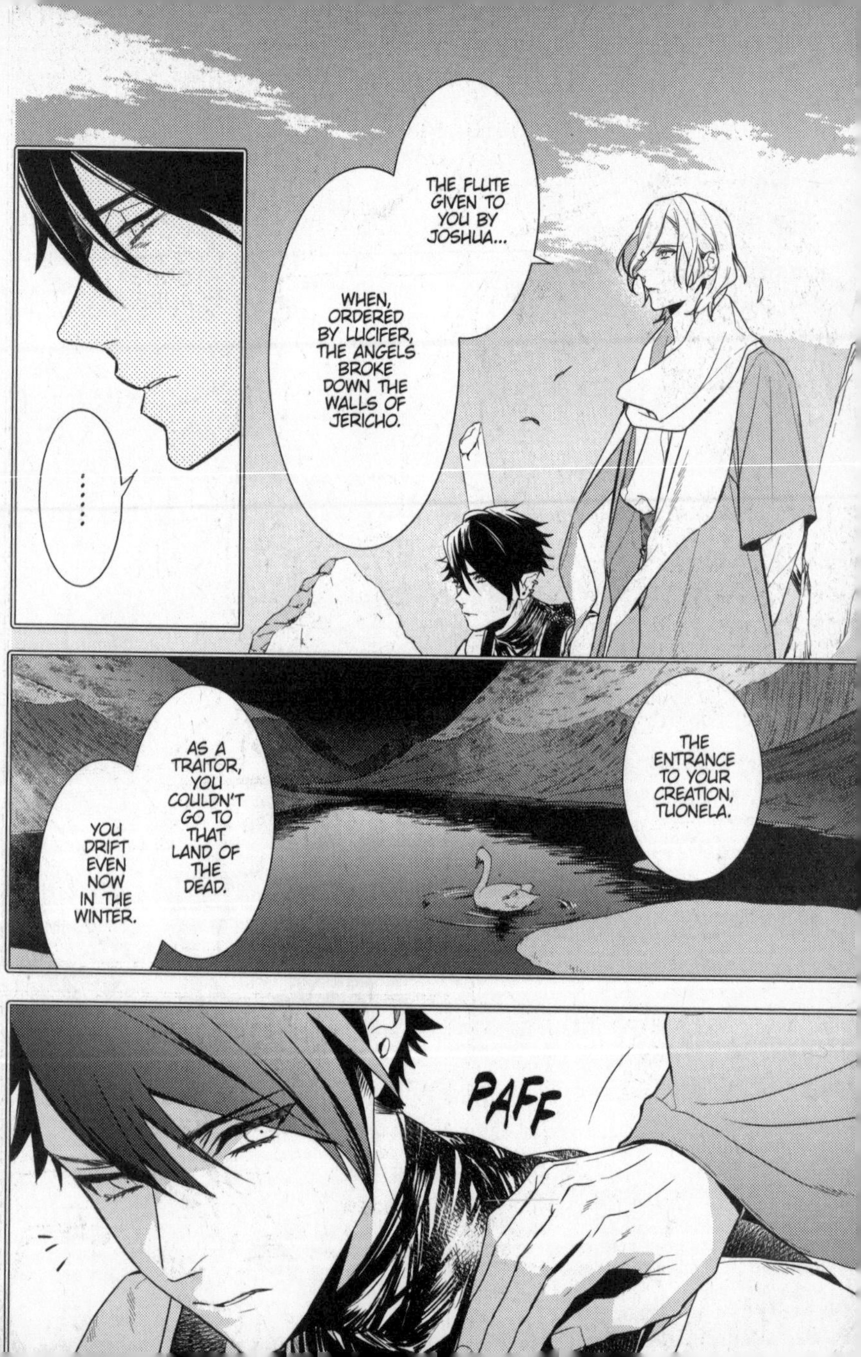
THE FLUTE GIVEN TO YOU BY JOSHUA...
WHEN, ORDERED BY LUCIFER, THE ANGELS BROKE DOWN THE WALLS OF JERICHO.
......
THE ENTRANCE TO YOUR CREATION, TUONELA.
AS A TRAITOR, YOU COULDN'T GO TO THAT LAND OF THE DEAD.
YOU DRIFT EVEN NOW IN THE WINTER.
PAFF

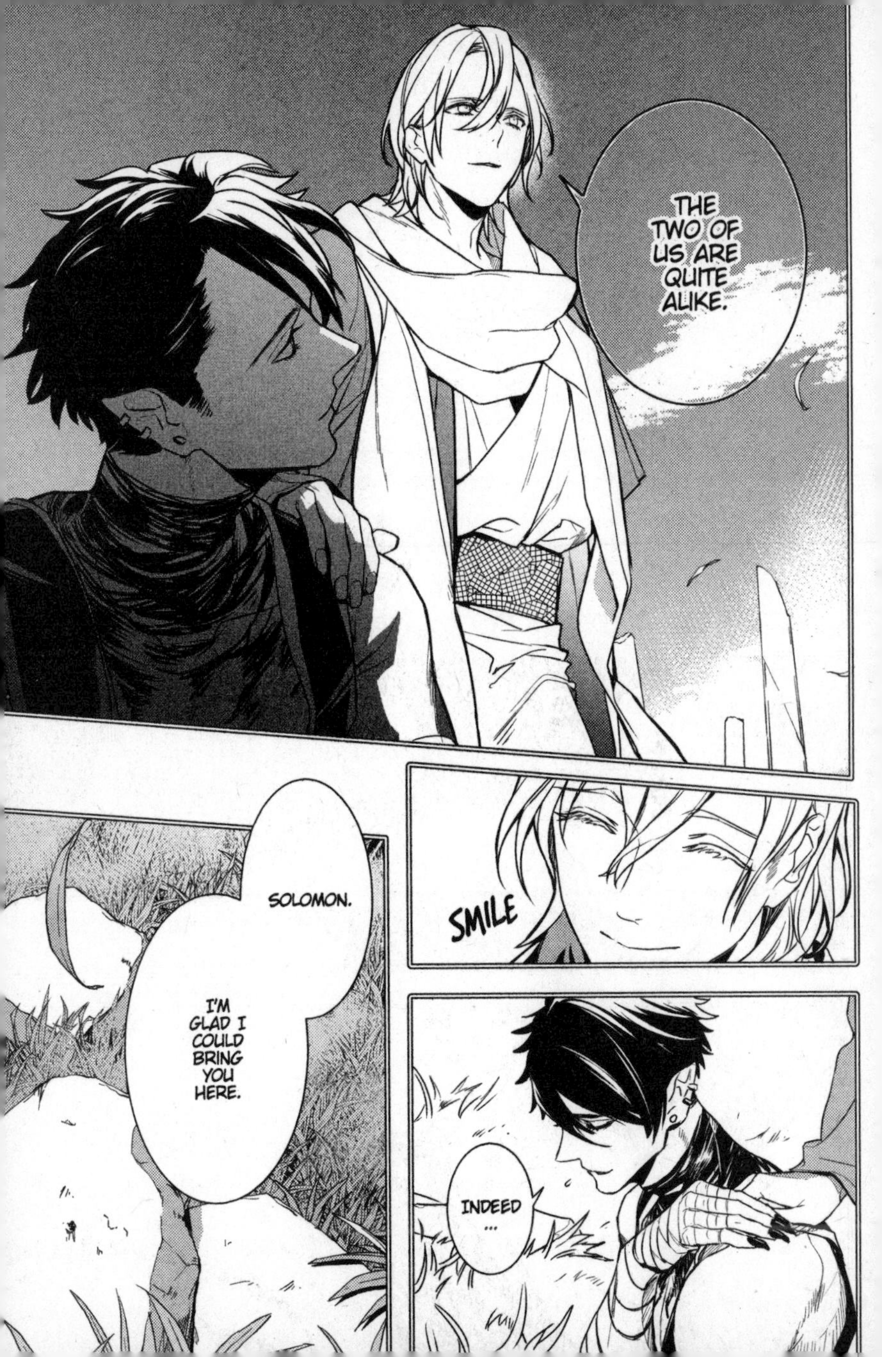
THE TWO OF US ARE QUITE ALIKE.
SMILE
INDEED...
SOLOMON.
I'M GLAD I COULD BRING YOU HERE.

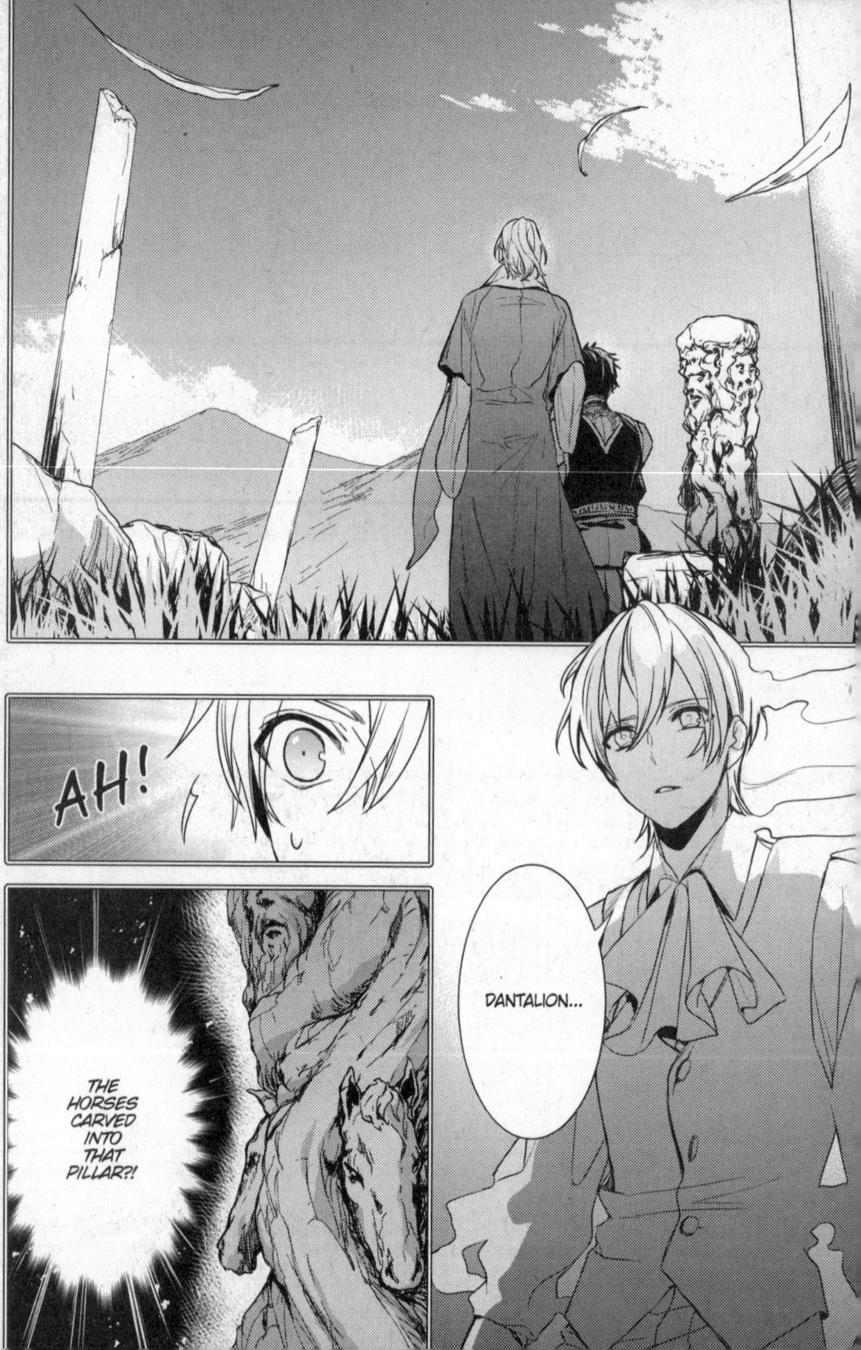
DANTALION...
AH!
THE HORSES CARVED INTO THAT PILLAR?!

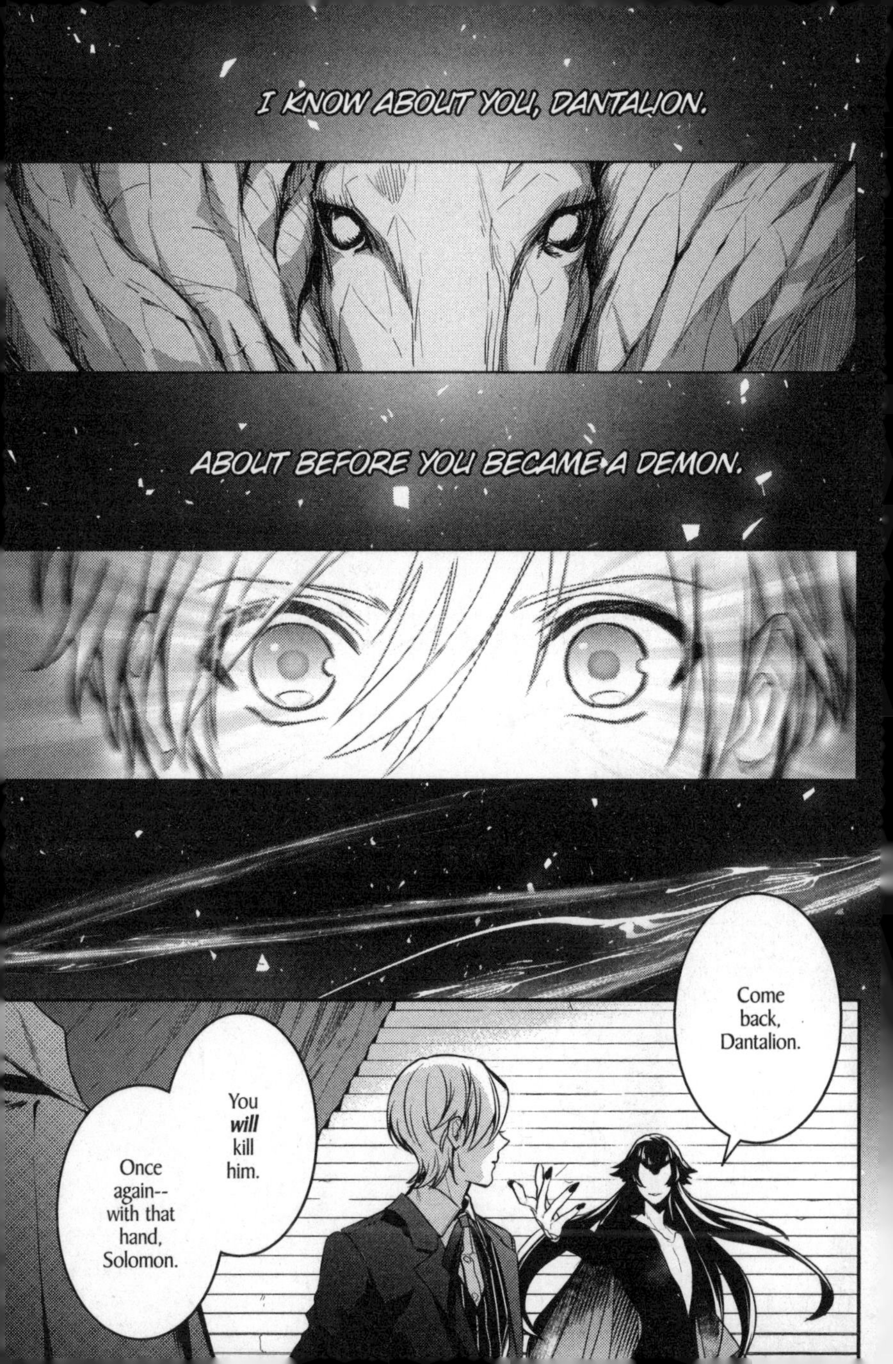
I KNOW ABOUT YOU, DANTALION.
ABOUT BEFORE YOU BECAME A DEMON.
Come back, Dantalion.
You *will* kill him.
Once again-- with that hand, Solomon.

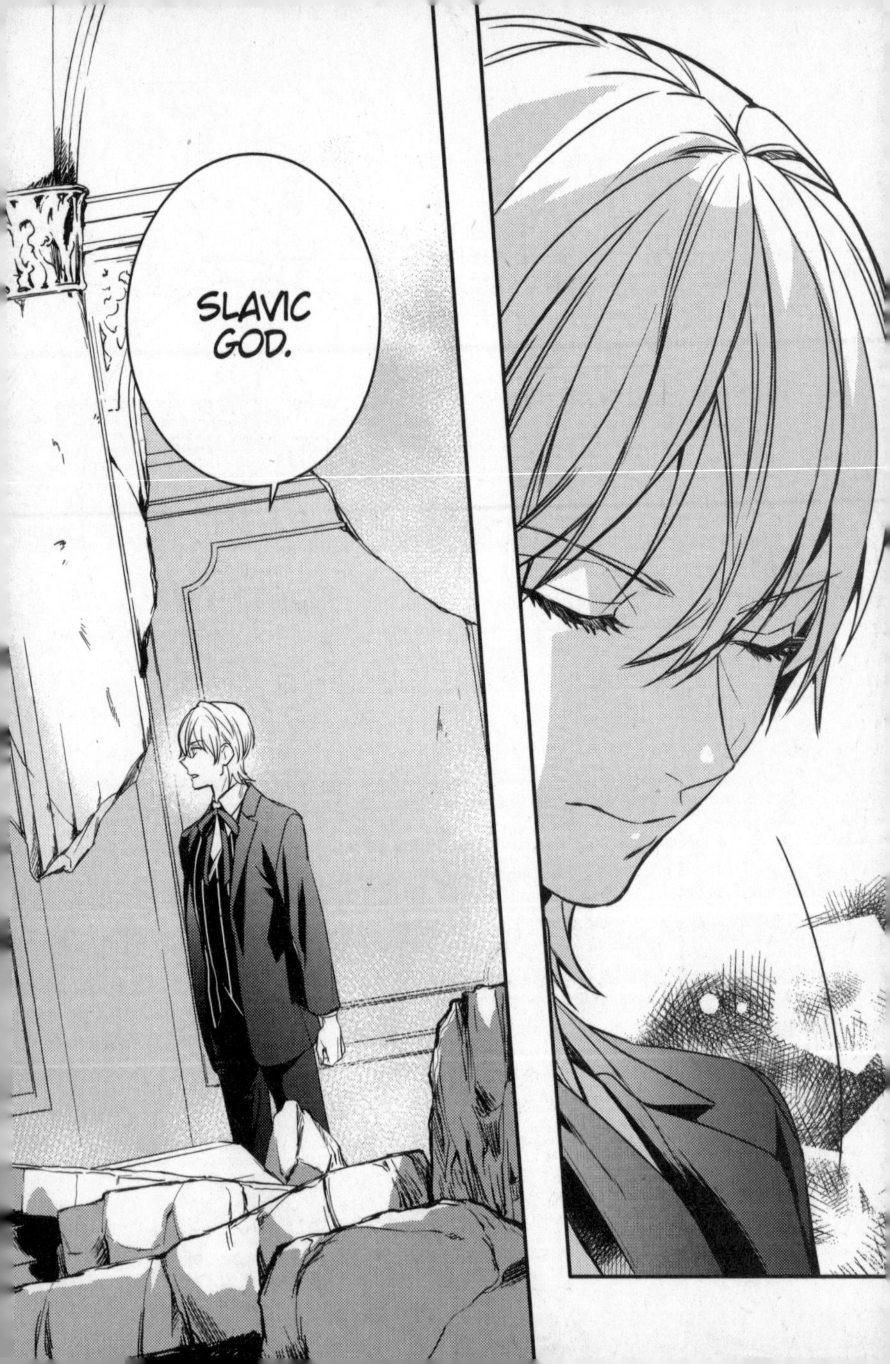
SLAVIC GOD.

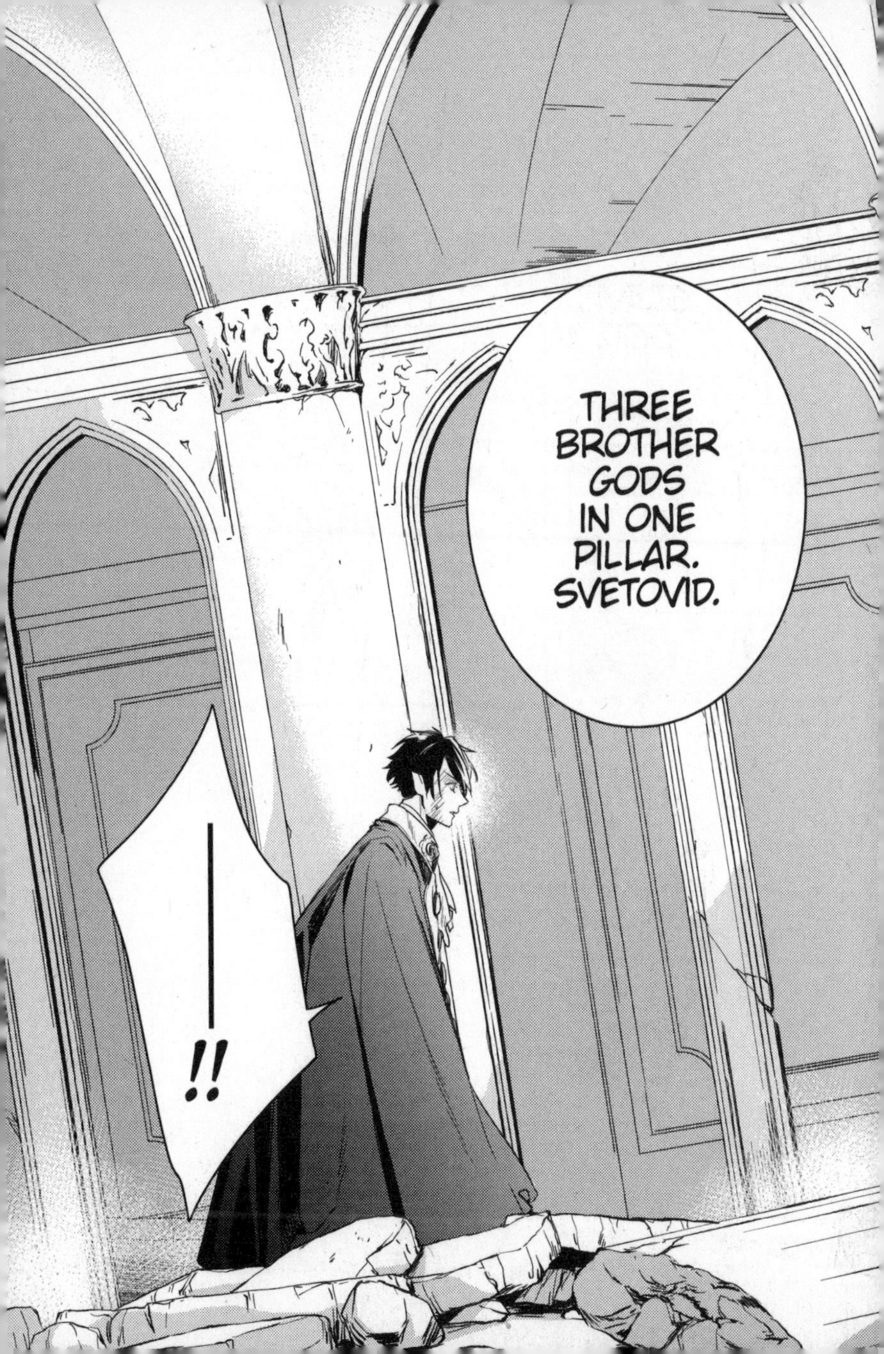
THREE BROTHER GODS IN ONE PILLAR. SVETOVID.
—!!

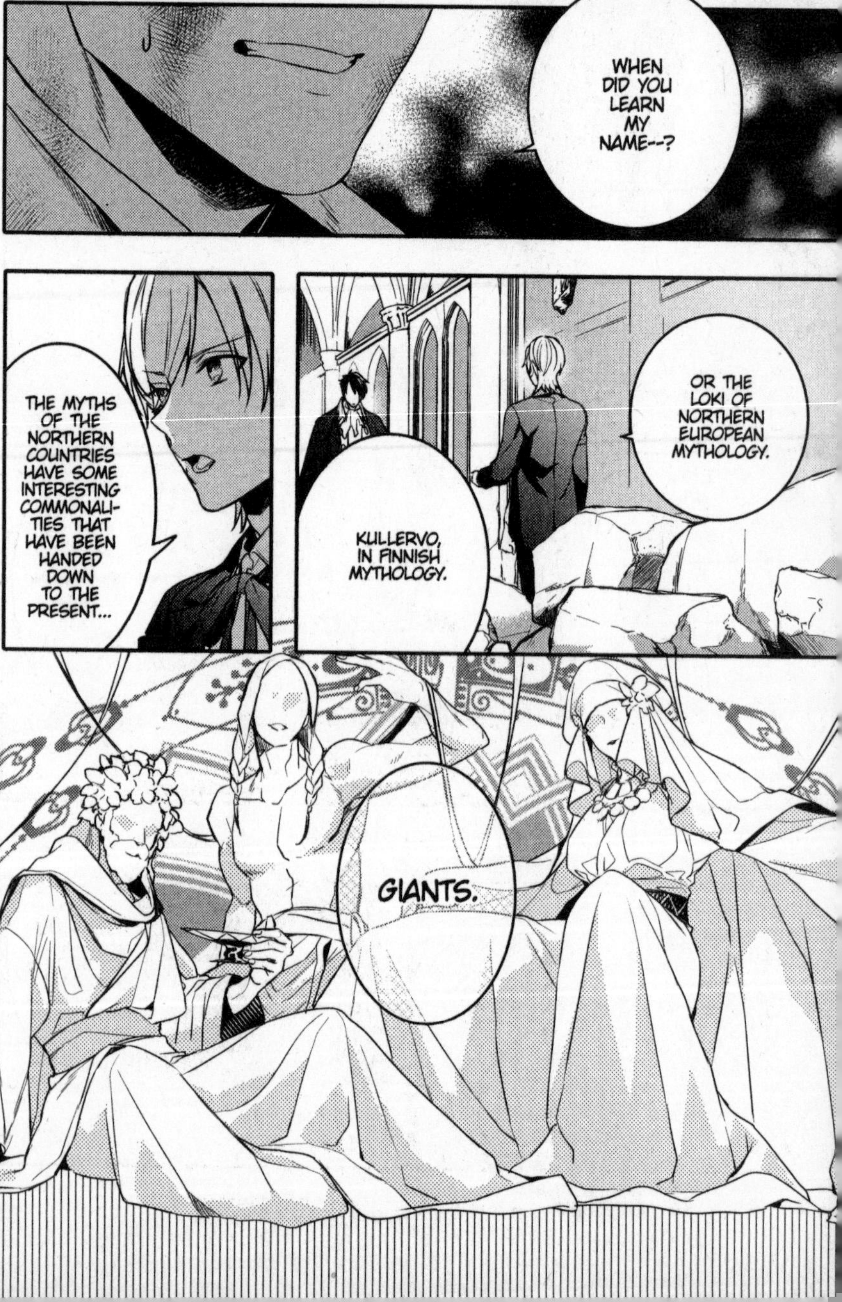
WHEN DID YOU LEARN MY NAME--?
OR THE LOKI OF NORTHERN EUROPEAN MYTHOLOGY.
KULLERVO, IN FINNISH MYTHOLOGY.
THE MYTHS OF THE NORTHERN COUNTRIES HAVE SOME INTERESTING COMMONALITIES THAT HAVE BEEN HANDED DOWN TO THE PRESENT...
GIANTS.

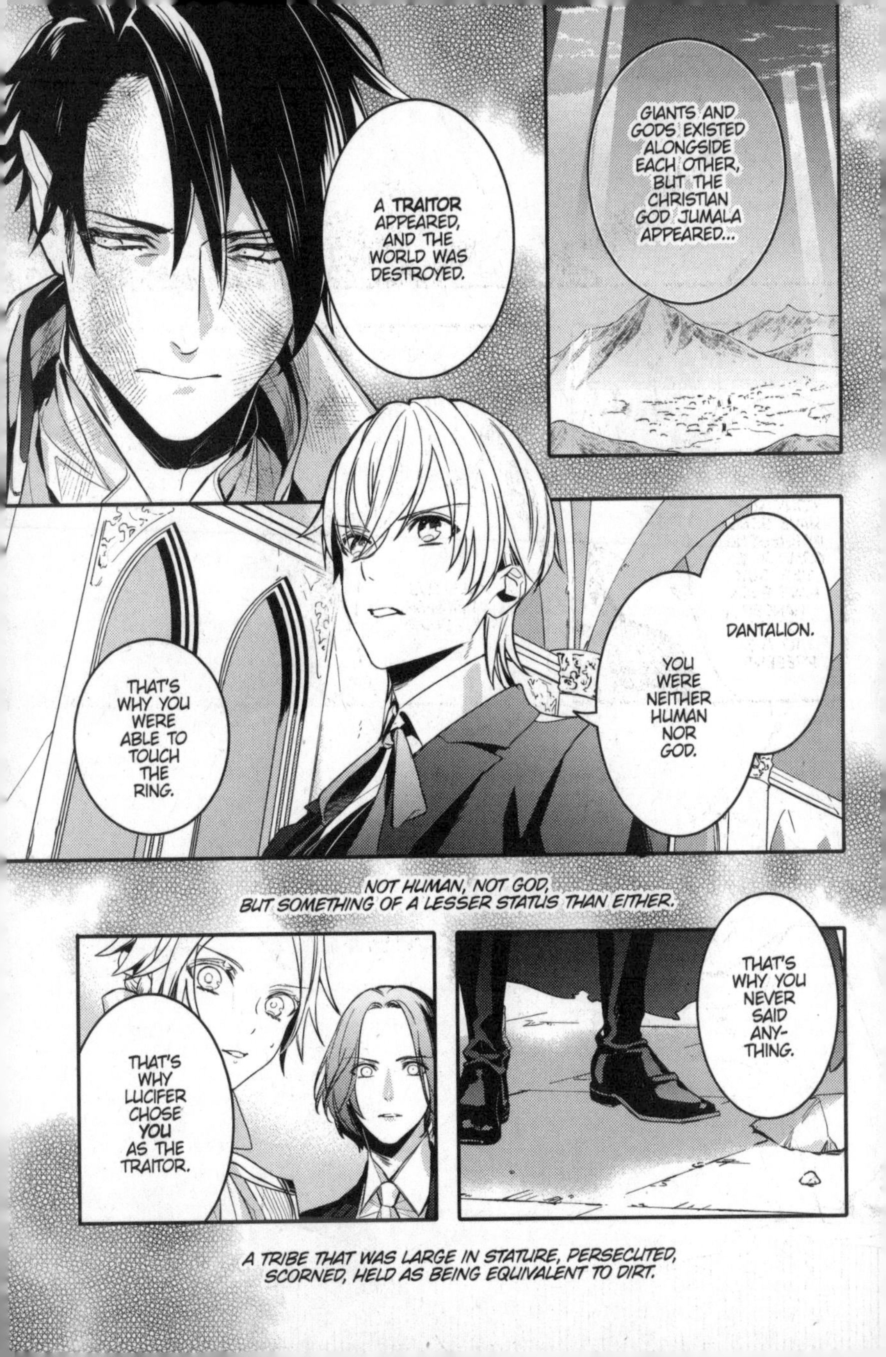
GIANTS AND GODS EXISTED ALONGSIDE EACH OTHER, BUT THE CHRISTIAN GOD JUMALA APPEARED...
A TRAITOR APPEARED, AND THE WORLD WAS DESTROYED.
DANTALION.
YOU WERE NEITHER HUMAN NOR GOD.
THAT'S WHY YOU WERE ABLE TO TOUCH THE RING.
NOT HUMAN, NOT GOD, BUT SOMETHING OF A LESSER STATUS THAN EITHER.
THAT'S WHY YOU NEVER SAID ANY-THING.
THAT'S WHY LUCIFER CHOSE YOU AS THE TRAITOR.
A TRIBE THAT WAS LARGE IN STATURE, PERSECUTED, SCORNED, HELD AS BEING EQUIVALENT TO DIRT.

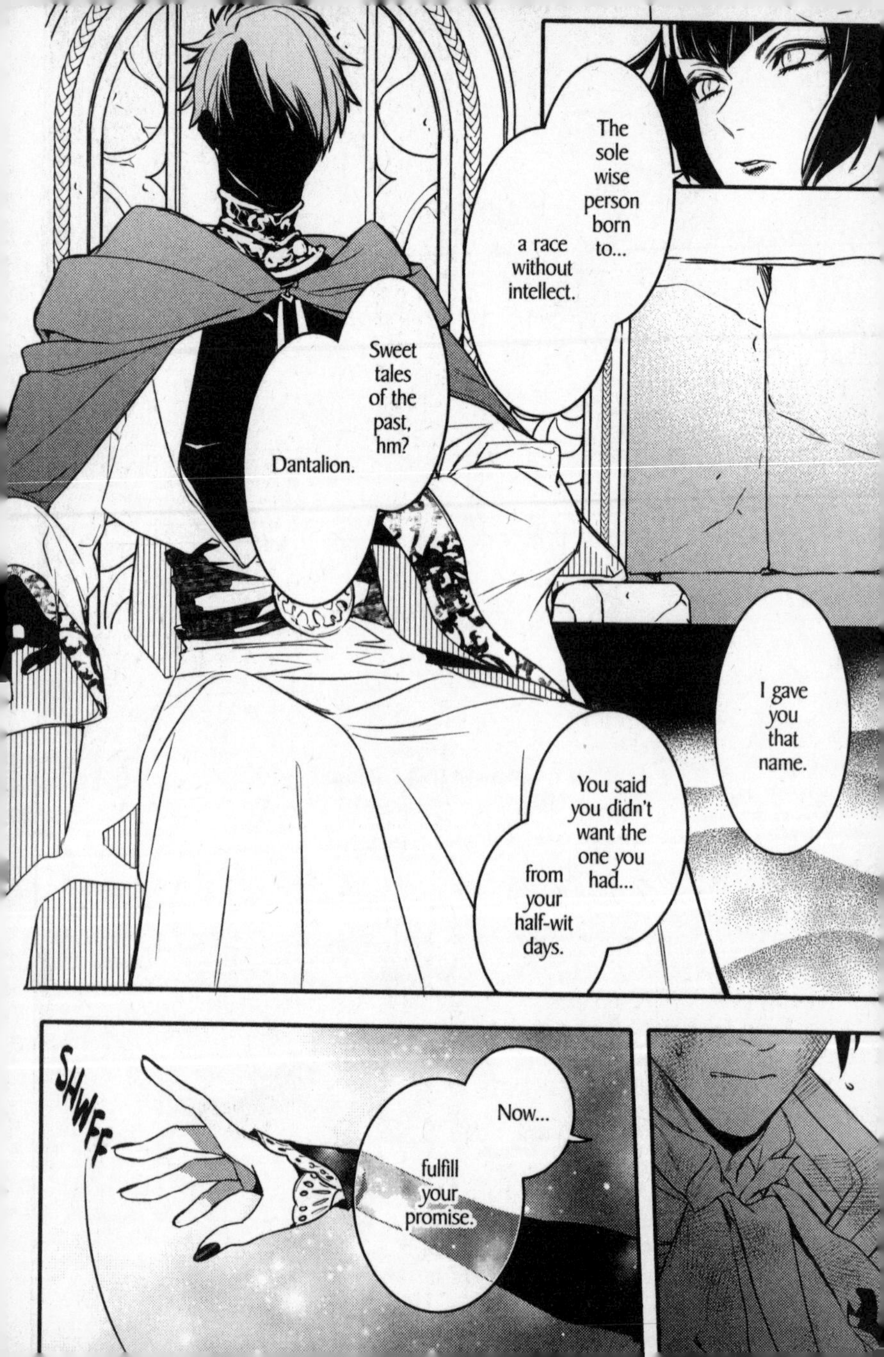
The sole wise person born to... a race without intellect.
Sweet tales of the past, hm? Dantalion.
I gave you that name.
You said you didn't want the one you had... from your half-wit days.
Now... fulfill your promise.
SHWFF

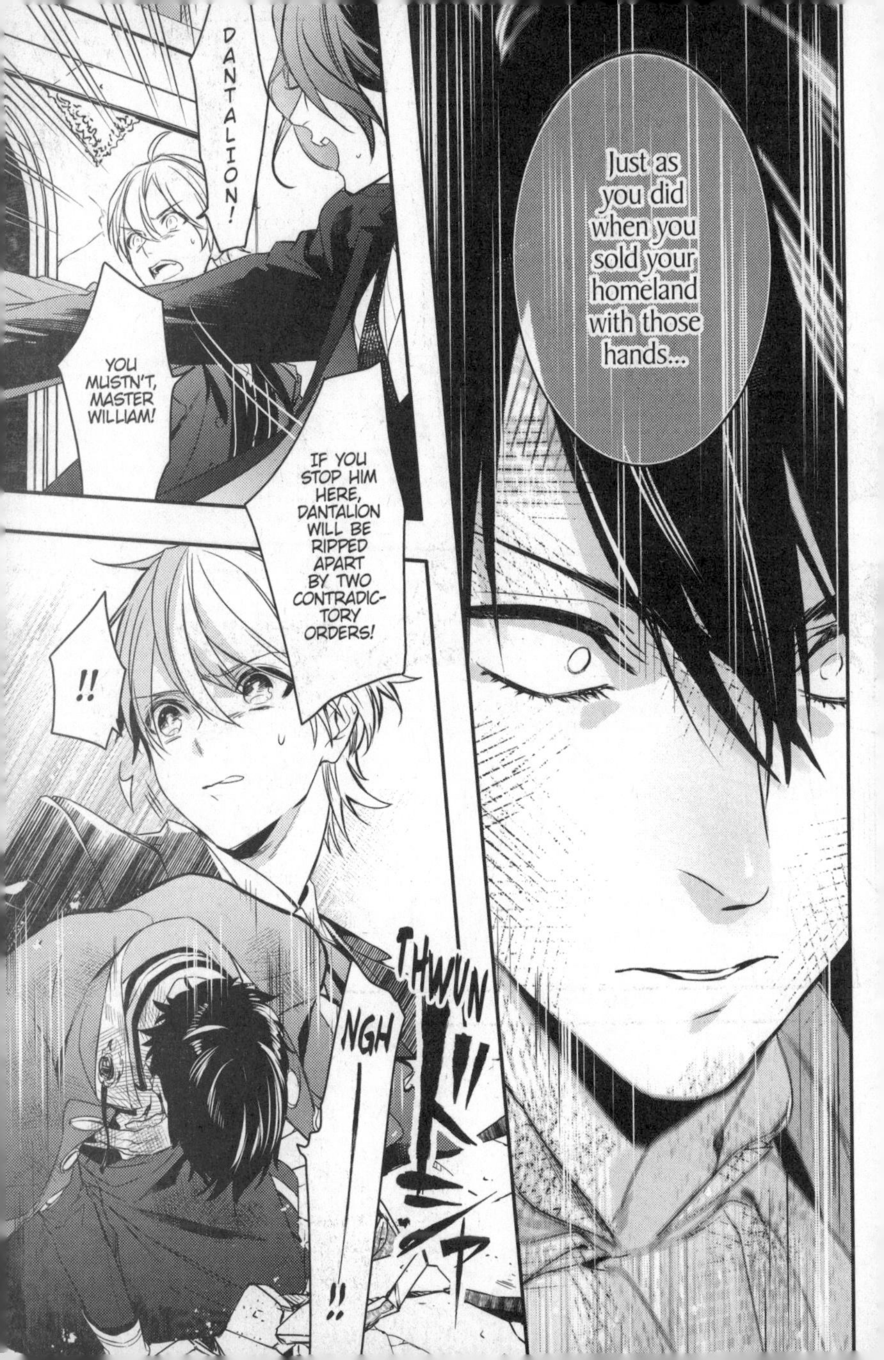
Just as you did when you sold your homeland with those hands...
DANTALION!
YOU MUSTN'T, MASTER WILLIAM!
IF YOU STOP HIM HERE, DANTALION WILL BE RIPPED APART BY TWO CONTRADICTORY ORDERS!
!!
THWUN
NGH!!

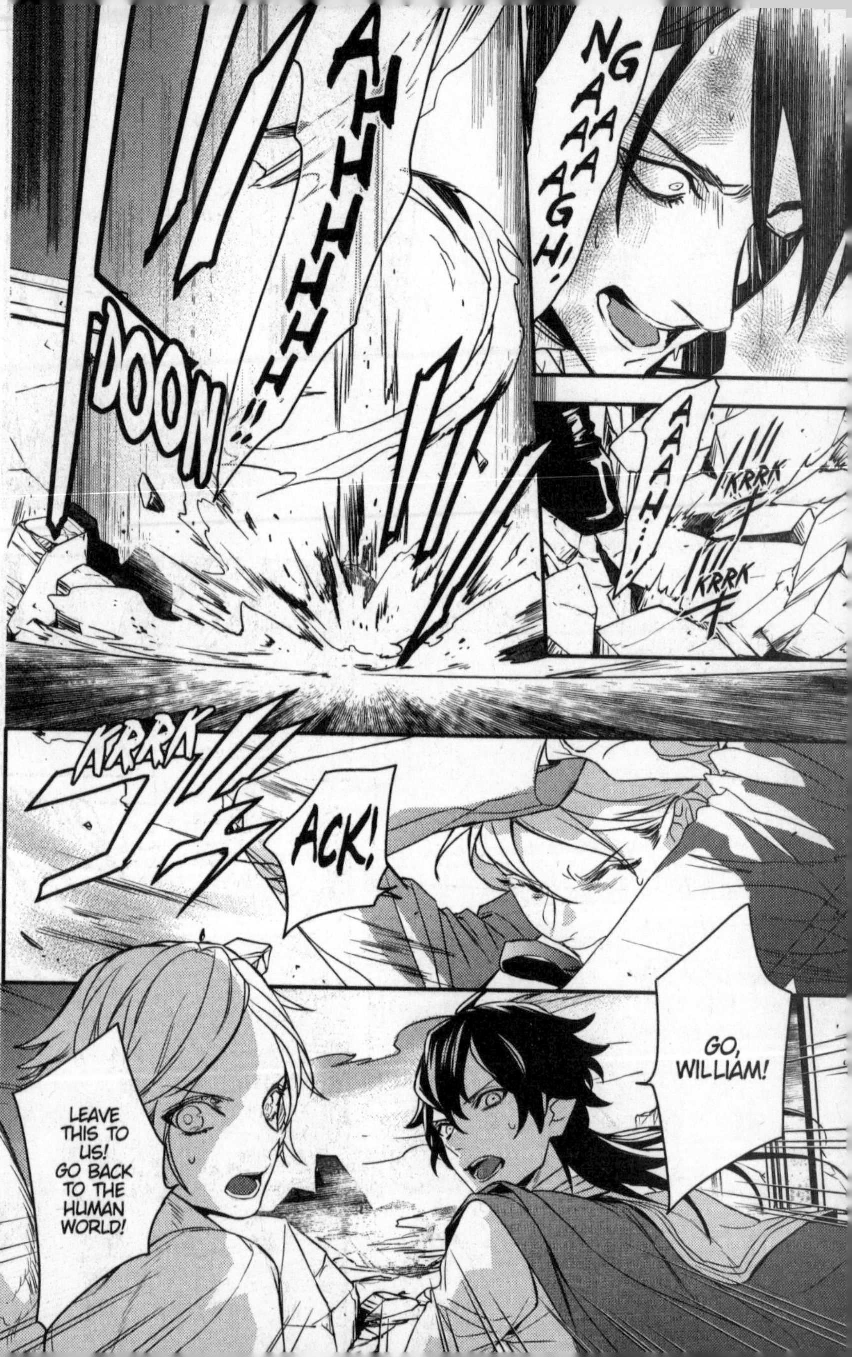
NGAAAAAGH!
AAAH...!
KRRK
KRRK
AHHHHHH...!!
DOON
KRRK
ACK!
GO, WILLIAM!
LEAVE THIS TO US! GO BACK TO THE HUMAN WORLD!

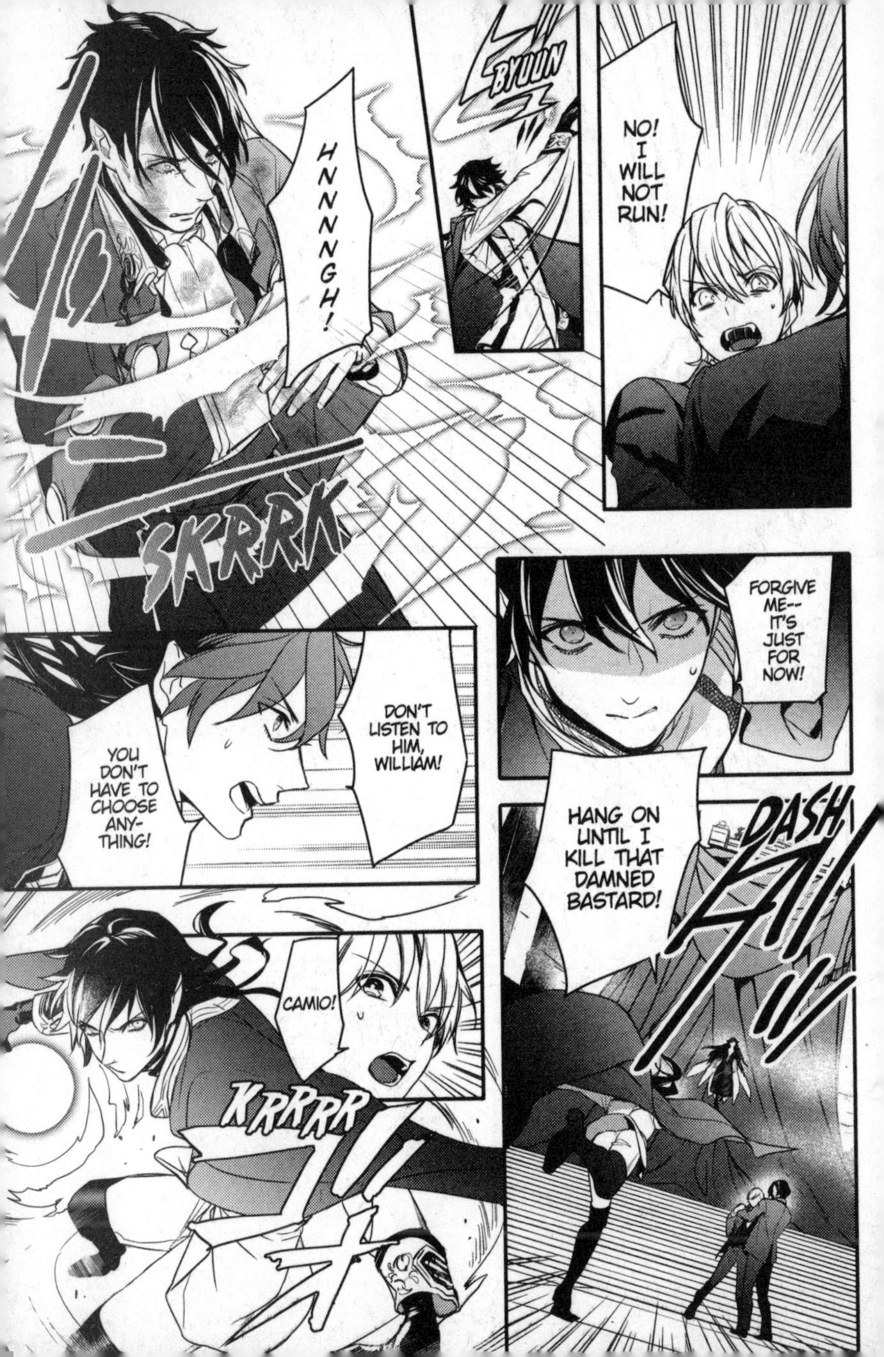
NO! I WILL NOT RUN!
BYUUN
HNNNNNGH!
SKRRK
FORGIVE ME-- IT'S JUST FOR NOW!
HANG ON UNTIL I KILL THAT DAMNED BASTARD!
DASH
DON'T LISTEN TO HIM, WILLIAM!
YOU DON'T HAVE TO CHOOSE ANYTHING!
CAMIO!
KRRRR

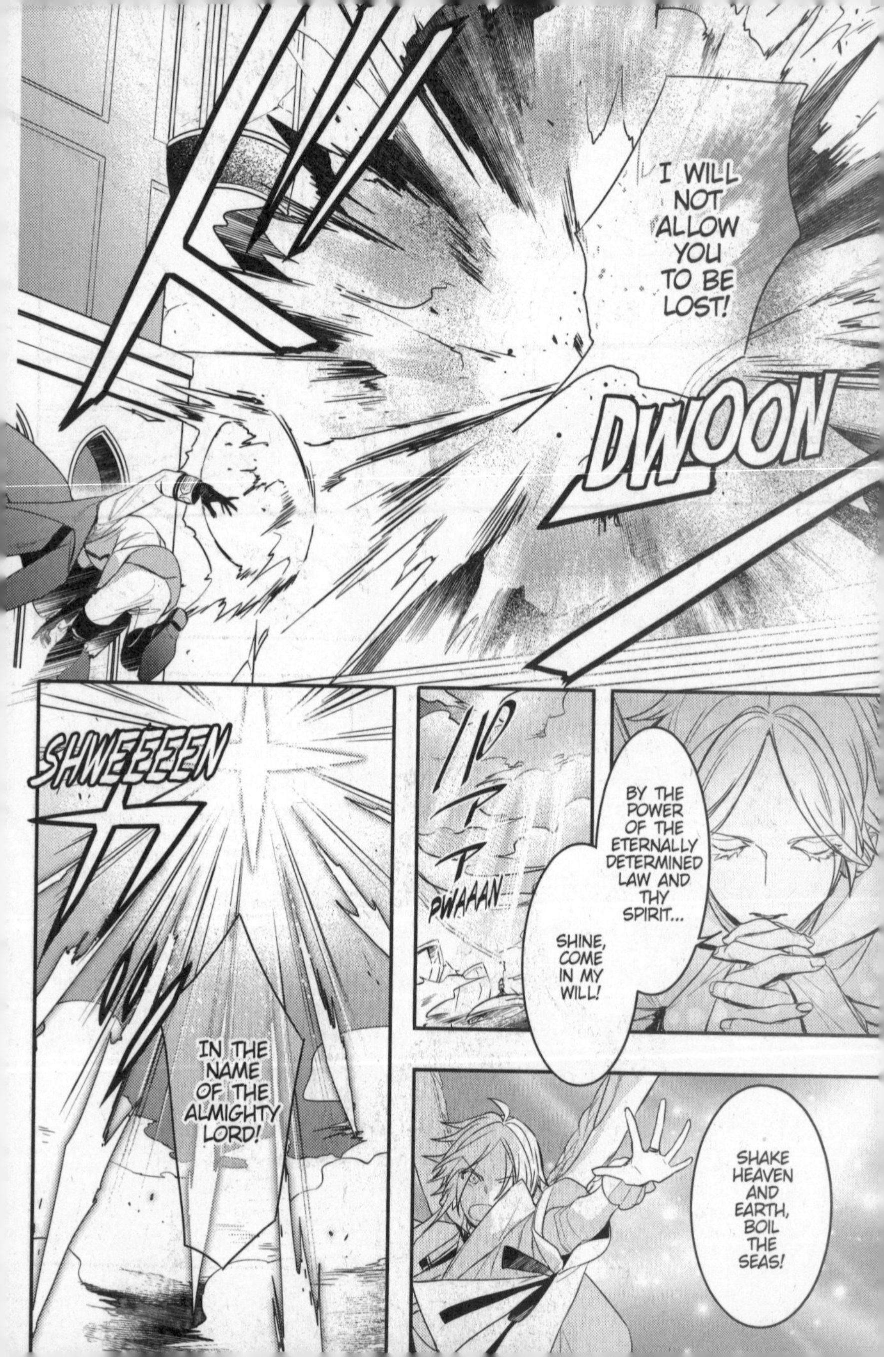
I WILL NOT ALLOW YOU TO BE LOST!
DWOON
BY THE POWER OF THE ETERNALLY DETERMINED LAW AND THY SPIRIT...
SHINE, COME IN MY WILL!
PWAAAN
SHAKE HEAVEN AND EARTH, BOIL THE SEAS!
SHWEEEEN
IN THE NAME OF THE ALMIGHTY LORD!

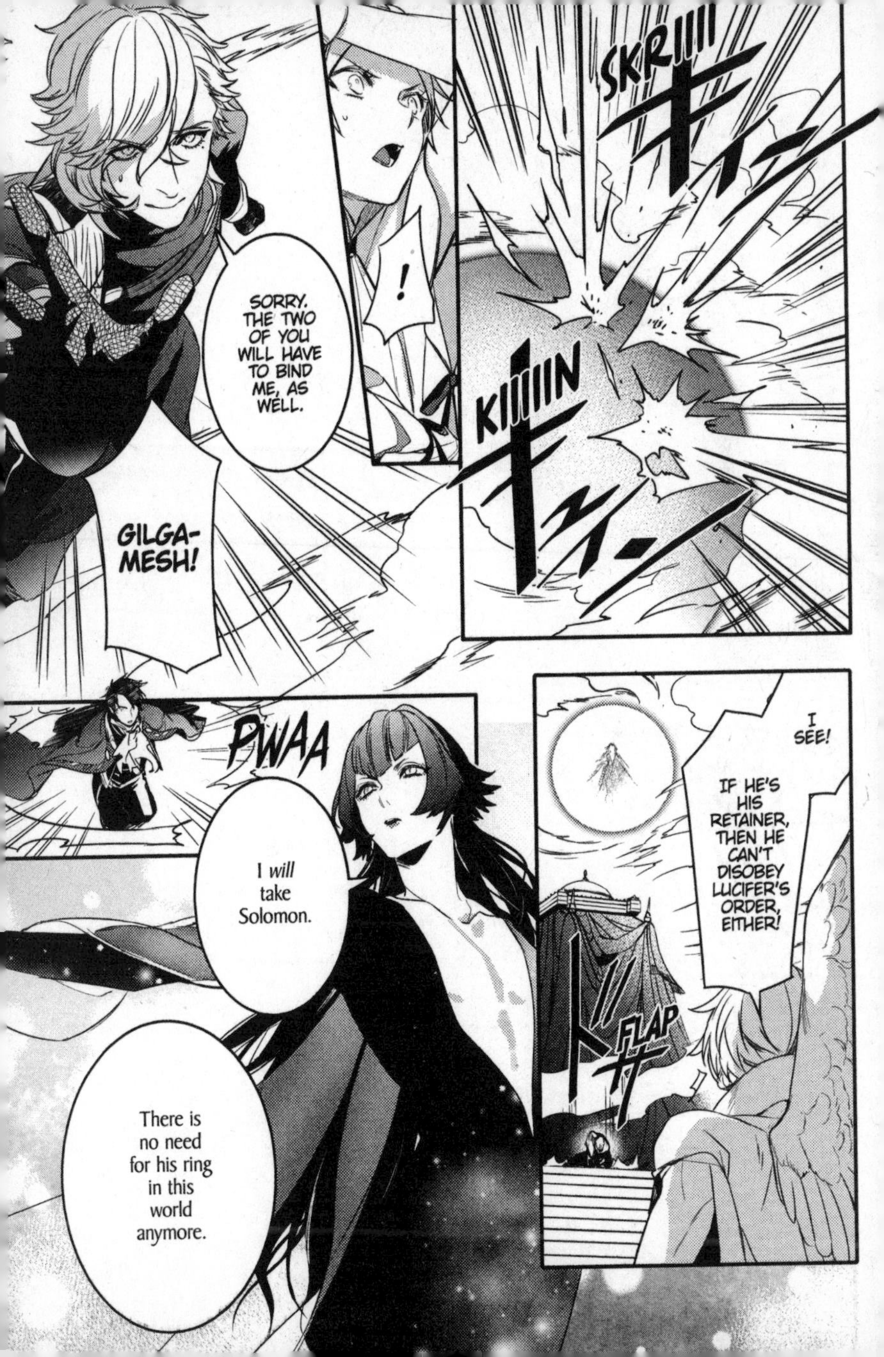
SKRIIII
KIIIIIN
!
SORRY. THE TWO OF YOU WILL HAVE TO BIND ME, AS WELL.
GILGA-MESH!
I SEE!
IF HE'S HIS RETAINER, THEN HE CAN'T DISOBEY LUCIFER'S ORDER, EITHER!
FLAP
PWAA
I *will* take Solomon.
There is no need for his ring in this world anymore.

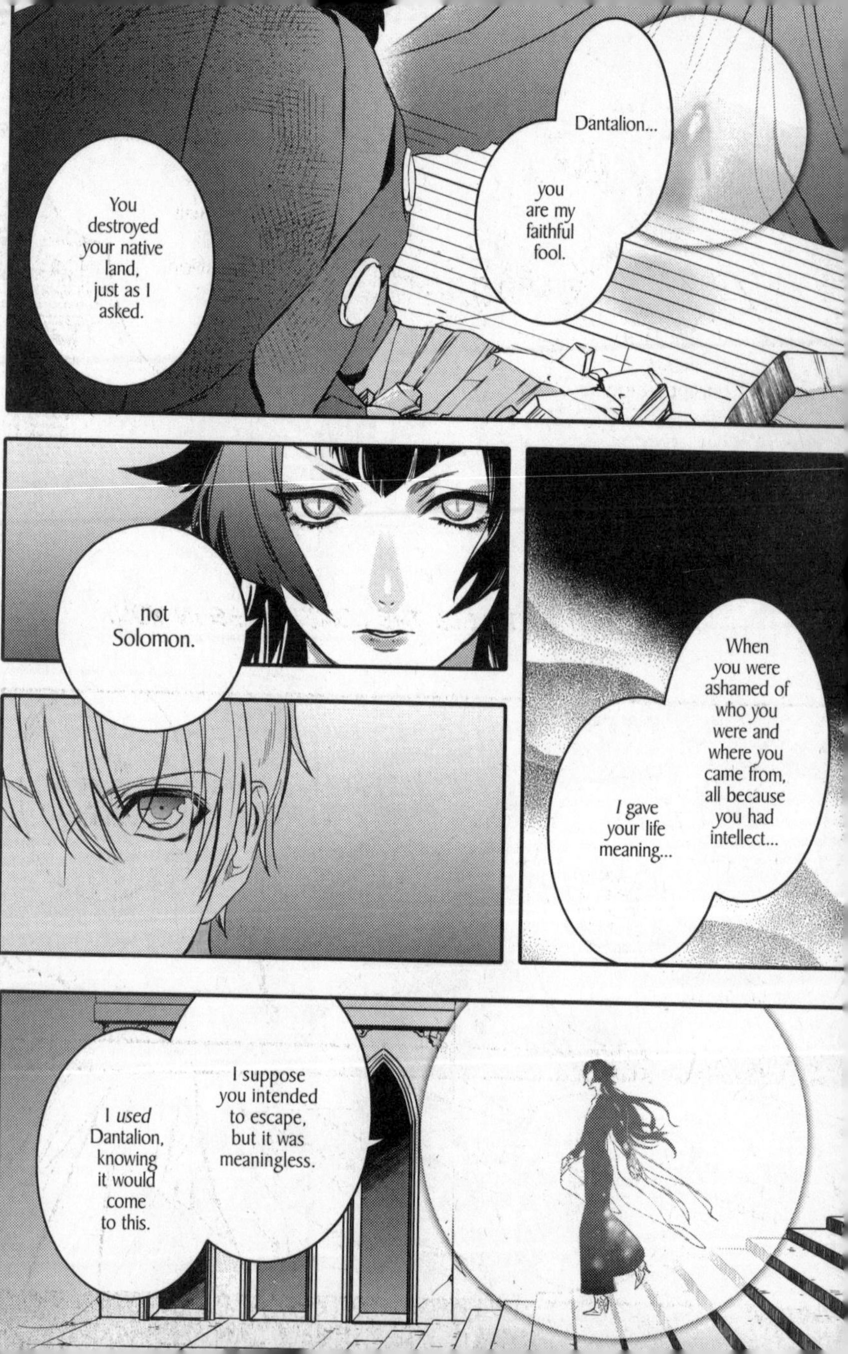
Dantalion... you are my faithful fool.
You destroyed your native land, just as I asked.
When you were ashamed of who you were and where you came from, all because you had intellect...
I gave your life meaning...
not Solomon.
I suppose you intended to escape, but it was meaningless.
I *used* Dantalion, knowing it would come to this.

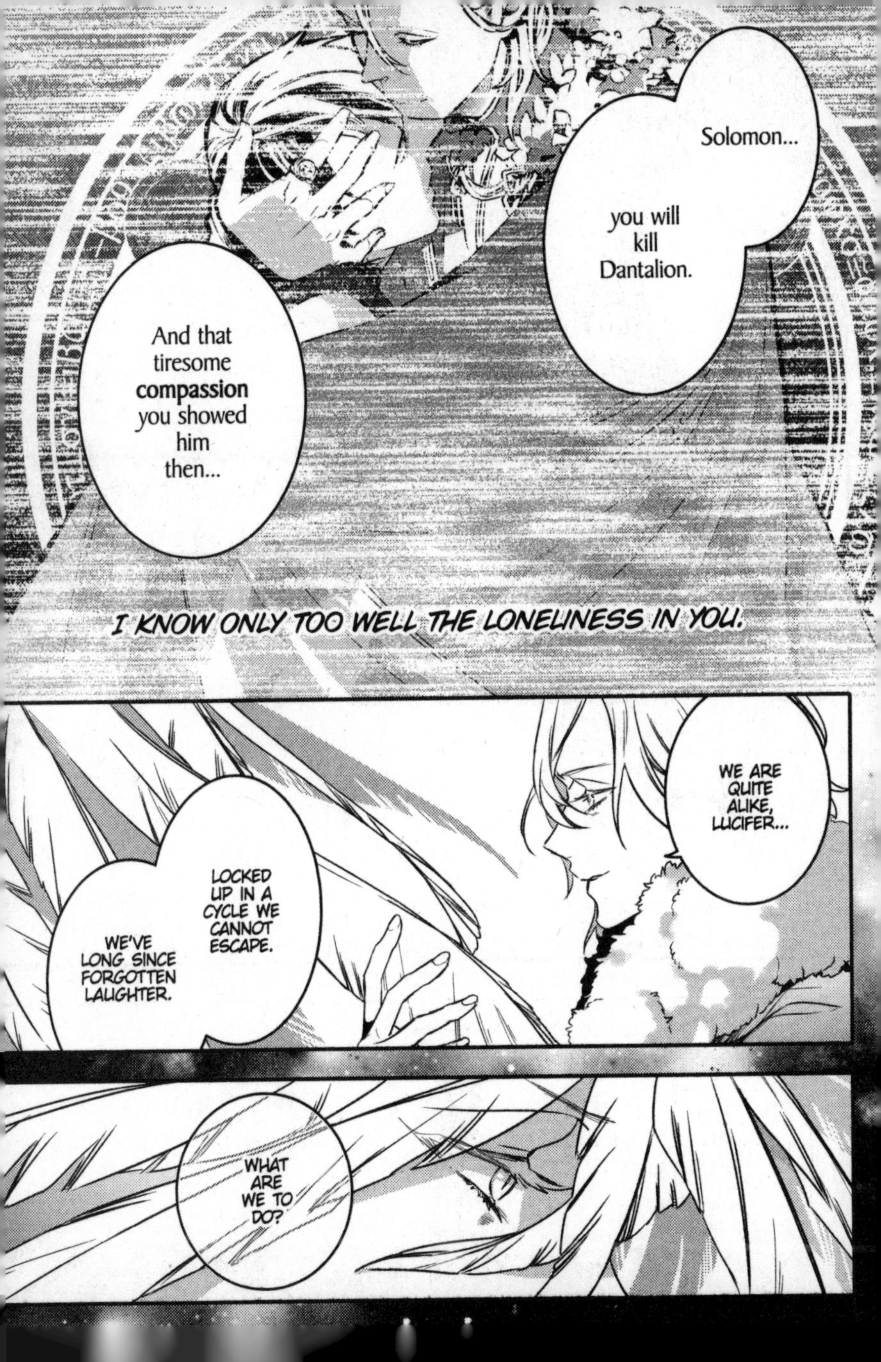
Solomon... you will kill Dantalion.
And that tiresome **compassion** you showed him then...
I KNOW ONLY TOO WELL THE LONELINESS IN YOU.
WE ARE QUITE ALIKE, LUCIFER...
LOCKED UP IN A CYCLE WE CANNOT ESCAPE.
WE'VE LONG SINCE FORGOTTEN LAUGHTER.
WHAT ARE WE TO DO?

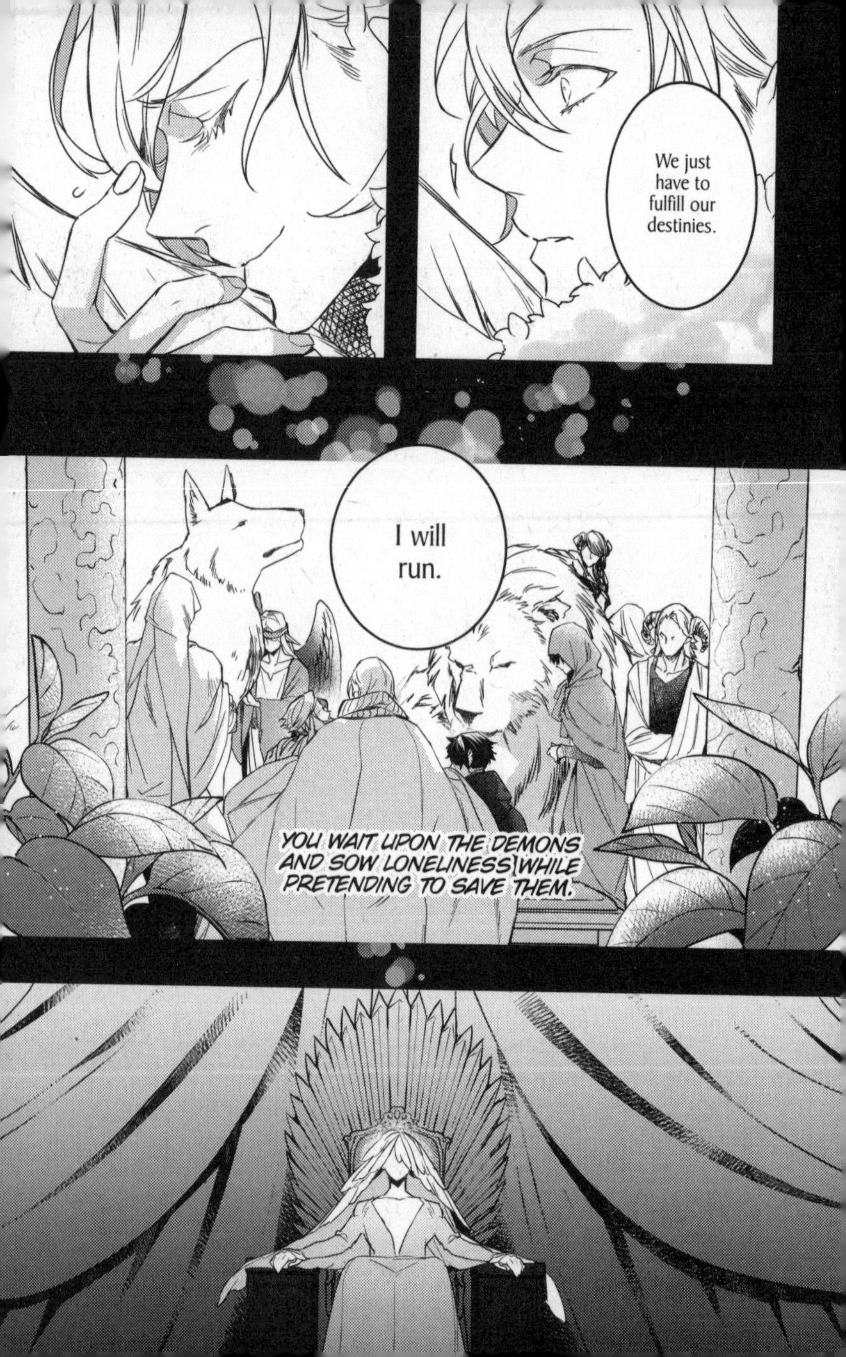
We just have to fulfill our destinies.
I will run.
YOU WAIT UPON THE DEMONS AND SOW LONELINESS WHILE PRETENDING TO SAVE THEM.

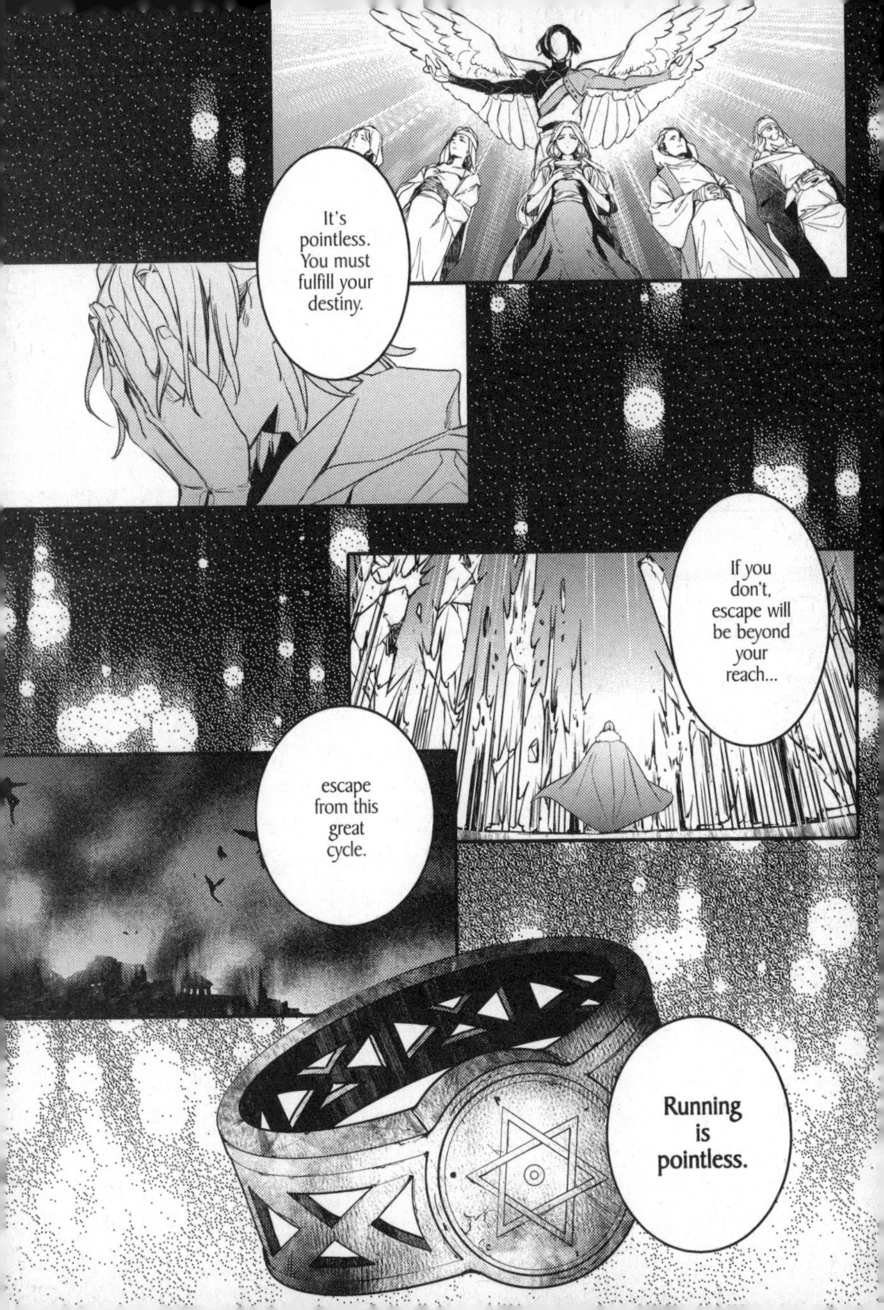
It's pointless. You must fulfill your destiny.
If you don't, escape will be beyond your reach...
escape from this great cycle.
Running is pointless.

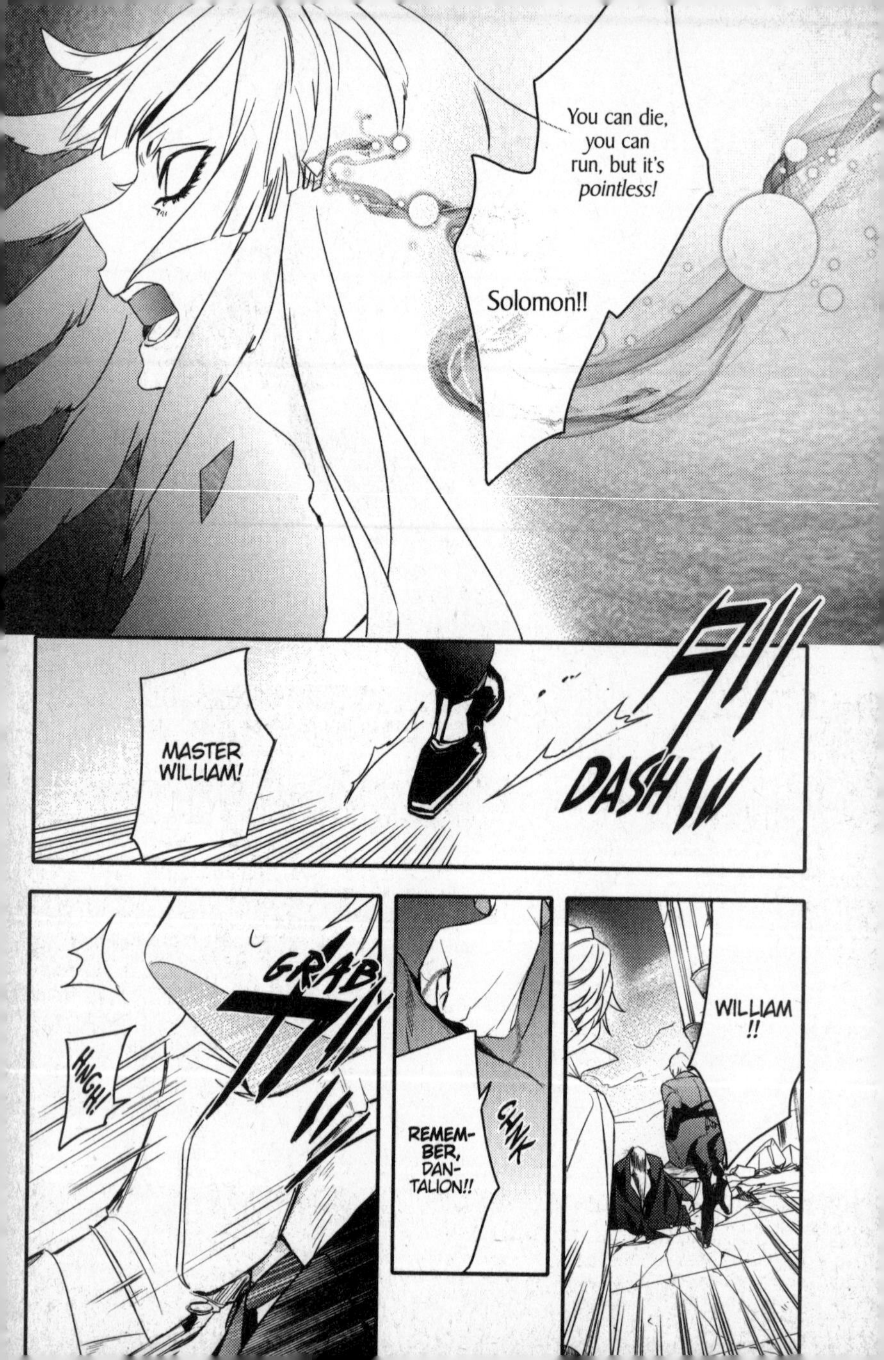
You can die, you can run, but it's *pointless!*
Solomon!!
DASH
MASTER WILLIAM!
WILLIAM !!
CHNK
REMEMBER, DANTALION!!
GRAB
HNGH!

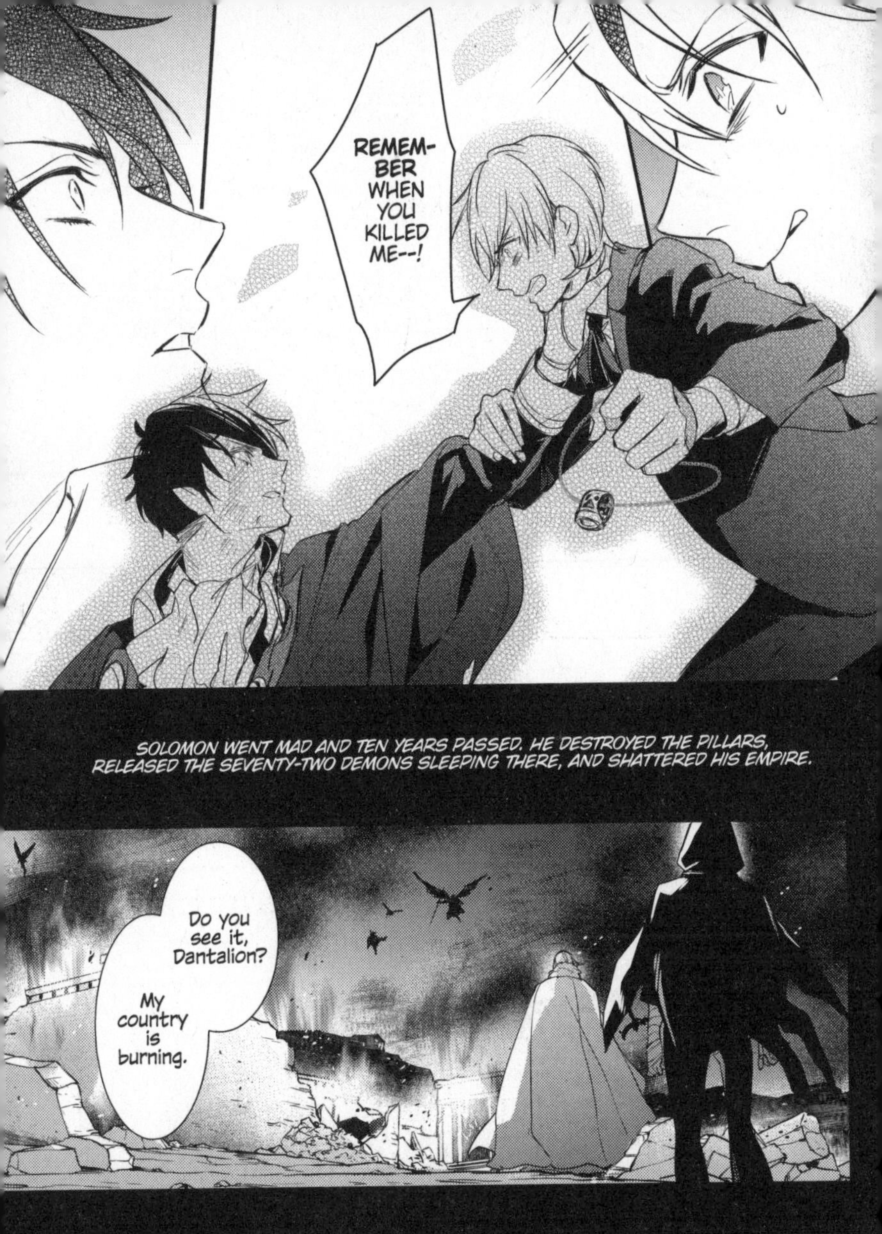
REMEMBER WHEN YOU KILLED ME--!
SOLOMON WENT MAD AND TEN YEARS PASSED. HE DESTROYED THE PILLARS, RELEASED THE SEVENTY-TWO DEMONS SLEEPING THERE, AND SHATTERED HIS EMPIRE.
Do you see it, Dantalion?
My country is burning.
THE GRANDEUR OF ISRAEL WAS GONE WITHOUT A TRACE.
IT WAS LIKE A BRITTLE CLAY RELIC, SIMPLY WAITING TO BE FORGOTTEN BY HISTORY.

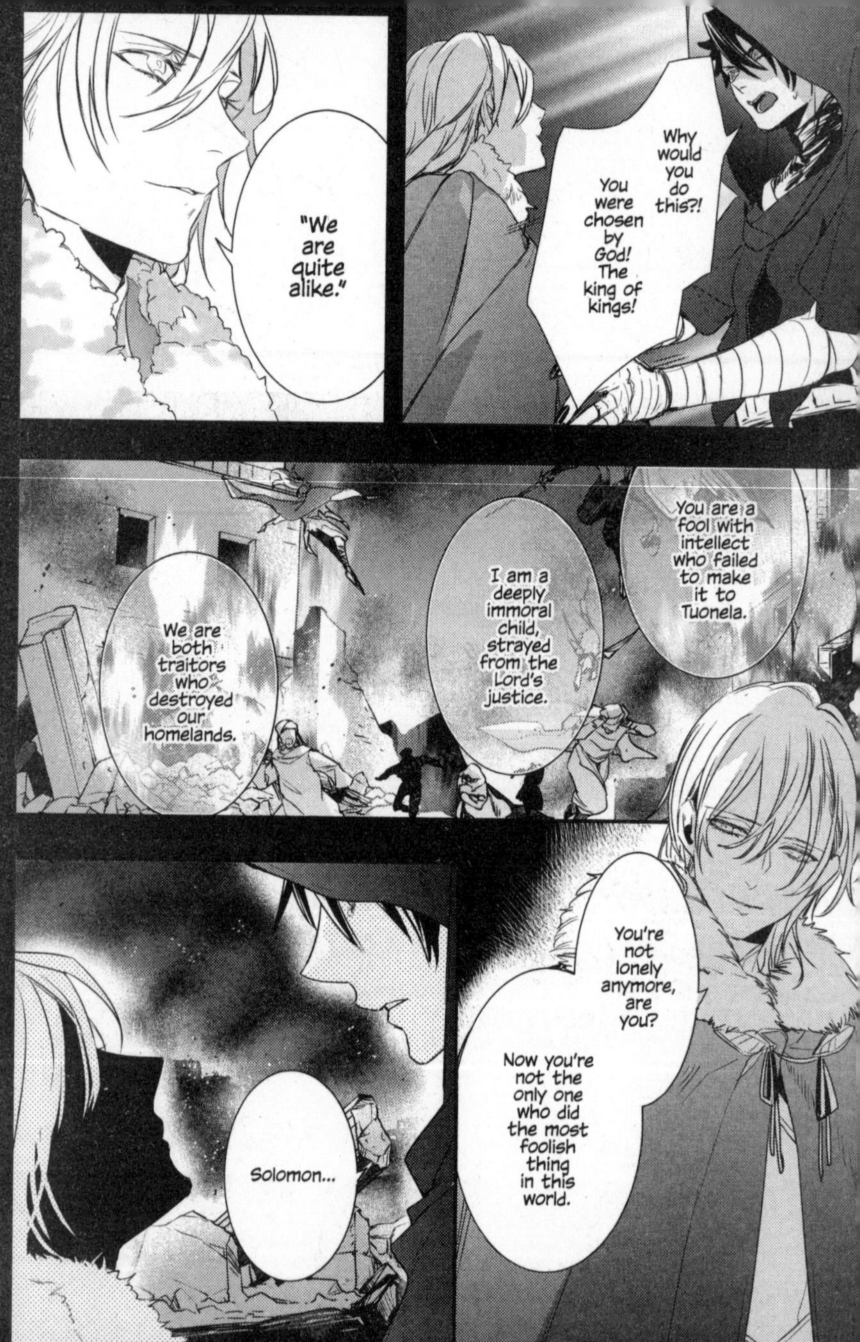
Why would you do this?!
You were chosen by God! The king of kings!
"We are quite alike."
You are a fool with intellect who failed to make it to Tuonela.
I am a deeply immoral child, strayed from the Lord's justice.
We are both traitors who destroyed our homelands.
You're not lonely anymore, are you?
Now you're not the only one who did the most foolish thing in this world.
Solomon...

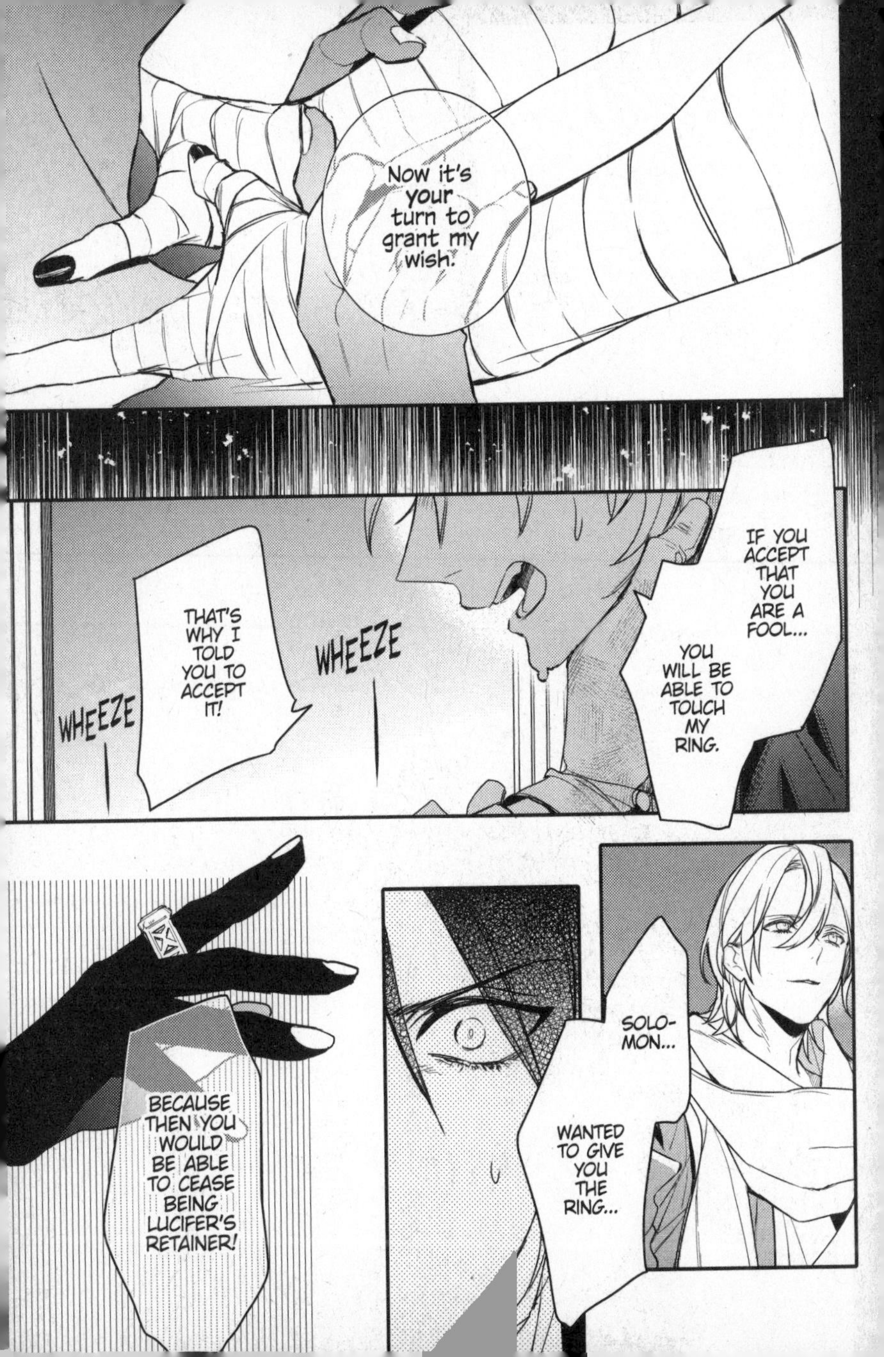
Now it's your turn to grant my wish!
IF YOU ACCEPT THAT YOU ARE A FOOL...
YOU WILL BE ABLE TO TOUCH MY RING.
WHEEZE
THAT'S WHY I TOLD YOU TO ACCEPT IT!
WHEEZE
SOLO-MON...
WANTED TO GIVE YOU THE RING...
BECAUSE THEN YOU WOULD BE ABLE TO CEASE BEING LUCIFER'S RETAINER!

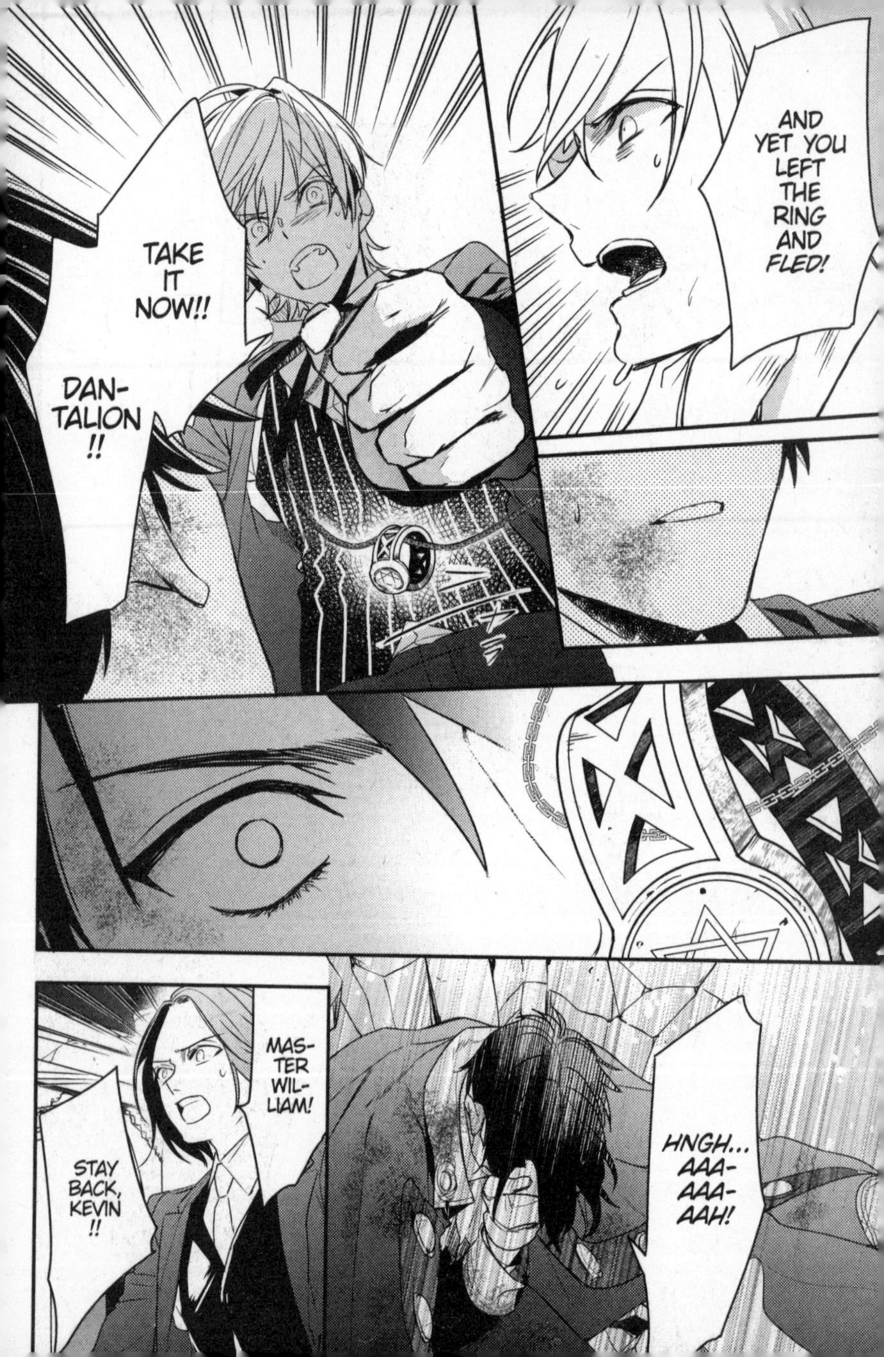
AND YET YOU LEFT THE RING AND FLED!
TAKE IT NOW!!
DAN-TALION!!
HNGH... AAA-AAA-AAH!
MAS-TER WIL-LIAM!
STAY BACK, KEVIN!!

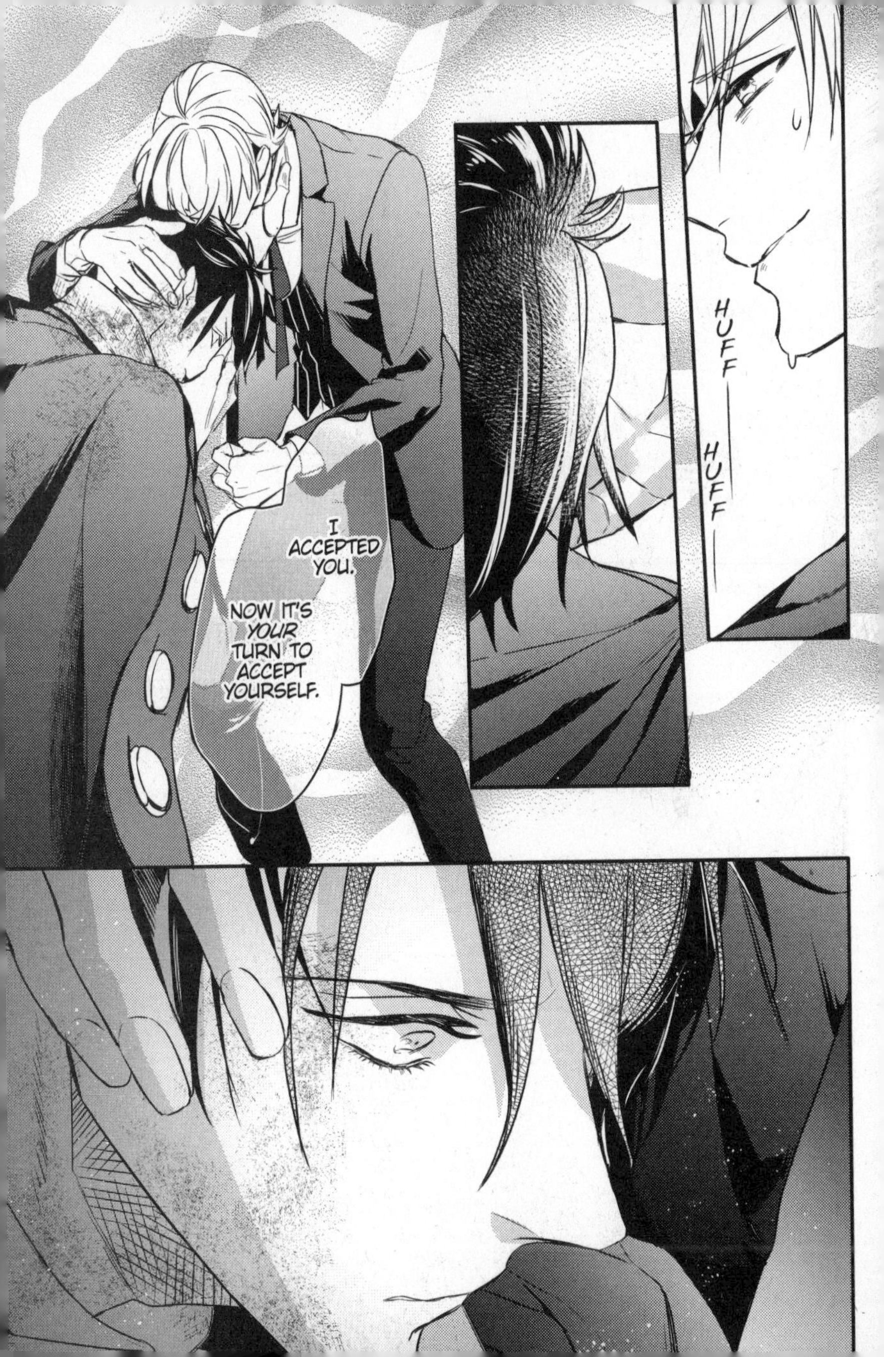
HUFF— HUFF—
I ACCEPTED YOU.
NOW IT'S *YOUR* TURN TO ACCEPT YOURSELF.

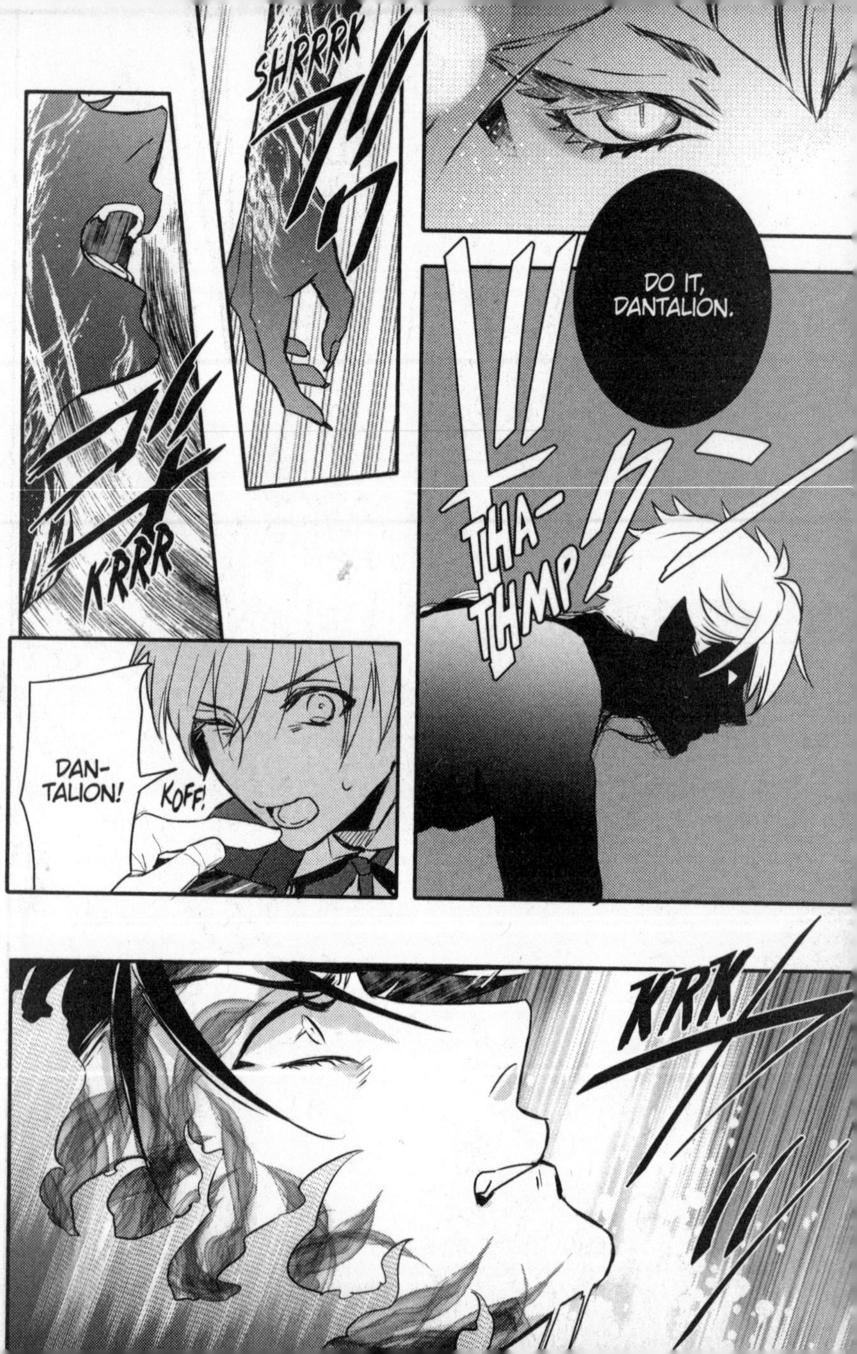
DO IT, DANTALION.
THA-THMP
SHRRRK
K'RRR
KOFF!
DAN-TALION!
K'RK

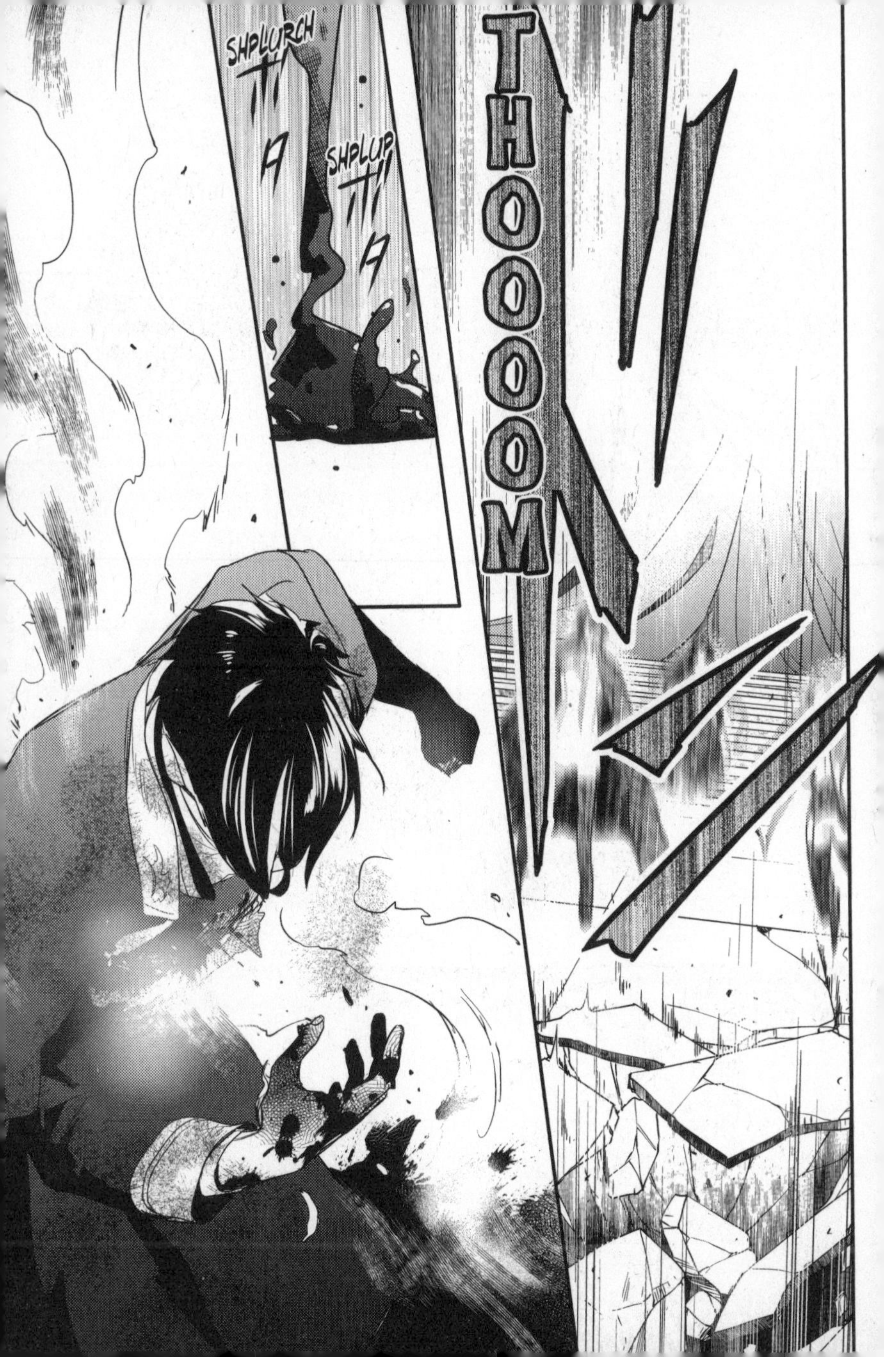
THOOOOOM
SHPLURCH
SHPLUP

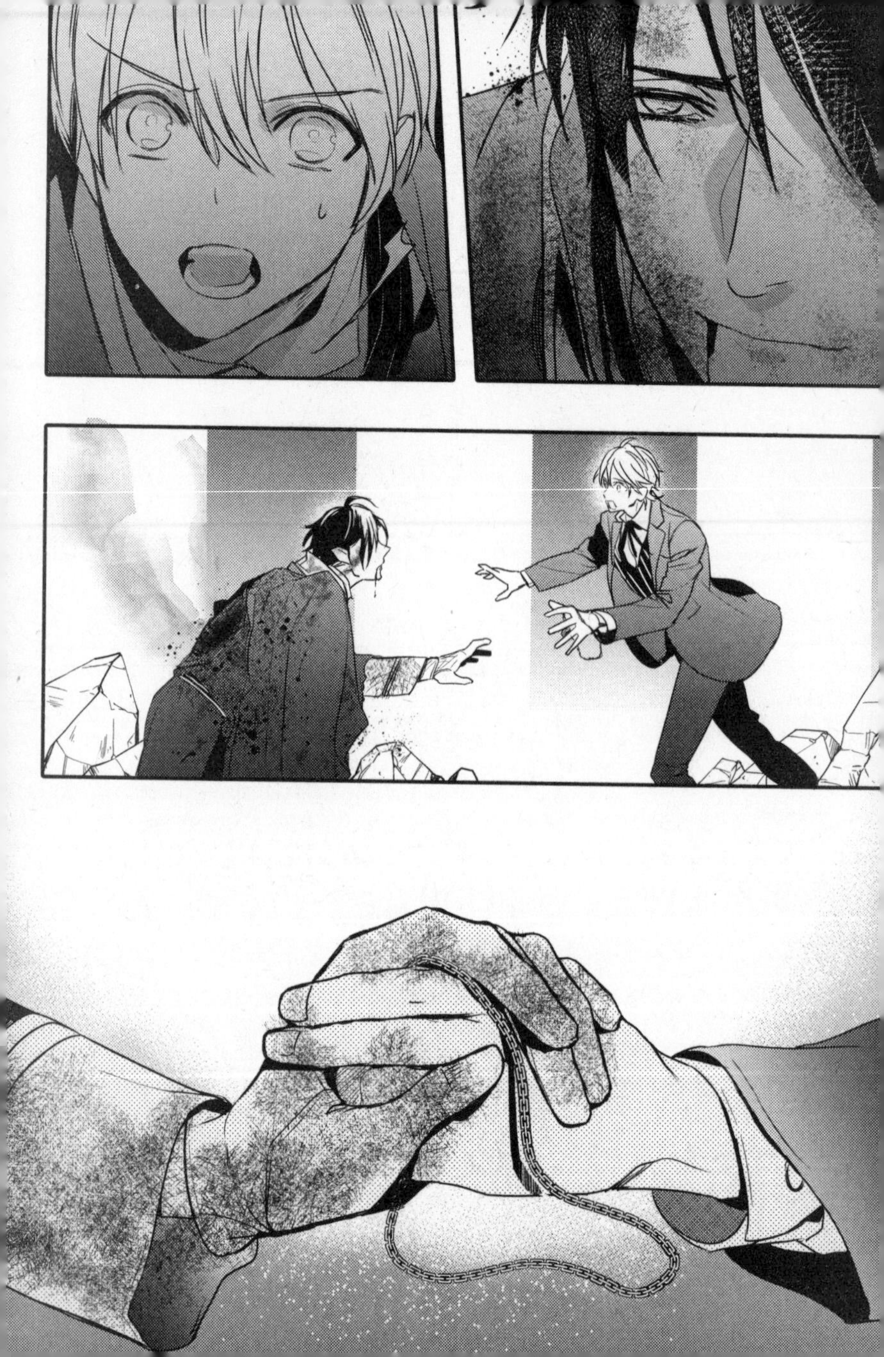

Pillar 94

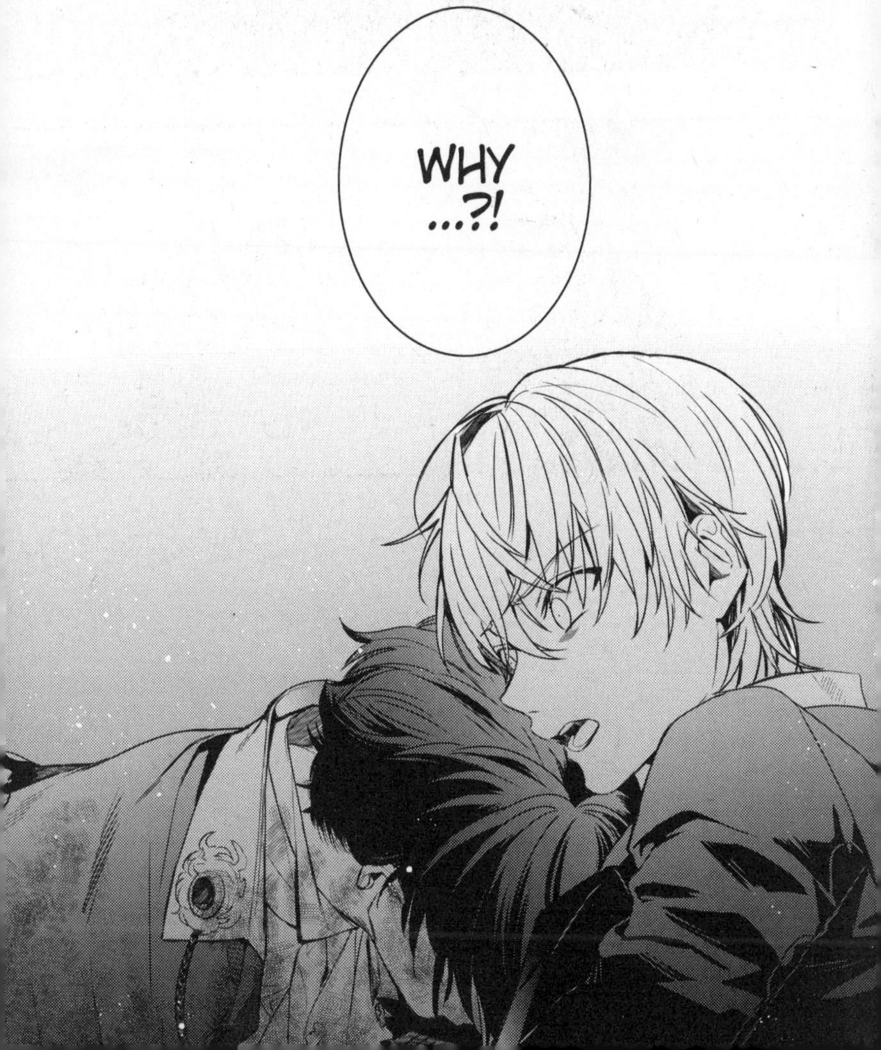
WHY
...?!

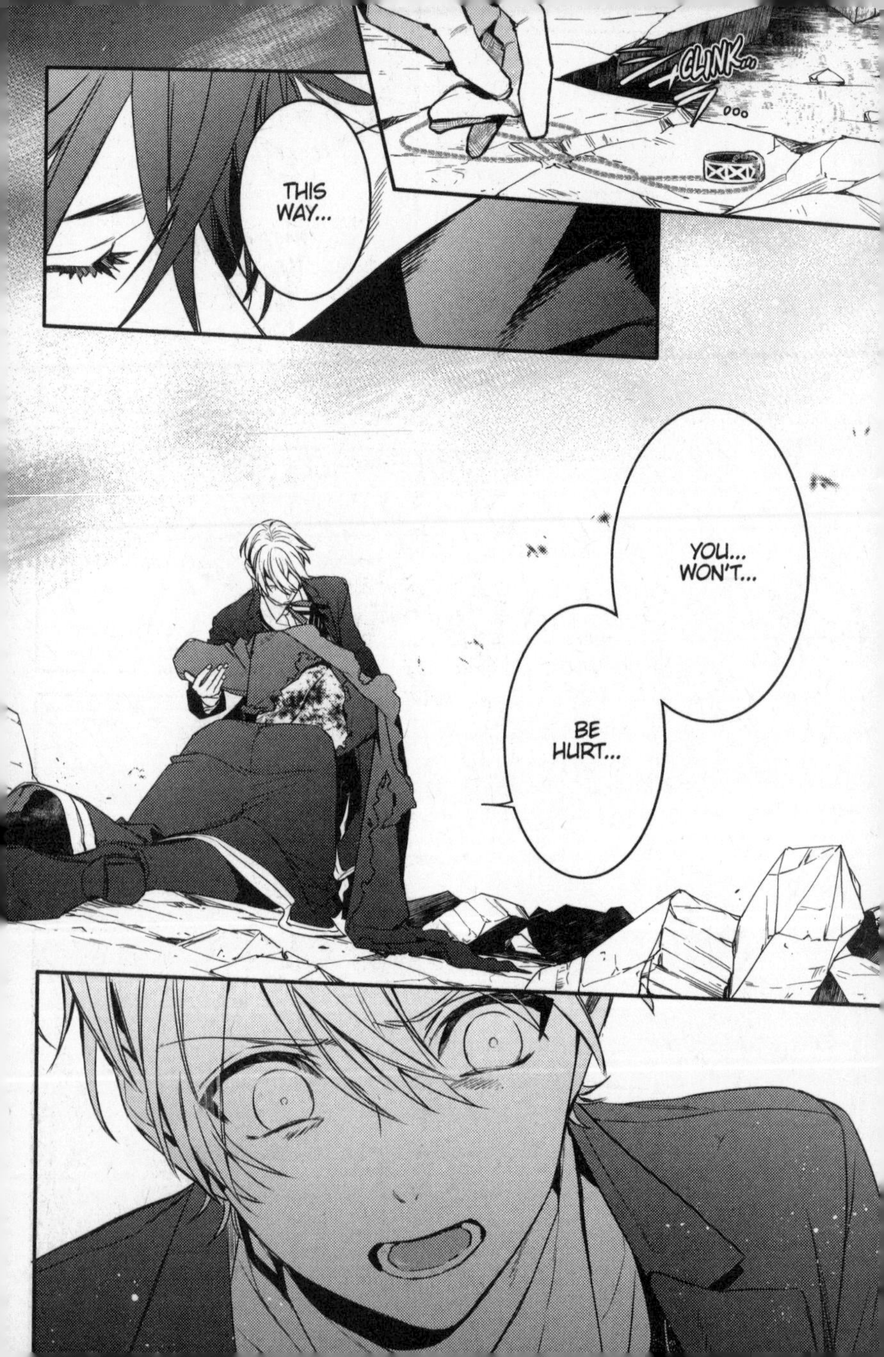
CLINK...
ooo
THIS WAY...
YOU... WON'T...
BE HURT...

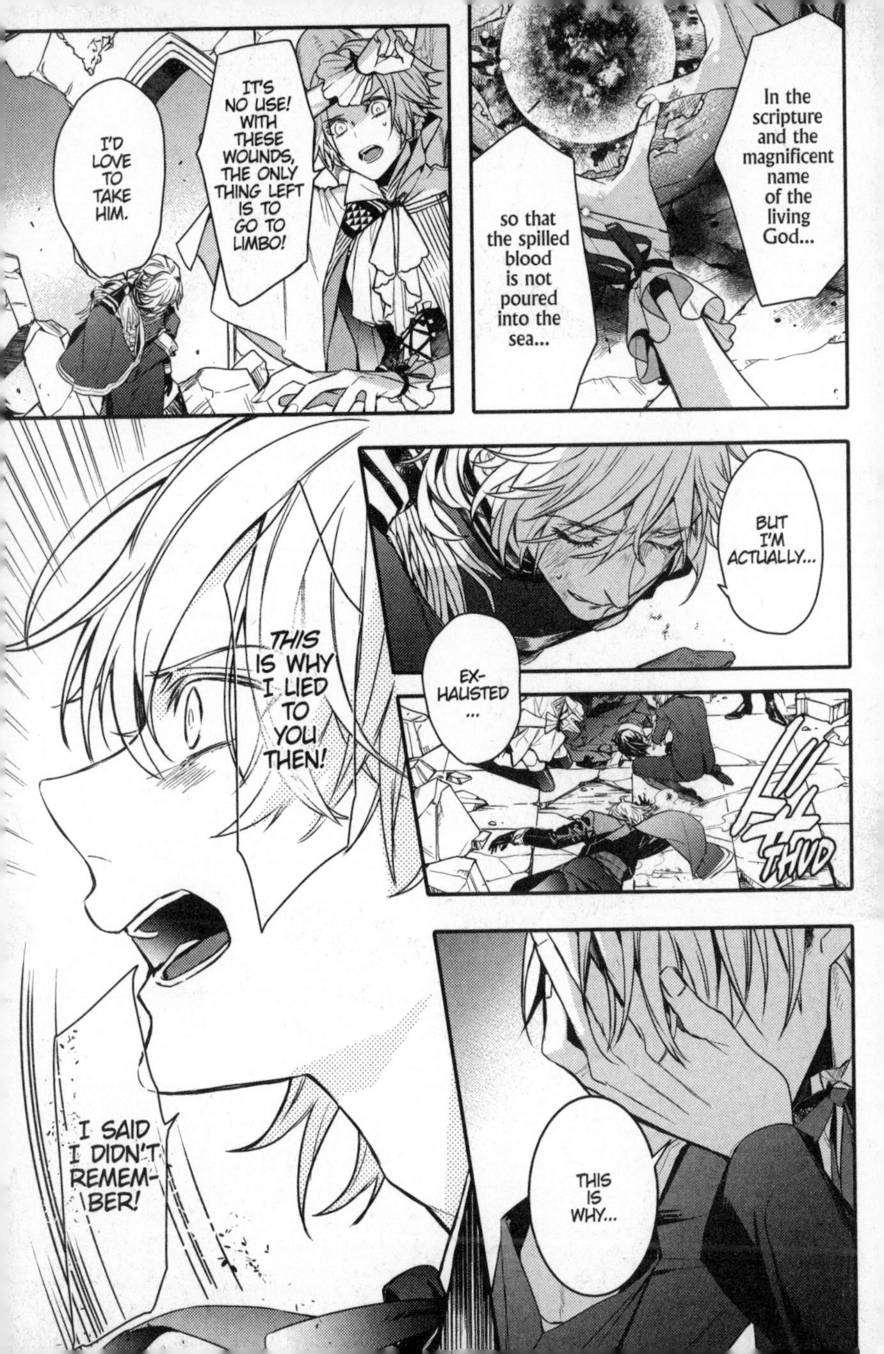

In the scripture and the magnificent name of the living God...
so that the spilled blood is not poured into the sea...
IT'S NO USE! WITH THESE WOUNDS, THE ONLY THING LEFT IS TO GO TO LIMBO!
I'D LOVE TO TAKE HIM.
BUT I'M ACTUALLY...
EX-HAUSTED...
THUD
THIS IS WHY...
THIS IS WHY I LIED TO YOU THEN!
I SAID I DIDN'T REMEMBER!

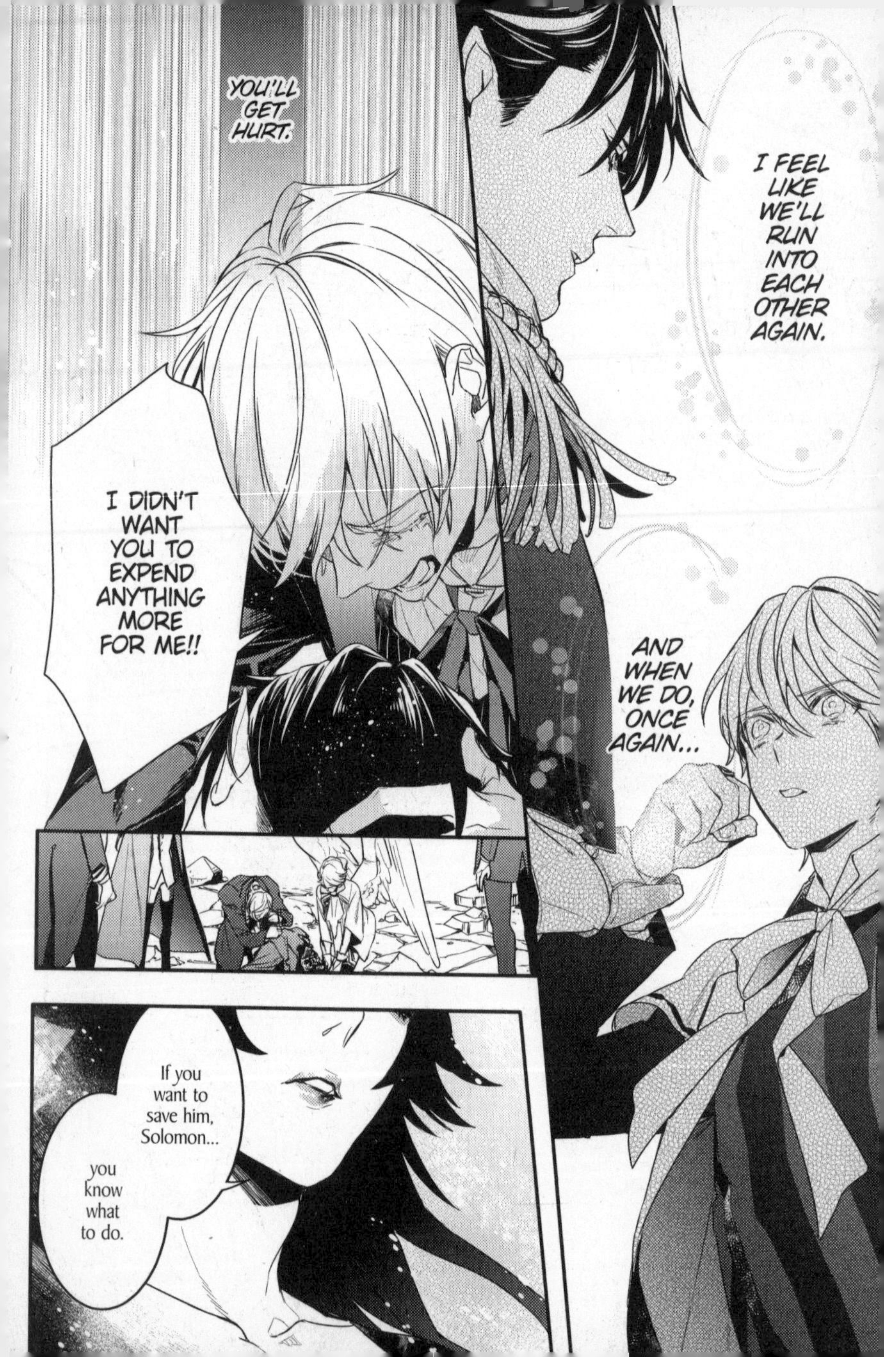
I FEEL LIKE WE'LL RUN INTO EACH OTHER AGAIN.
AND WHEN WE DO, ONCE AGAIN...
YOU'LL GET HURT.
I DIDN'T WANT YOU TO EXPEND ANYTHING MORE FOR ME!!
If you want to save him, Solomon...
you know what to do.

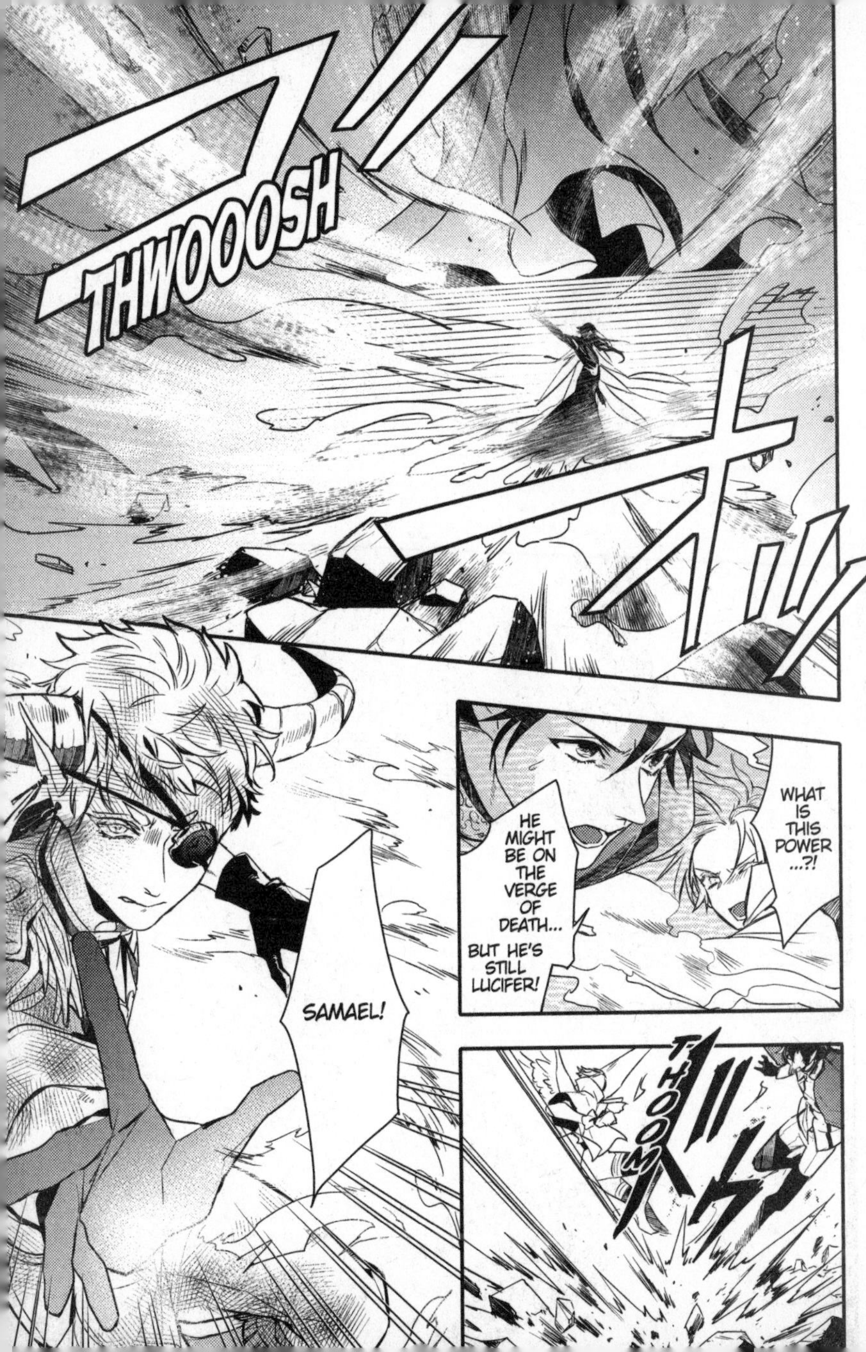
THWOOOSH
WHAT IS THIS POWER ...?!
HE MIGHT BE ON THE VERGE OF DEATH...
BUT HE'S STILL LUCIFER!
THOOOM
SAMAEL!

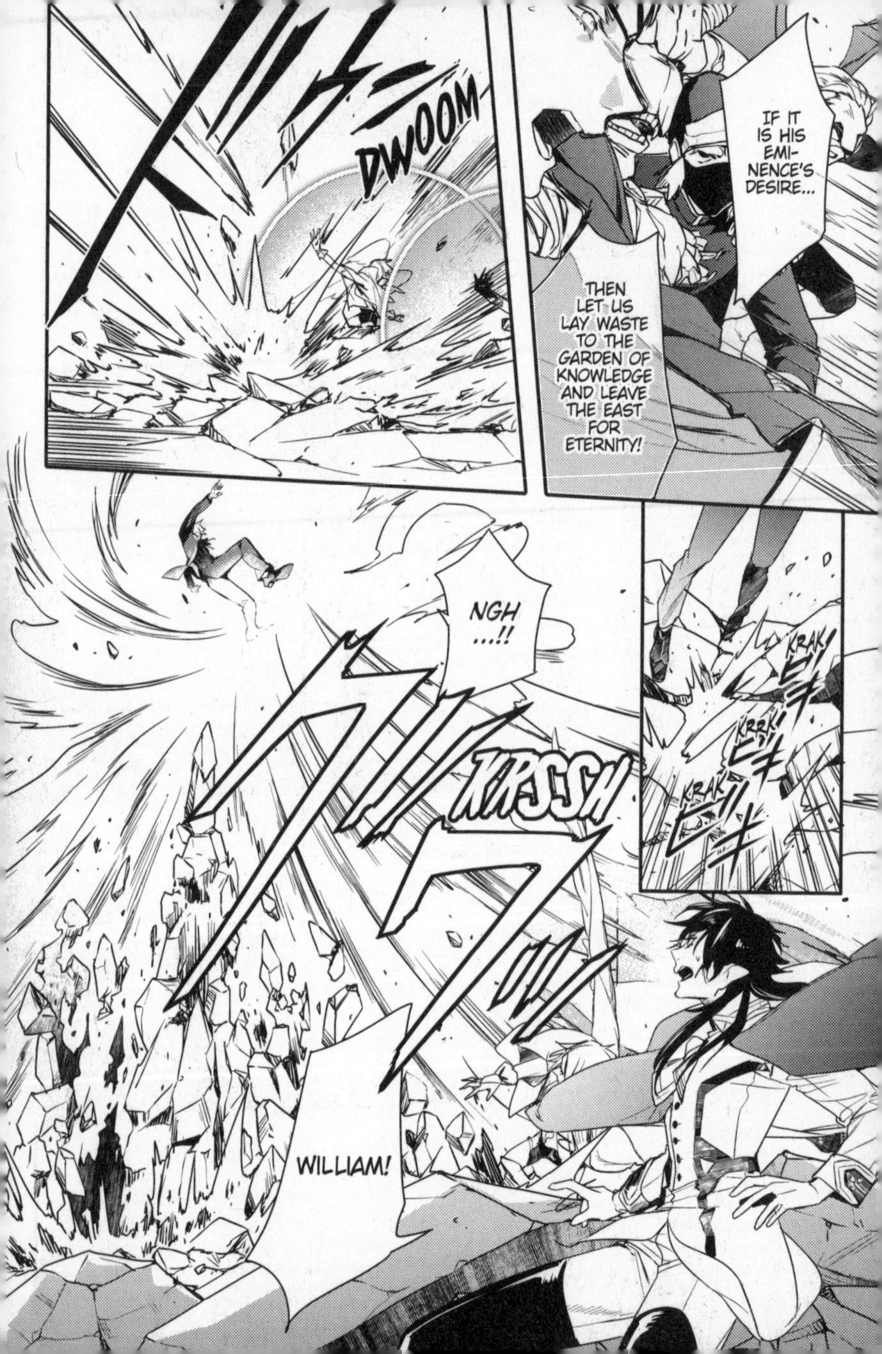
IF IT IS HIS EMINENCE'S DESIRE...
THEN LET US LAY WASTE TO THE GARDEN OF KNOWLEDGE AND LEAVE THE EAST FOR ETERNITY!
DWOOM
KRAK
KRRK
KRAK
NGH ...!!
KRSSH
WILLIAM!

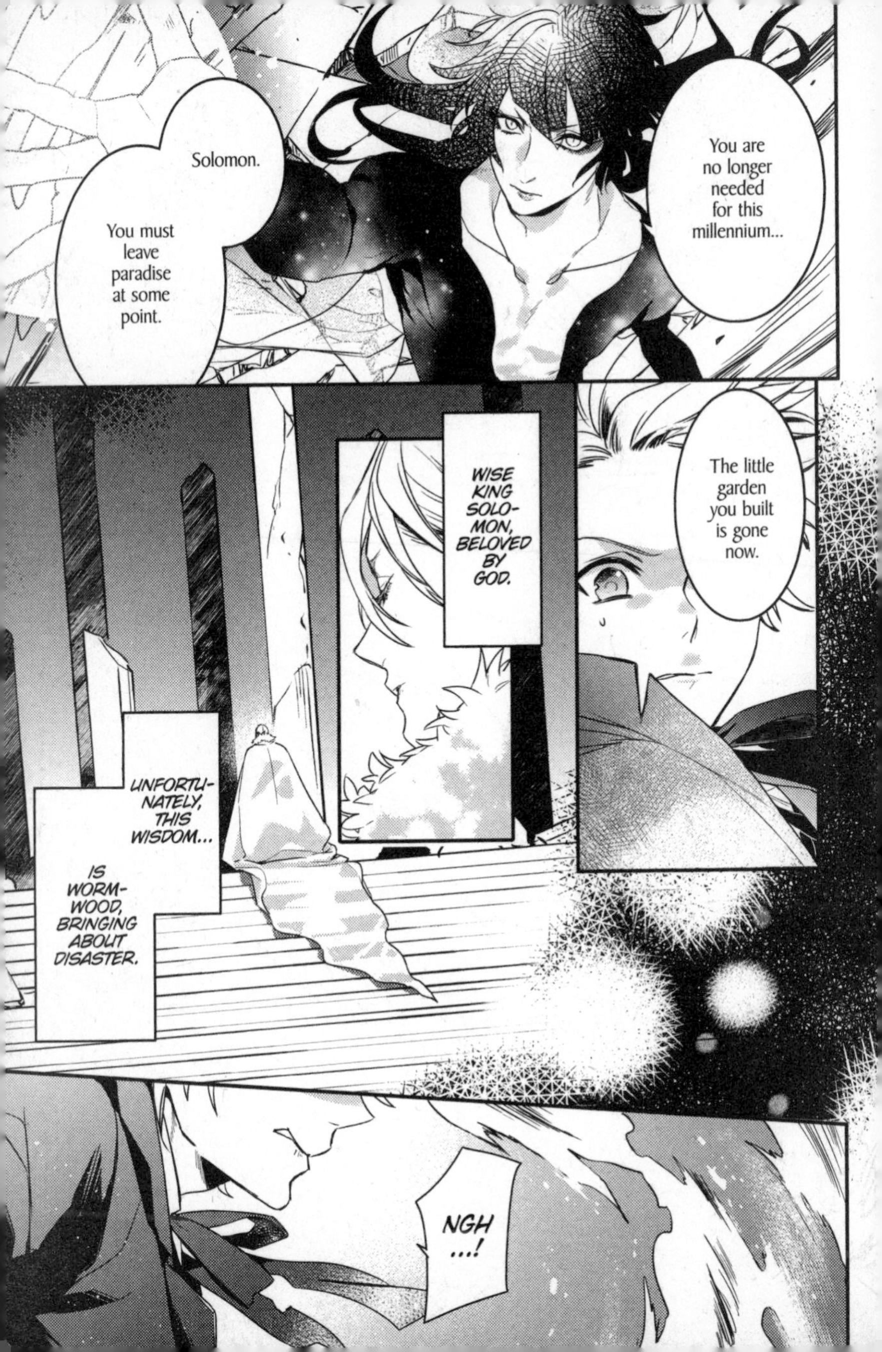
You are no longer needed for this millennium...
Solomon.
You must leave paradise at some point.
The little garden you built is gone now.
WISE KING SOLOMON, BELOVED BY GOD.
UNFORTUNATELY, THIS WISDOM...
IS WORMWOOD, BRINGING ABOUT DISASTER.
NGH...!

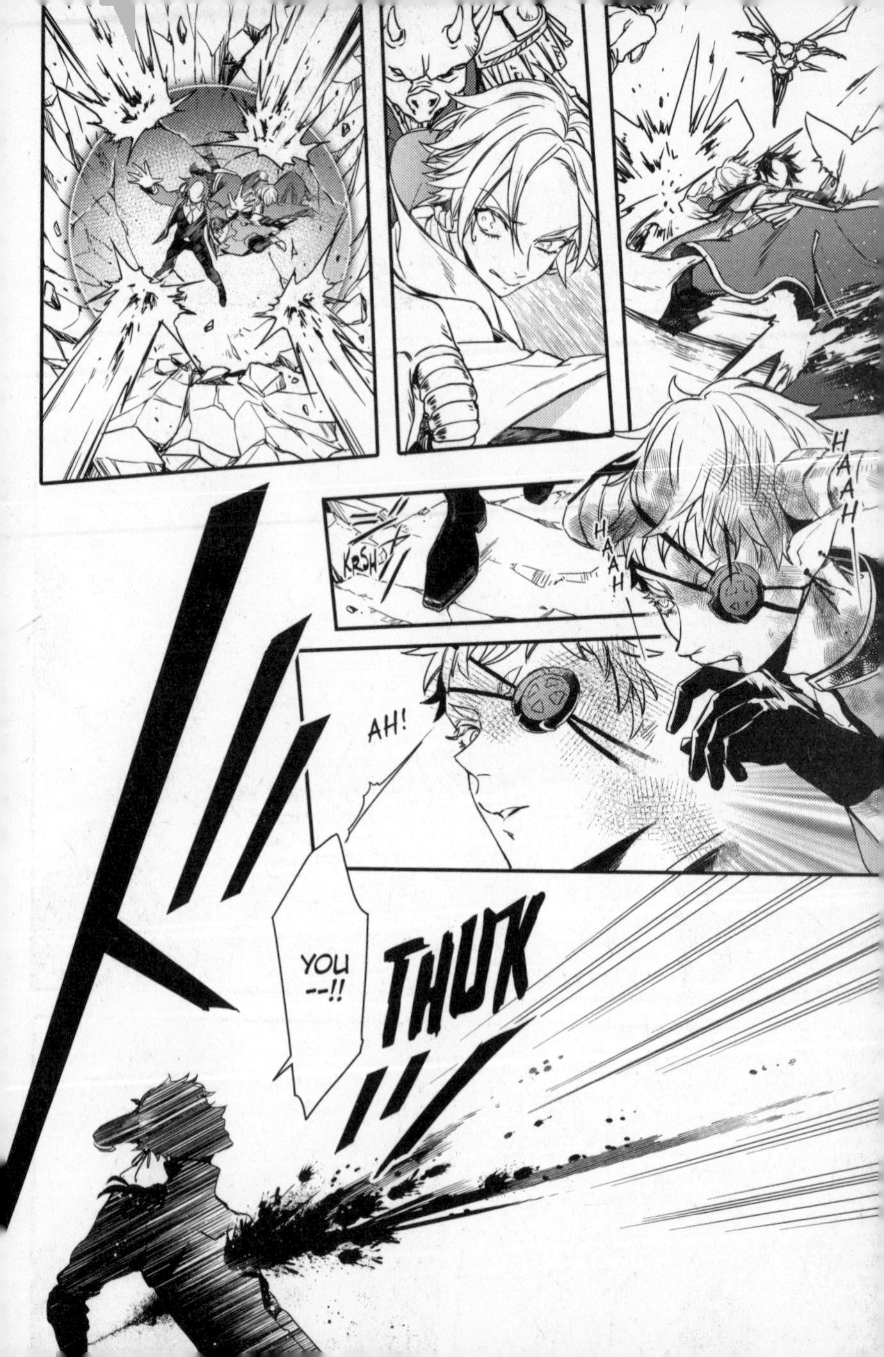

HAAH
HAAH
KRSH
AH!
YOU --!!
THUK

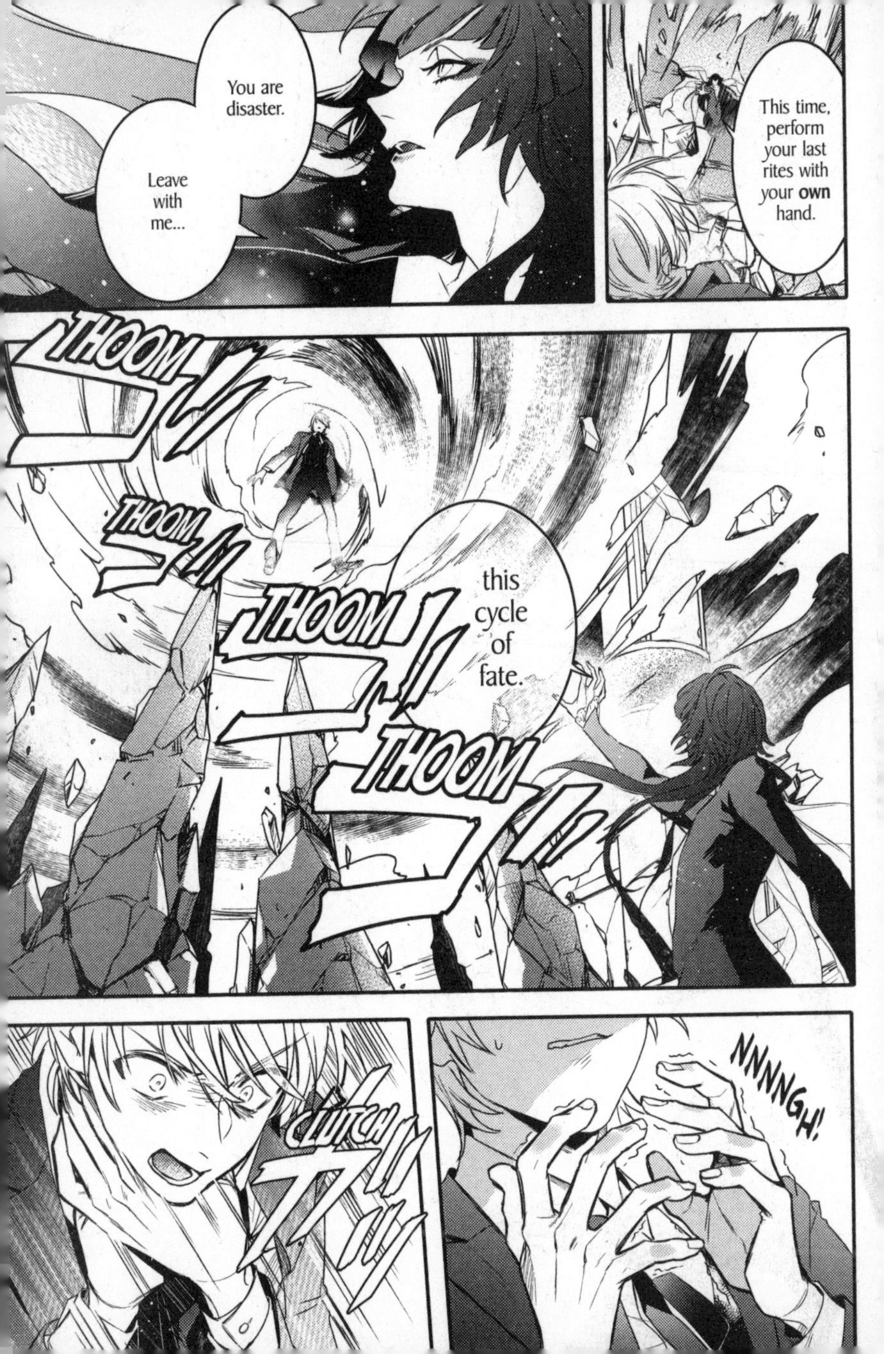
This time, perform your last rites with your own hand.
You are disaster.
Leave with me...
this cycle of fate.
THOOM
THOOM
THOOM
THOOM
NNNNGH!
CLUTCH

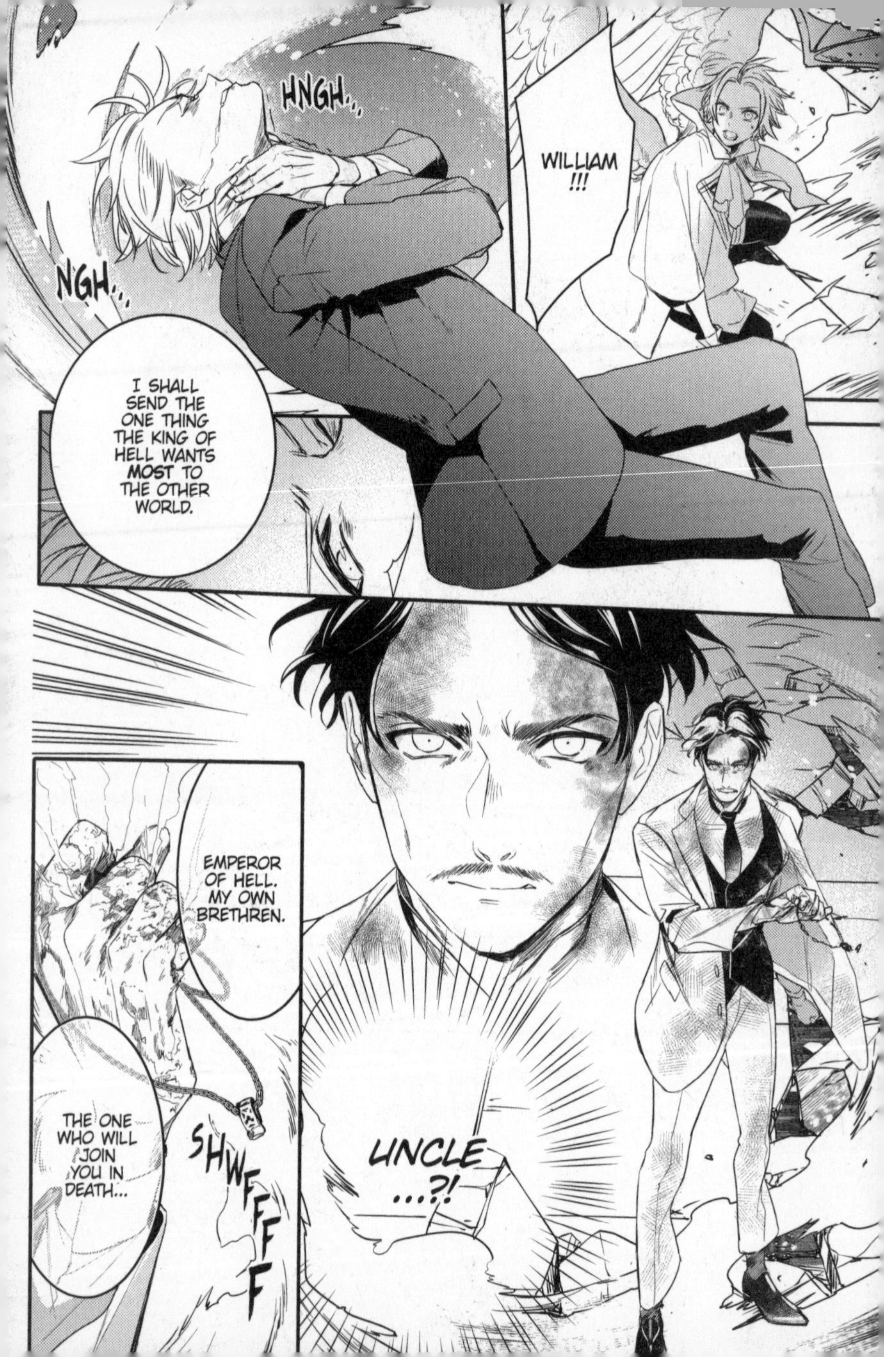

WILLIAM !!!
HNGH...
NGH...
I SHALL SEND THE ONE THING THE KING OF HELL WANTS MOST TO THE OTHER WORLD.
UNCLE ...?!
EMPEROR OF HELL. MY OWN BRETHREN.
THE ONE WHO WILL JOIN YOU IN DEATH...
SHWFFFF

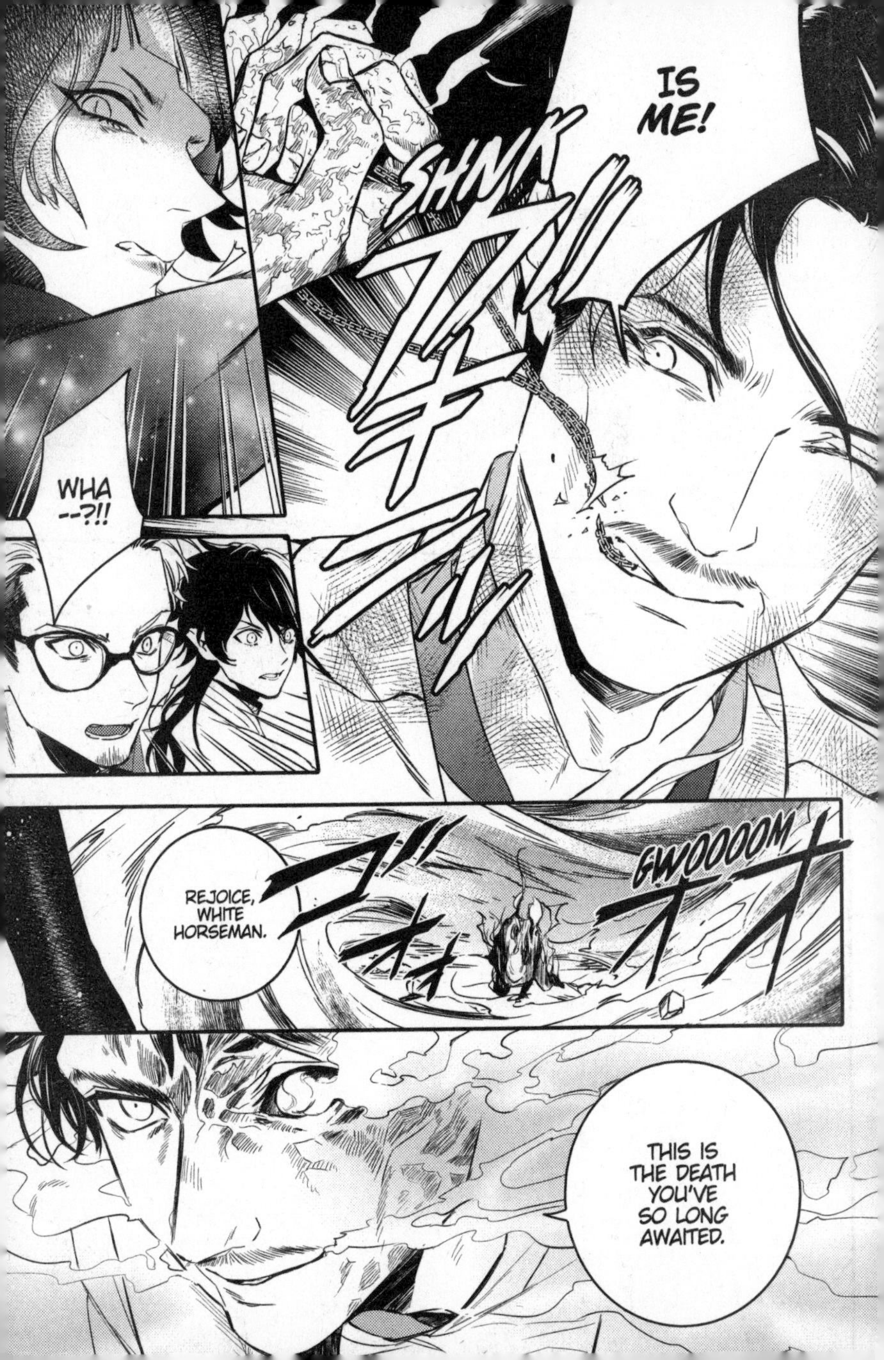
IS ME!
SHINK
WHA--?!!
GWOOOOM
REJOICE, WHITE HORSEMAN.
THIS IS THE DEATH YOU'VE SO LONG AWAITED.

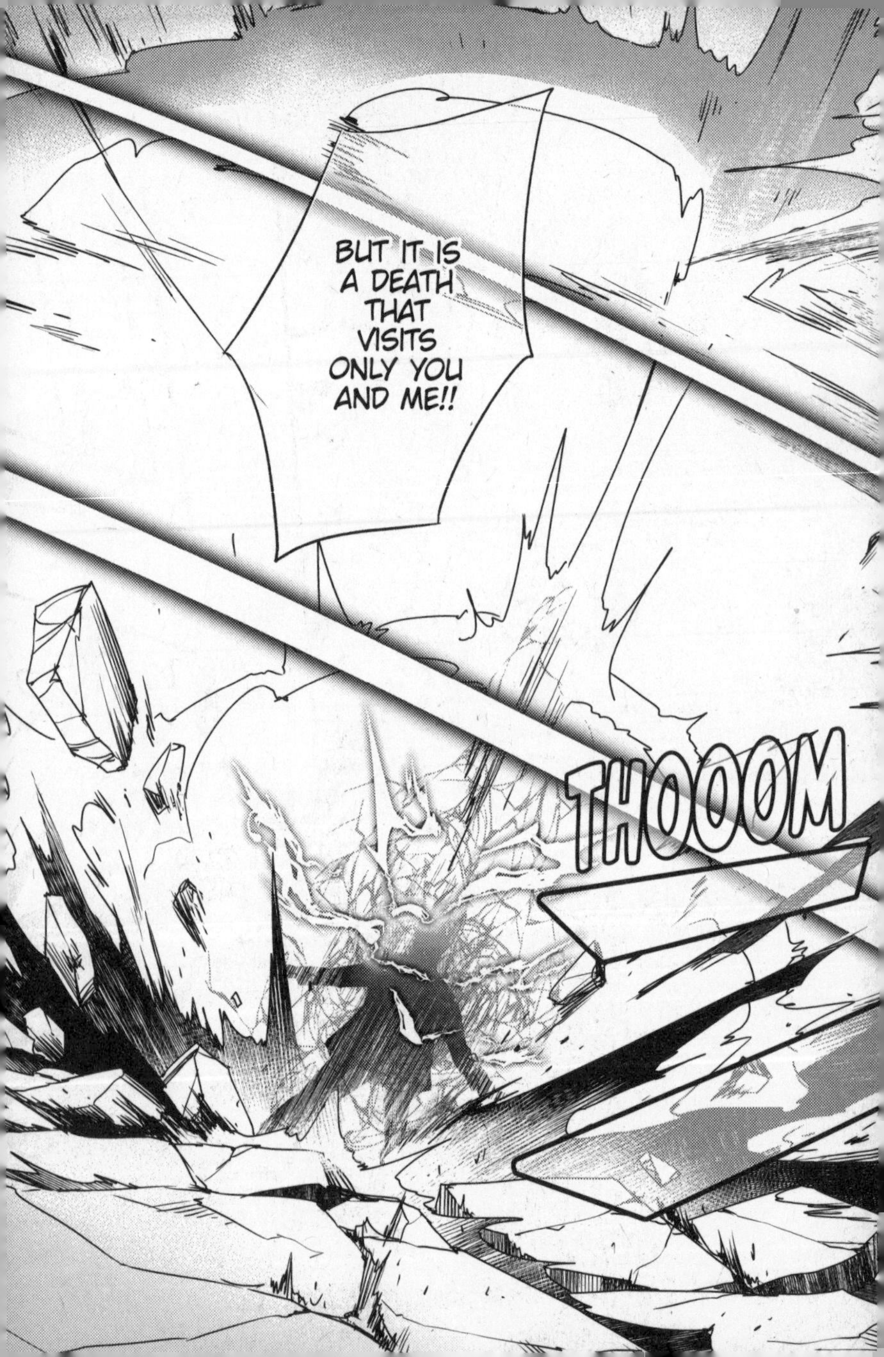
BUT IT IS A DEATH THAT VISITS ONLY YOU AND ME!!
THOOOM

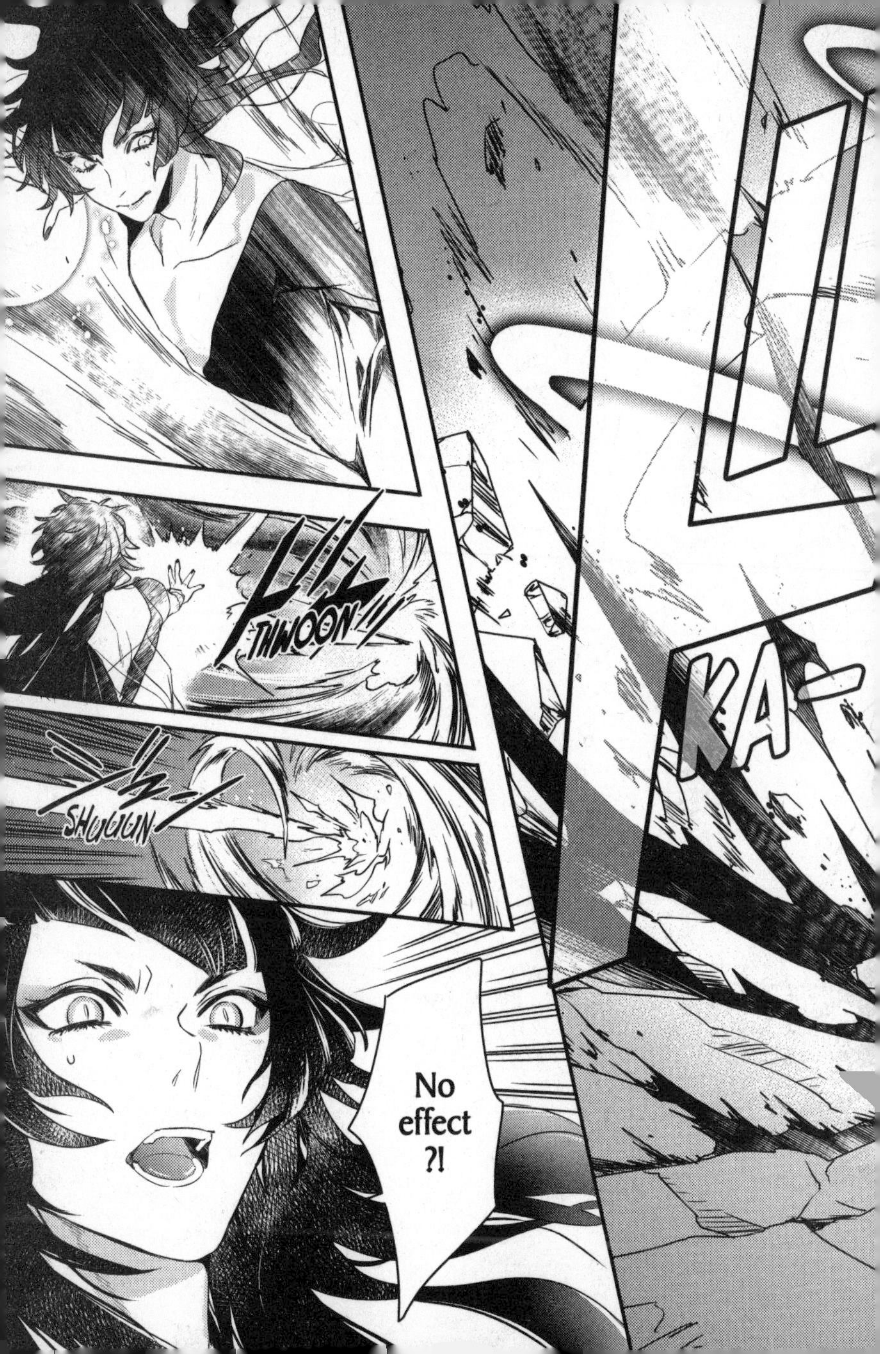
KA-
THWOON!!!
SHUUUN
No effect ?!

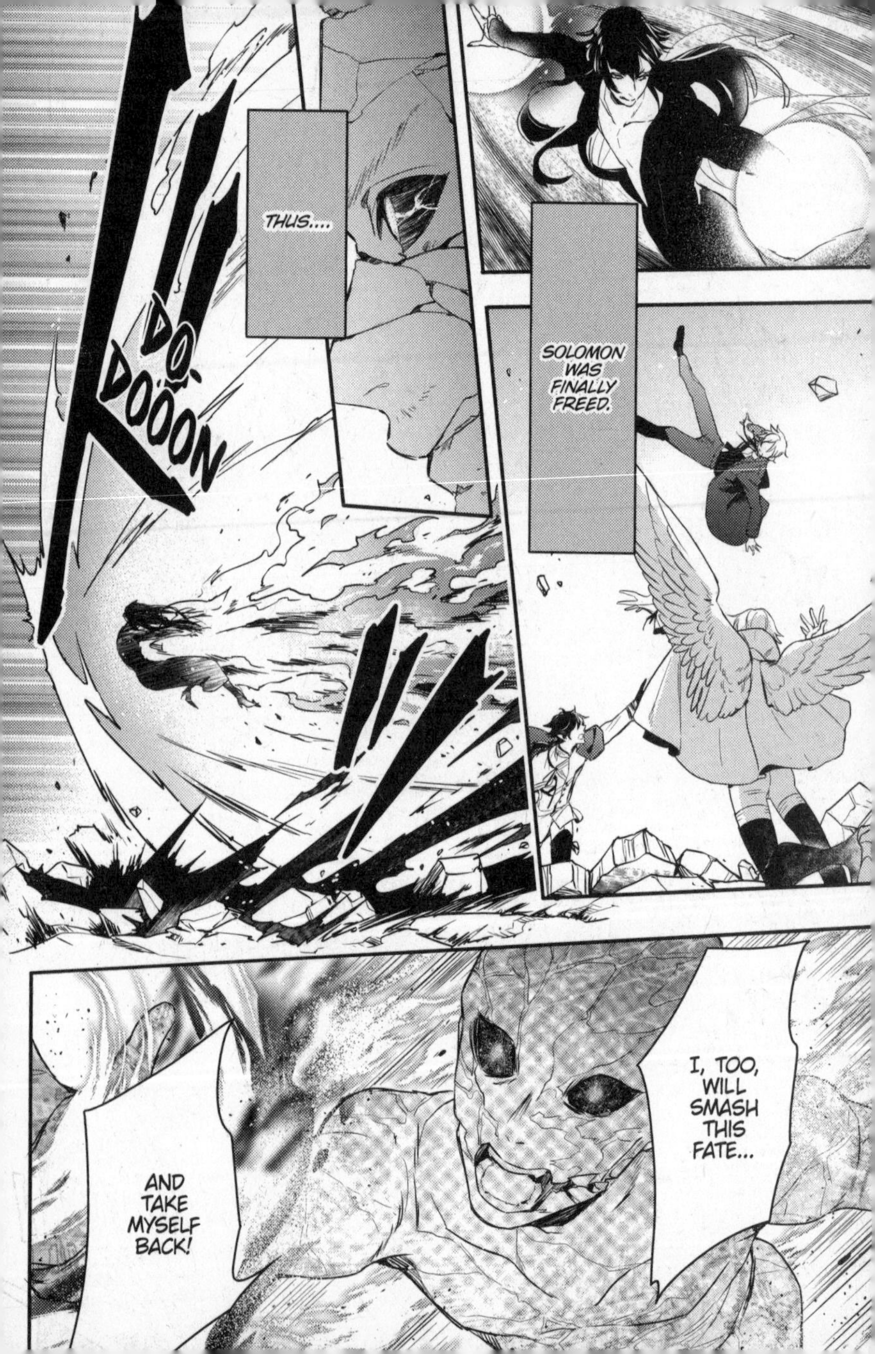
THUS....
SOLOMON WAS FINALLY FREED.
DO-DOOON
I, TOO, WILL SMASH THIS FATE...
AND TAKE MYSELF BACK!

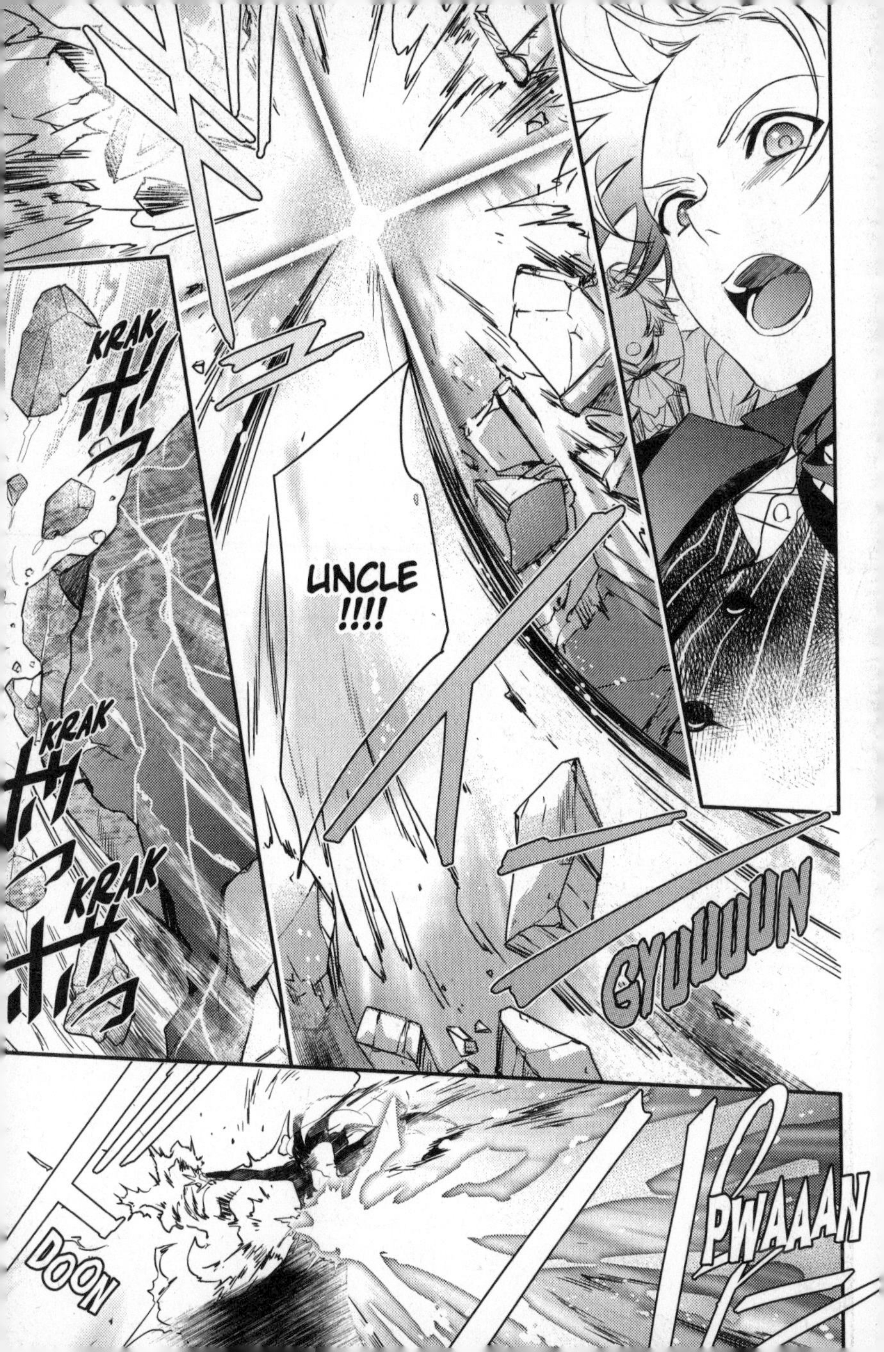

UNCLE!!!!
GYUUUUN
KRAK
KRAK
KRAK
PWAAAN
DOON

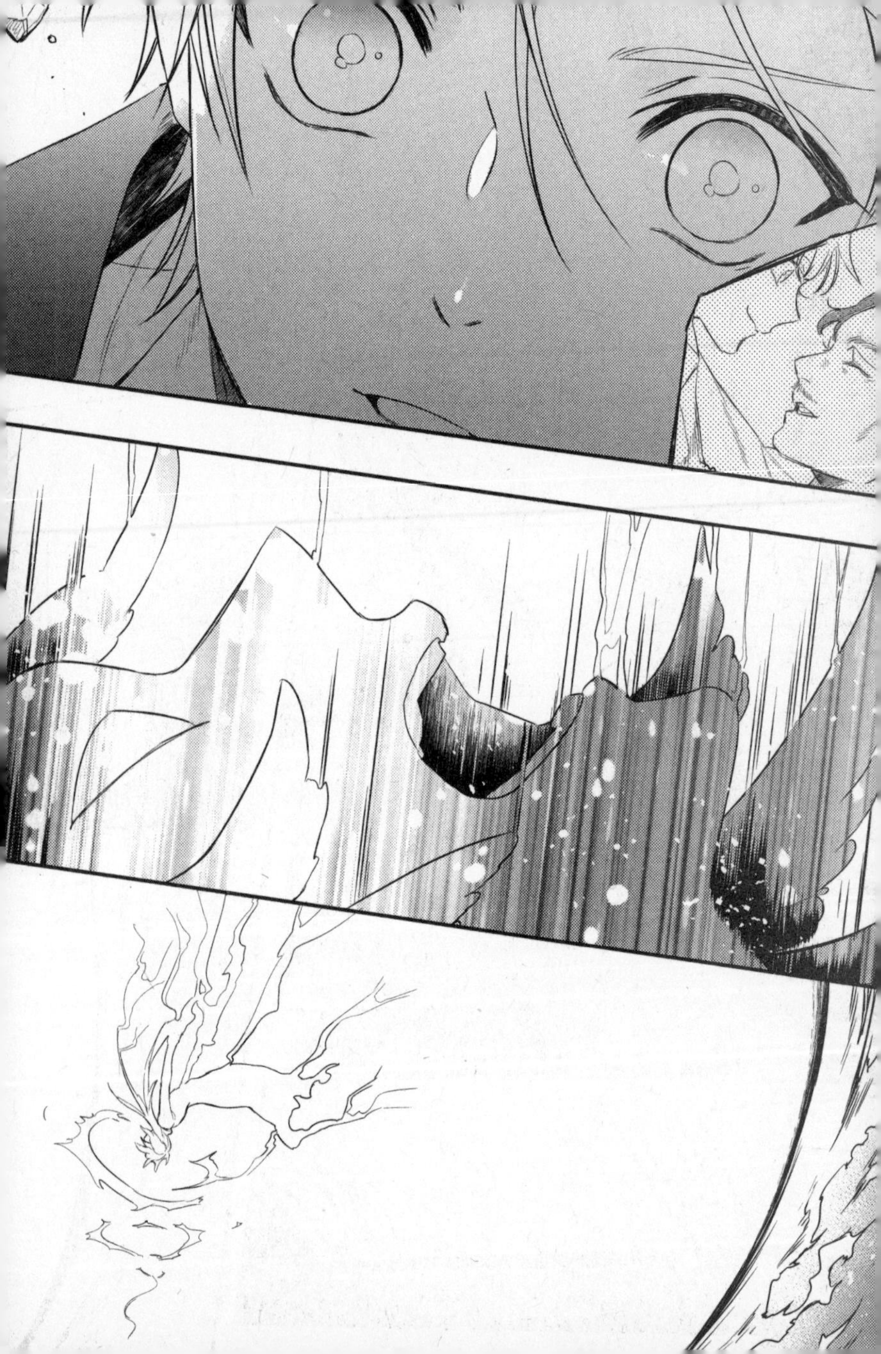

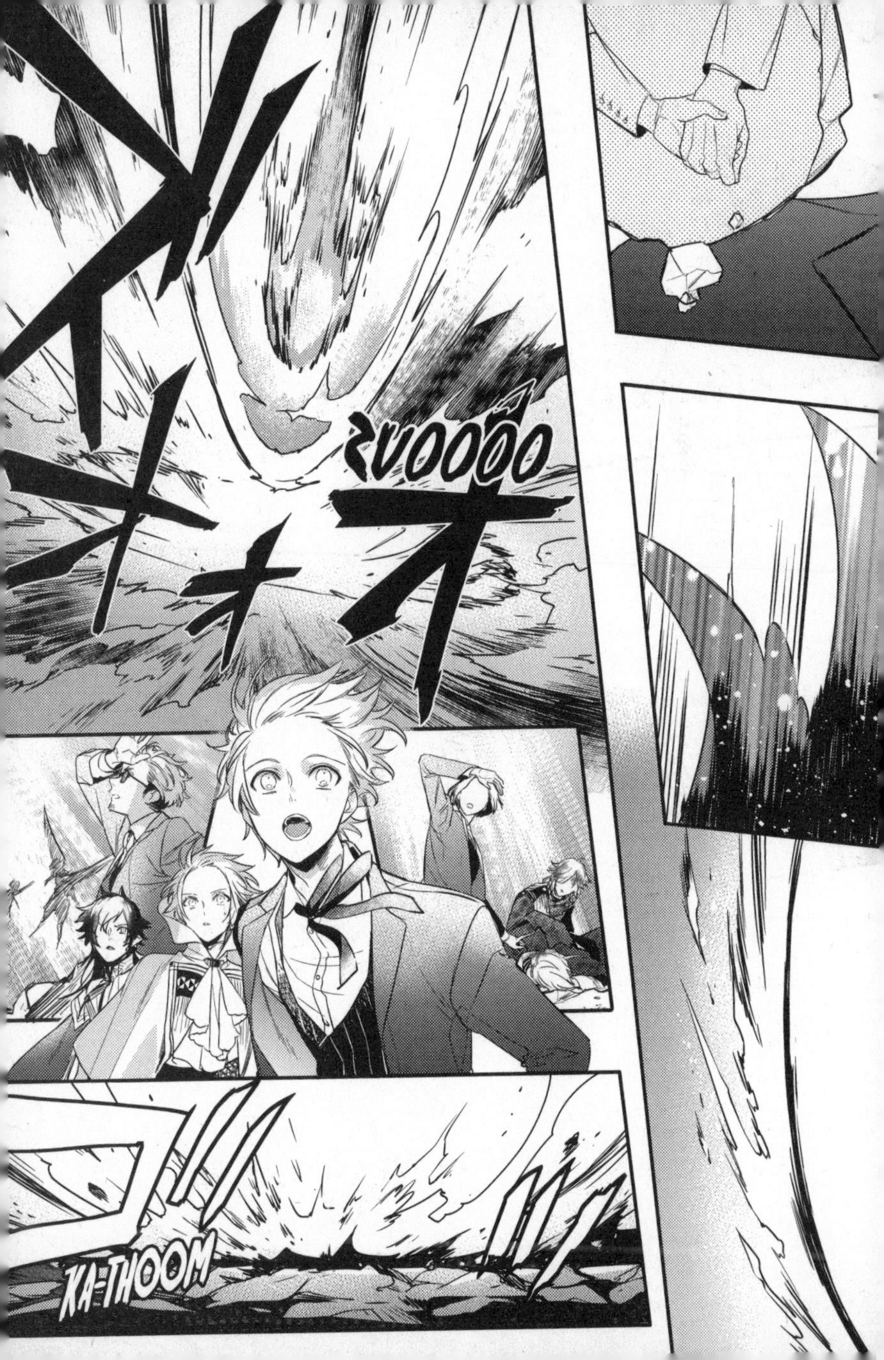
ZVOOOO
KA-THOOM

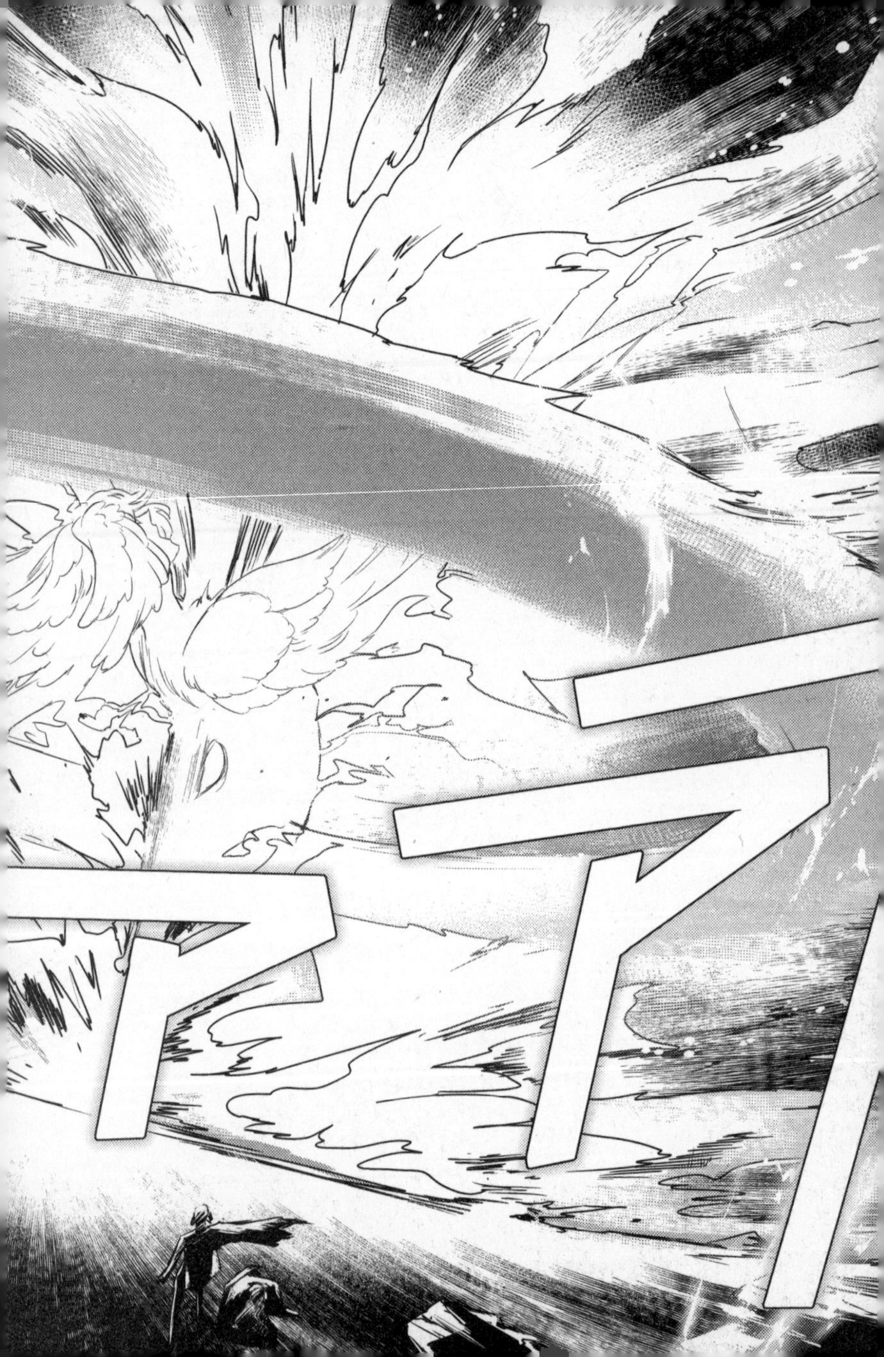
アア

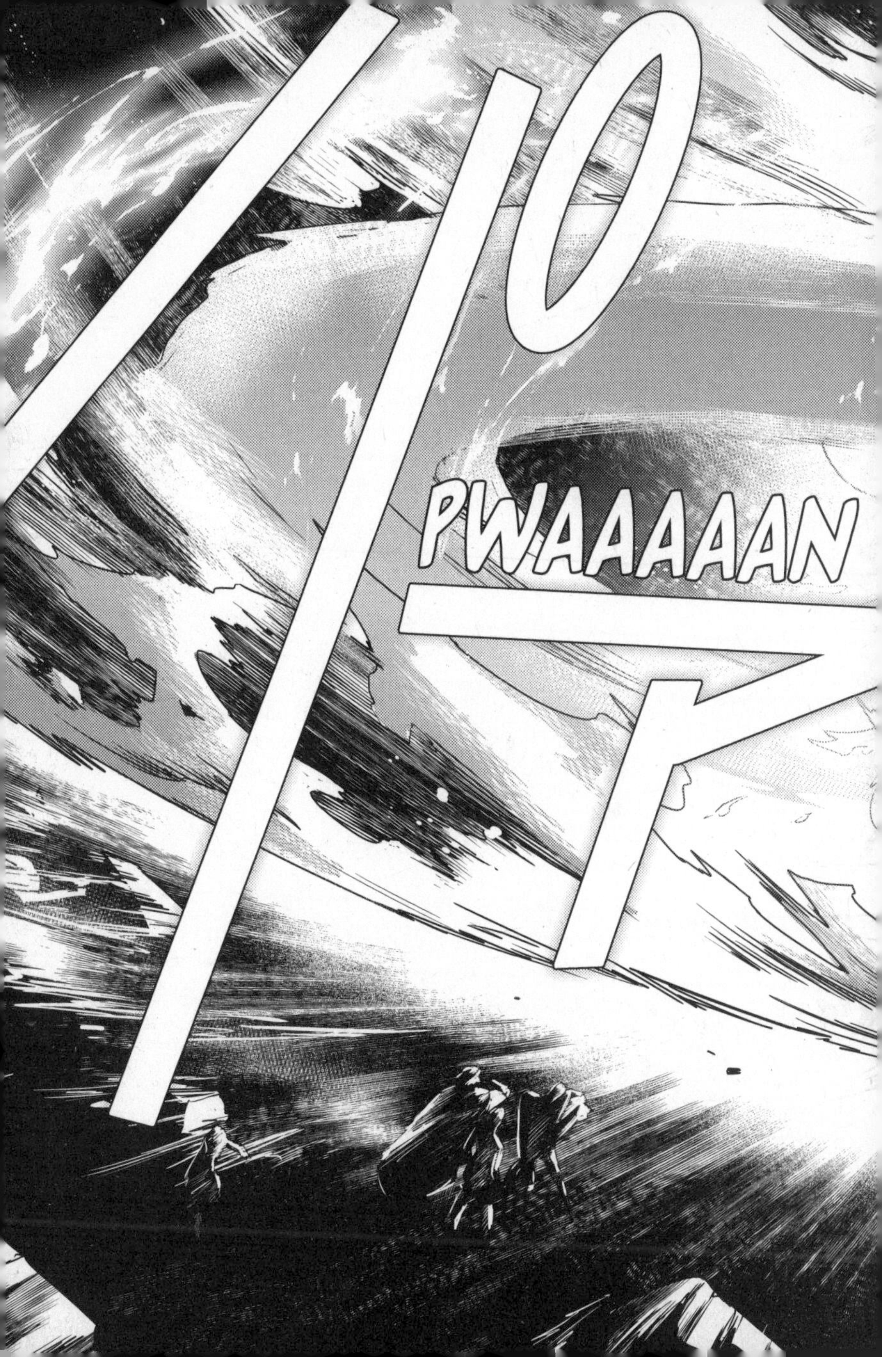
PWAAAAAN

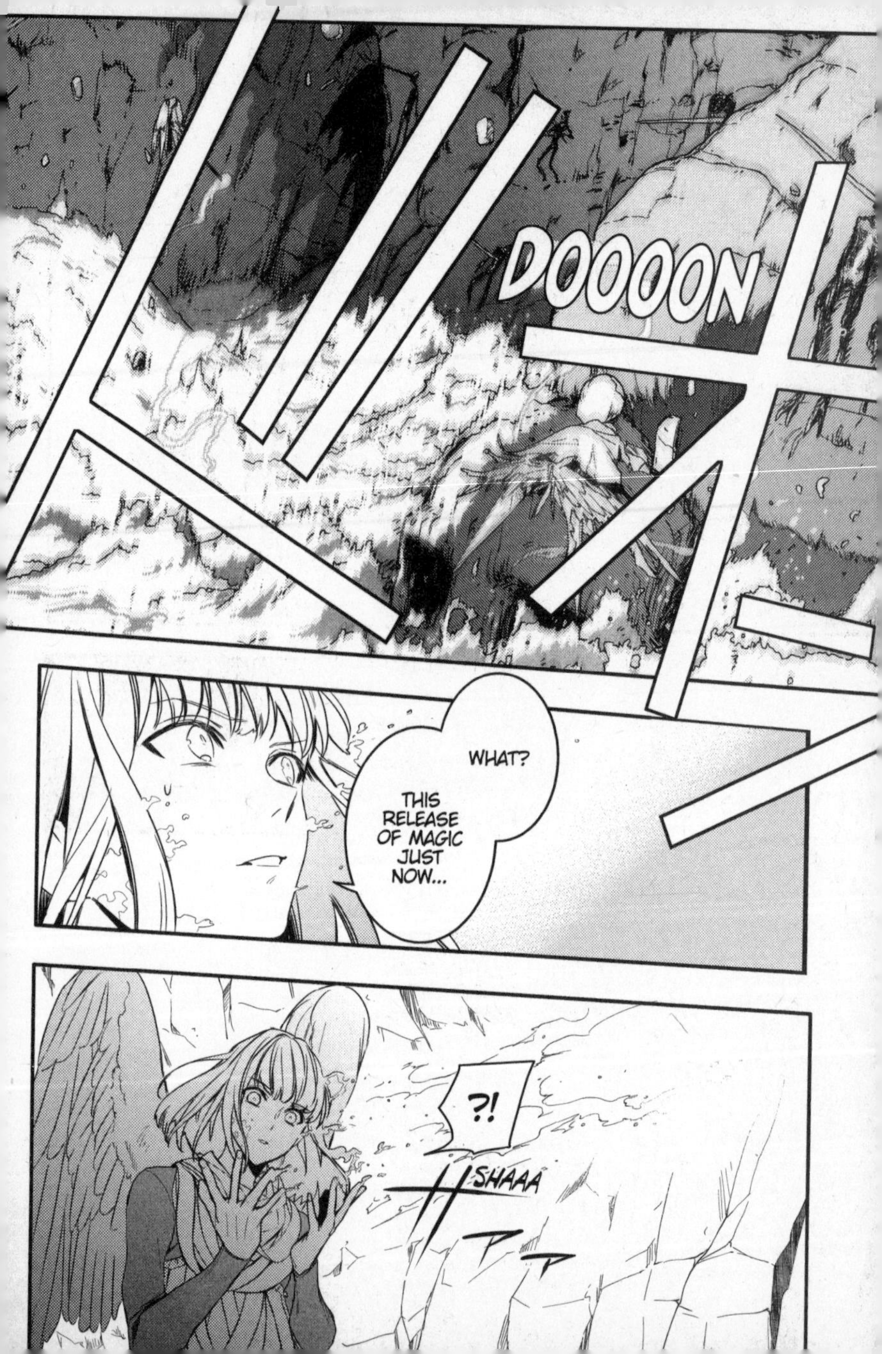
DOOOON
WHAT?
THIS RELEASE OF MAGIC JUST NOW...
?!
SHAAA

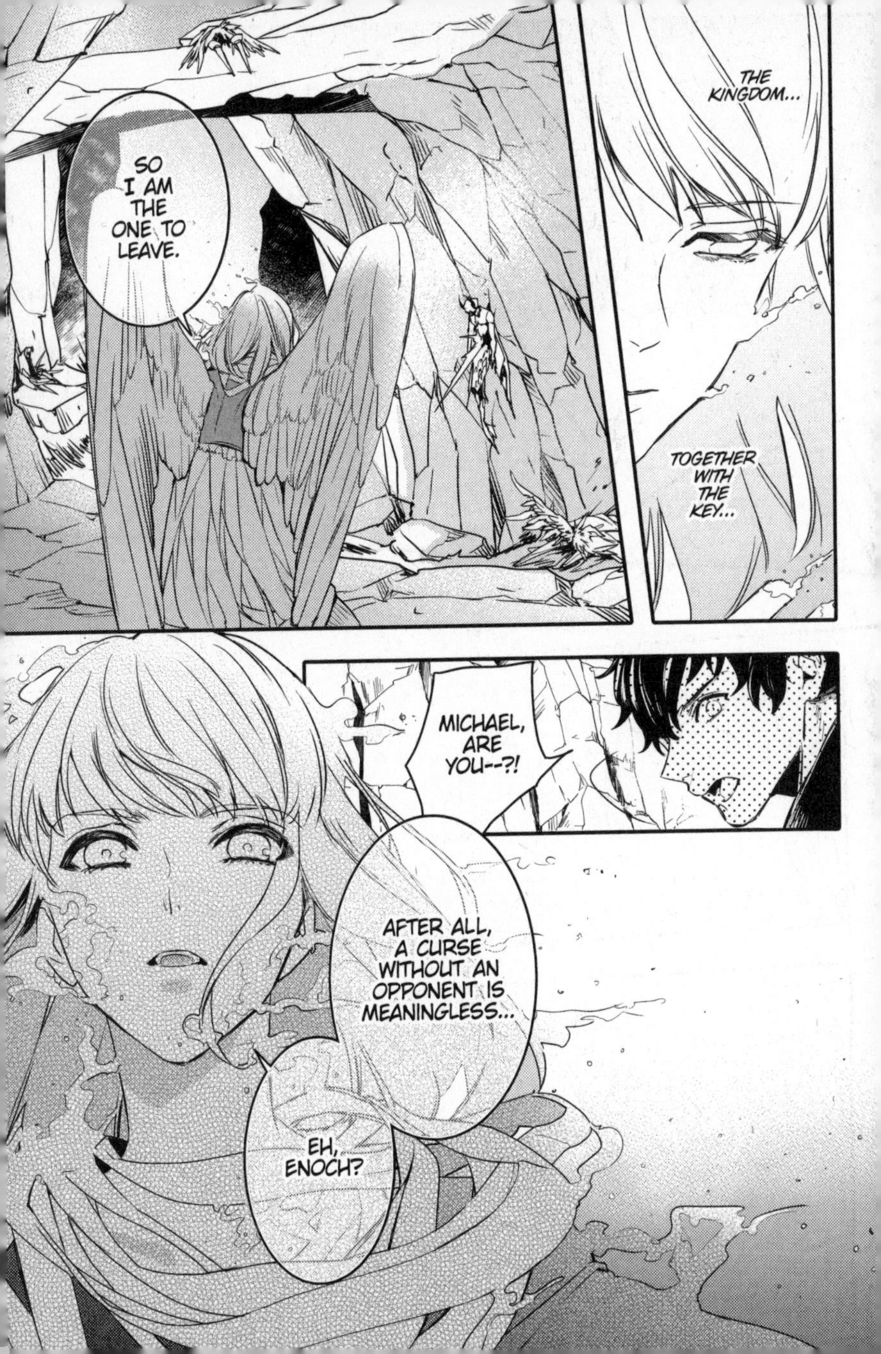
THE KINGDOM...
TOGETHER WITH THE KEY...
SO I AM THE ONE TO LEAVE.
MICHAEL, ARE YOU--?!
AFTER ALL, A CURSE WITHOUT AN OPPONENT IS MEANINGLESS...
EH, ENOCH?

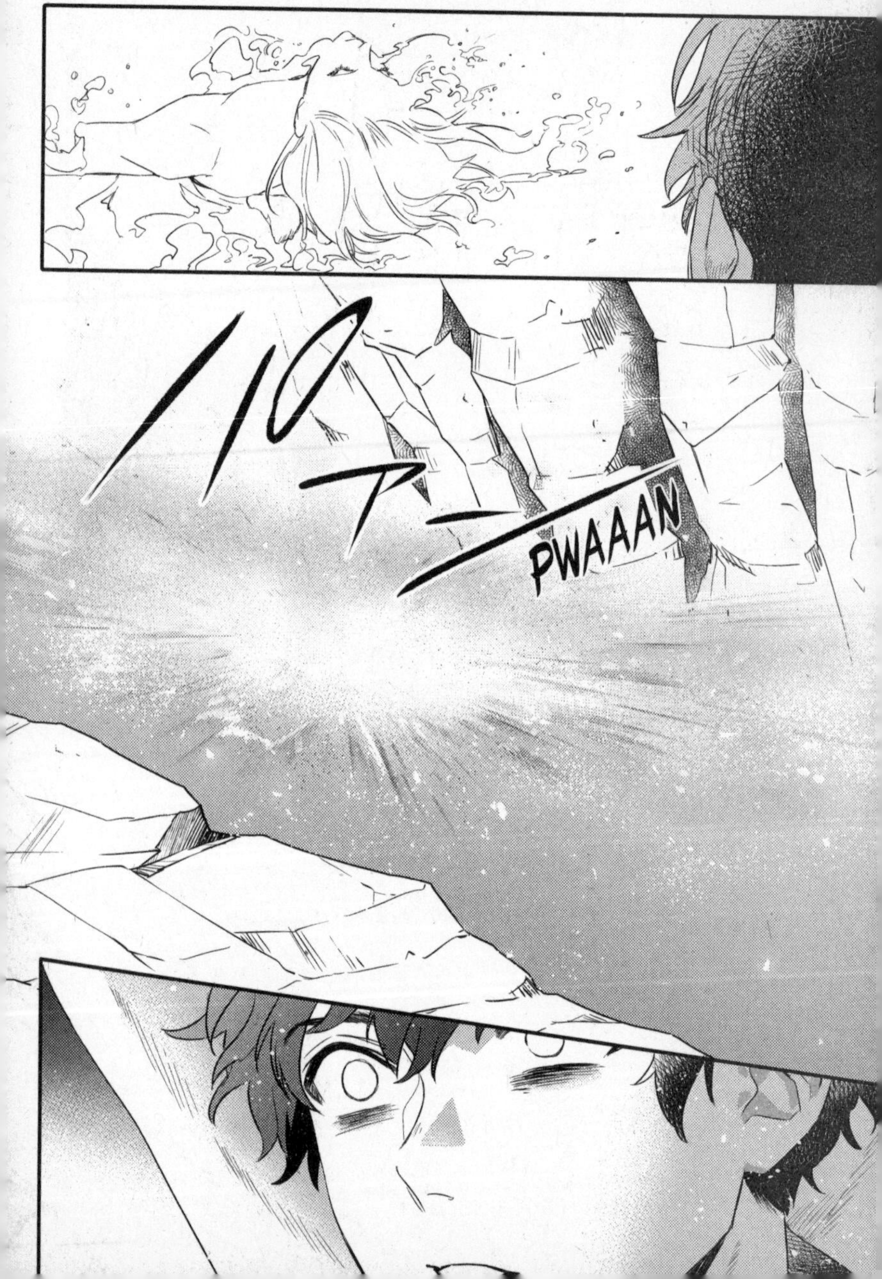
パァー
PWAAAN

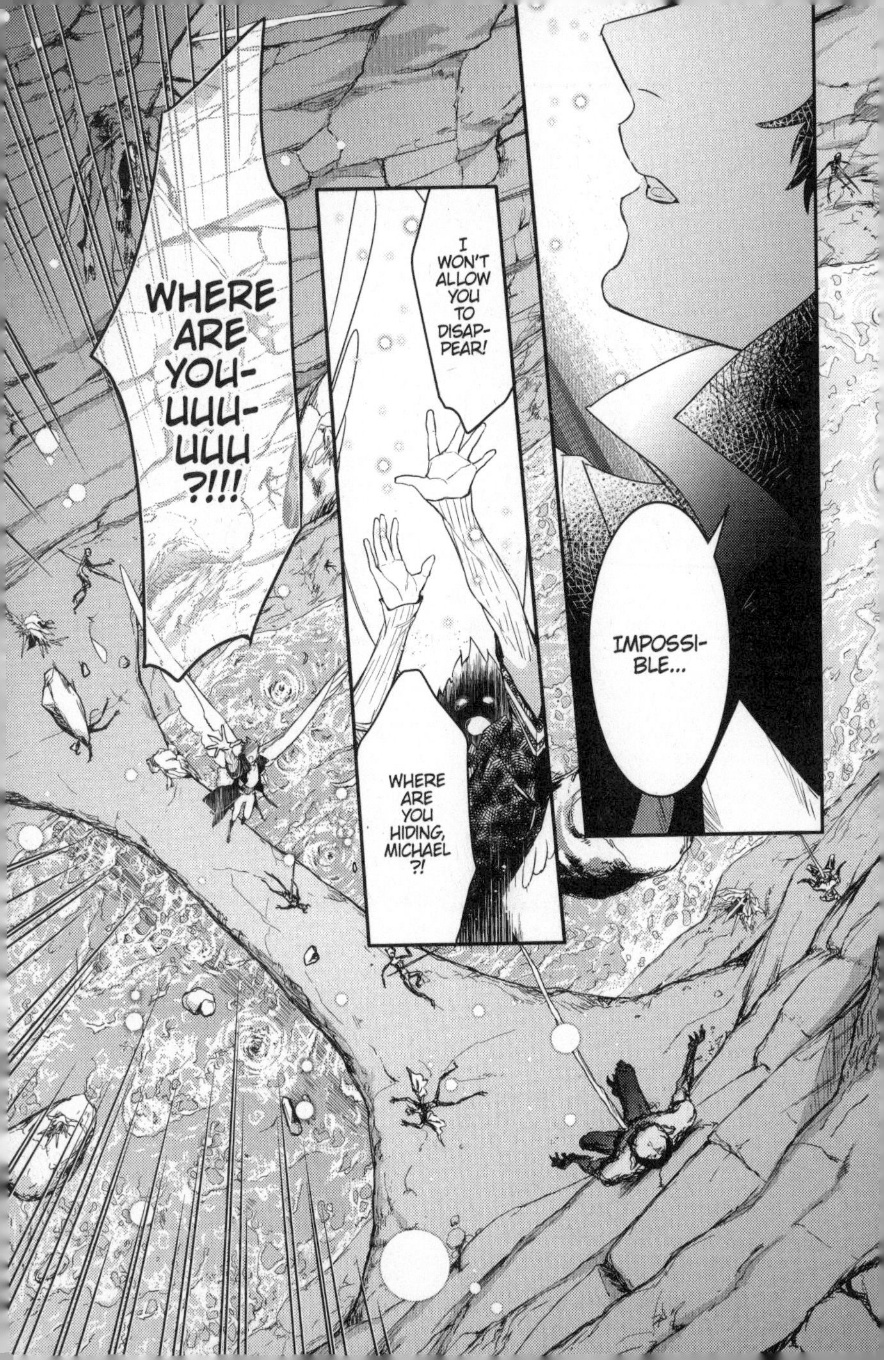
IMPOSSIBLE...
I WON'T ALLOW YOU TO DISAPPEAR!
WHERE ARE YOU HIDING, MICHAEL?!
WHERE ARE YOU-UUUU-UUUU?!!!

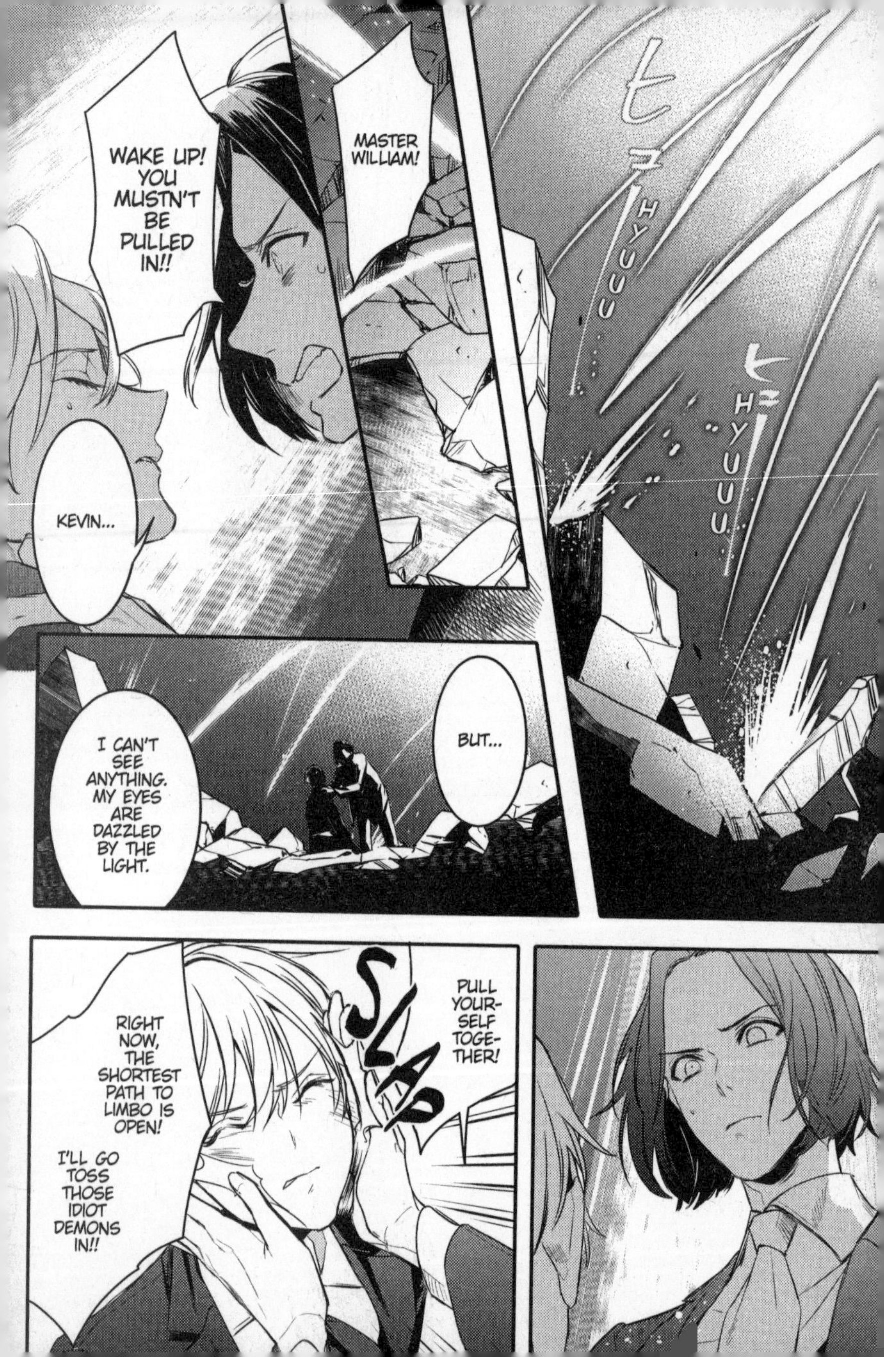

ヒュ
HYUUUU
ヒュ
HYUUUU
MASTER WILLIAM!
WAKE UP! YOU MUSTN'T BE PULLED IN!!
KEVIN...
BUT...
I CAN'T SEE ANYTHING. MY EYES ARE DAZZLED BY THE LIGHT.
PULL YOURSELF TOGETHER!
SLAP
RIGHT NOW, THE SHORTEST PATH TO LIMBO IS OPEN!
I'LL GO TOSS THOSE IDIOT DEMONS IN!!

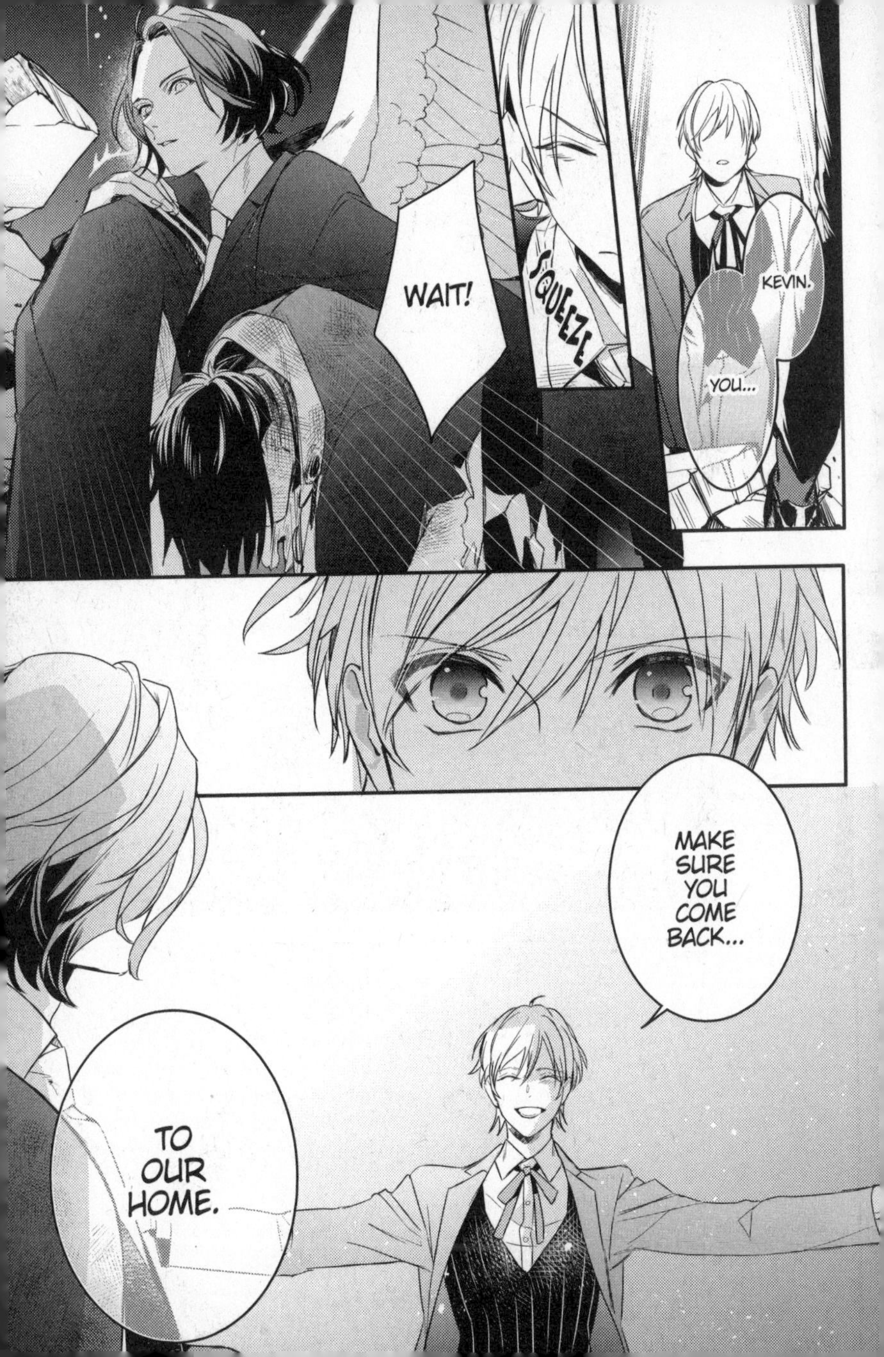
KEVIN.
YOU...
SQUEEZE
WAIT!
MAKE SURE YOU COME BACK...
TO OUR HOME.

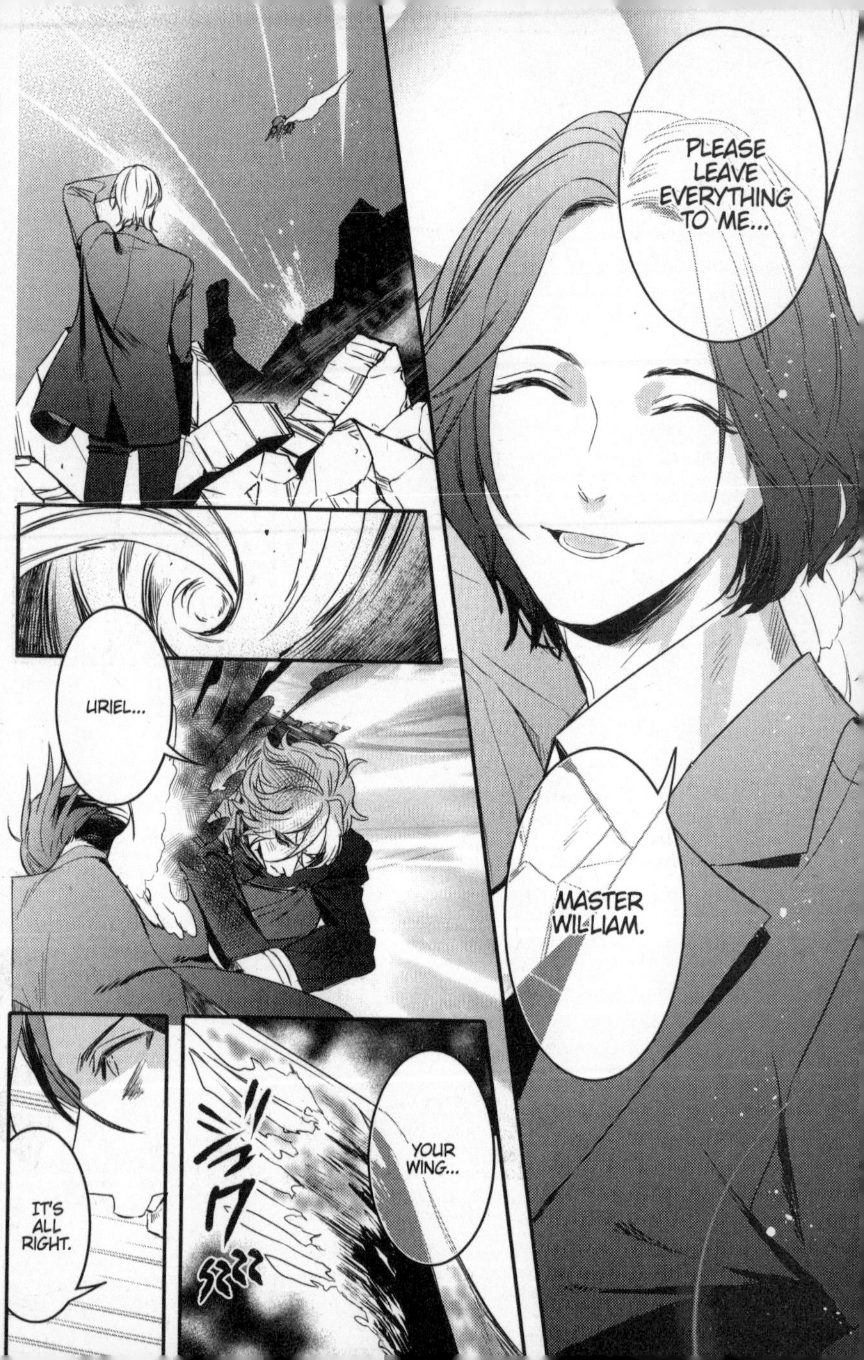
PLEASE LEAVE EVERYTHING TO ME...
MASTER WILLIAM.
URIEL...
YOUR WING...
IT'S ALL RIGHT.

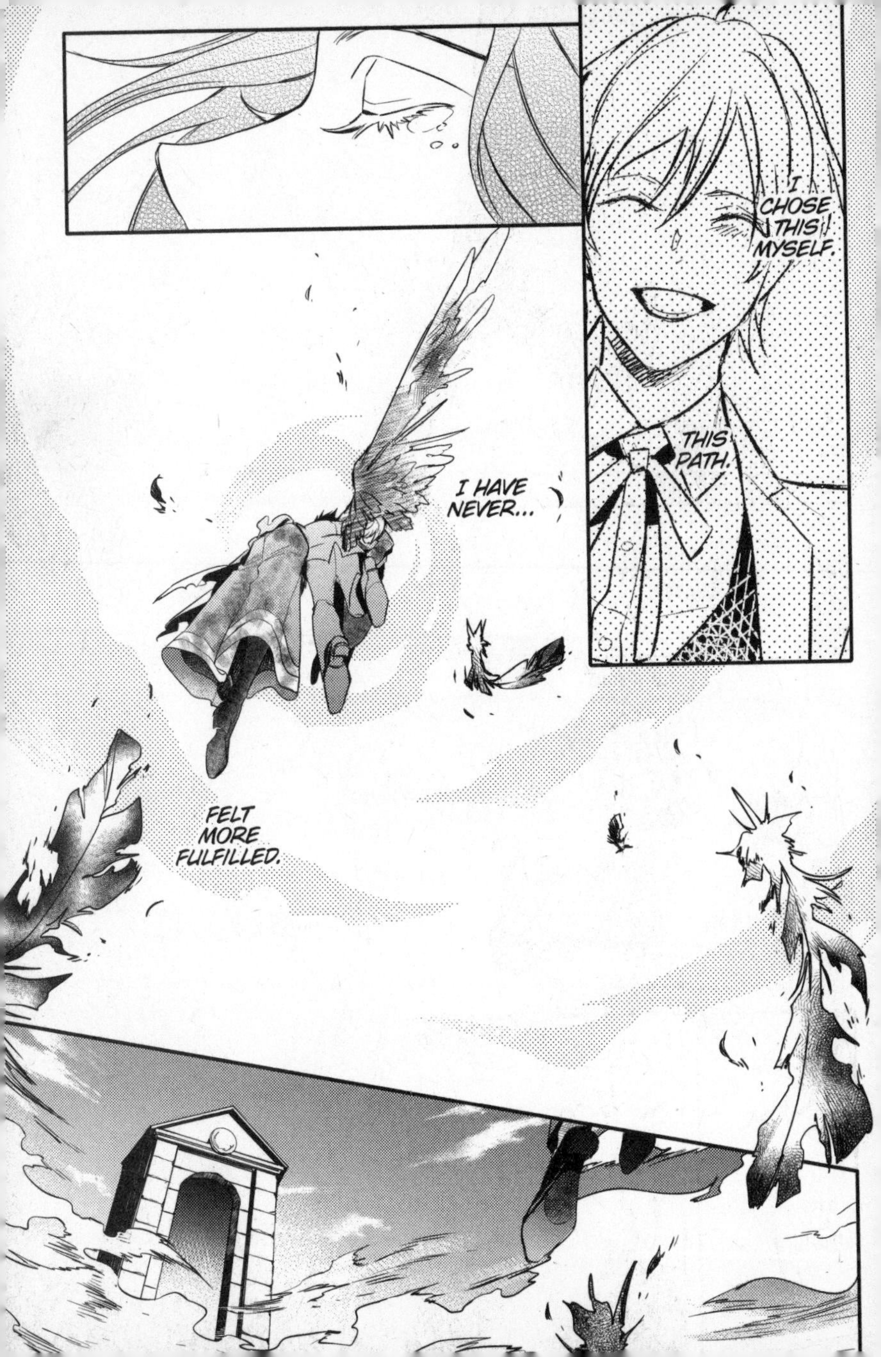
I CHOSE THIS MYSELF.
THIS PATH.
I HAVE NEVER...
FELT MORE FULFILLED.

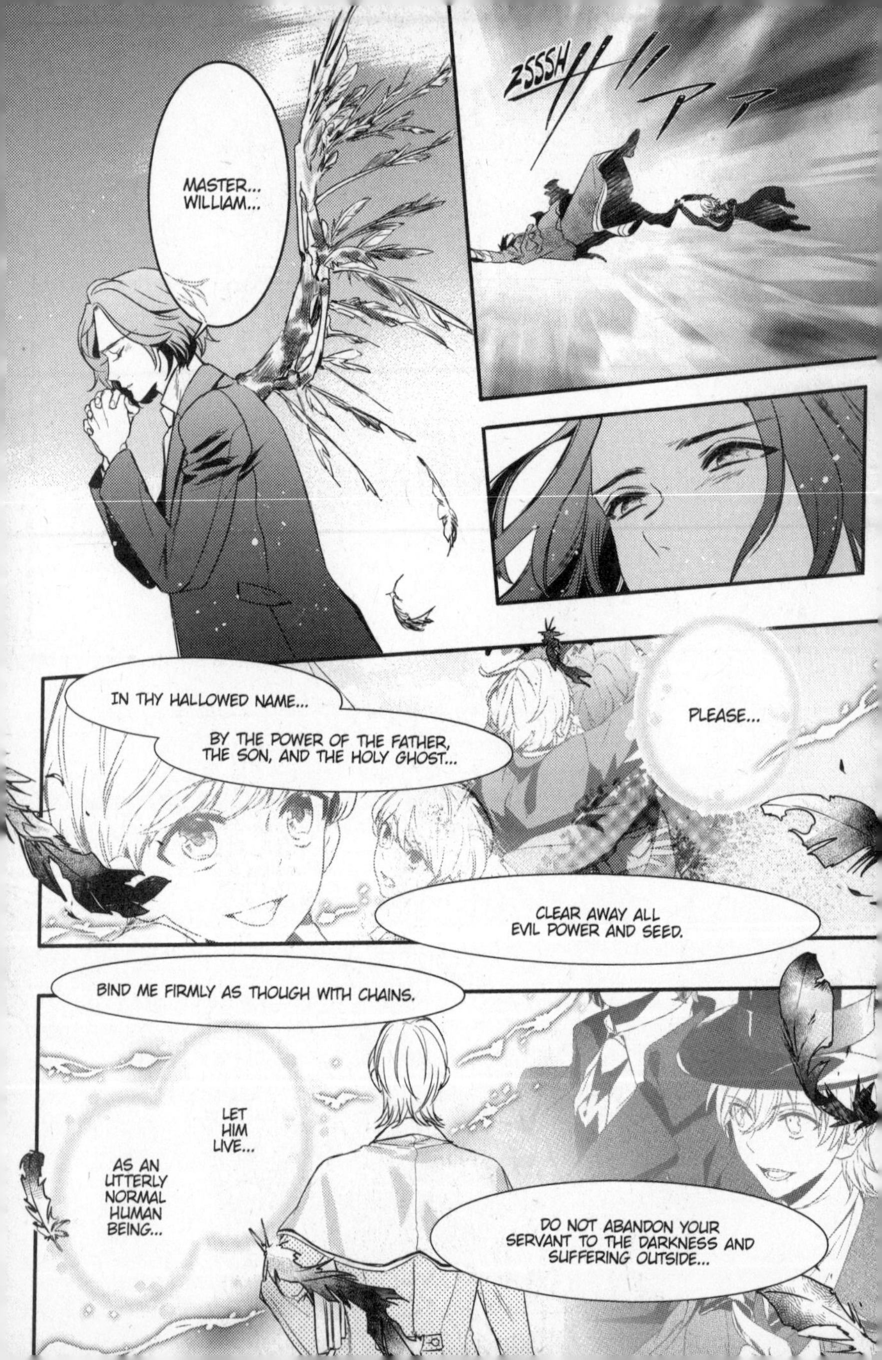
ZSSSH
MASTER... WILLIAM...
PLEASE...
IN THY HALLOWED NAME...
BY THE POWER OF THE FATHER, THE SON, AND THE HOLY GHOST...
CLEAR AWAY ALL EVIL POWER AND SEED.
BIND ME FIRMLY AS THOUGH WITH CHAINS.
DO NOT ABANDON YOUR SERVANT TO THE DARKNESS AND SUFFERING OUTSIDE...
LET HIM LIVE...
AS AN UTTERLY NORMAL HUMAN BEING...

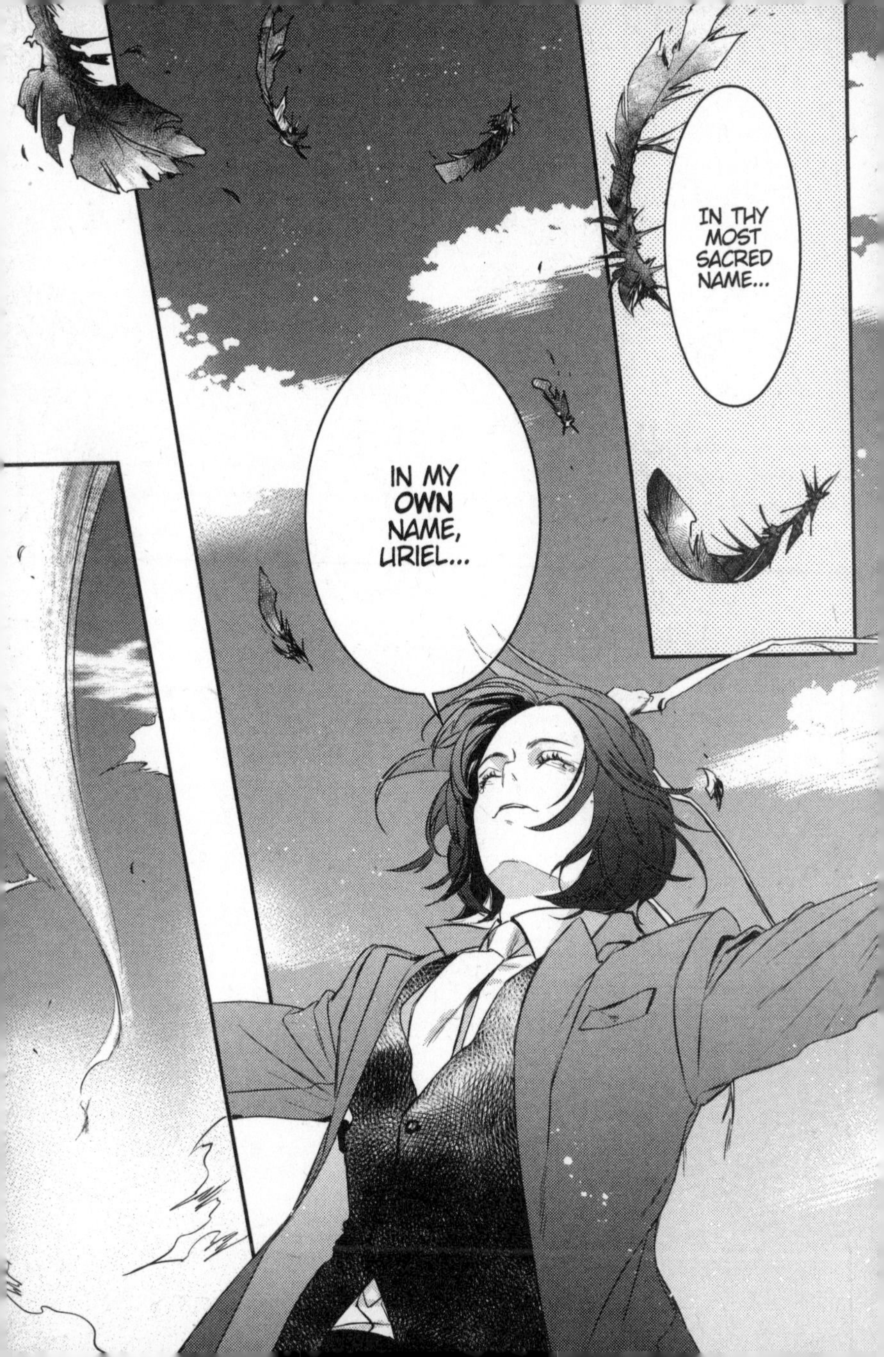
IN THY MOST SACRED NAME...
IN MY OWN NAME, URIEL...

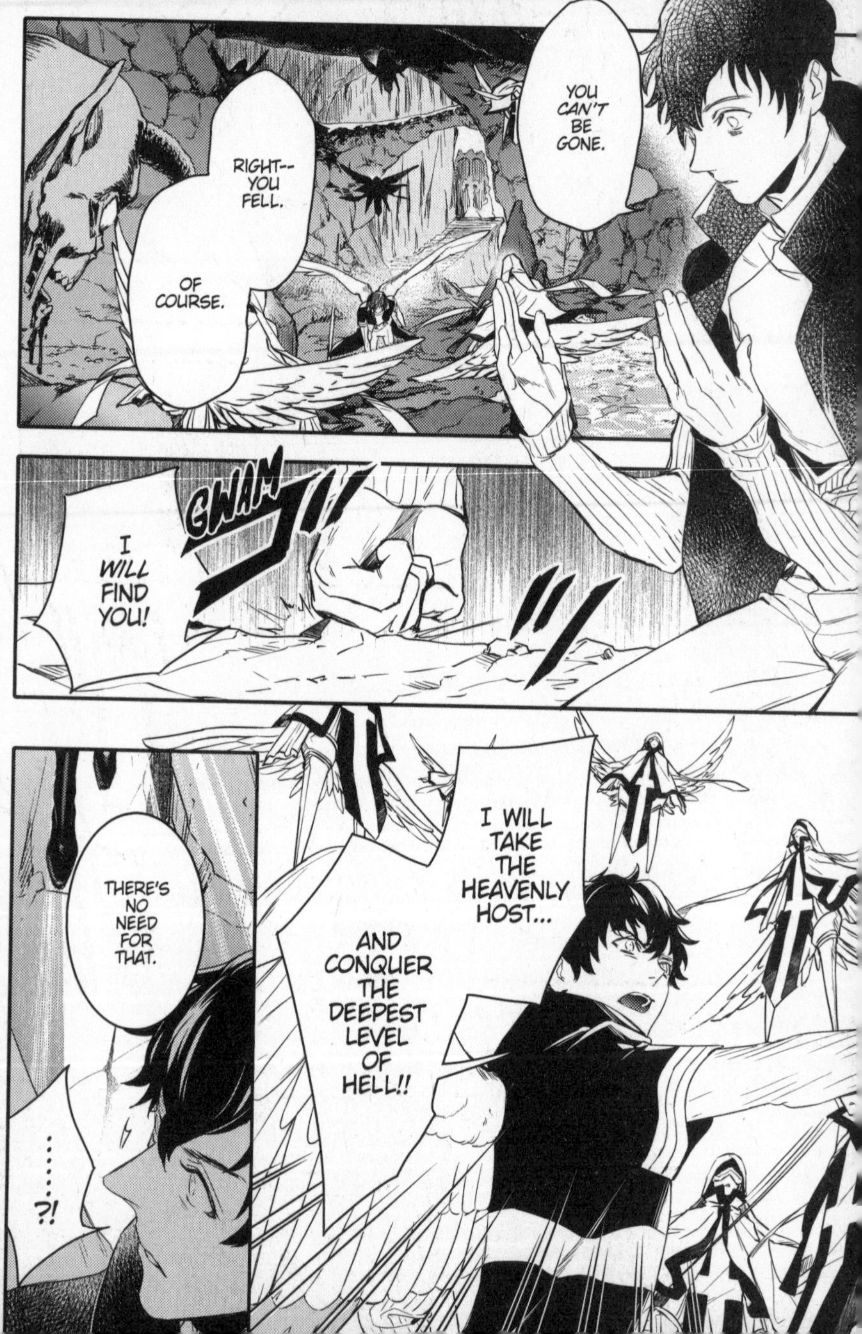
YOU CAN'T BE GONE.
RIGHT-- YOU FELL.
OF COURSE.
GWAM
I WILL FIND YOU!
I WILL TAKE THE HEAVENLY HOST...
AND CONQUER THE DEEPEST LEVEL OF HELL!!
THERE'S NO NEED FOR THAT.
......?!

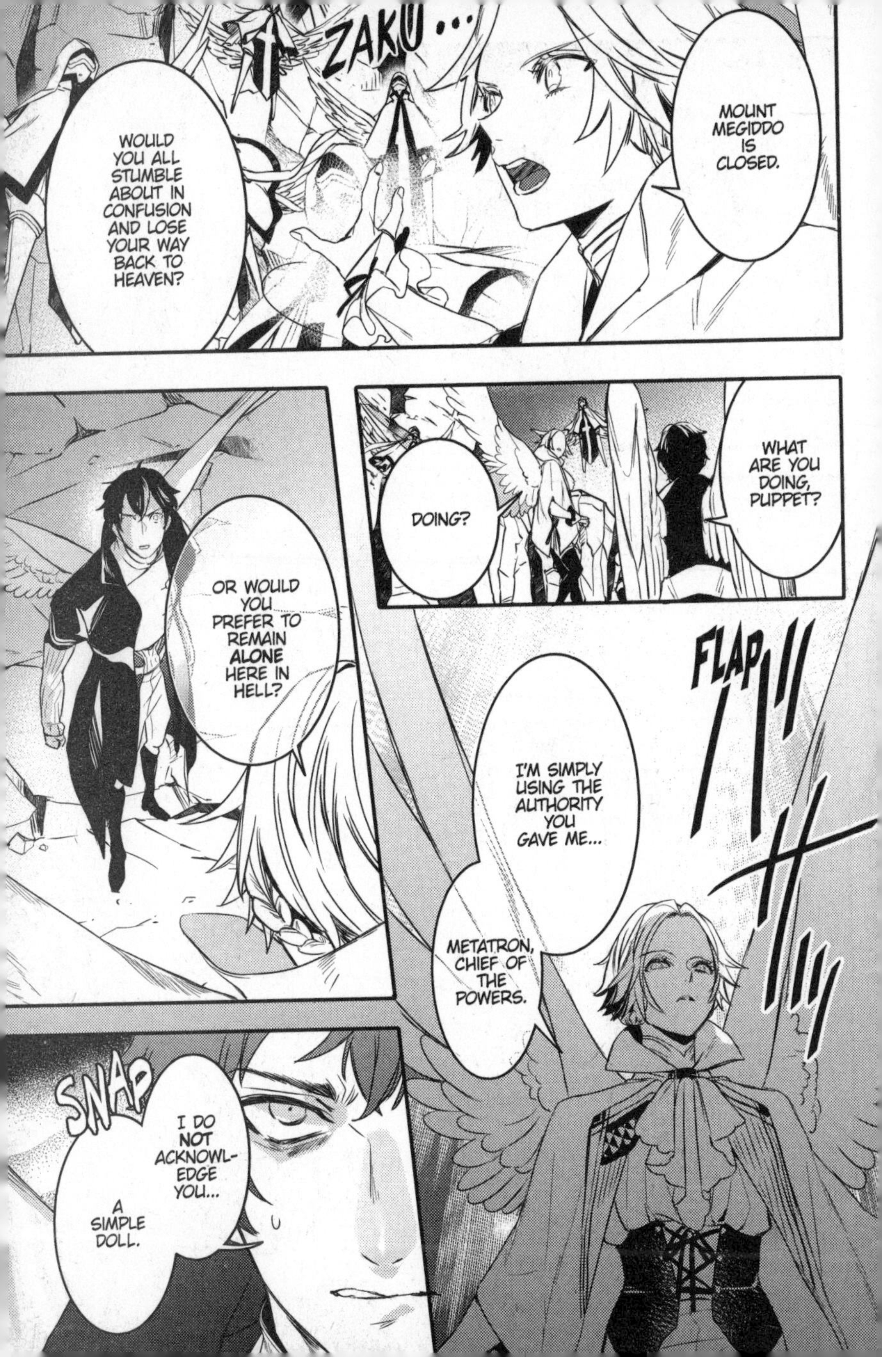
MOUNT MEGIDDO IS CLOSED.
ZAKU...
WOULD YOU ALL STUMBLE ABOUT IN CONFUSION AND LOSE YOUR WAY BACK TO HEAVEN?
WHAT ARE YOU DOING, PUPPET?
DOING?
OR WOULD YOU PREFER TO REMAIN **ALONE** HERE IN HELL?
FLAP
I'M SIMPLY USING THE AUTHORITY YOU GAVE ME...
METATRON, CHIEF OF THE POWERS.
SNAP
I DO **NOT** ACKNOWL-EDGE YOU...
A SIMPLE DOLL.

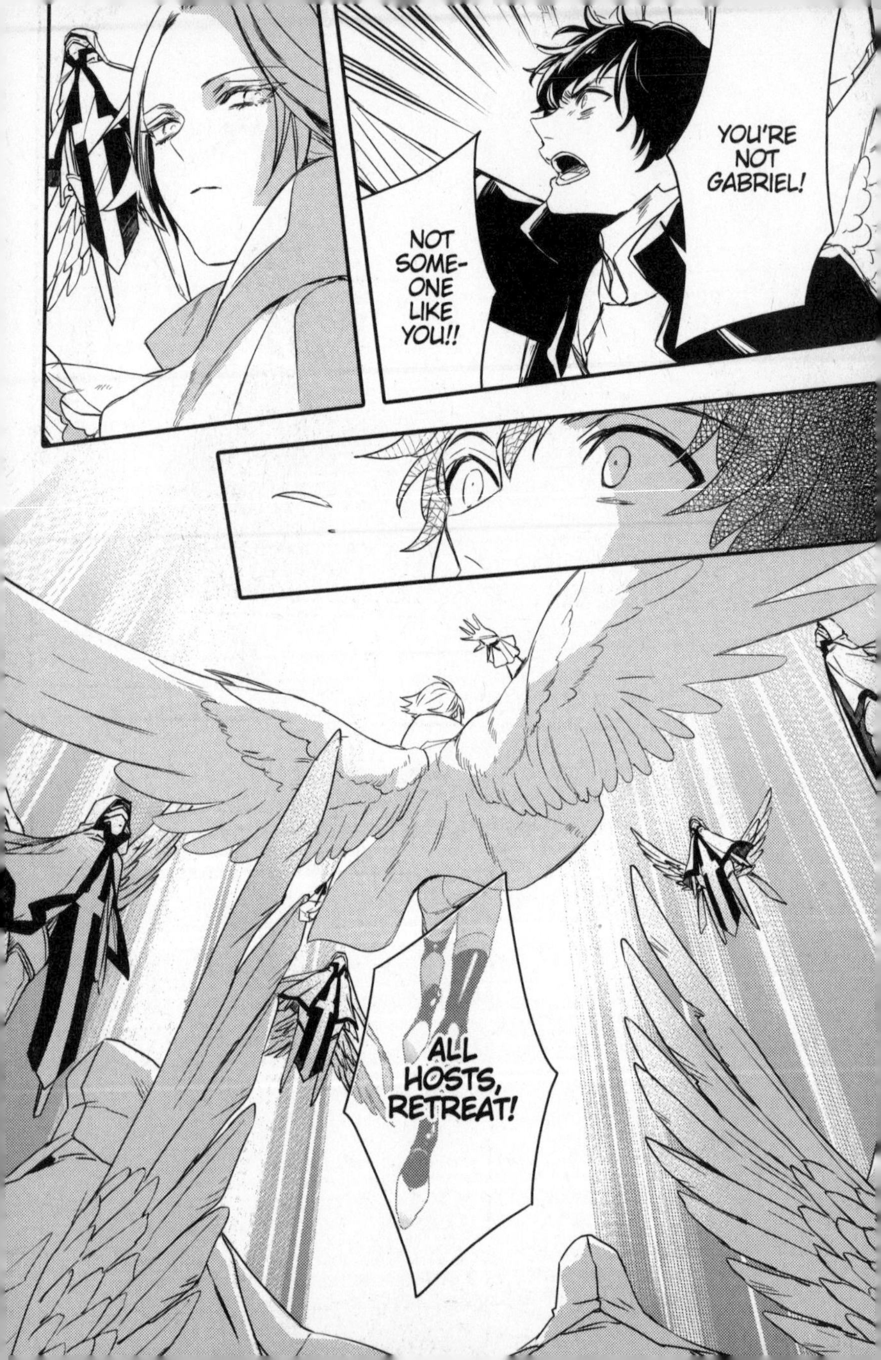
YOU'RE NOT GABRIEL!
NOT SOME-ONE LIKE YOU!!
ALL HOSTS, RETREAT!

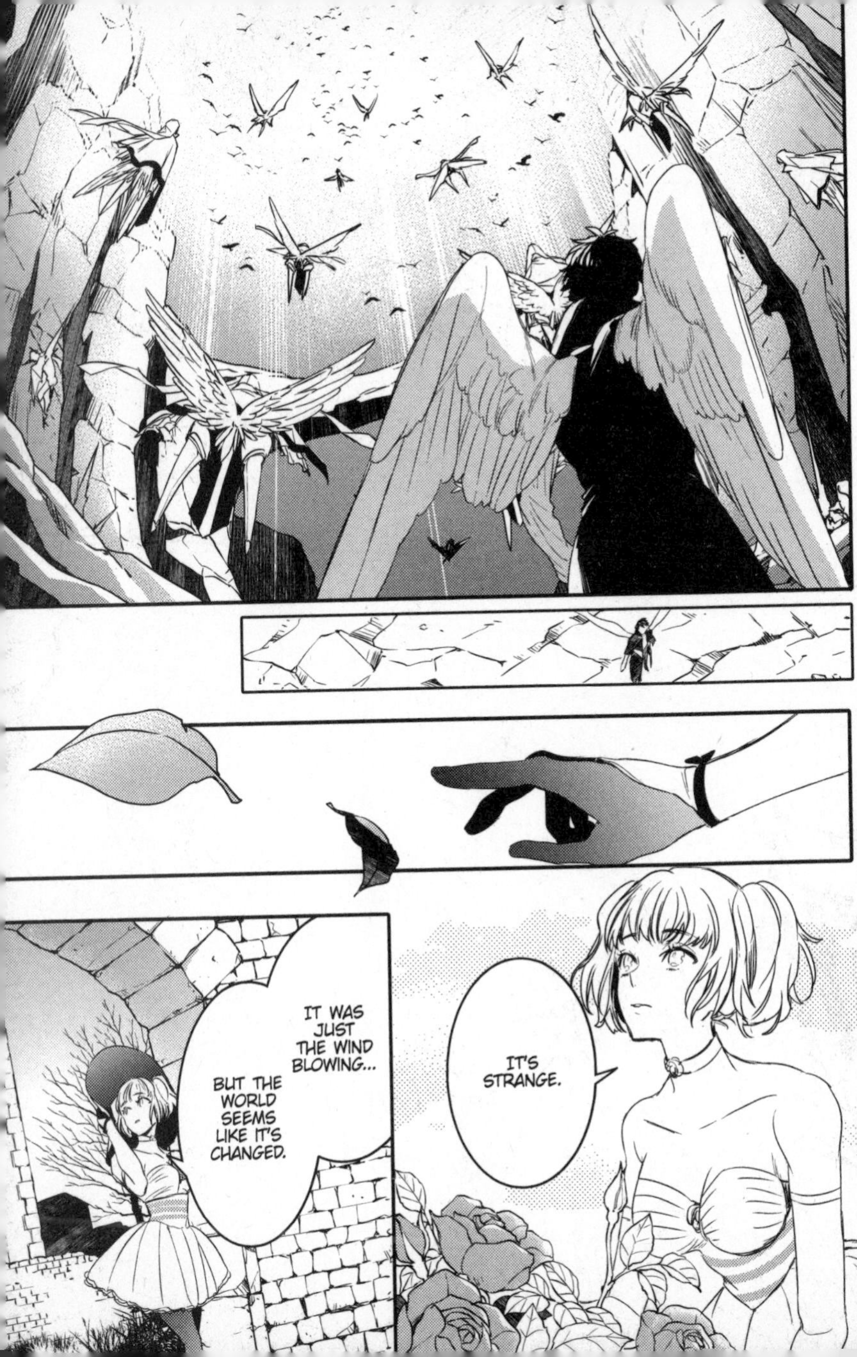
IT'S STRANGE.
IT WAS JUST THE WIND BLOWING...
BUT THE WORLD SEEMS LIKE IT'S CHANGED.

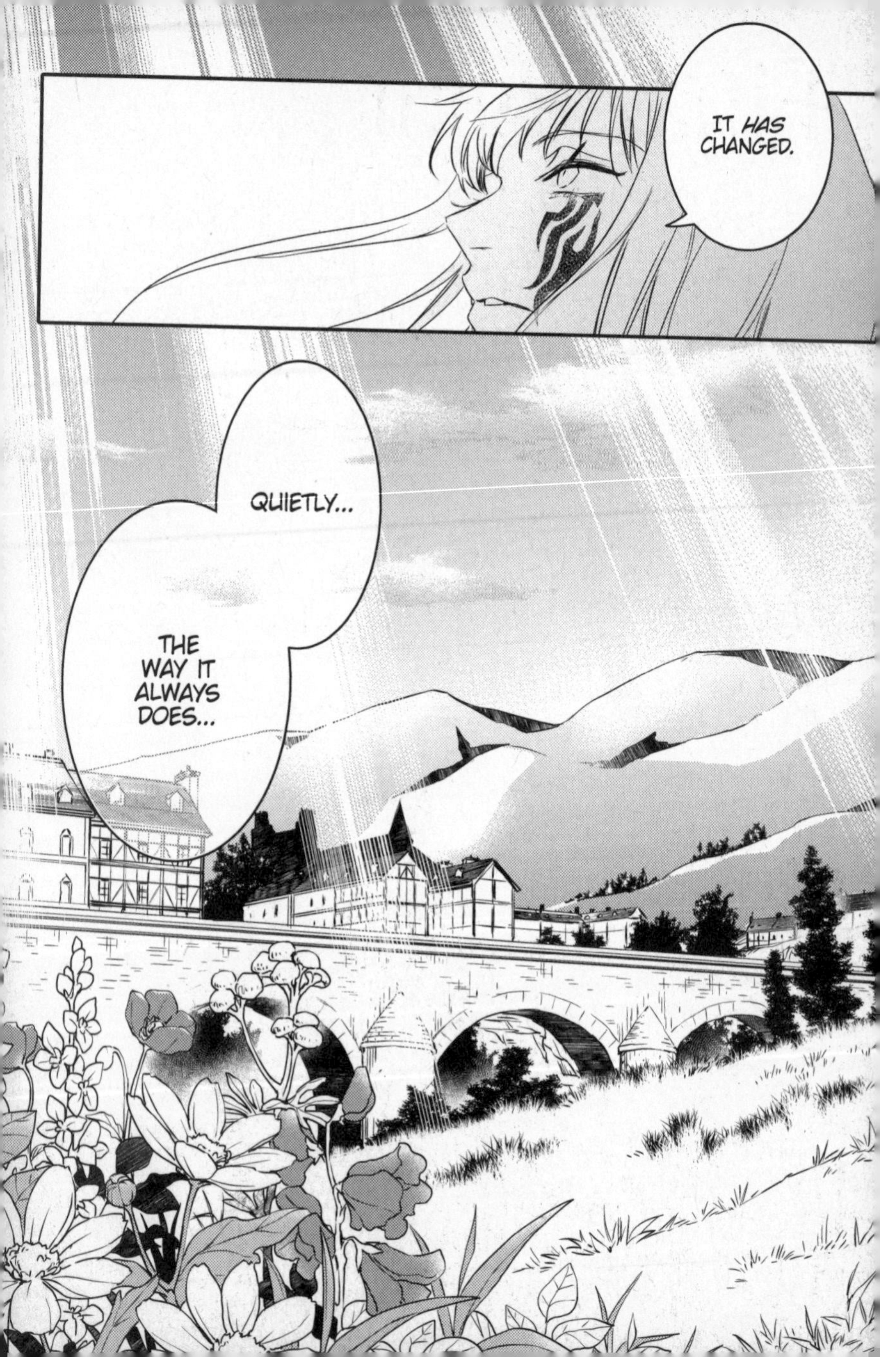
IT *HAS* CHANGED.
QUIETLY...
THE WAY IT ALWAYS DOES...

Final Pillar

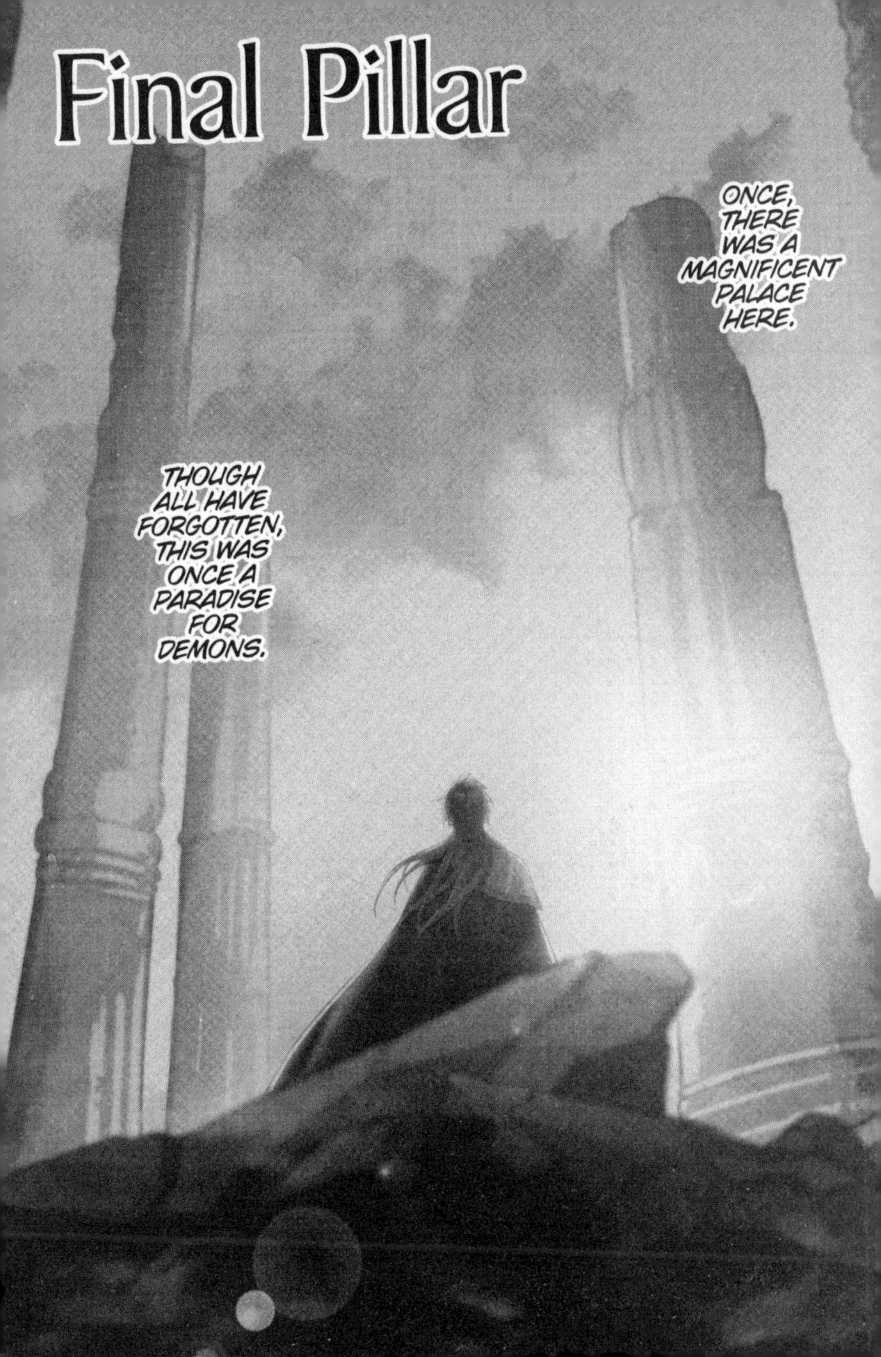
ONCE, THERE WAS A MAGNIFICENT PALACE HERE.
THOUGH ALL HAVE FORGOTTEN, THIS WAS ONCE A PARADISE FOR DEMONS.

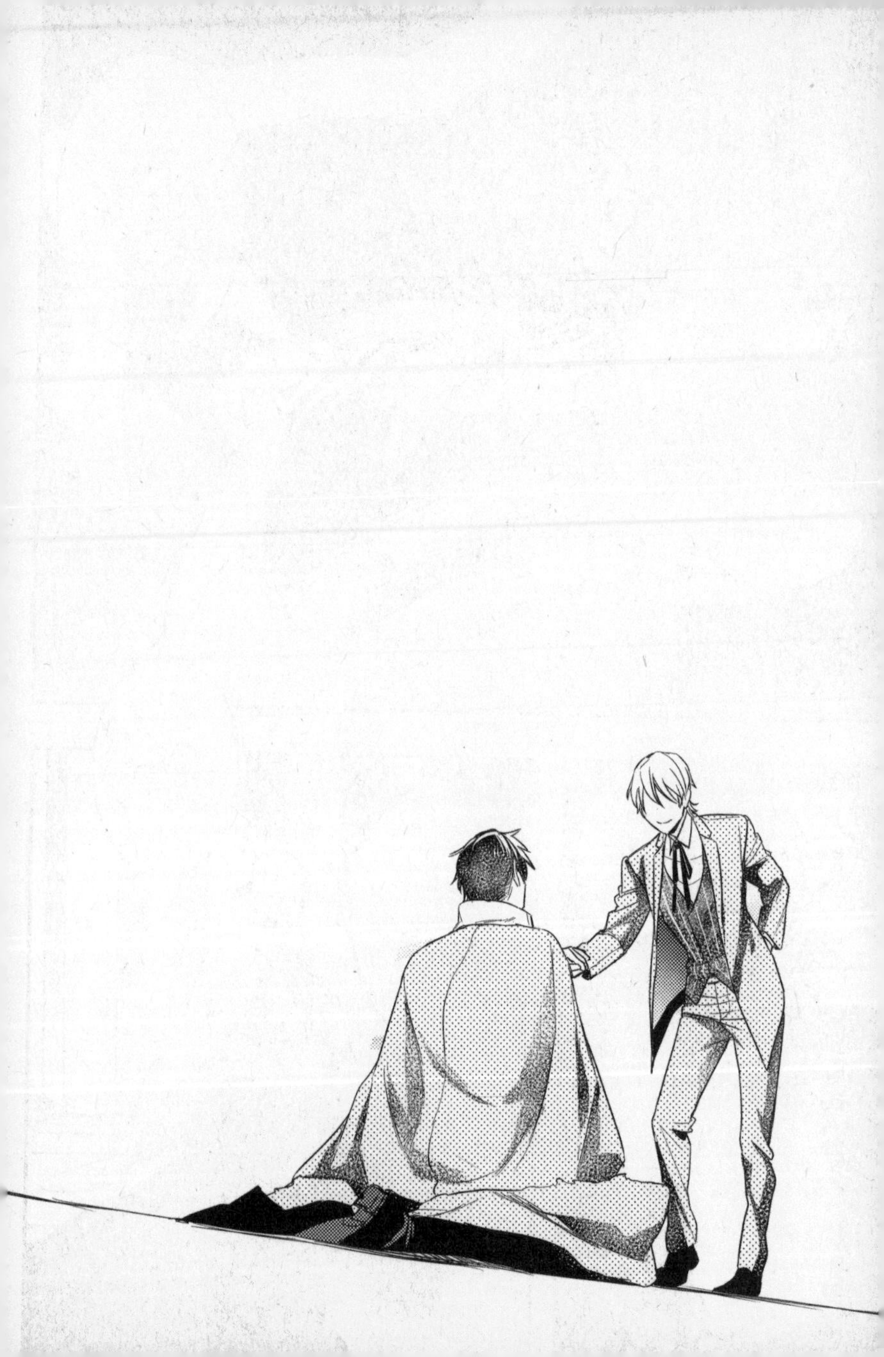

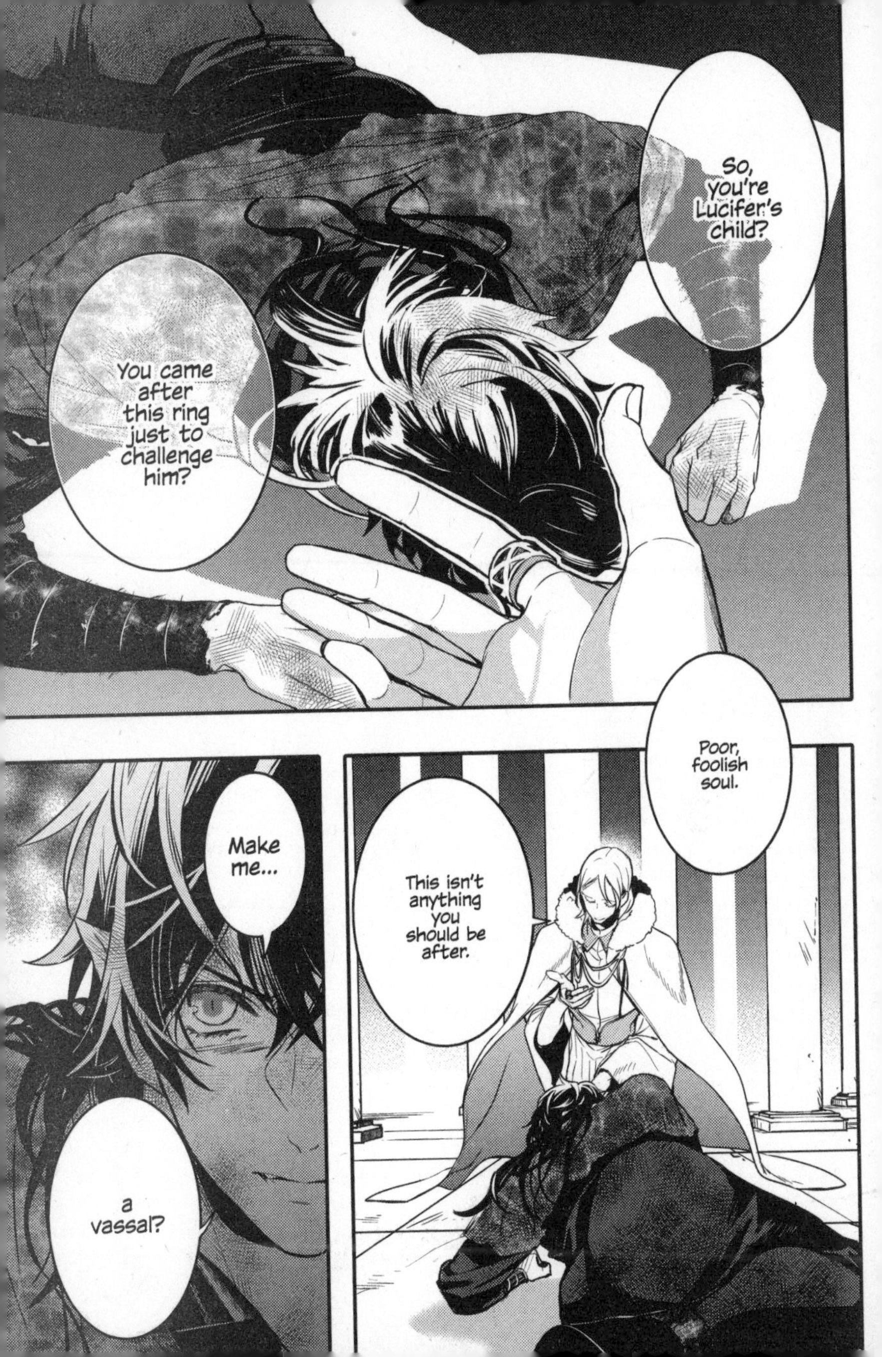
So, you're Lucifer's child?
You came after this ring just to challenge him?
Poor, foolish soul.
This isn't anything you should be after.
Make me...
a vassal?

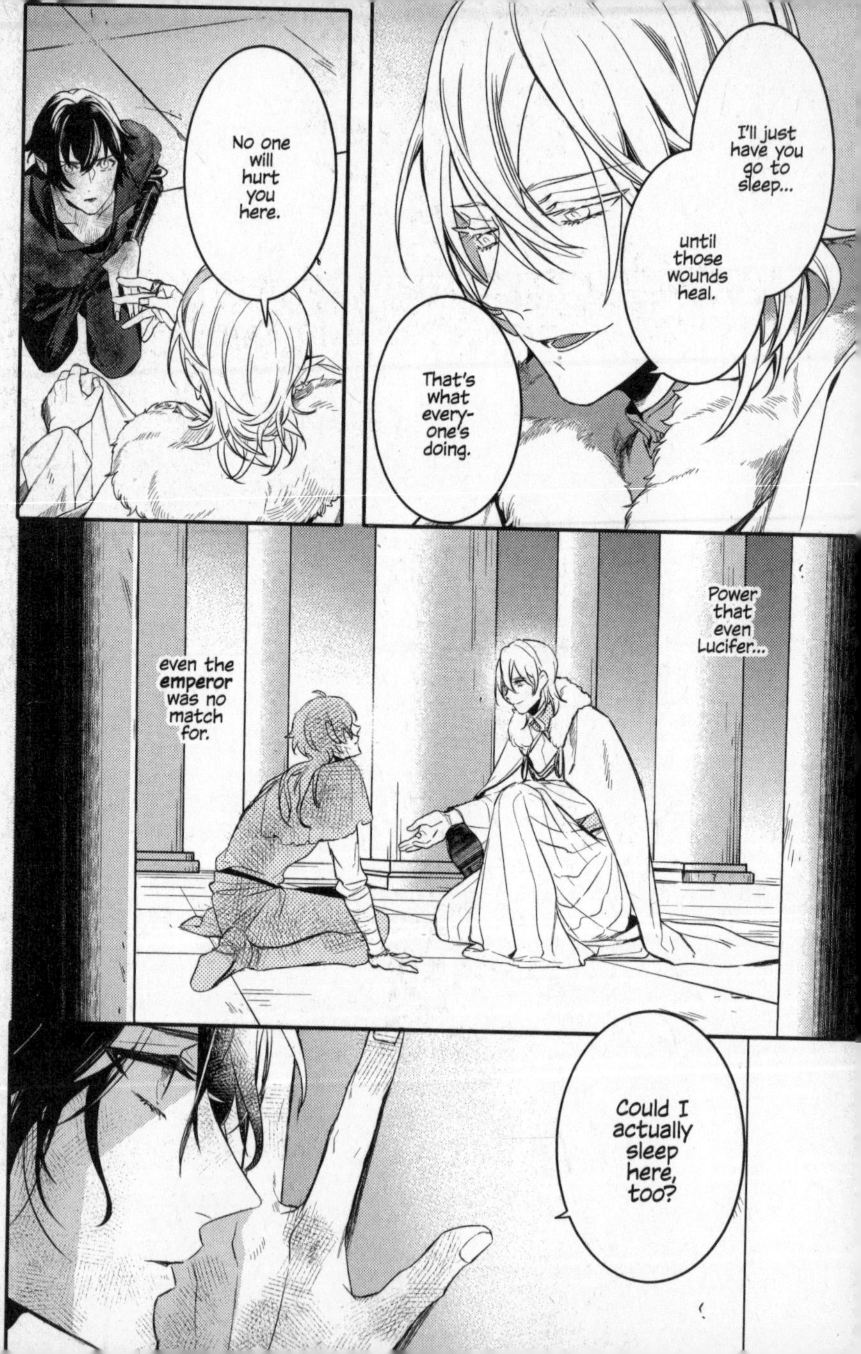
I'll just have you go to sleep...
until those wounds heal.
That's what every-one's doing.
No one will hurt you here.
Power that even Lucifer...
even the emperor was no match for.
Could I actually sleep here, too?

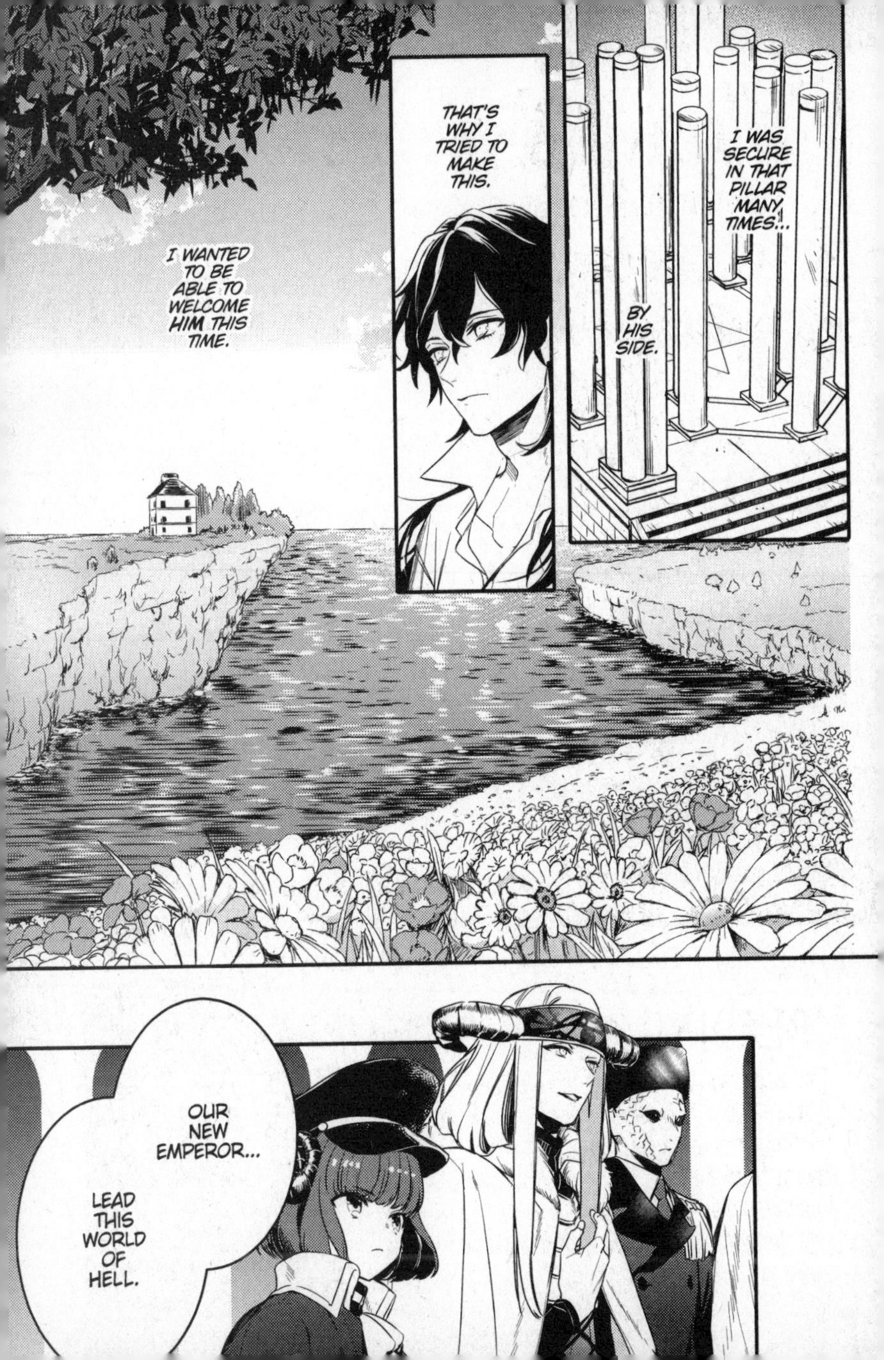
I WAS SECURE IN THAT PILLAR MANY TIMES...
BY HIS SIDE.
THAT'S WHY I TRIED TO MAKE THIS.
I WANTED TO BE ABLE TO WELCOME HIM THIS TIME.
OUR NEW EMPEROR...
LEAD THIS WORLD OF HELL.

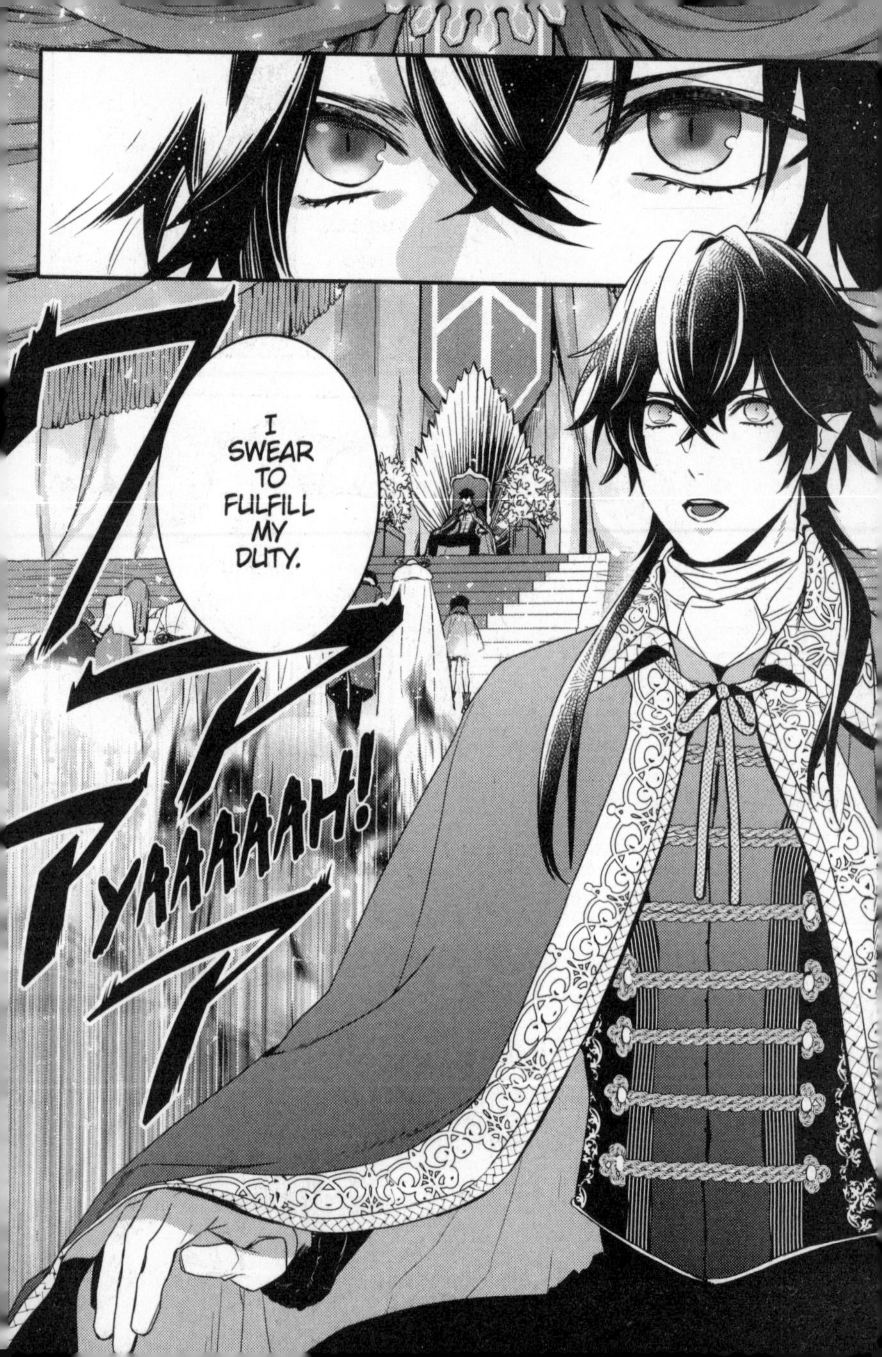
I SWEAR TO FULFILL MY DUTY.
YAAAAAH!

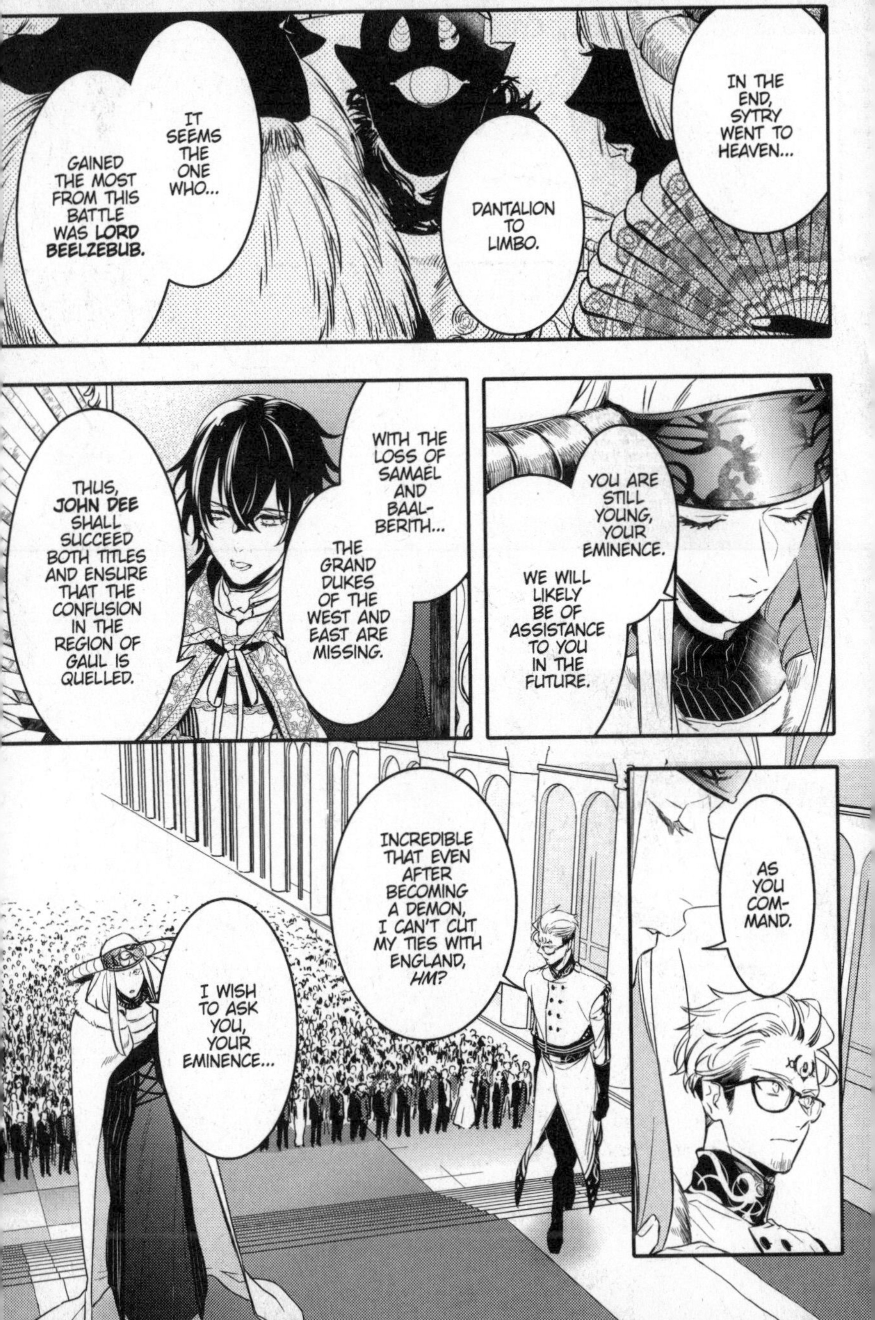
IN THE END, SYTRY WENT TO HEAVEN...
DANTALION TO LIMBO.
IT SEEMS THE ONE WHO...
GAINED THE MOST FROM THIS BATTLE WAS **LORD BEELZEBUB.**
YOU ARE STILL YOUNG, YOUR EMINENCE.
WE WILL LIKELY BE OF ASSISTANCE TO YOU IN THE FUTURE.
WITH THE LOSS OF SAMAEL AND BAAL-BERITH...
THE GRAND DUKES OF THE WEST AND EAST ARE MISSING.
THUS, **JOHN DEE** SHALL SUCCEED BOTH TITLES AND ENSURE THAT THE CONFUSION IN THE REGION OF GAUL IS QUELLED.
AS YOU COM-MAND.
INCREDIBLE THAT EVEN AFTER BECOMING A DEMON, I CAN'T CUT MY TIES WITH ENGLAND, *HM?*
I WISH TO ASK YOU, YOUR EMINENCE...

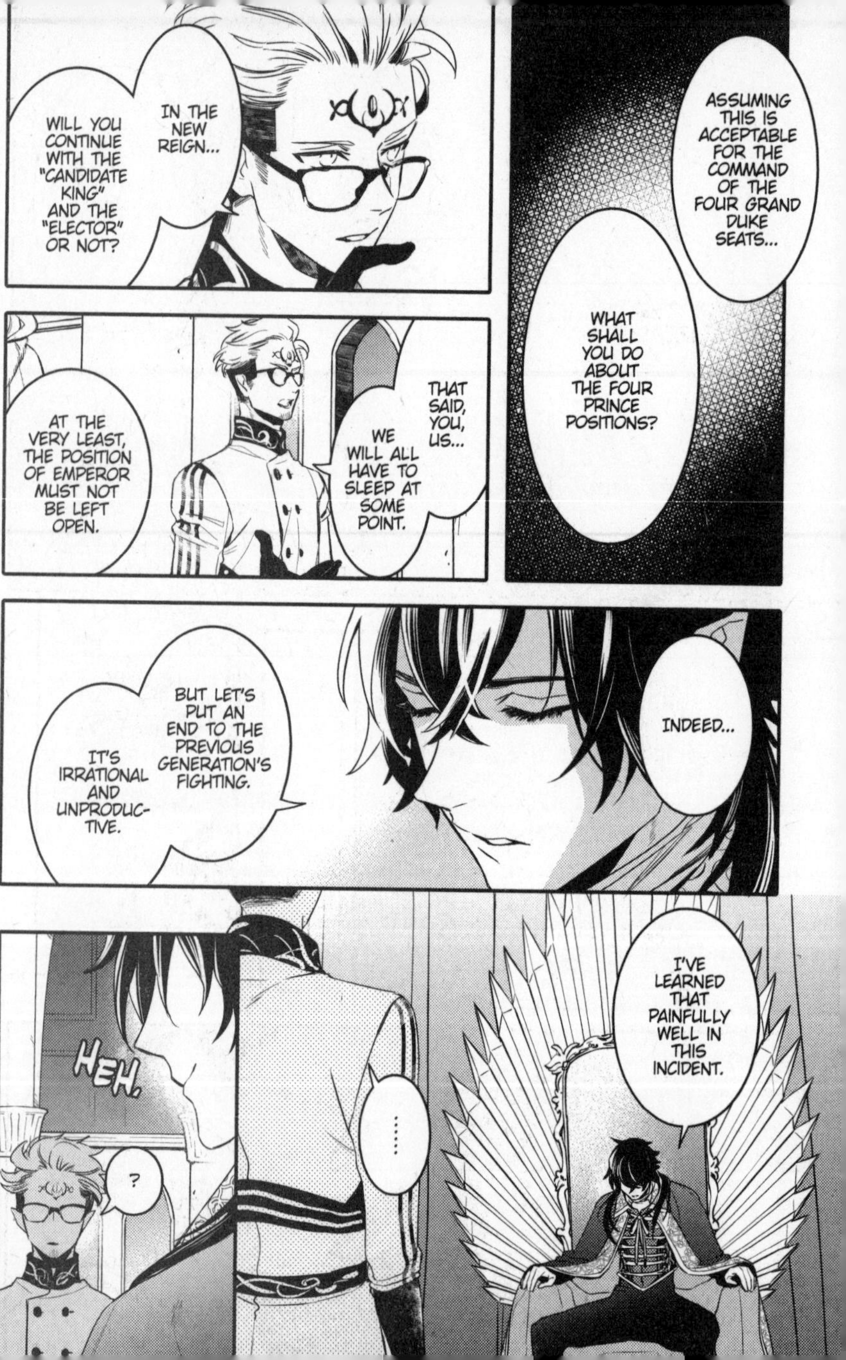
ASSUMING THIS IS ACCEPTABLE FOR THE COMMAND OF THE FOUR GRAND DUKE SEATS...
WHAT SHALL YOU DO ABOUT THE FOUR PRINCE POSITIONS?
IN THE NEW REIGN...
WILL YOU CONTINUE WITH THE "CANDIDATE KING" AND THE "ELECTOR" OR NOT?
THAT SAID, YOU, US...
WE WILL ALL HAVE TO SLEEP AT SOME POINT.
AT THE VERY LEAST, THE POSITION OF EMPEROR MUST NOT BE LEFT OPEN.
INDEED...
BUT LET'S PUT AN END TO THE PREVIOUS GENERATION'S FIGHTING.
IT'S IRRATIONAL AND UNPRODUCTIVE.
I'VE LEARNED THAT PAINFULLY WELL IN THIS INCIDENT.
......
HEH.
?

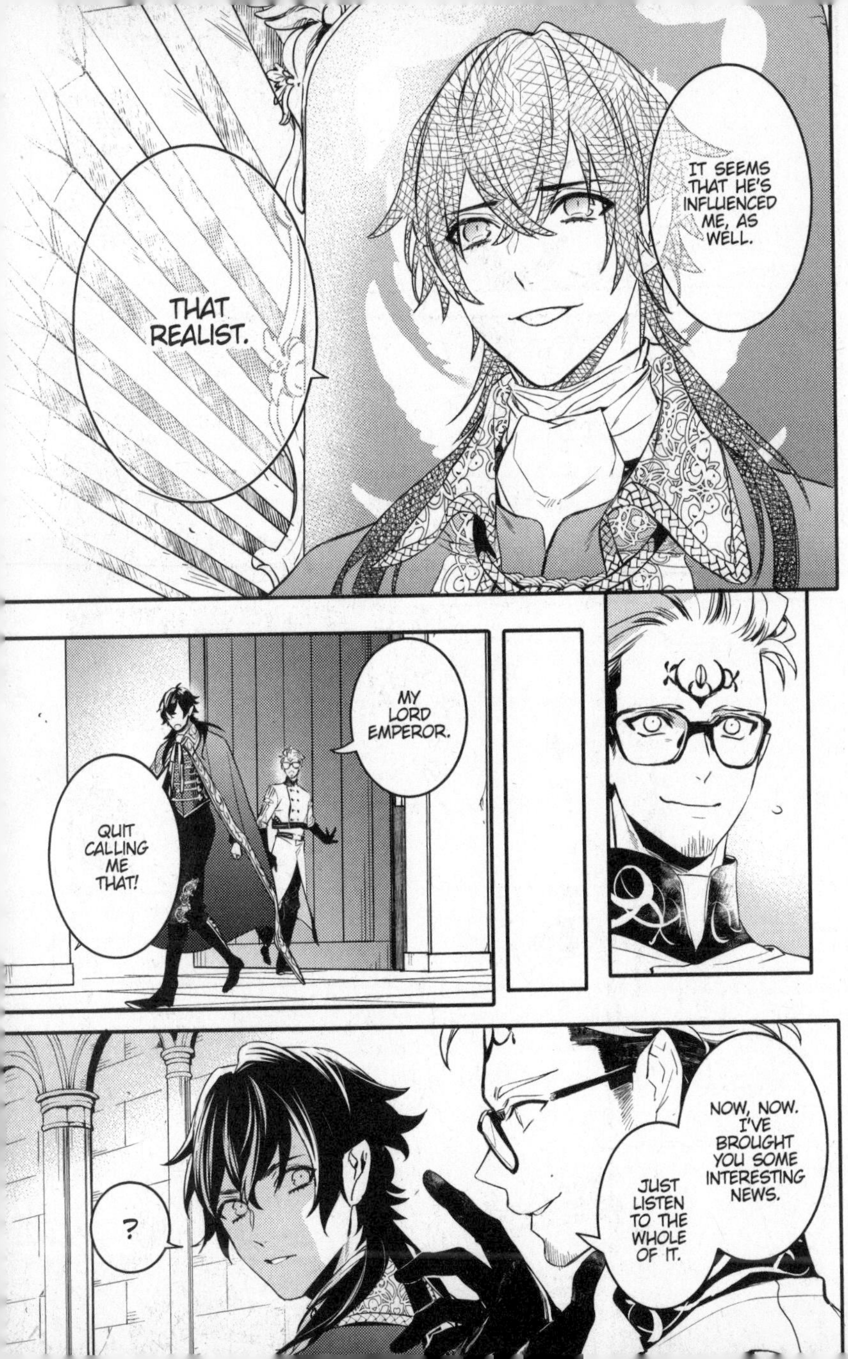
IT SEEMS THAT HE'S INFLUENCED ME, AS WELL.
THAT REALIST.
MY LORD EMPEROR.
QUIT CALLING ME THAT!
NOW, NOW. I'VE BROUGHT YOU SOME INTERESTING NEWS.
JUST LISTEN TO THE WHOLE OF IT.
?

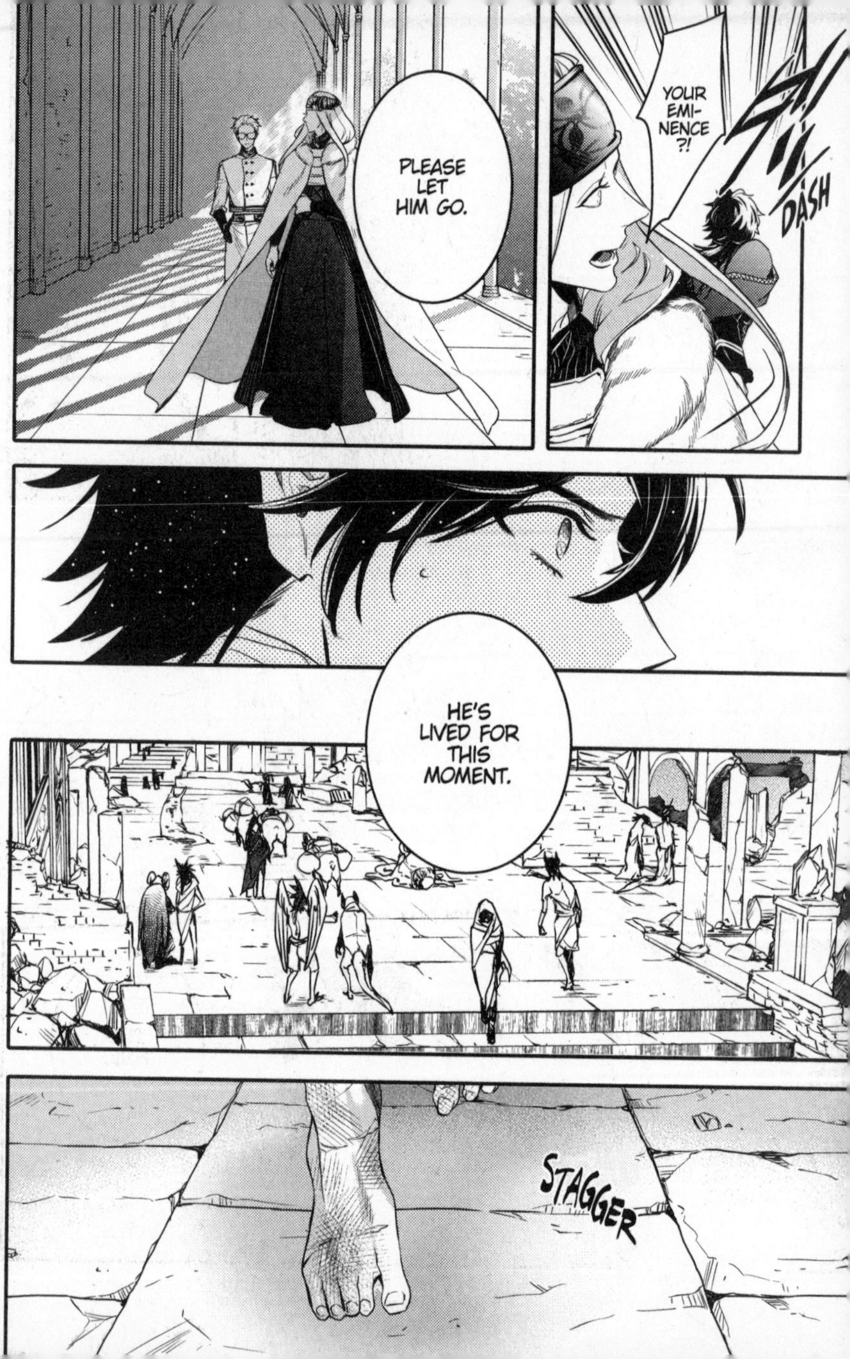
YOUR EMINENCE?!
DASH
PLEASE LET HIM GO.
HE'S LIVED FOR THIS MOMENT.
STAGGER

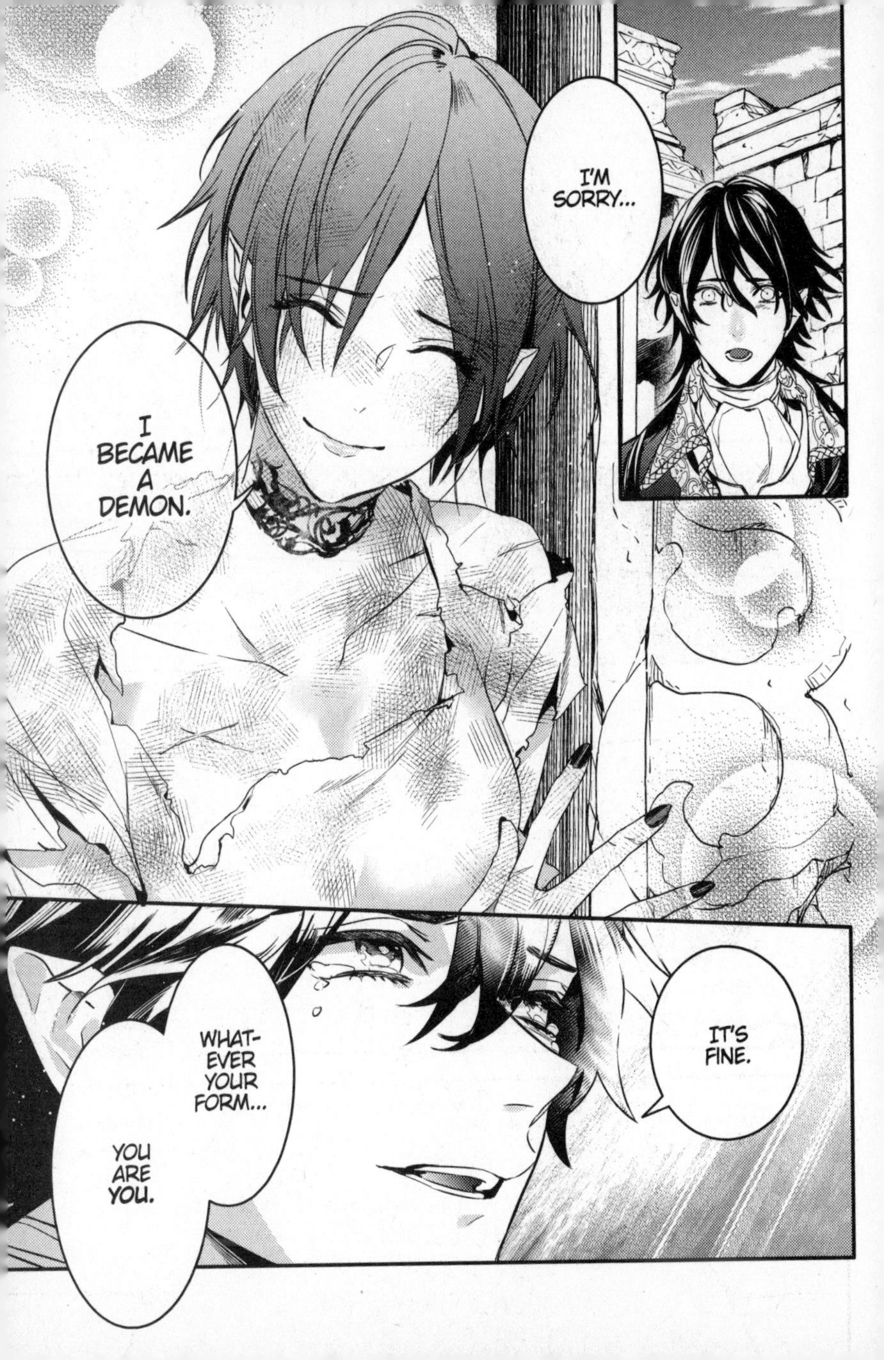

I'M SORRY...
I BECAME A DEMON.
IT'S FINE.
WHAT-EVER YOUR FORM...
YOU ARE YOU.

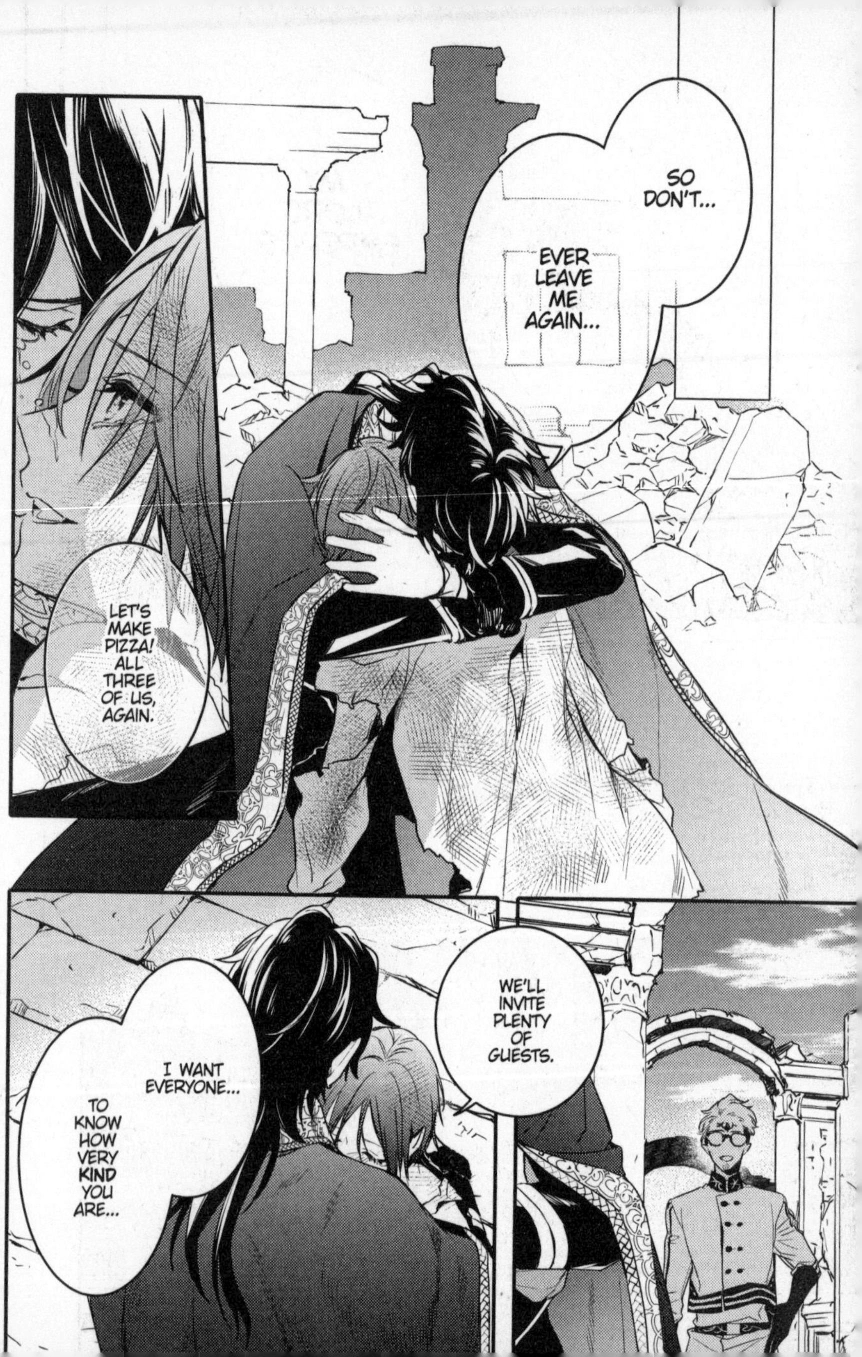
SO DON'T...
EVER LEAVE ME AGAIN...
LET'S MAKE PIZZA! ALL THREE OF US, AGAIN.
WE'LL INVITE PLENTY OF GUESTS.
I WANT EVERYONE...
TO KNOW HOW VERY KIND YOU ARE...

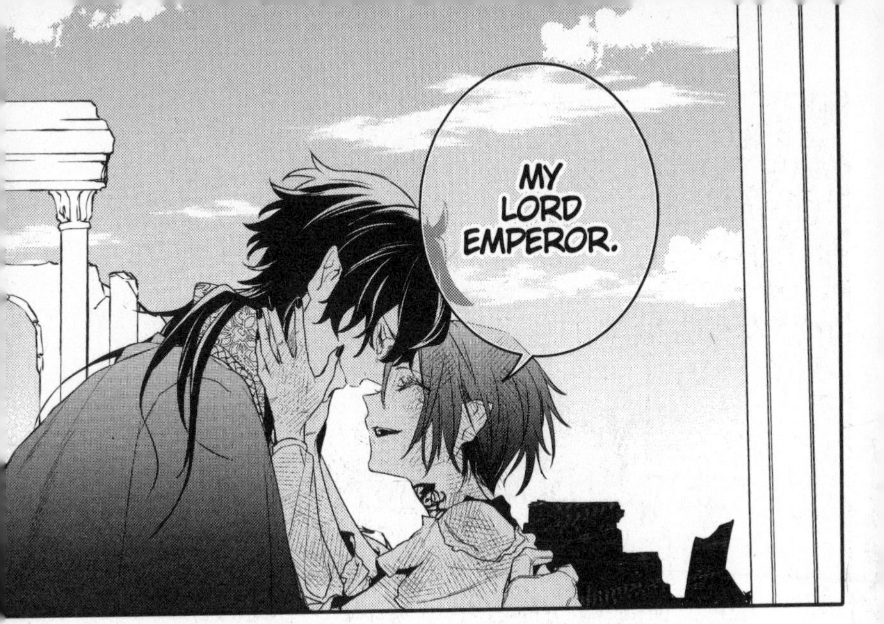
MY LORD EMPEROR.

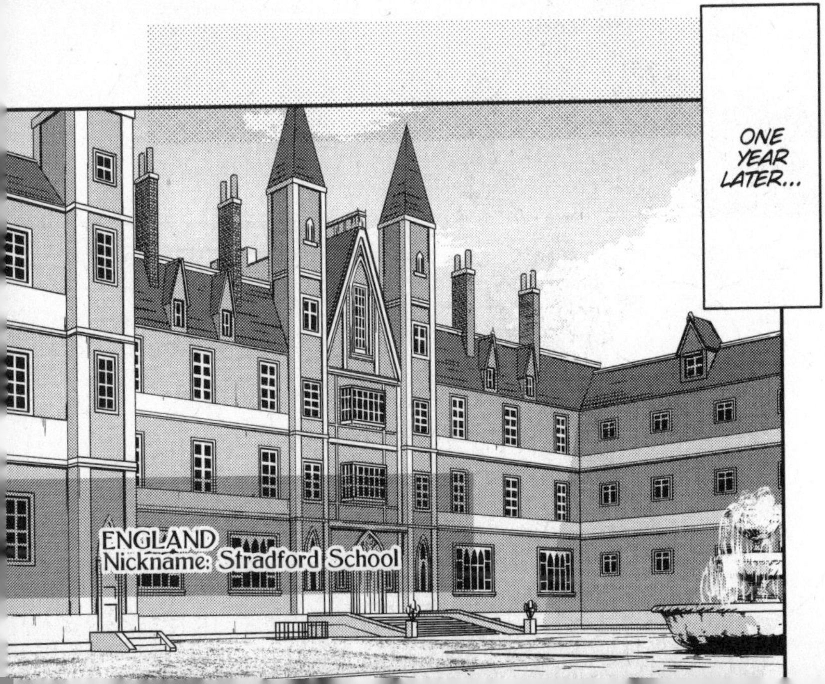
ONE YEAR LATER...
ENGLAND
Nickname: Stradford School

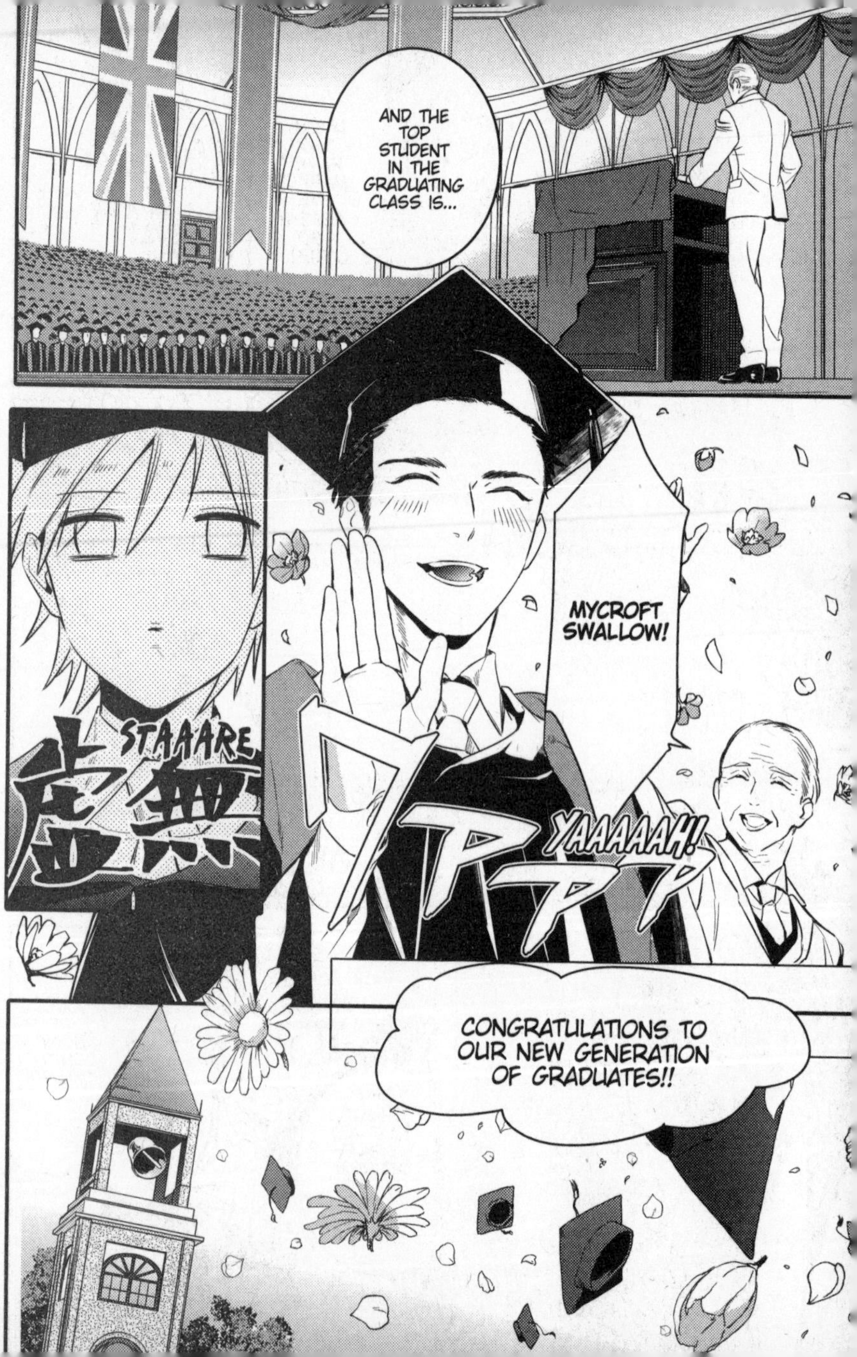
AND THE TOP STUDENT IN THE GRADUATING CLASS IS...
MYCROFT SWALLOW!
YAAAAAH!
STAAARE
虚無
CONGRATULATIONS TO OUR NEW GENERATION OF GRADUATES!!

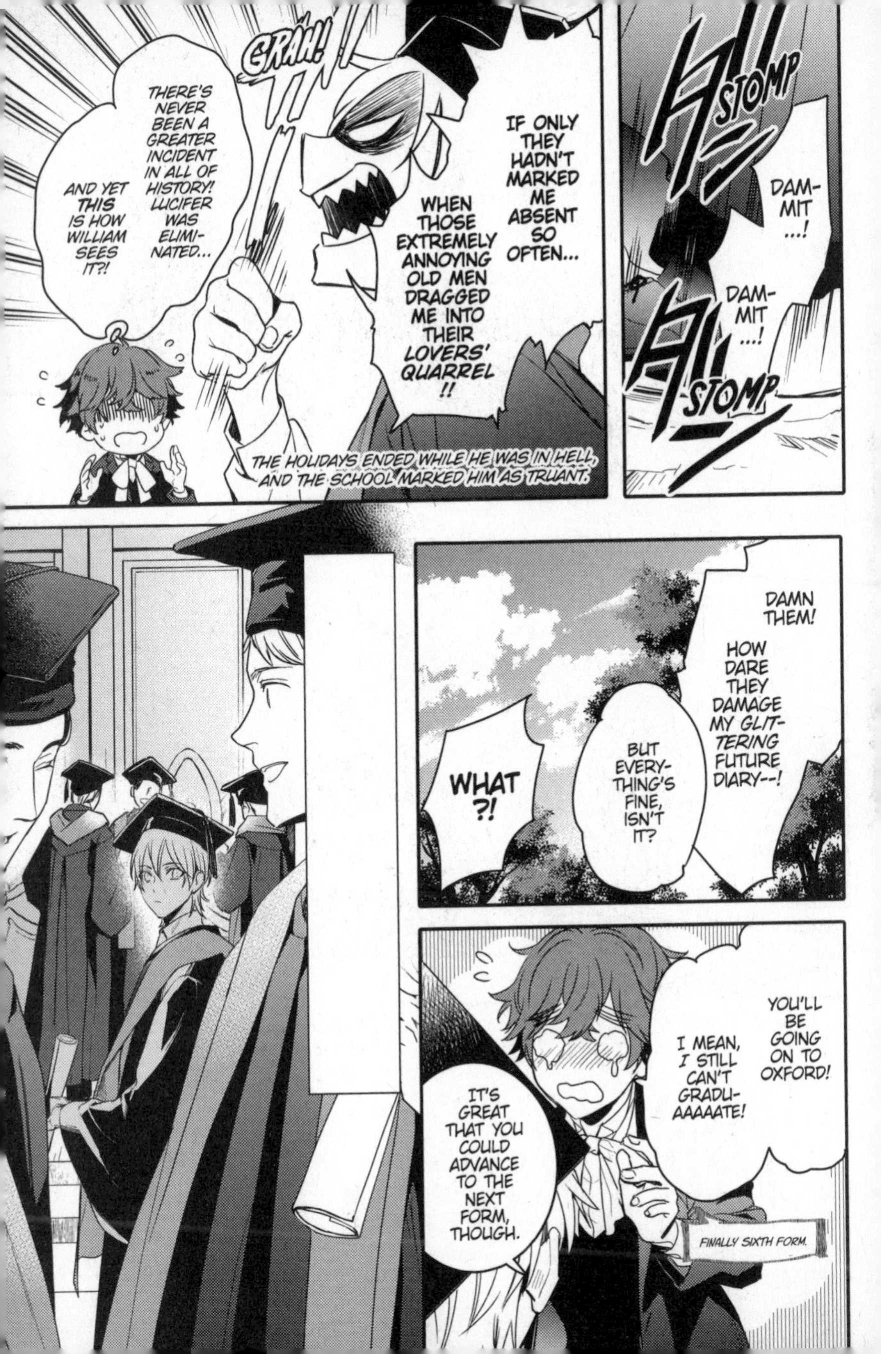
STOMP
DAMMIT ...!
DAMMIT ...!
STOMP
GRAH!
IF ONLY THEY HADN'T MARKED ME ABSENT SO OFTEN...
WHEN THOSE EXTREMELY ANNOYING OLD MEN DRAGGED ME INTO THEIR *LOVERS' QUARREL*!!
THERE'S NEVER BEEN A GREATER INCIDENT IN ALL OF HISTORY! LUCIFER WAS ELIMINATED...
AND YET *THIS* IS HOW WILLIAM SEES IT?!
THE HOLIDAYS ENDED WHILE HE WAS IN HELL, AND THE SCHOOL MARKED HIM AS TRUANT.
DAMN THEM!
HOW DARE THEY DAMAGE MY *GLITTERING* FUTURE DIARY--!
BUT EVERYTHING'S FINE, ISN'T IT?
WHAT?!
YOU'LL BE GOING ON TO OXFORD!
I MEAN, *I* STILL CAN'T GRADUAAAAATE!
IT'S GREAT THAT YOU COULD ADVANCE TO THE NEXT FORM, THOUGH.
FINALLY SIXTH FORM.

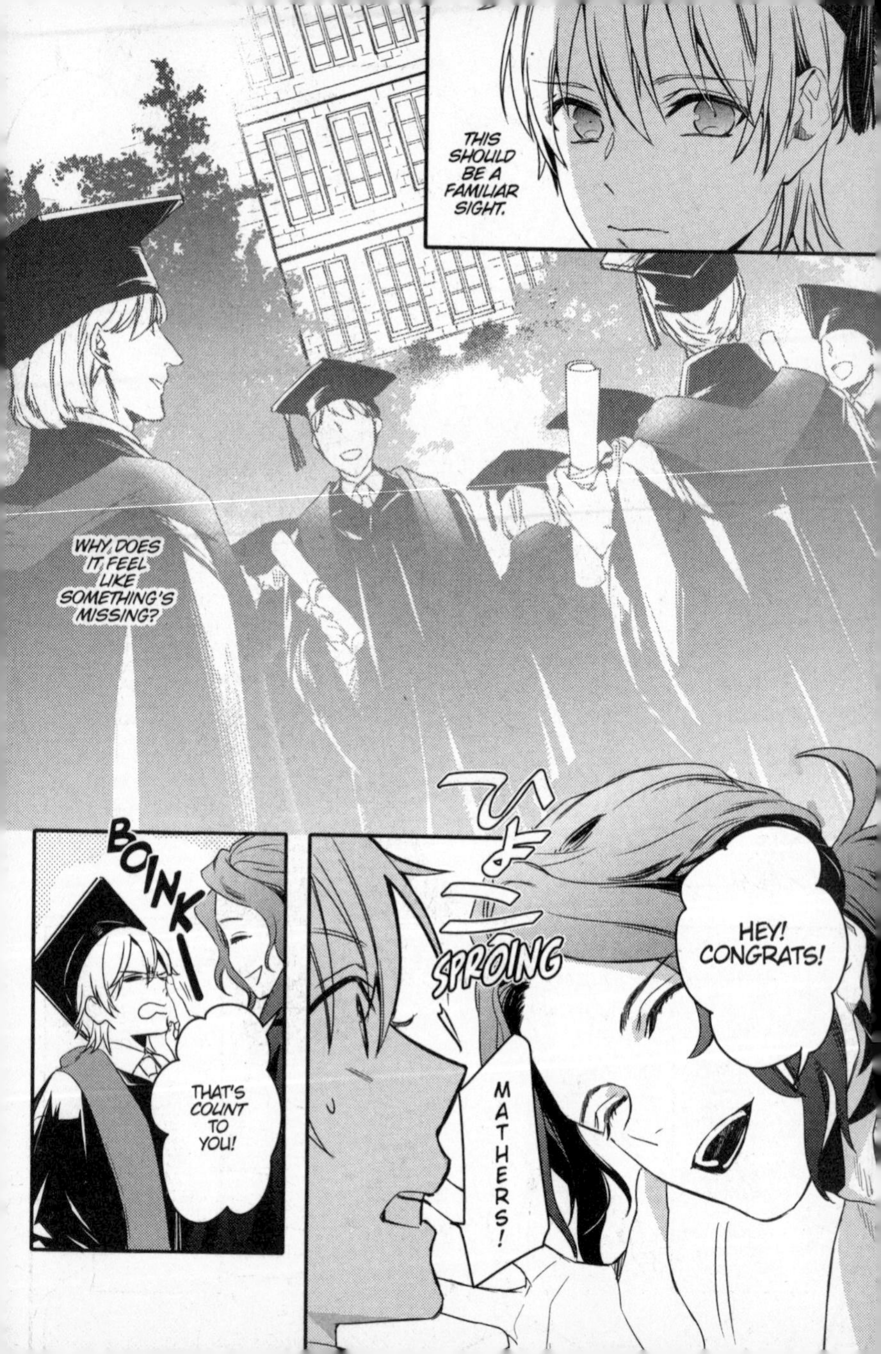
THIS SHOULD BE A FAMILIAR SIGHT.
WHY DOES IT FEEL LIKE SOMETHING'S MISSING?
ひょこ
SPROING
HEY! CONGRATS!
MATHERS!
BOINK!
THAT'S COUNT TO YOU!

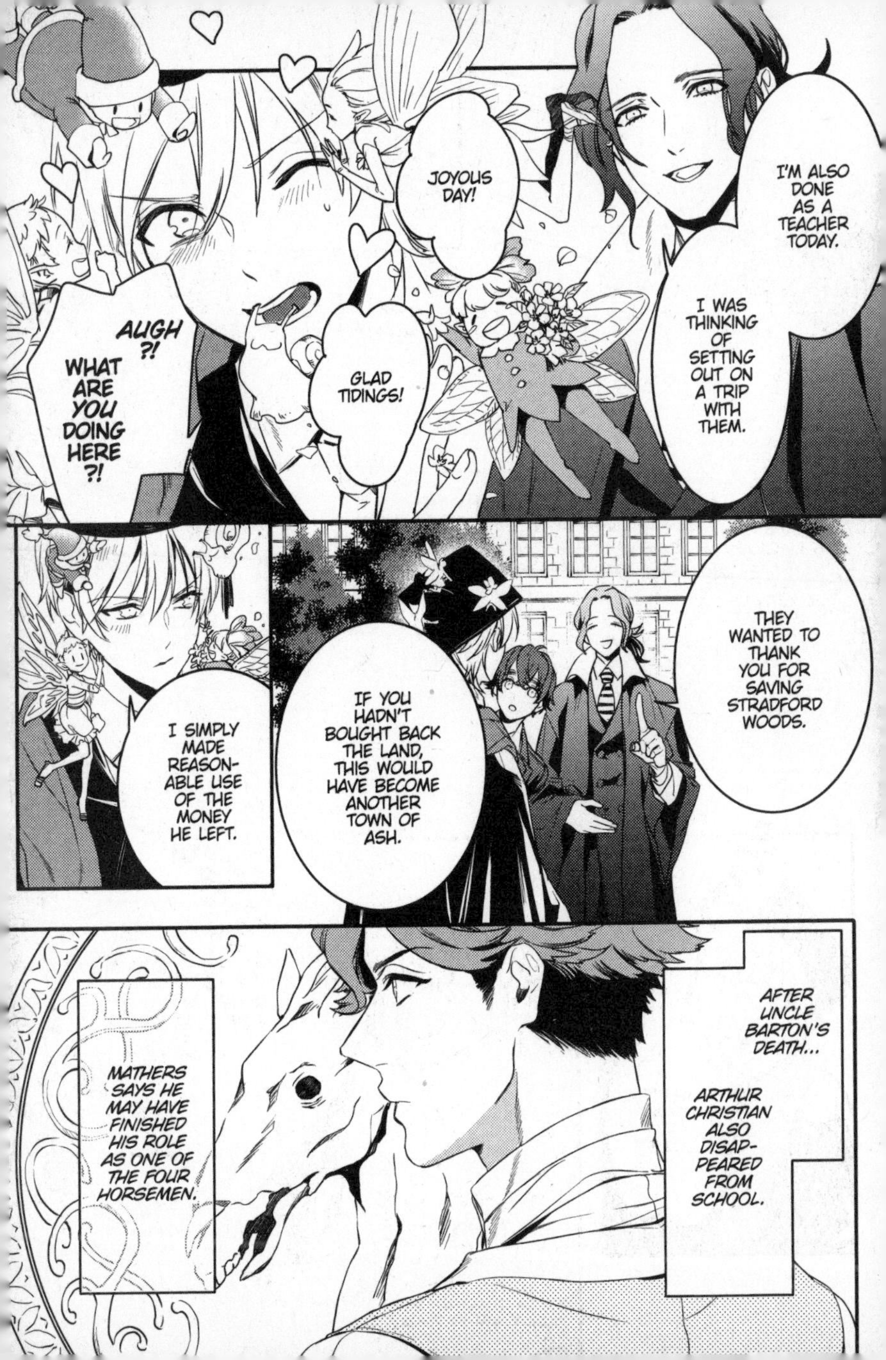
I'M ALSO DONE AS A TEACHER TODAY.
I WAS THINKING OF SETTING OUT ON A TRIP WITH THEM.
JOYOUS DAY!
GLAD TIDINGS!
AUGH?! WHAT ARE YOU DOING HERE?!
THEY WANTED TO THANK YOU FOR SAVING STRADFORD WOODS.
IF YOU HADN'T BOUGHT BACK THE LAND, THIS WOULD HAVE BECOME ANOTHER TOWN OF ASH.
I SIMPLY MADE REASON-ABLE USE OF THE MONEY HE LEFT.
AFTER UNCLE BARTON'S DEATH...
ARTHUR CHRISTIAN ALSO DISAP-PEARED FROM SCHOOL.
MATHERS SAYS HE MAY HAVE FINISHED HIS ROLE AS ONE OF THE FOUR HORSEMEN.

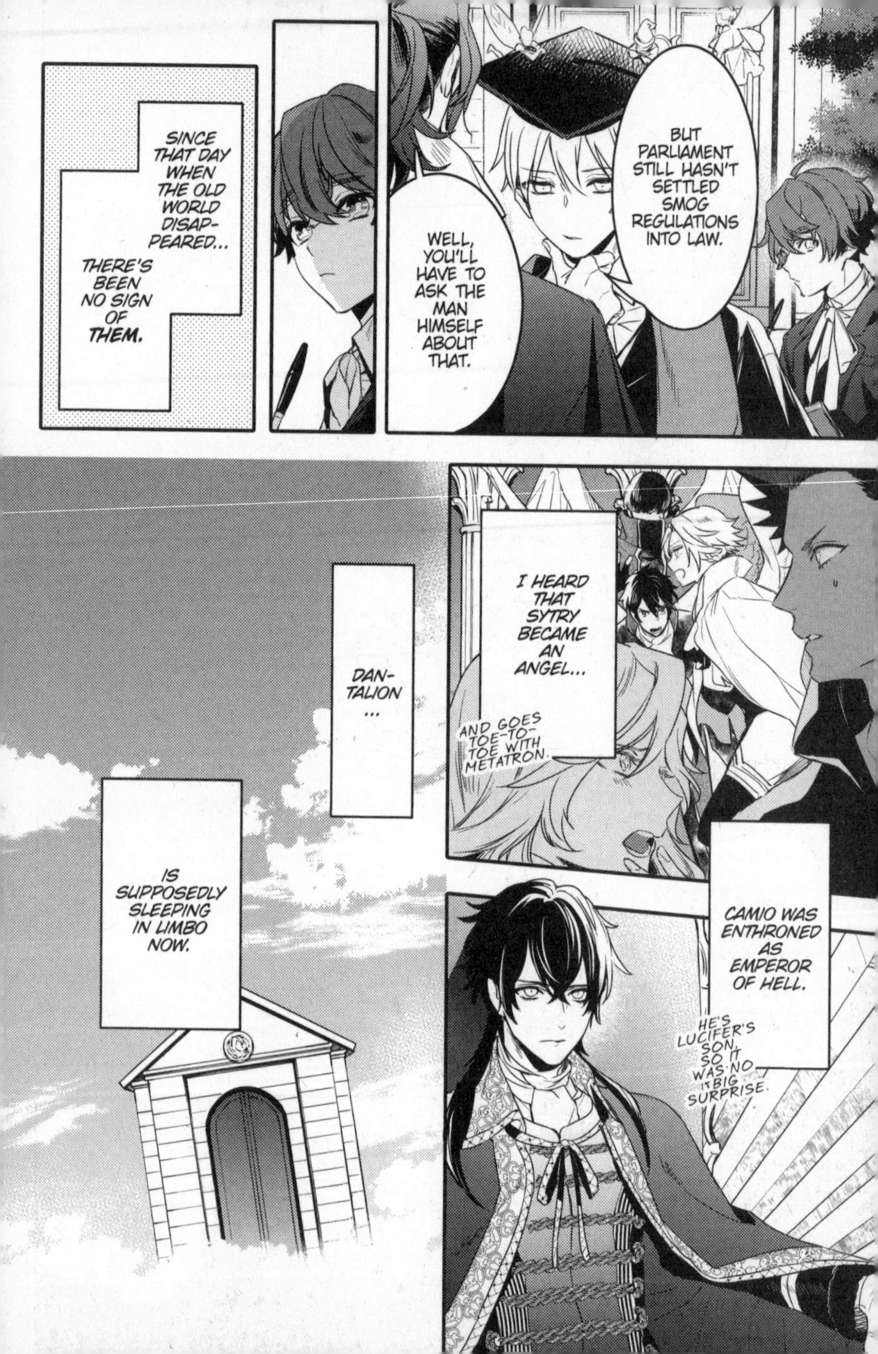
BUT PARLIAMENT STILL HASN'T SETTLED SMOG REGULATIONS INTO LAW.
WELL, YOU'LL HAVE TO ASK THE MAN HIMSELF ABOUT THAT.
SINCE THAT DAY WHEN THE OLD WORLD DISAPPEARED...
THERE'S BEEN NO SIGN OF THEM.
I HEARD THAT SYTRY BECAME AN ANGEL...
AND GOES TOE-TO-TOE WITH METATRON.
CAMIO WAS ENTHRONED AS EMPEROR OF HELL.
HE'S LUCIFER'S SON, SO IT WAS NO BIG SURPRISE.
DANTALION...
IS SUPPOSEDLY SLEEPING IN LIMBO NOW.

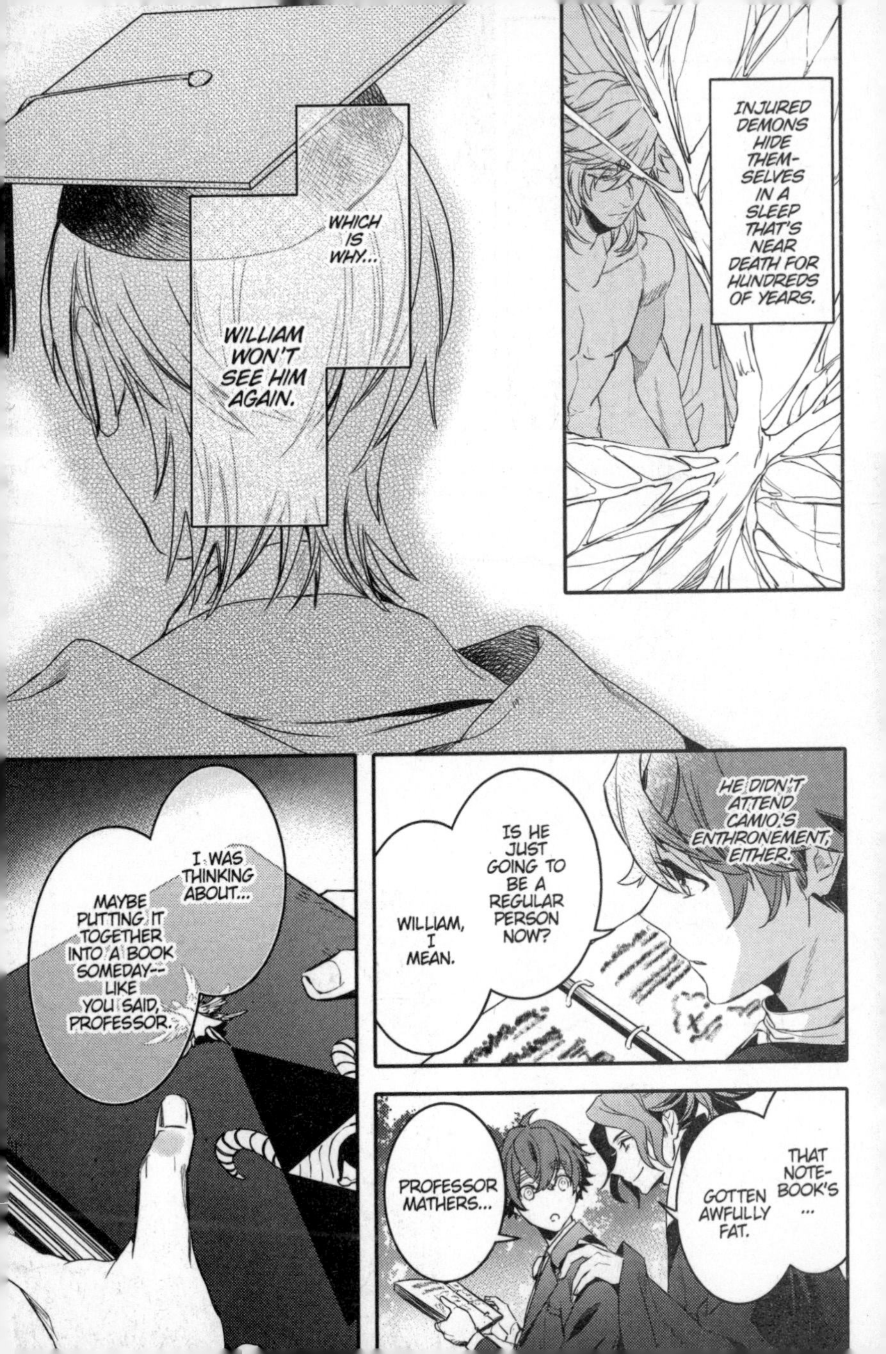
INJURED DEMONS HIDE THEM-SELVES IN A SLEEP THAT'S NEAR DEATH FOR HUNDREDS OF YEARS.
WHICH IS WHY...
WILLIAM WON'T SEE HIM AGAIN.
HE DIDN'T ATTEND CAMIO'S ENTHRONEMENT, EITHER.
IS HE JUST GOING TO BE A REGULAR PERSON NOW?
WILLIAM, I MEAN.
THAT NOTE-BOOK'S...
GOTTEN AWFULLY FAT.
PROFESSOR MATHERS...
I WAS THINKING ABOUT...
MAYBE PUTTING IT TOGETHER INTO A BOOK SOMEDAY--LIKE YOU SAID, PROFESSOR.

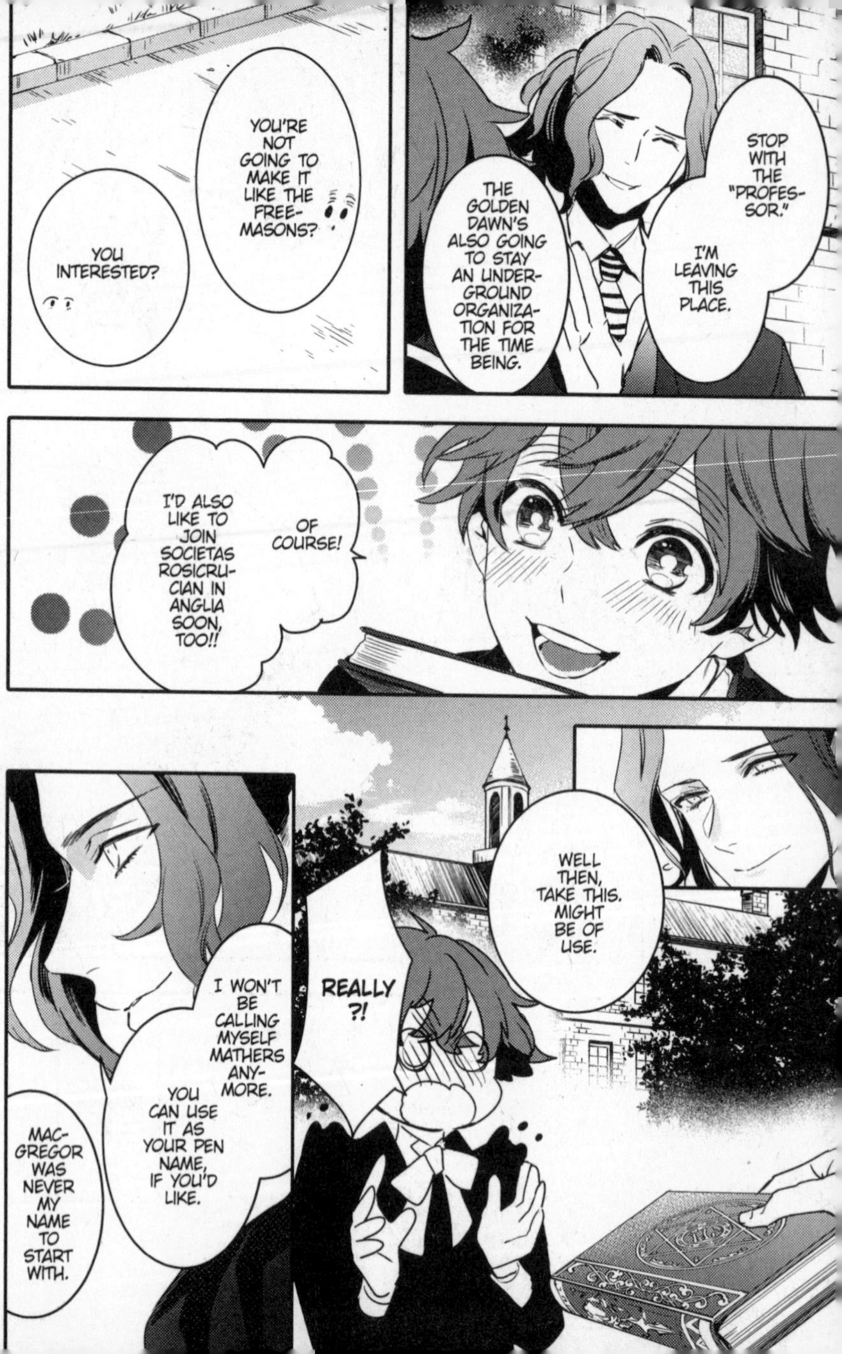
STOP WITH THE "PROFESSOR."
I'M LEAVING THIS PLACE.
THE GOLDEN DAWN'S ALSO GOING TO STAY AN UNDERGROUND ORGANIZATION FOR THE TIME BEING.
YOU'RE NOT GOING TO MAKE IT LIKE THE FREEMASONS?
YOU INTERESTED?
OF COURSE!
I'D ALSO LIKE TO JOIN SOCIETAS ROSICRUCIAN IN ANGLIA SOON, TOO!!
WELL THEN, TAKE THIS. MIGHT BE OF USE.
REALLY?!
I WON'T BE CALLING MYSELF MATHERS ANYMORE.
YOU CAN USE IT AS YOUR PEN NAME, IF YOU'D LIKE.
MACGREGOR WAS NEVER MY NAME TO START WITH.

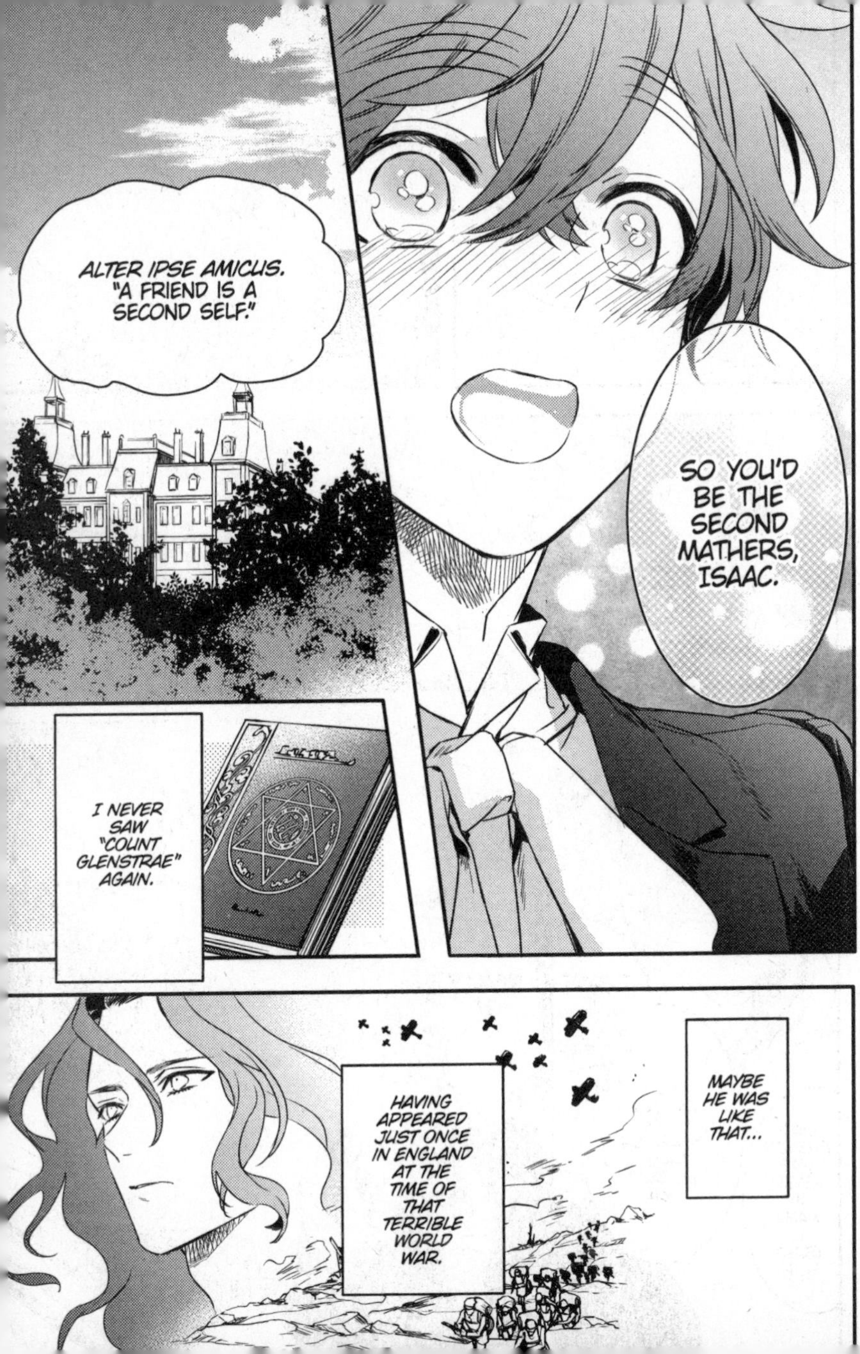
SO YOU'D BE THE SECOND MATHERS, ISAAC.
ALTER IPSE AMICUS. "A FRIEND IS A SECOND SELF."
I NEVER SAW "COUNT GLENSTRAE" AGAIN.
MAYBE HE WAS LIKE THAT...
HAVING APPEARED JUST ONCE IN ENGLAND AT THE TIME OF THAT TERRIBLE WORLD WAR.

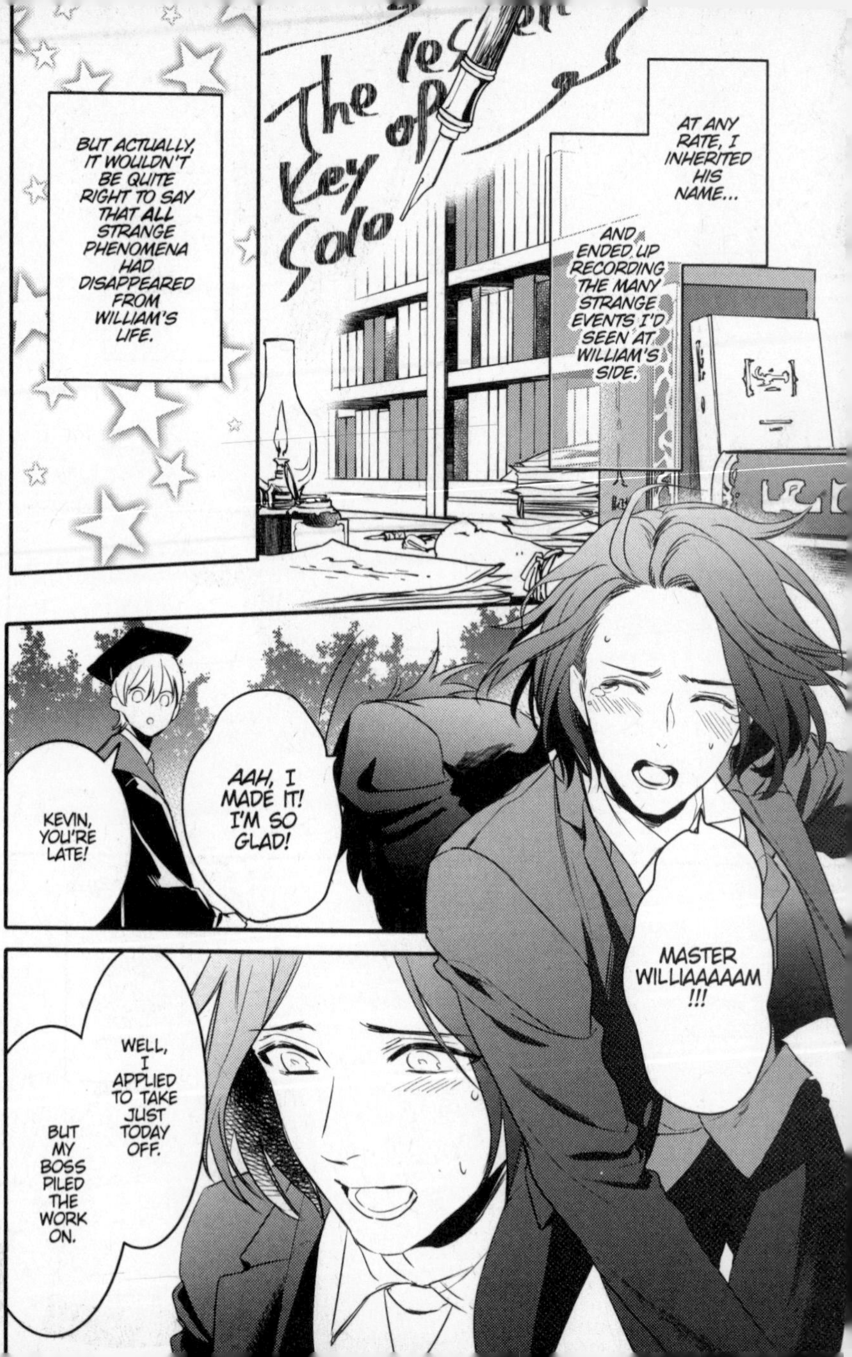
AT ANY RATE, I INHERITED HIS NAME...
AND ENDED UP RECORDING THE MANY STRANGE EVENTS I'D SEEN AT WILLIAM'S SIDE.
BUT ACTUALLY, IT WOULDN'T BE QUITE RIGHT TO SAY THAT ALL STRANGE PHENOMENA HAD DISAPPEARED FROM WILLIAM'S LIFE.
MASTER WILLIAAAAAM!!!
AAH, I MADE IT! I'M SO GLAD!
KEVIN, YOU'RE LATE!
WELL, I APPLIED TO TAKE JUST TODAY OFF.
BUT MY BOSS PILED THE WORK ON.

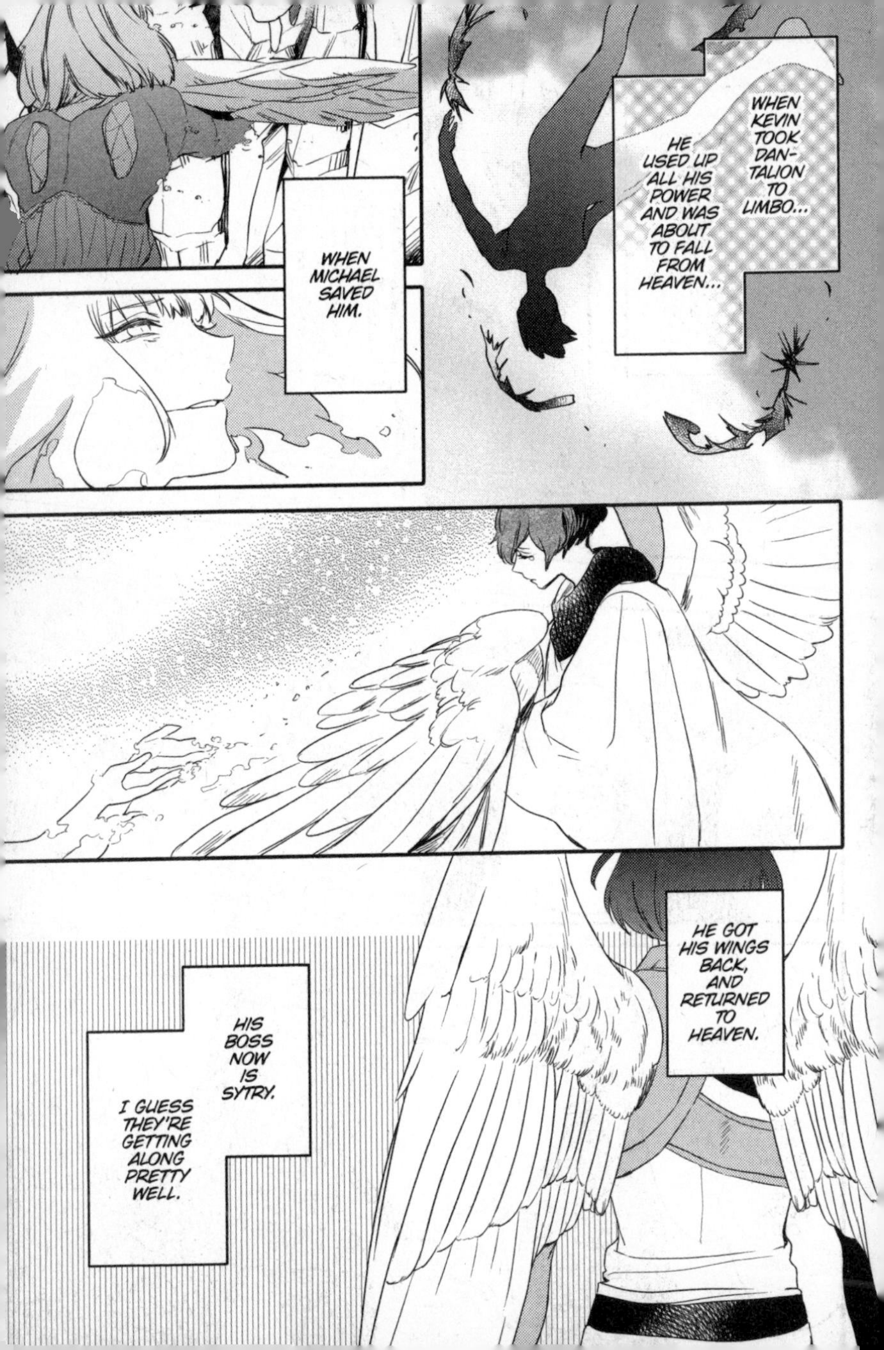
WHEN KEVIN TOOK DANTALION TO LIMBO...
HE USED UP ALL HIS POWER AND WAS ABOUT TO FALL FROM HEAVEN...
WHEN MICHAEL SAVED HIM.
HE GOT HIS WINGS BACK, AND RETURNED TO HEAVEN.
HIS BOSS NOW IS SYTRY.
I GUESS THEY'RE GETTING ALONG PRETTY WELL.

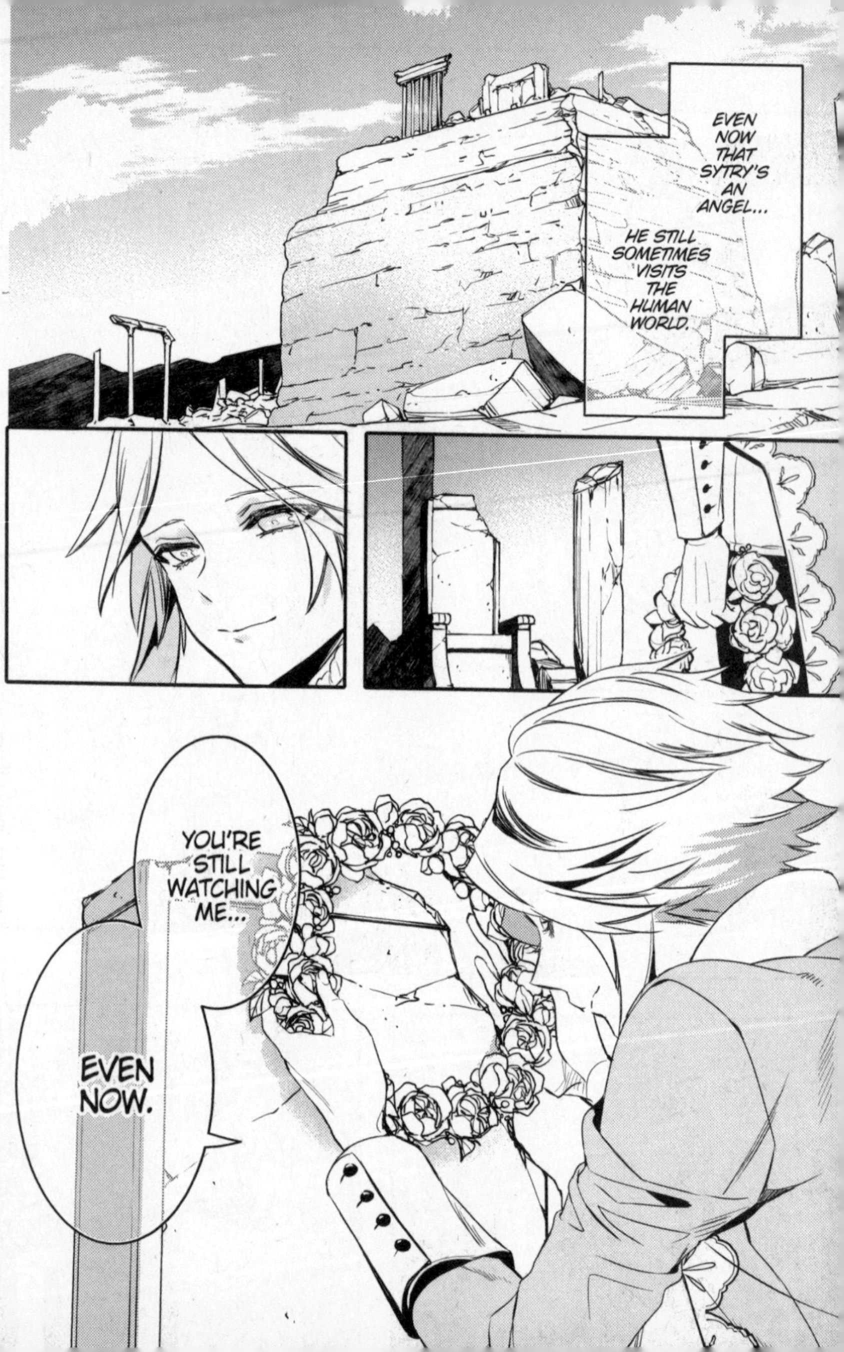
EVEN NOW THAT SYTRY'S AN ANGEL...
HE STILL SOMETIMES VISITS THE HUMAN WORLD.
YOU'RE STILL WATCHING ME...
EVEN NOW.

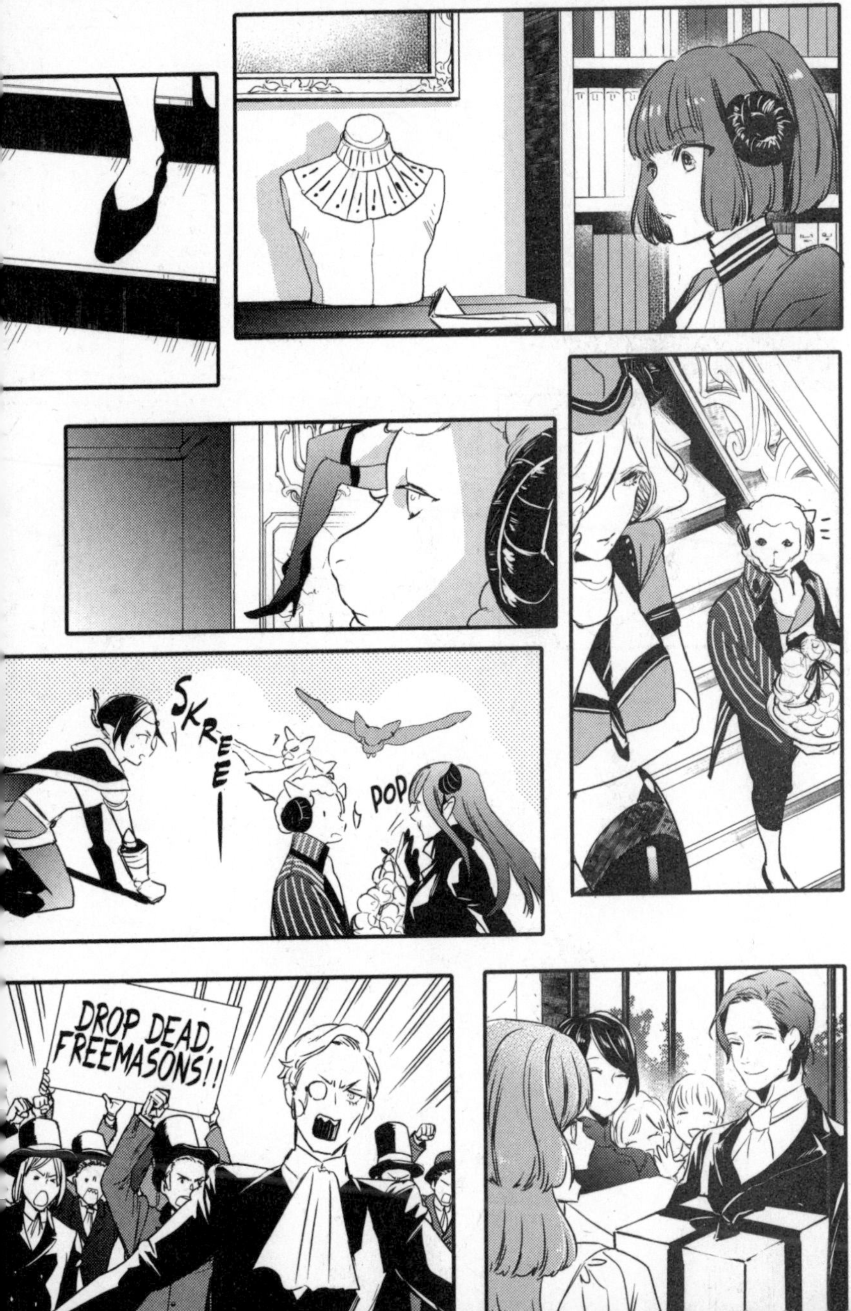
SKREE—
POP
DROP DEAD, FREEMASONS!!

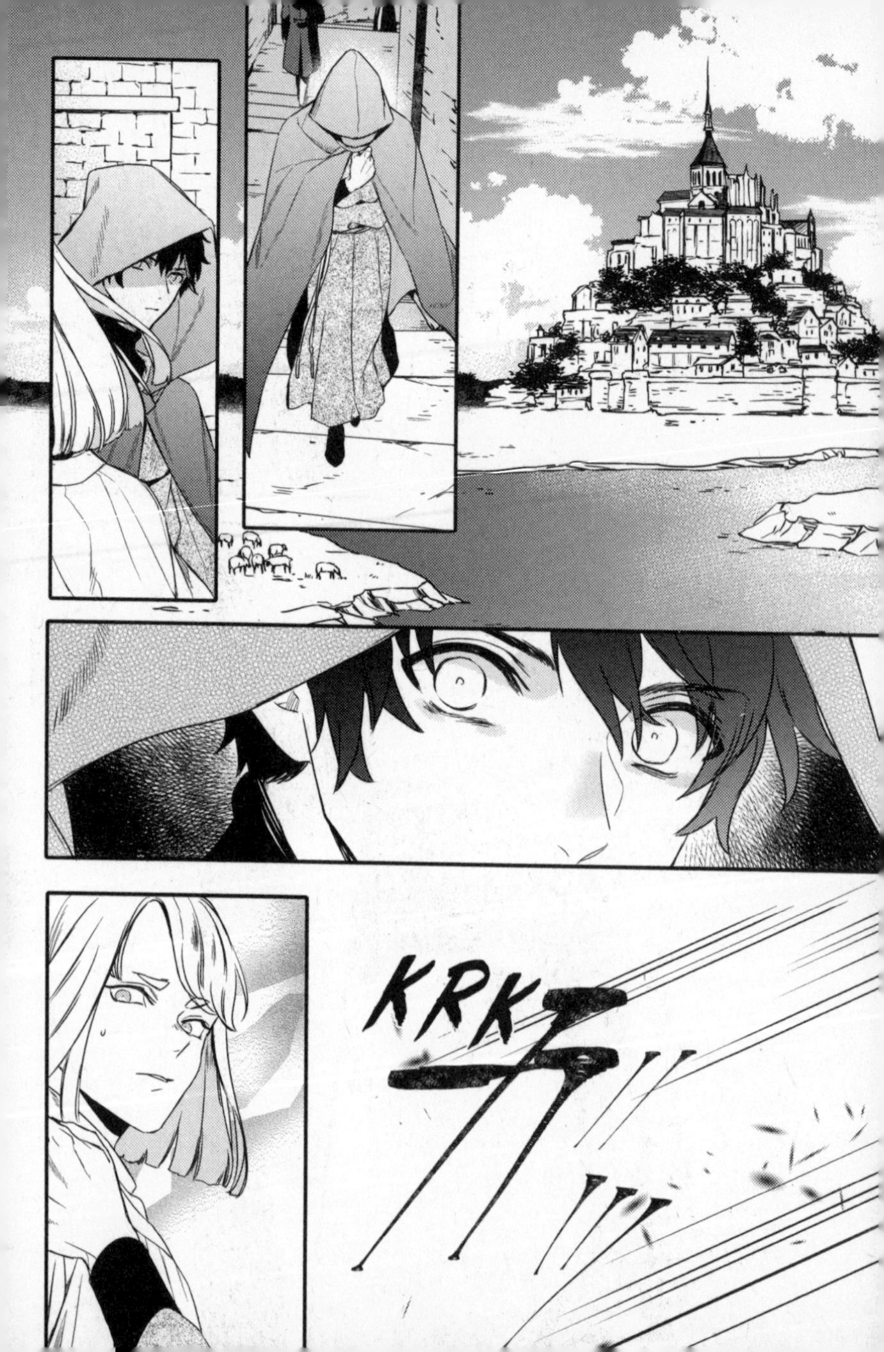
KRK

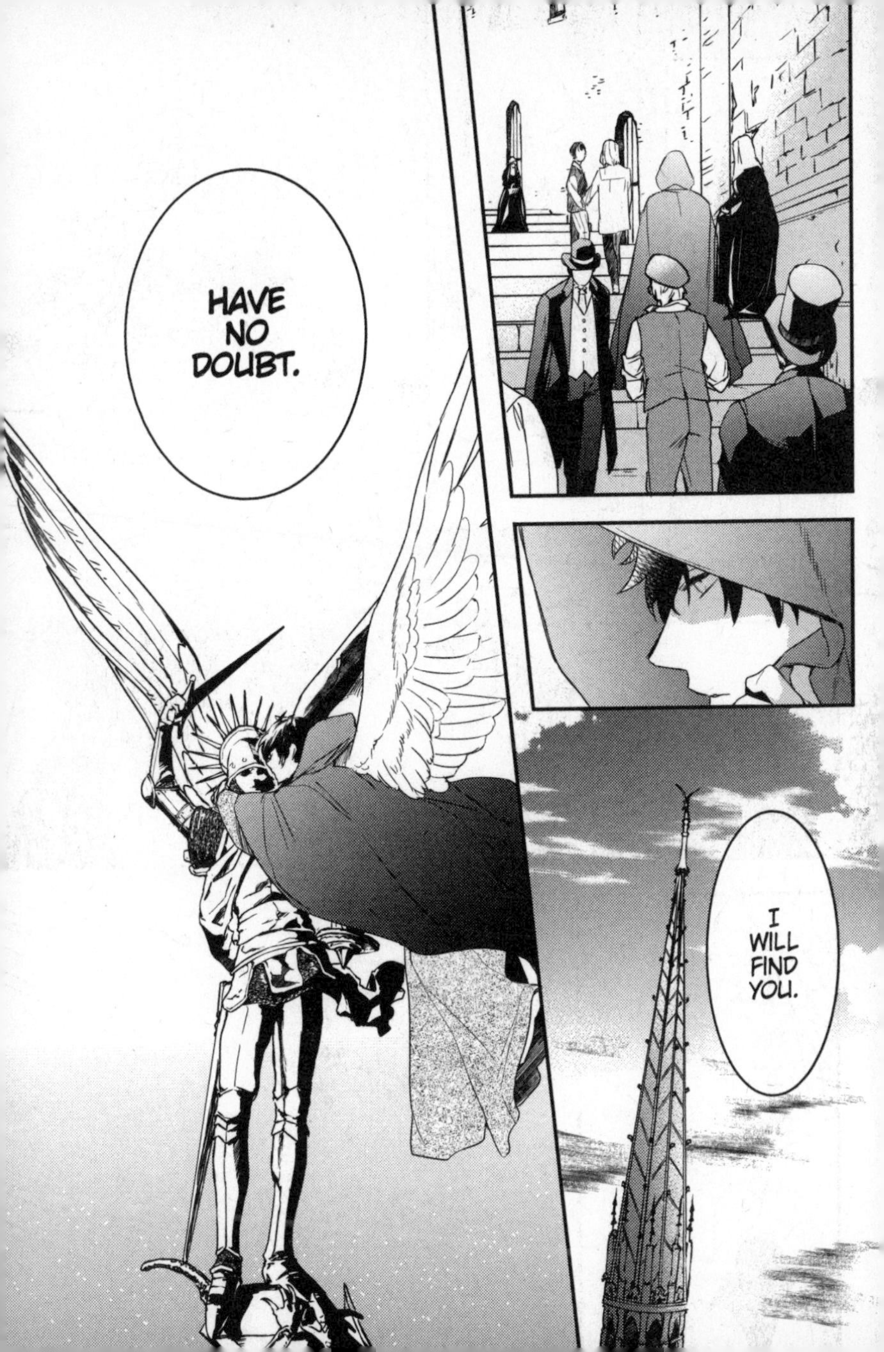
HAVE NO DOUBT.
I WILL FIND YOU.

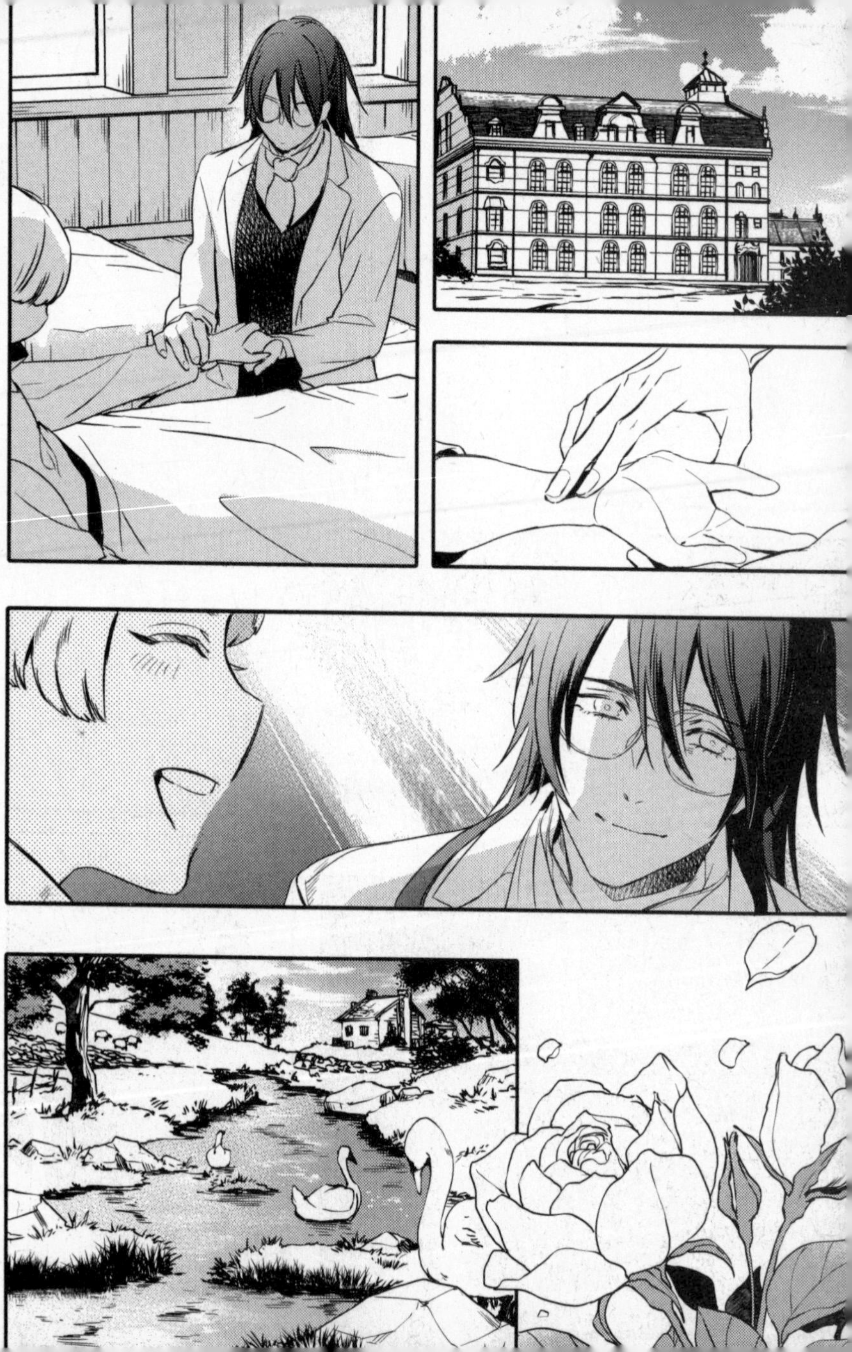

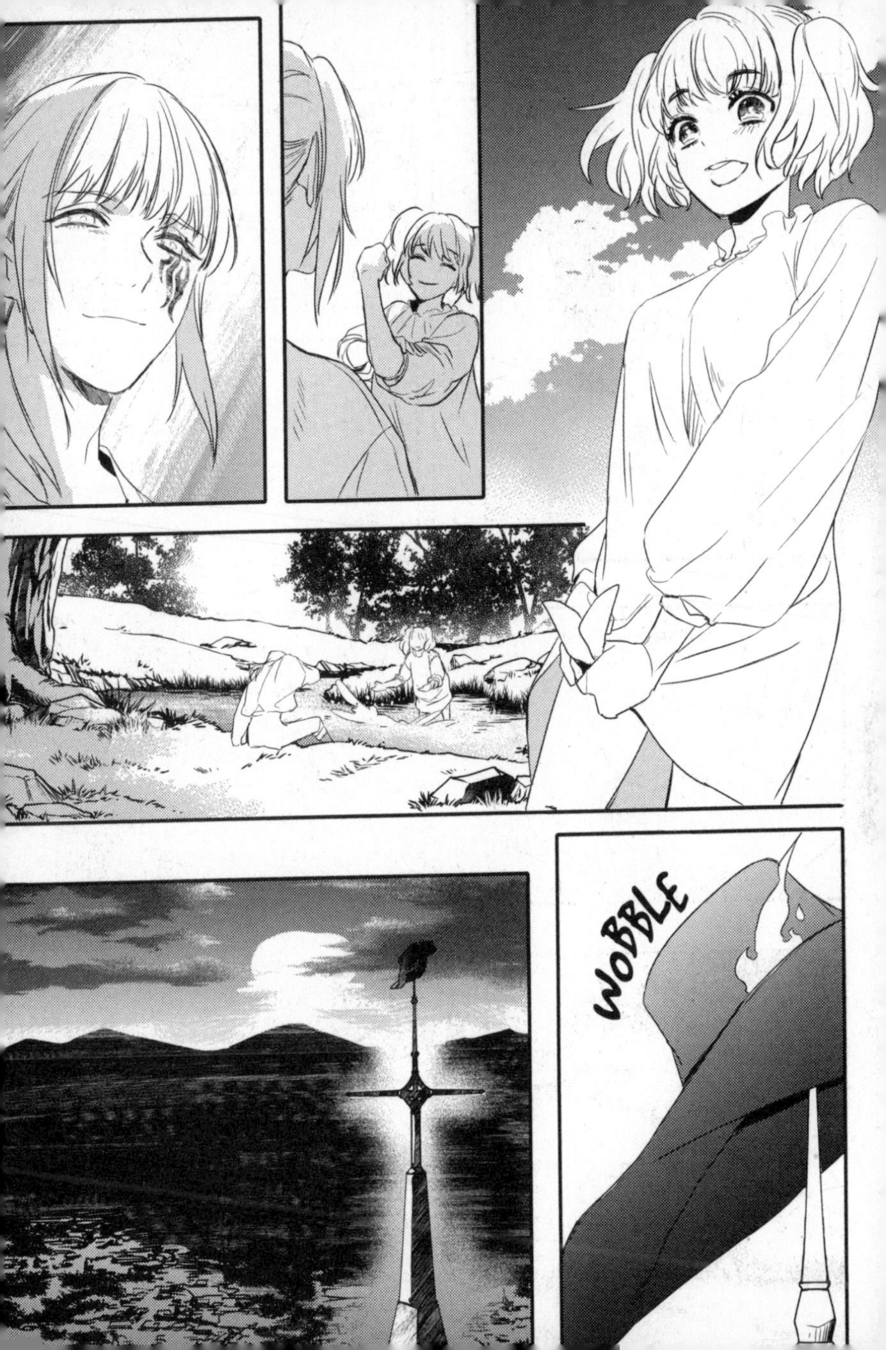
WOBBLE

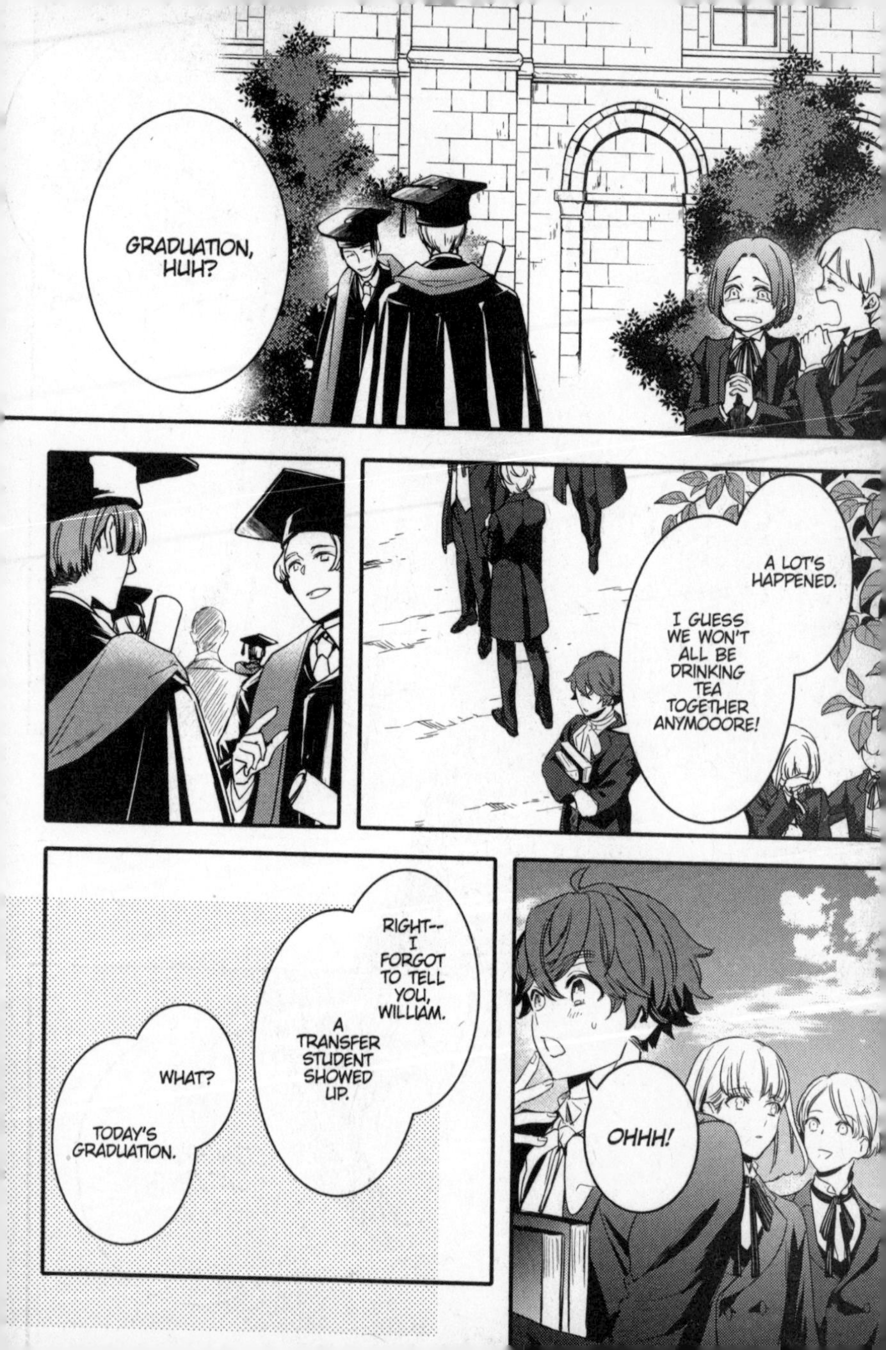
GRADUATION, HUH?
A LOT'S HAPPENED.
I GUESS WE WON'T ALL BE DRINKING TEA TOGETHER ANYMOOORE!
OHHH!
RIGHT-- I FORGOT TO TELL YOU, WILLIAM.
A TRANSFER STUDENT SHOWED UP.
WHAT?
TODAY'S GRADUATION.

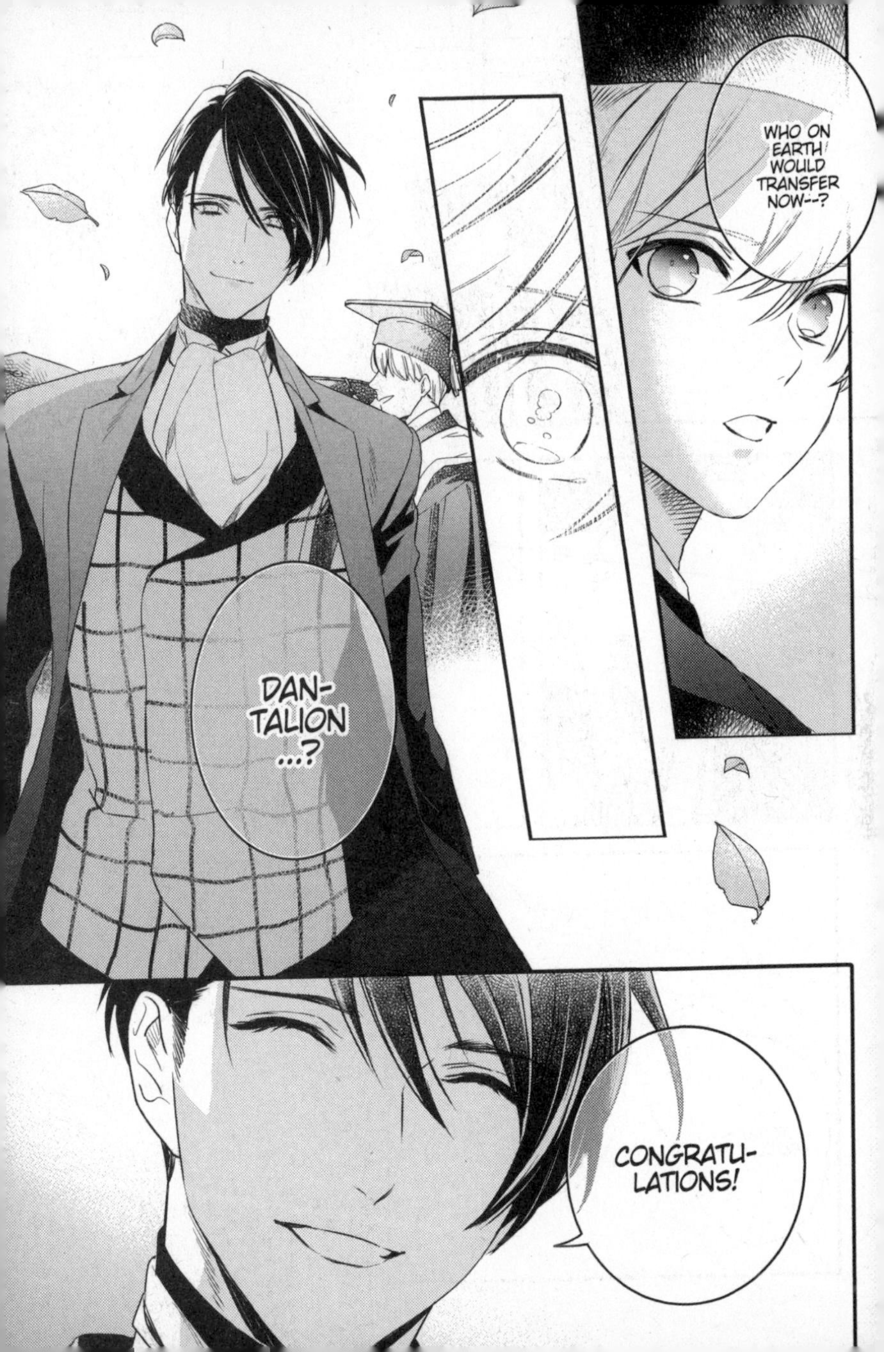
WHO ON EARTH WOULD TRANSFER NOW--?
DAN-TALION ...?
CONGRATU-LATIONS!

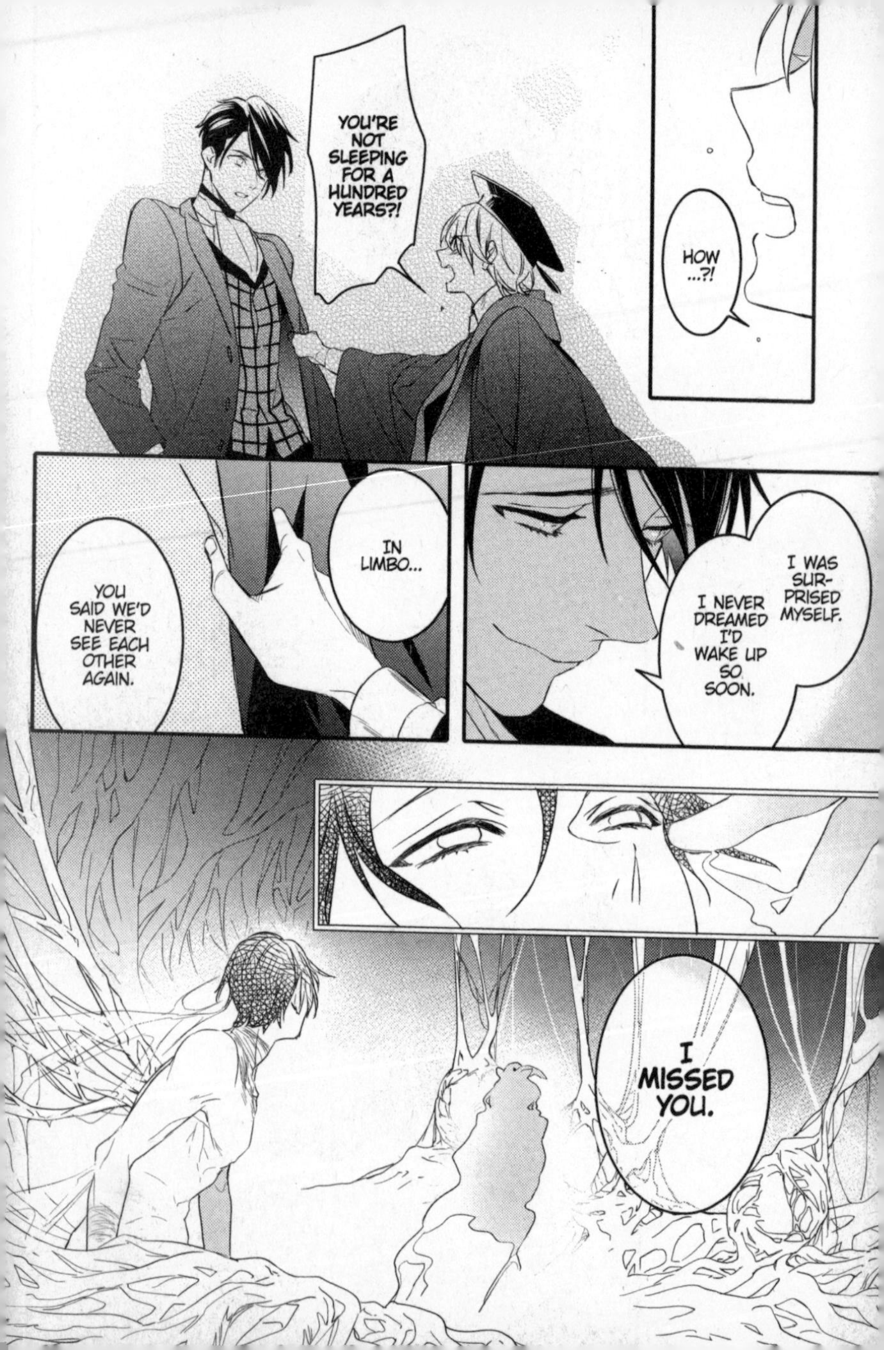
HOW ...?!
YOU'RE NOT SLEEPING FOR A HUNDRED YEARS?!
I WAS SUR-PRISED MYSELF.
I NEVER DREAMED I'D WAKE UP SO SOON.
IN LIMBO...
YOU SAID WE'D NEVER SEE EACH OTHER AGAIN.
I MISSED YOU.

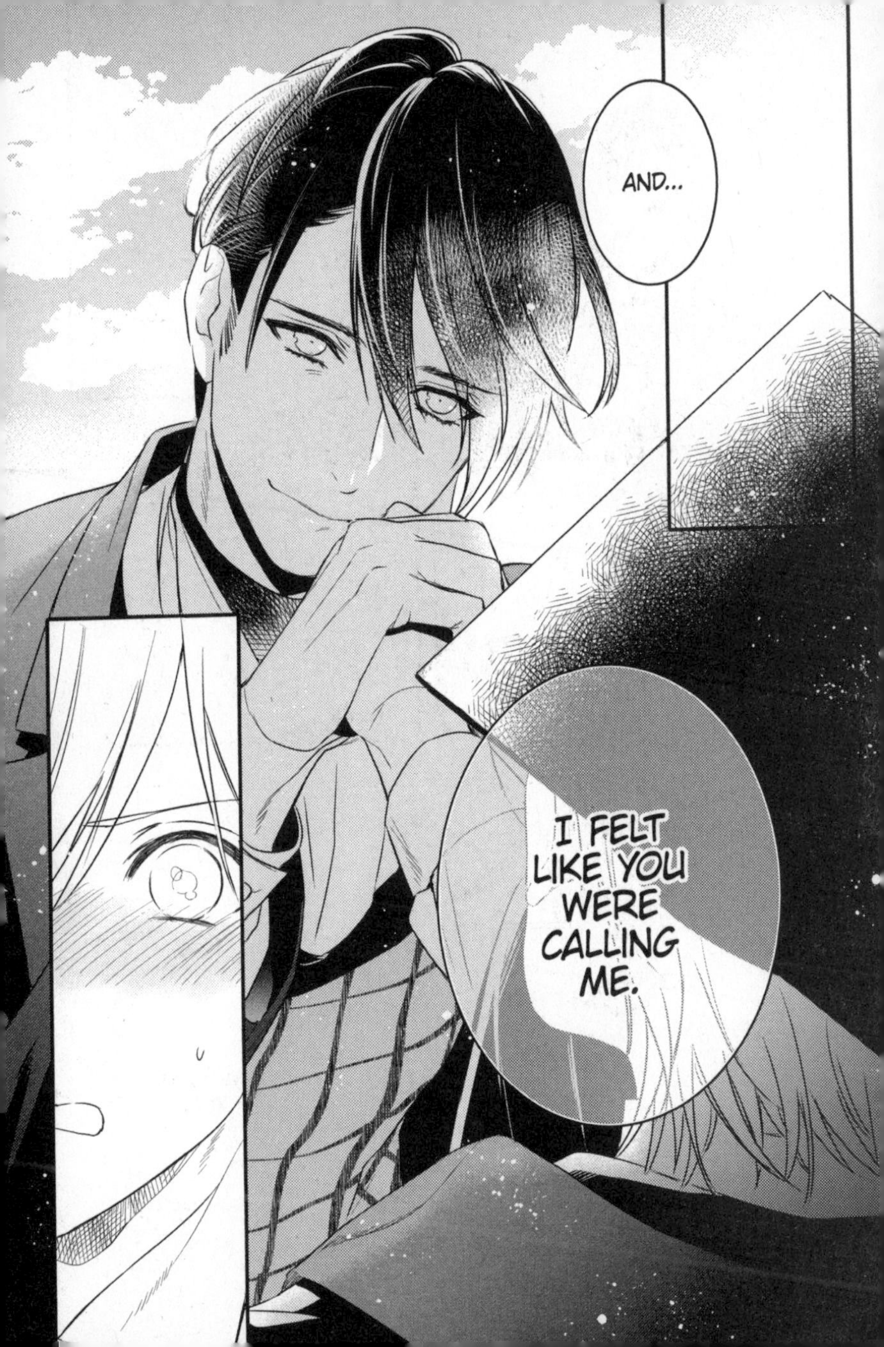
AND...
I FELT LIKE YOU WERE CALLING ME.

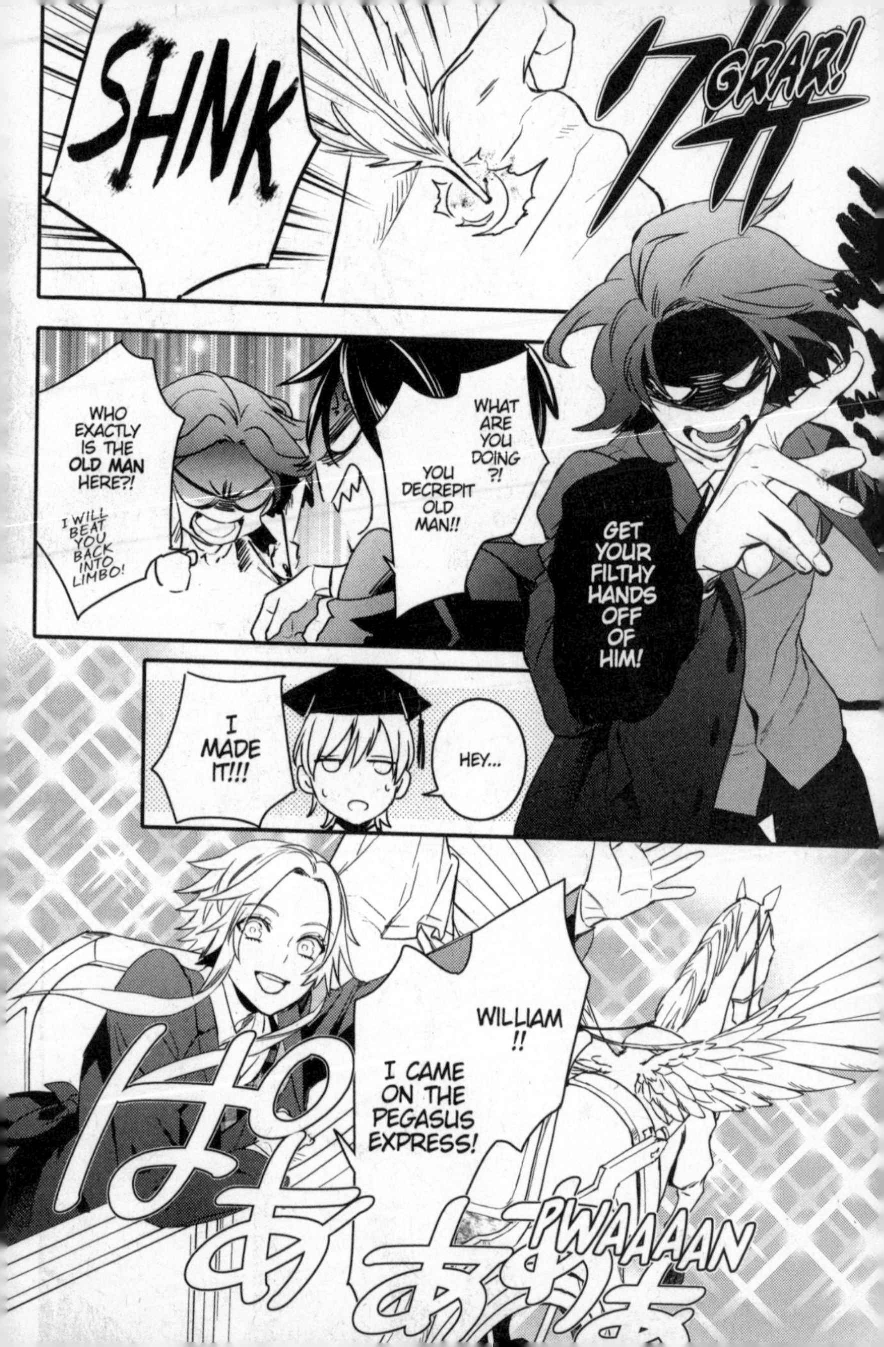

GRAR!
SHINK
GET YOUR FILTHY HANDS OFF OF HIM!
WHAT ARE YOU DOING?!
YOU DECREPIT OLD MAN!!
WHO EXACTLY IS THE OLD MAN HERE?!
I WILL BEAT YOU BACK INTO LIMBO!
HEY...
I MADE IT!!!
WILLIAM!!
I CAME ON THE PEGASUS EXPRESS!
PWAAAAN

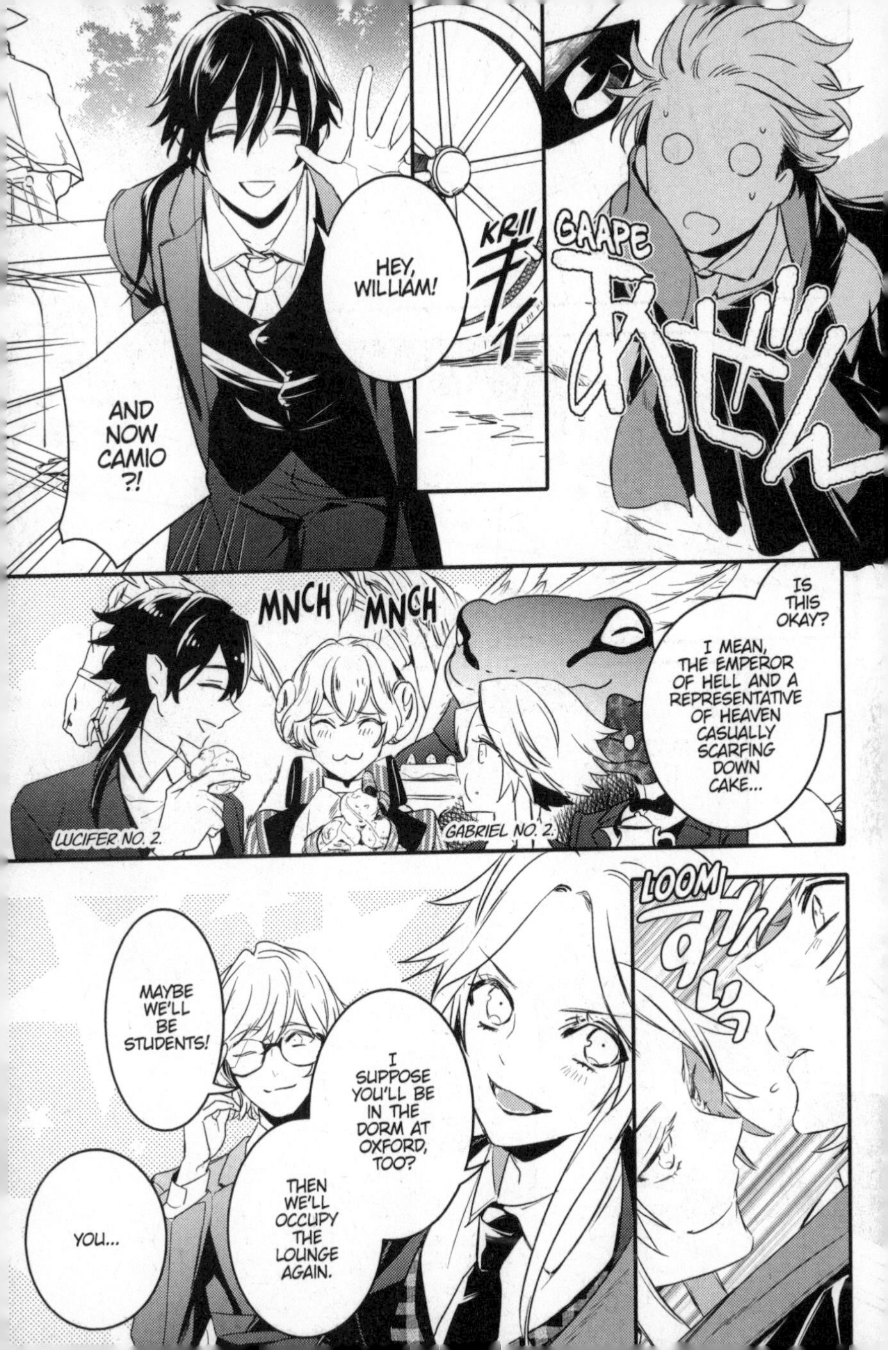
GAAPE
HEY, WILLIAM!
KRII
AND NOW CAMIO ?!
IS THIS OKAY?
I MEAN, THE EMPEROR OF HELL AND A REPRESENTATIVE OF HEAVEN CASUALLY SCARFING DOWN CAKE...
MNCH MNCH
GABRIEL NO. 2.
LUCIFER NO. 2.
LOOM
I SUPPOSE YOU'LL BE IN THE DORM AT OXFORD, TOO?
THEN WE'LL OCCUPY THE LOUNGE AGAIN.
MAYBE WE'LL BE STUDENTS!
YOU...

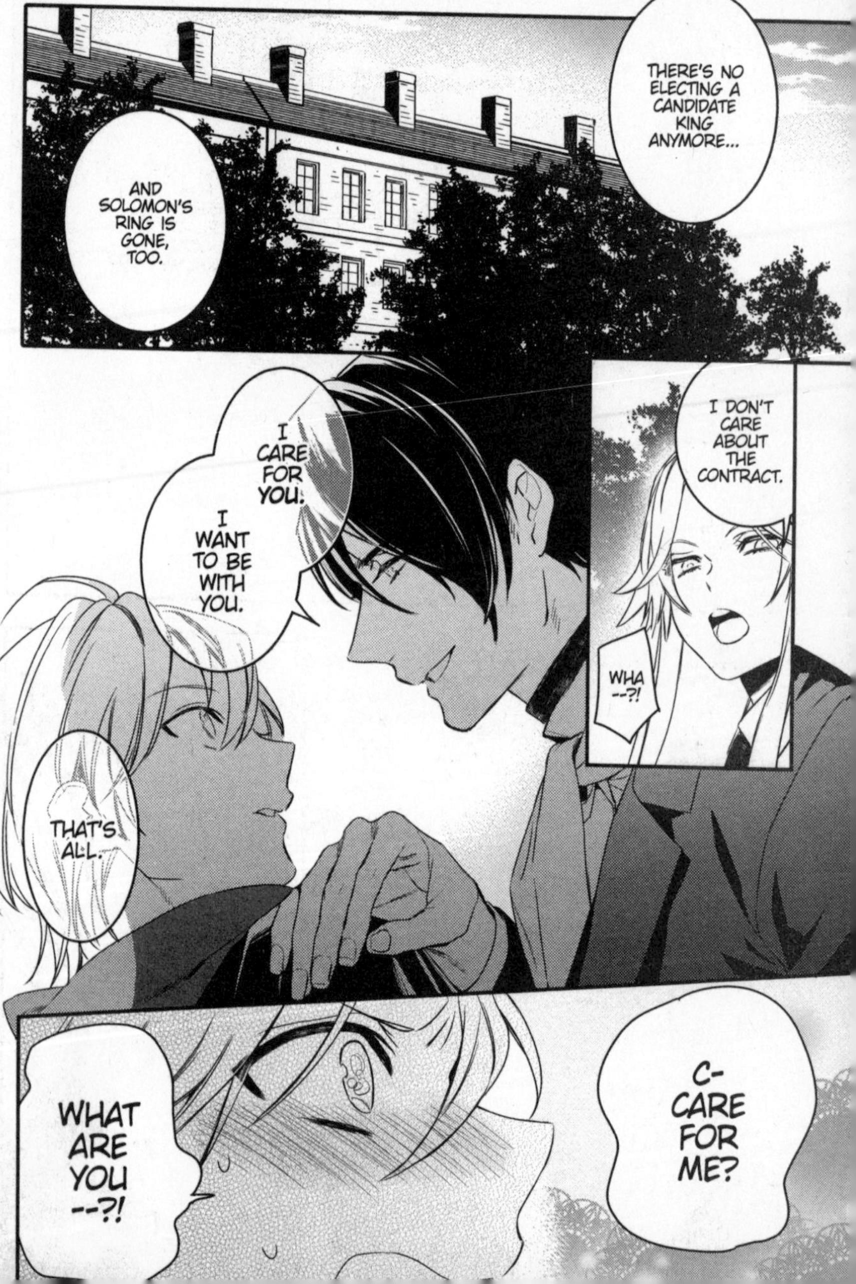
THERE'S NO ELECTING A CANDIDATE KING ANYMORE...
AND SOLOMON'S RING IS GONE, TOO.
I DON'T CARE ABOUT THE CONTRACT.
WHA--?!
I CARE FOR YOU.
I WANT TO BE WITH YOU.
THAT'S ALL.
C-CARE FOR ME?
WHAT ARE YOU--?!

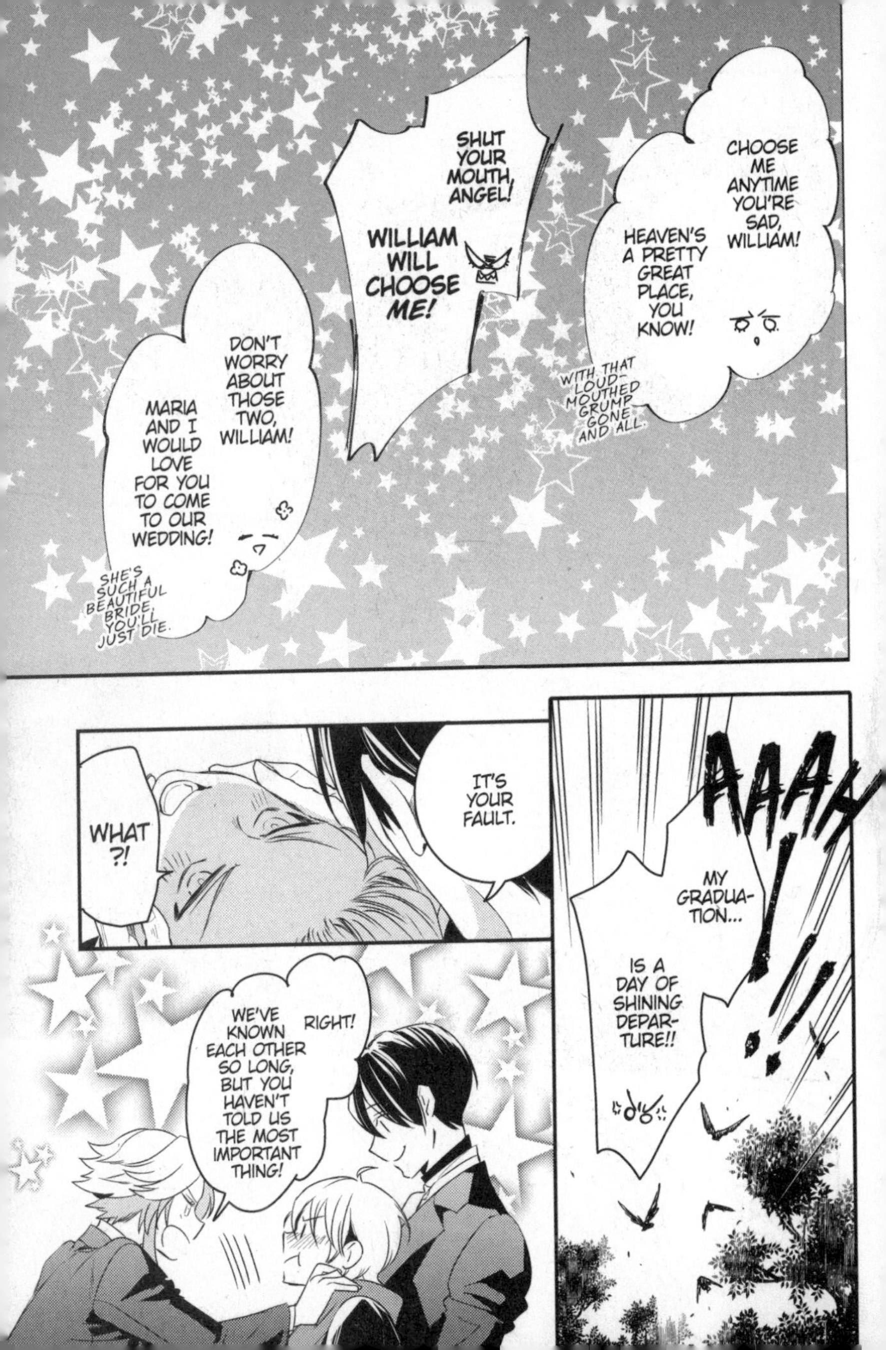
CHOOSE ME ANYTIME YOU'RE SAD, WILLIAM!
HEAVEN'S A PRETTY GREAT PLACE, YOU KNOW!
WITH THAT LOUD-MOUTHED GRUMP GONE AND ALL.
SHUT YOUR MOUTH, ANGEL!
WILLIAM WILL CHOOSE ME!
DON'T WORRY ABOUT THOSE TWO, WILLIAM!
MARIA AND I WOULD LOVE FOR YOU TO COME TO OUR WEDDING!
SHE'S SUCH A BEAUTIFUL BRIDE, YOU'LL JUST DIE.
AAAH!!!
MY GRADUATION...
IS A DAY OF SHINING DEPARTURE!!
IT'S YOUR FAULT.
WHAT?!
RIGHT!
WE'VE KNOWN EACH OTHER SO LONG, BUT YOU HAVEN'T TOLD US THE MOST IMPORTANT THING!

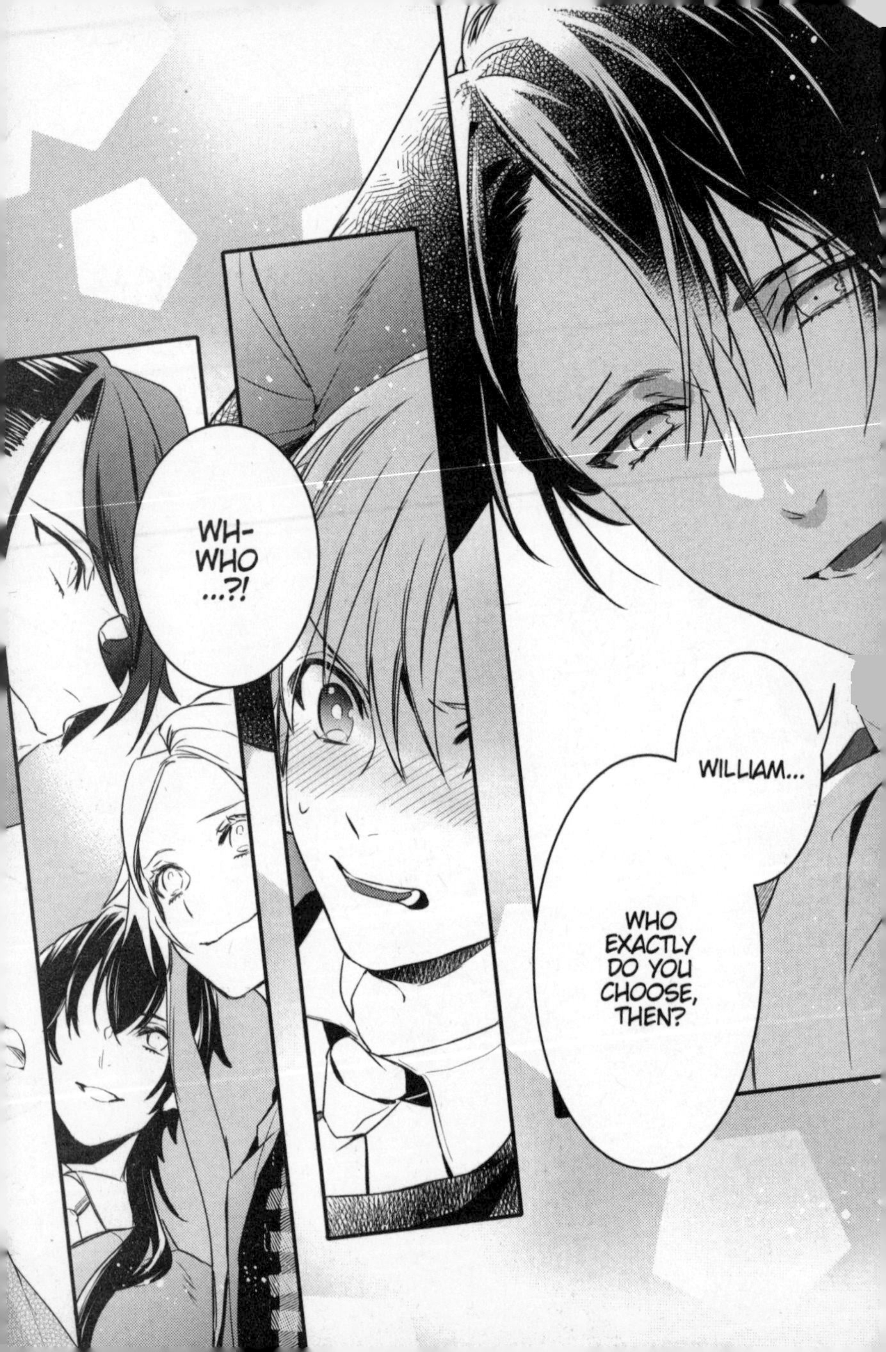
WILLIAM...
WHO EXACTLY DO YOU CHOOSE, THEN?
WH- WHO ...?!

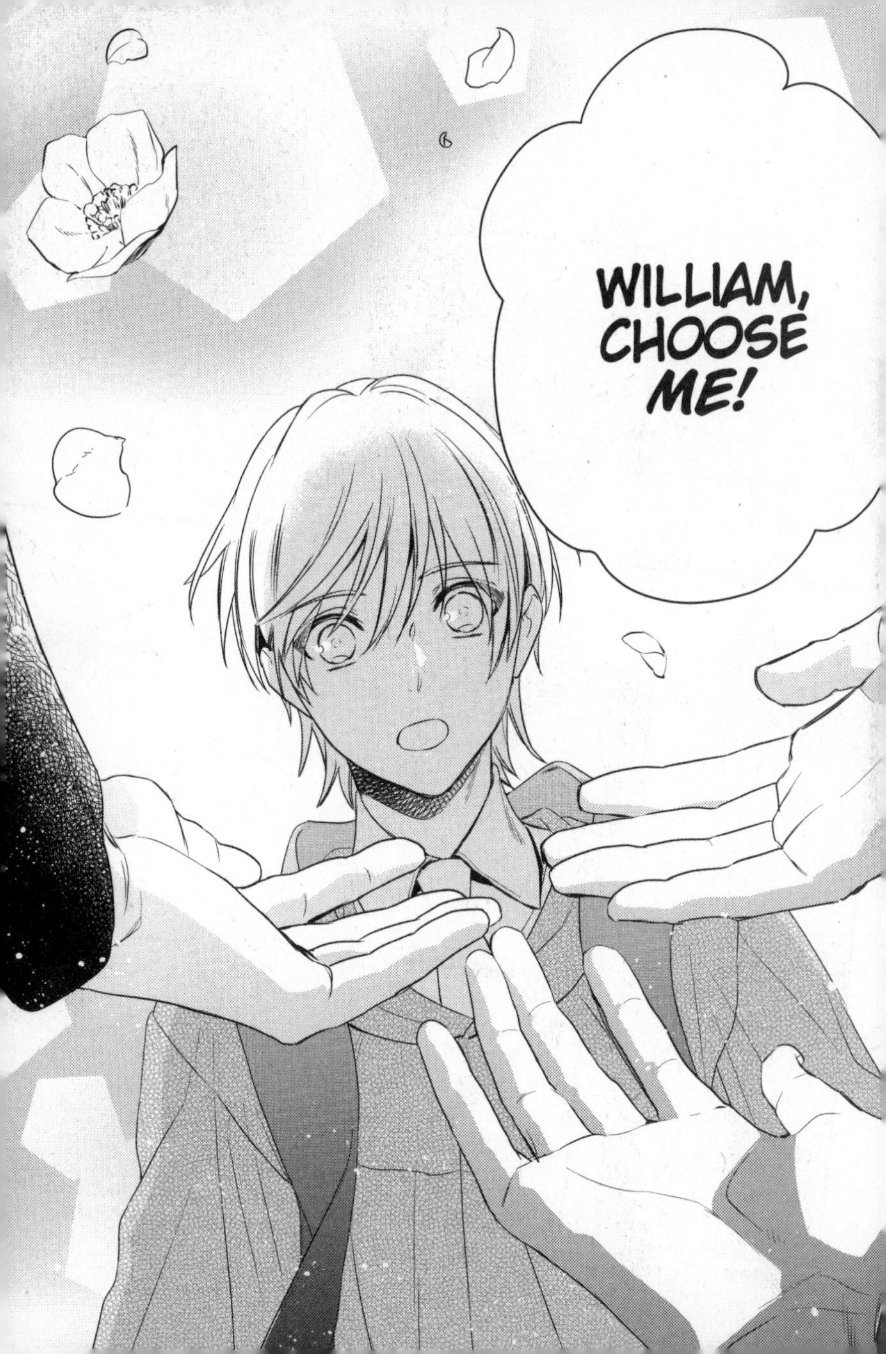
WILLIAM, CHOOSE ME!

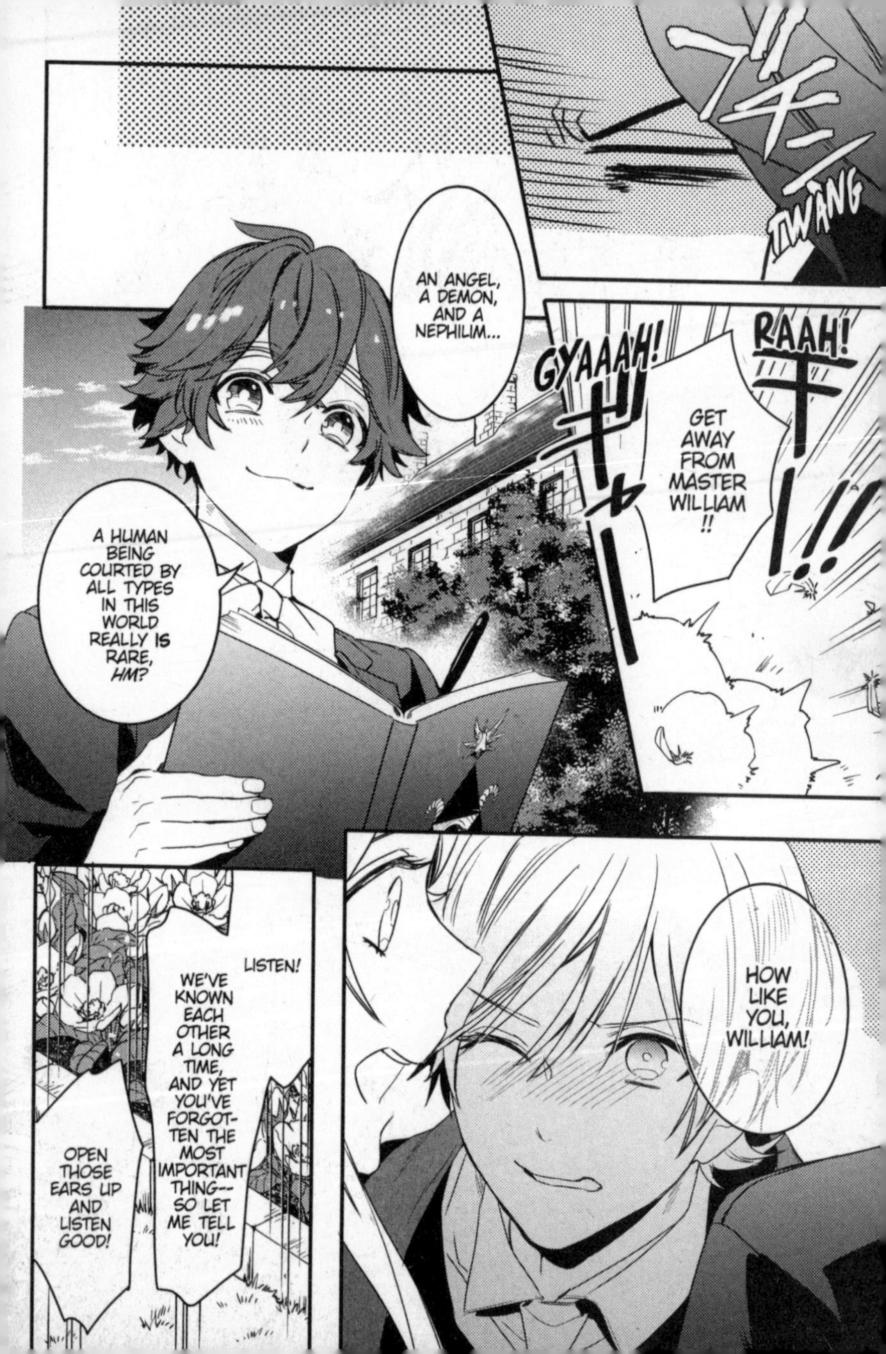

TWANG
RAAH!
GYAAAH!
GET AWAY FROM MASTER WILLIAM!!
AN ANGEL, A DEMON, AND A NEPHILIM...
A HUMAN BEING COURTED BY ALL TYPES IN THIS WORLD REALLY IS RARE, *HM?*
HOW LIKE YOU, WILLIAM!
LISTEN!
WE'VE KNOWN EACH OTHER A LONG TIME, AND YET YOU'VE FORGOT-TEN THE MOST IMPORTANT THING-- SO LET ME TELL YOU!
OPEN THOSE EARS UP AND LISTEN GOOD!

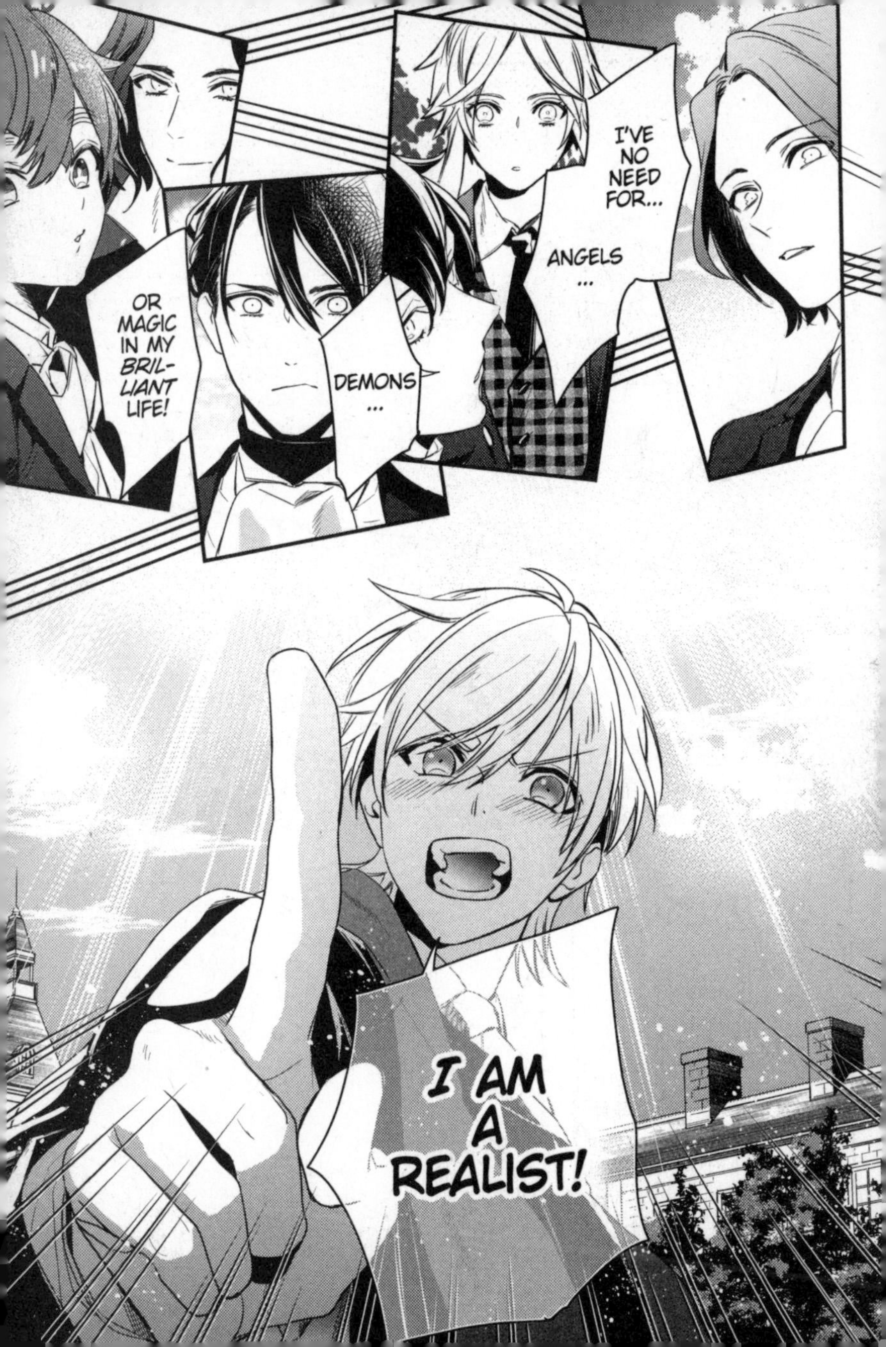
I'VE NO NEED FOR...
ANGELS...
DEMONS...
OR MAGIC IN MY BRILLIANT LIFE!
I AM A REALIST!

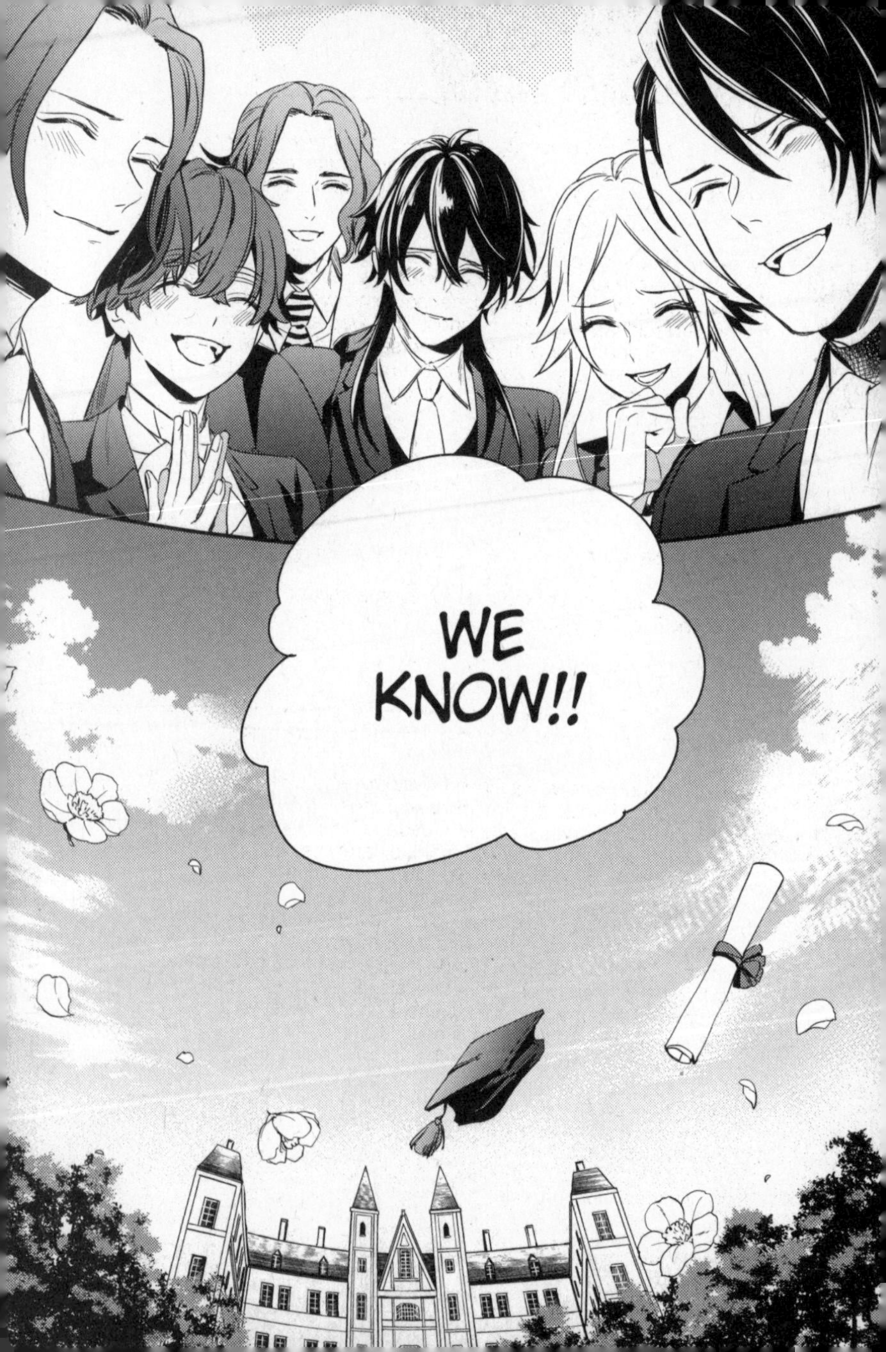
WE KNOW!!

Utako Yukihiro

I was in the middle of working on a one-shot story when I got the plan for *Devils and Realist*. The script for the first chapter and the character profiles I got were quite interesting... I remember reading it in a trance, totally absorbed.

When the first book came out, I was told we could probably keep going for three volumes, and when volume three came out, I was told we might make it to five. Every time the comic was released, my heart would leap up into my chest like I was about to be executed. It still does. Before I knew it, we'd been serialized for nine years. I've had so many experiences I never could have dreamed of happening, thanks to the illustration collection, various media mixes, and publication overseas.

A huge thank you to everyone who supported us! And to the divine protection of Gabriel! (Although he seems to specialize in sweet things!)

Thank you so much for coming all the way to the end with us.

If you remember it out of the blue for even a second, the story will live on forever. That's my hope.

We'll meet again someday!

It's already been nine years since I pleaded with my editor in the Tokyo Dome Hotel café to let me do *Tokimeki Tonight* in a boys' boarding school. And then I blinked and it's almost a decade later. The series was turned into an anime and a musical. So many different things have happened, and I've been so glad to be a part of it.

The story of a human being manipulated by Heaven and Hell was in my head as a sort of chronicle, and William was only one part of that. (In another time, probably, there will also be the story of the other seventy-two pillar demons and Solomon's vessels.) Even so, I'm grateful we were able to close the curtain without incident on this dense story-- we piled up fifteen volumes! Even now, I have nothing but gratitude in my heart. I pray we meet again in another story.

This tale has had its finale for now, and going forward, I'd like to travel around to the regions in *Devils and Realist* and the Bible and enjoy the story from a different direction.

Thank you. See you someday.

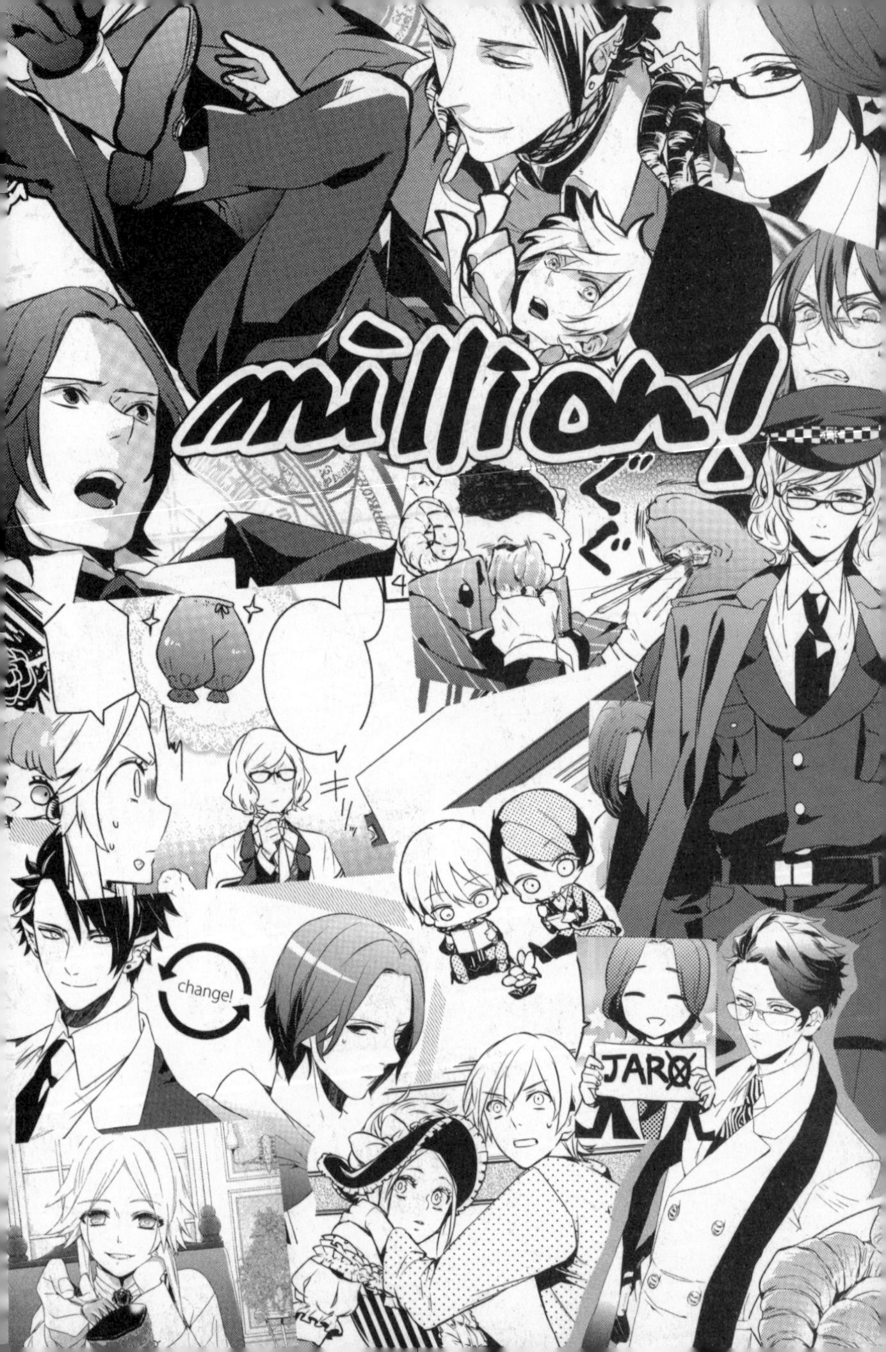
million!
ぐ ぐ
4
change!
JARO

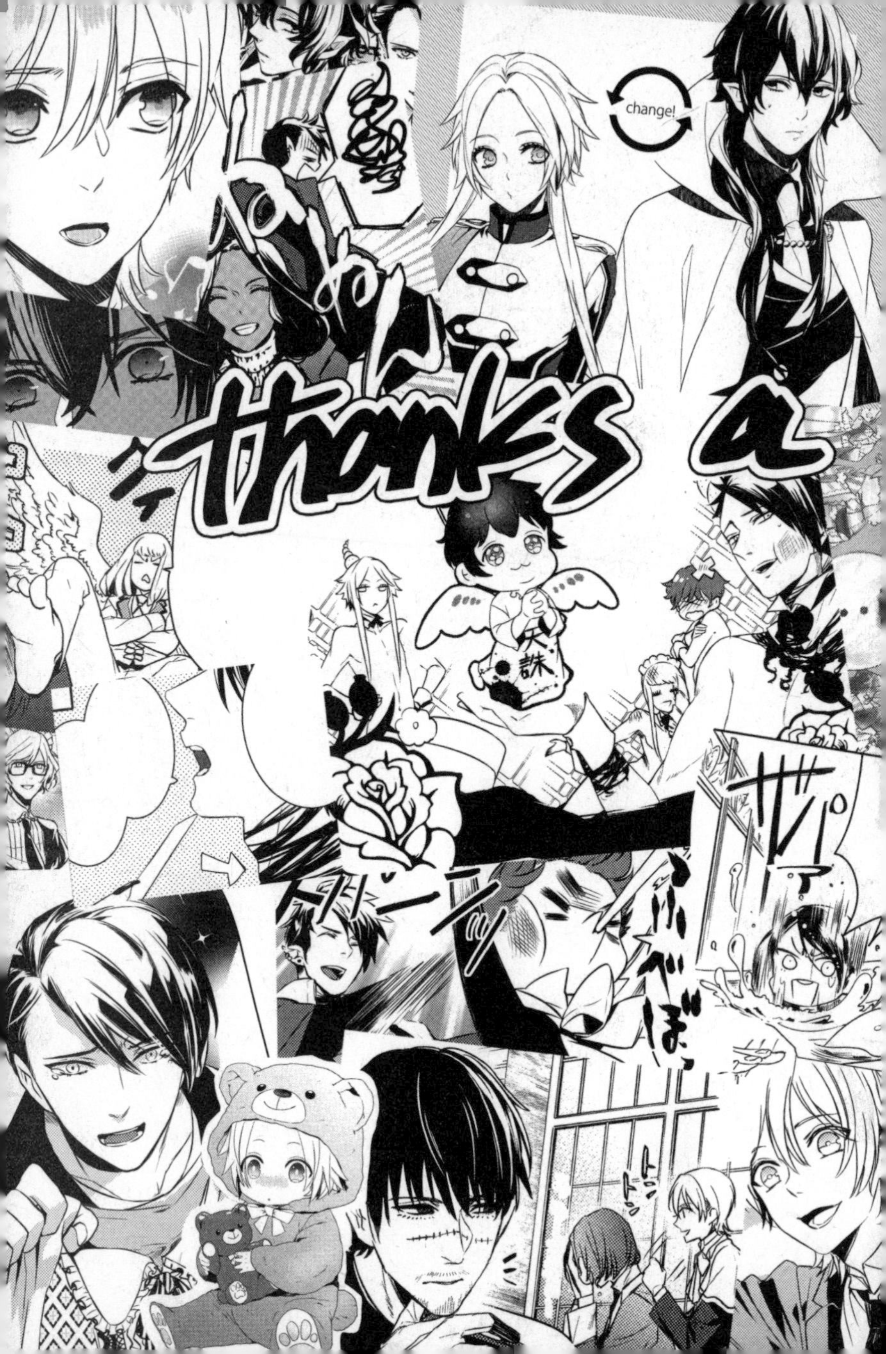
change!
thanks a

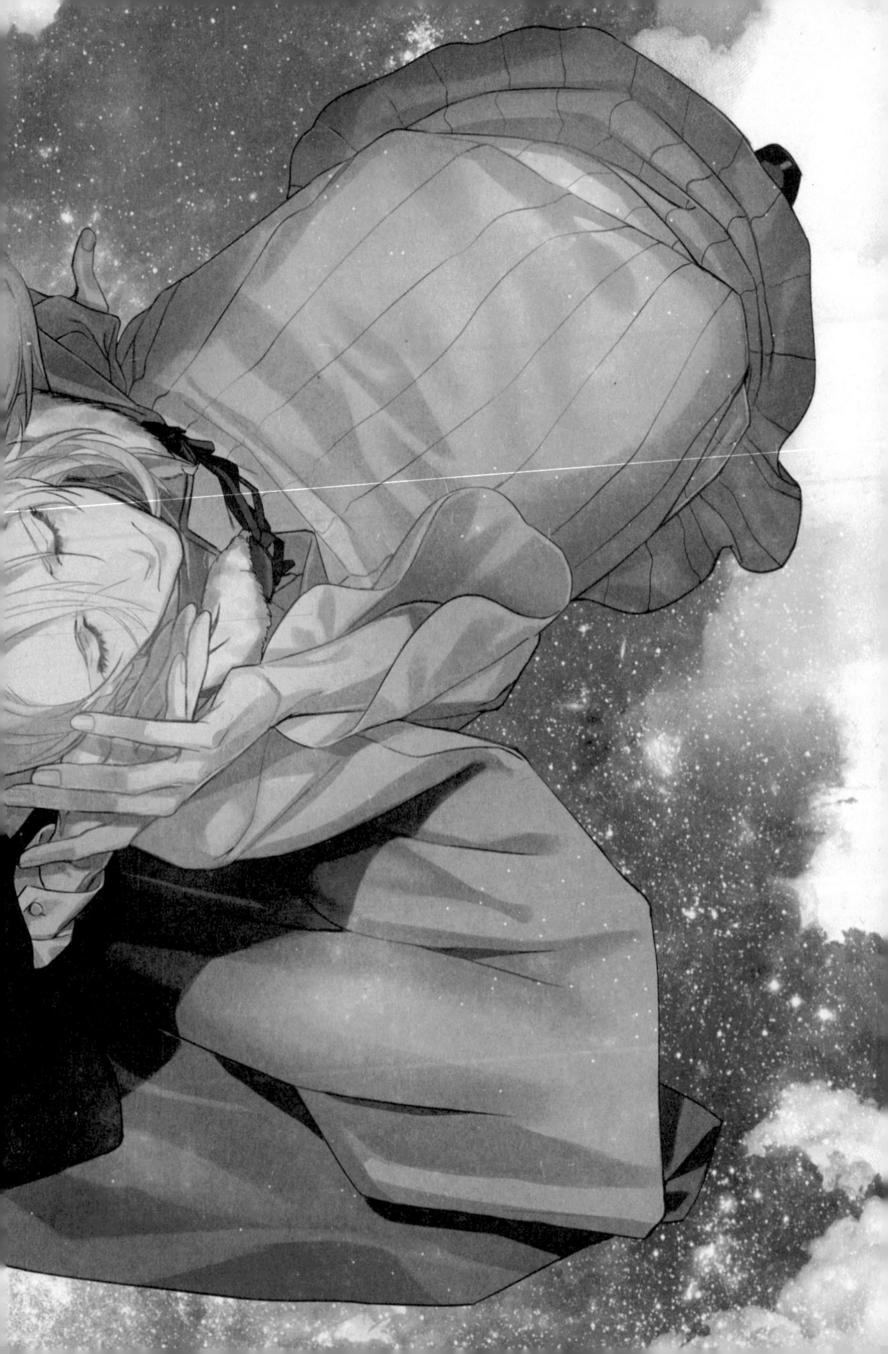

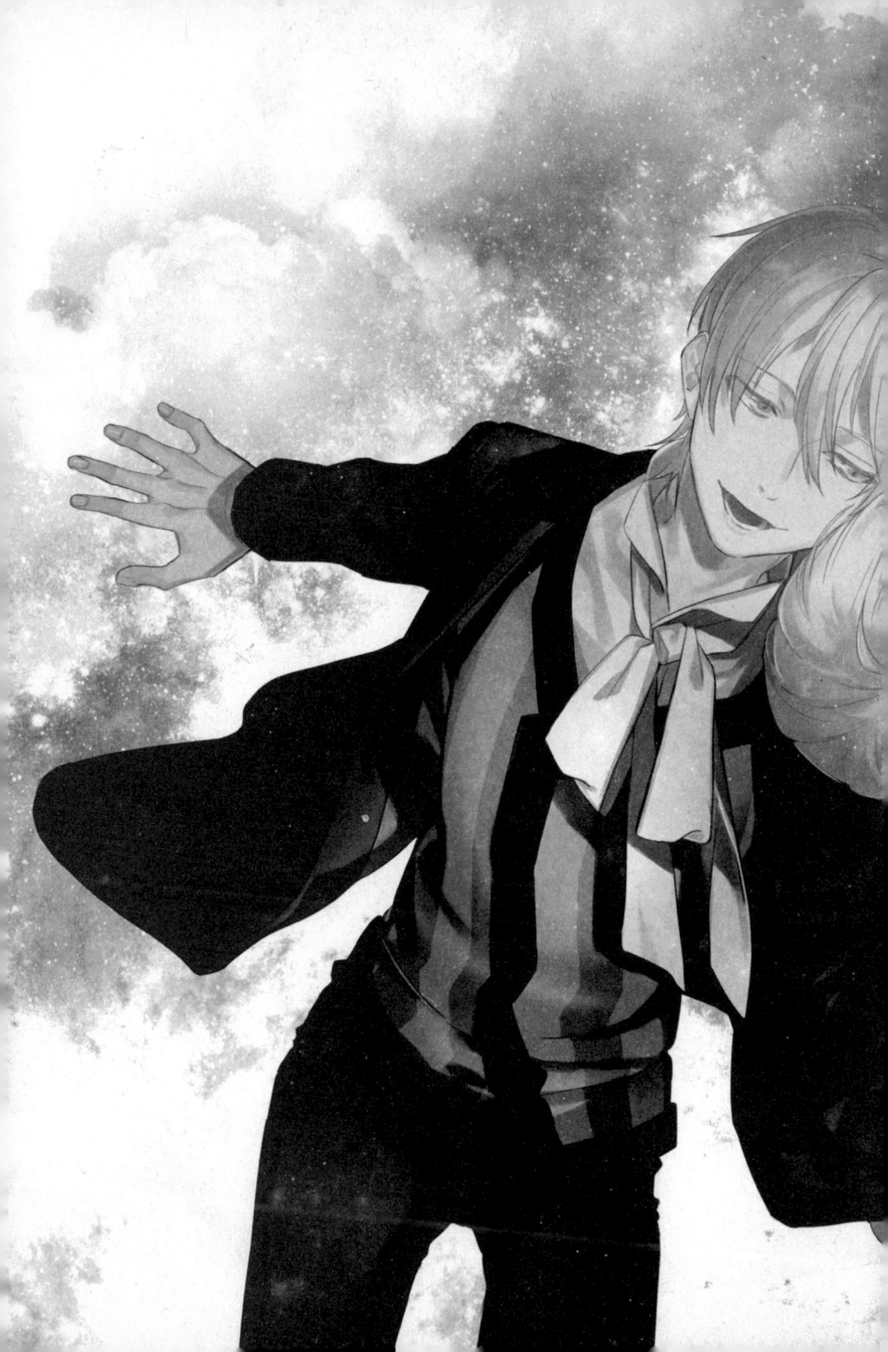

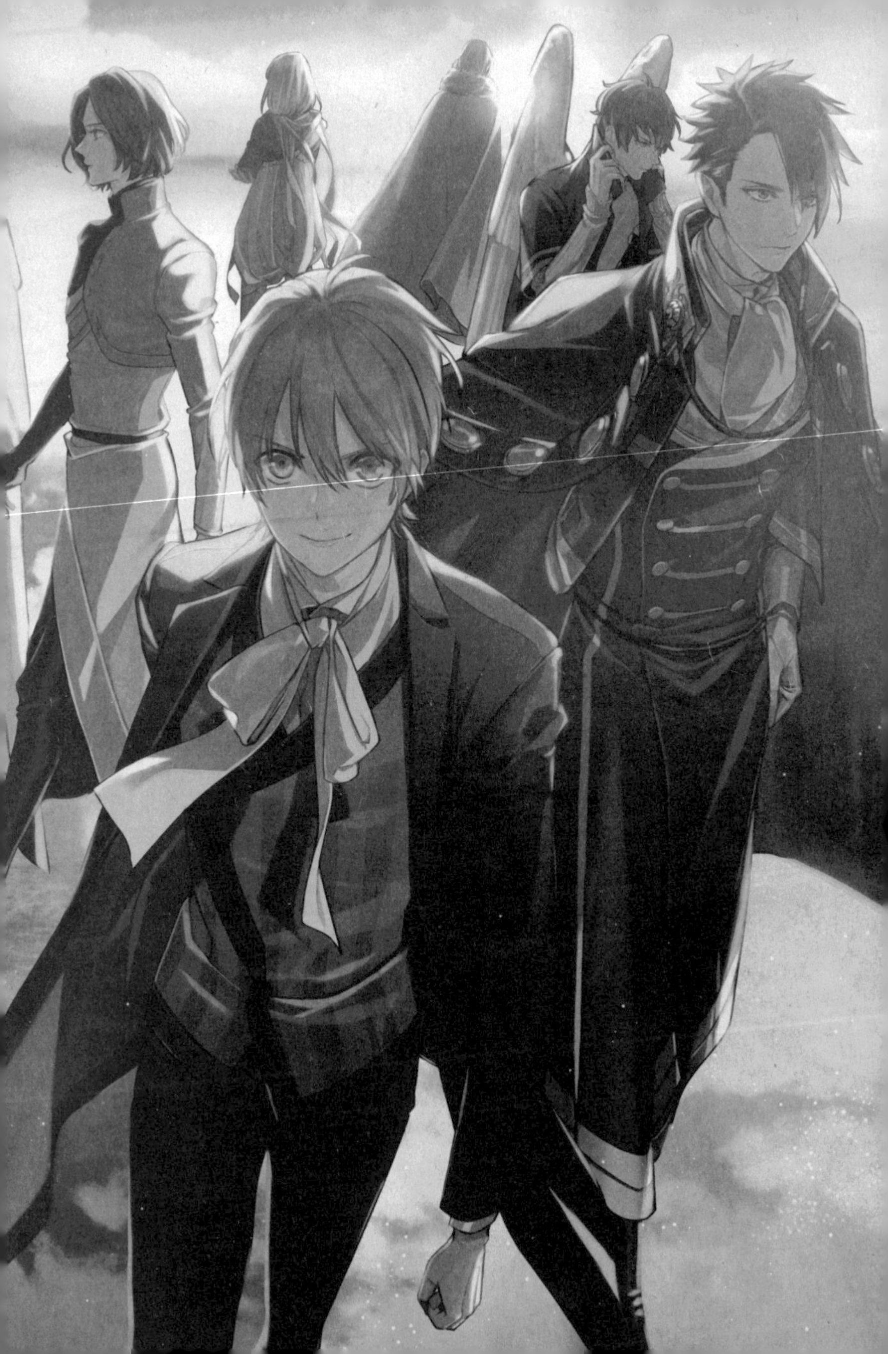

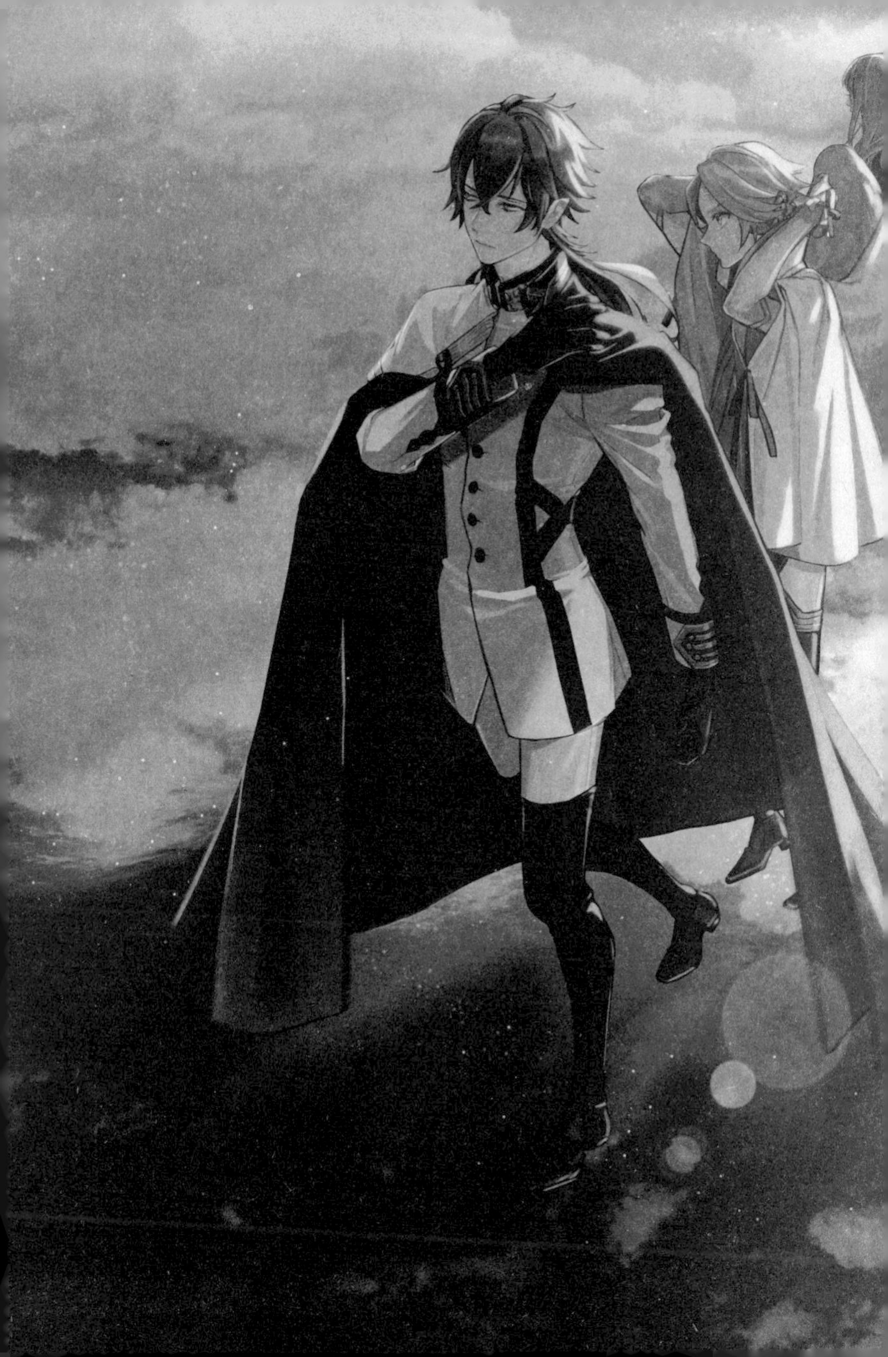

Devils
and Realist

The End

SEVEN SEAS ENTERTAINMENT PRESENTS

Devils and Realist

art by **UTAKO YUKIHIRO** / story by **MADOKA TAKADONO**　　VOLUME 15

TRANSLATION
Jocelyne Allen

ADAPTATION
Danielle King

LETTERING AND RETOUCH
Roland Amago
Bambi Eloriaga-Amago

COVER DESIGN
Nicky Lim

PROOFREADER
B. Lana Guggenheim
Danielle King

EDITOR
Jenn Grunigen

PRODUCTION ASSISTANT
CK Russell

PRODUCTION MANAGER
Lissa Pattillo

EDITOR-IN-CHIEF
Adam Arnold

PUBLISHER
Jason DeAngelis

MAKAI OUJI: DEVILS AND REALIST VOL. 15
© Utako Yukihiro/Madoka Takadono 2018
First published in Japan in 2018 by ICHIJINSHA Inc., Tokyo.
English translation rights arranged with ICHIJINSHA Inc., Tokyo, Japan.

Seven Seas books may be purchased in bulk for promotional, educational, or business use. Please contact your local bookseller or the Macmillan Corporate and Premium Sales Department at 1-800-221-7945, extension 5442, or by e-mail at MacmillanSpecialMarkets@macmillan.com.

Seven Seas and the Seven Seas logo are trademarks of Seven Seas Entertainment, LLC. All rights reserved.

ISBN: 978-1-626926-99-8

Printed in Canada

First Printing: January 2019

10 9 8 7 6 5 4 3 2 1

FOLLOW US ONLINE: *www.sevenseasentertainment.com*

READING DIRECTIONS

This book reads from *right to left*, Japanese style. If this is your first time reading manga, you start reading from the top right panel on each page and take it from there. If you get lost, just follow the numbered diagram here. It may seem backwards at first, but you'll get the hang of it! Have fun!!

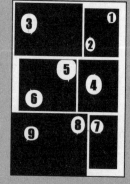